D0079556

Foundations of Criminal Science

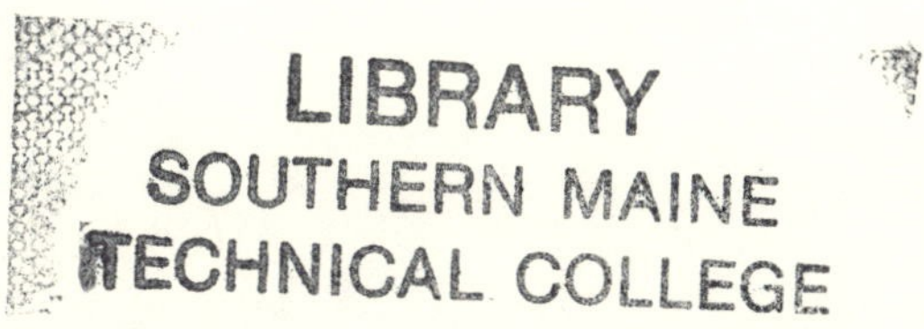

FOUNDATIONS OF CRIMINAL SCIENCE

VOLUME 1:
The Development of Knowledge

GLENN D. WALTERS

PRAEGER

New York
Westport, Connecticut
London

Library of Congress Cataloging-in-Publication Data

Walters, Glenn D.
Foundations of criminal science.

Includes bibliographical references and indexes.
Contents: v. 1. The development of knowledge—
v. 2. The use of knowledge.
1. Criminology. 2. Crime—United States.
I. Title.
HV6025.W37 1992 364 91–4202
ISBN 0–275–94128–0 (set)
ISBN 0–275–93953–7 (v. 1 : alk. paper)
ISBN 0–275–93954–5 (v. 2 : alk. paper)

British Library Cataloguing in Publication Data is available.

Library of Congress Catalog Card Number: 91–4202
ISBN: 0–275–94128–0 (set)
0–275–93953–7 (vol. 1)

First published in 1992

Praeger Publishers, One Madison Avenue, New York, NY 10010
An imprint of Greenwood Publishing Group, Inc.

Printed in the United States of America

The paper used in this book complies with the
Permanent Paper Standard issued by the National
Information Standards Organization (Z39.48–1984).

10 9 8 7 6 5 4 3 2 1

Contents

Tables and Figures

TABLES

FIGURES

Preface

In 1989 police had their first "viable suspect" in the Green River murders. A 38-year-old former law student was alleged by police to have been responsible for the mutilation deaths of 48 young women, although further investigation revealed that this individual could not have been responsible for the deaths of the majority of these young women. In the spring of the same year a 28-year-old female investment banker was assaulted by a group of nine 14- to 17-year-old males as she jogged through New York's Central Park. This woman was beaten, raped, and left for dead in a highly publicized case of what would soon become known as "wilding." It was also during the spring of 1989 that residents of Atlanta, Georgia, were warned of the continuing machinations of a female burglar who has been given the nickname "Catwoman" because she has avoided apprehension in the past by using the ruse of searching for her pet Siamese with persons who happen to catch her in the act of burglarizing their homes. Police maintain that the Catwoman has visited Atlanta for ten springs and during that time has made off with $1 million in valuables, though she has only been convicted for burglary once. Finally, on October 24, 1989, a federal judge in Charlotte, North Carolina, sentenced television evangelist Jim Bakker to a 45-year sentence and fined him $500,000 for defrauding thousands of his followers out of several million dollars.

What do these four true-life situations have in common? First, though statistics show that the amount of violent crime has decreased slightly since 1980, criminals continue to exact a heavy toll on their victims, not to mention society as a whole. These cases also illustrate that crime is a genuinely serious problem in need of bona fide solutions, not bipartisan bickering, courtroom histrionics, or pseudoscientific triviality. Too long have we allowed ourselves to be diverted from investigating the pertinent areas of criminal science endeavor by political, forensic, or guild interests. I would therefore like to take this opportunity to introduce the reader to my own biases and beliefs concerning the proper study of crime-related issues. While it would be foolhardy to deny the role society, the courts, the police, or the victims of crime play in the criminal justice scenario, I submit that the proper focus of study is on the element common to all categories and forms of crime—the criminal him or herself, hence the term *criminal science*.

Criminal science can best be conceptualized as the holistic and interdisciplinary study of crime and criminals. Criminal science is holistic in the sense that all major features of criminal development are taken into account via specific person, situation, interactive, and choice variables. The criminal science effort is interdisciplinary in the sense that it does not exclude any means of knowledge acquisition from consideration, although all are subject to disconfirmation under the rules of scientific exposition and analysis. As such, medical, legal, sociological, ecological, and psychological sources of data are all potentially capable of contributing to the growing system of knowledge that is criminal science. Armed with this knowledge, the criminal scientist centers his or her investigation energies on the individual offender, cognizant that this individual is part of a wider network of interacting physical, social, and psychological influences.

The reader may recall that the field of criminology was established for the purpose of scientifically probing the causes of crime and the behavior of criminals. Unfortunately it took a decidedly sociological turn (at least in the United States) several decades ago and no longer appears to address the full spectrum of criminal science concerns. Consequently, criminology is viewed as a vital link in the interrelated fields of knowledge that have grown up around crime and criminals, although it is only one of several avenues by which the criminal science agenda might be advanced. In the end, it is knowledge, not any one particular perspective, which is of primary concern to the criminal scientist.

This first volume of a two-volume text on criminal science is dedicated to the development of knowledge. Information and knowledge acquisition are of prime significance to the criminal scientist because they provide a foundation for all future avenues of scientific inquiry. Specific to criminal science, this foundation is expressed in five ways: context, research, theory, assessment/prediction, and intervention. The first three foundations (context, research, theory) are scrutinized in the present volume while the fourth and fifth foundations (assessment/prediction, intervention) are covered in Volume 2. Without the structural guidance of these five foundations, our efforts, no matter how well intended, will likely fall short of adequately addressing the pertinent issues in any field of endeavor involving the scientific study of crime and criminals.

The author would like to thank Dr. Donald Denney for his assistance with several of the figures in this volume. Gratitude is also extended to my wife, Patti, and our two children, Christopher and Tara, whose patience and understanding permitted me the time and opportunity to write this two-volume text.

The assertions contained herein are the private views of the author and should in no way be construed as official or as necessarily reflecting the views of the Department of Justice or Federal Bureau of Prisons.

PART I

INTRODUCTION

1

Questions About Crime

WHAT IS CRIME?

Webster's New World Dictionary defines *crime* as ''an act committed in violation of a law prohibiting it, or omitted in violation of a law ordering it'' (Neufeldt, 1988, p. 328). This definition is misleading, however, insofar as it conceals the complexity of the act it supposedly defines. Crime can also serve as a mirror that often reveals as much about society as it does about the individual offender. The societal context is therefore of paramount significance in understanding the evolution of criminal behavior, although I hasten to add that this does not absolve the individual offender of responsibility for his or her violations of societal rules and standards. Since society establishes what is and is not criminal, it, in a sense, creates its own criminals. There are certain laws and mores, however, common to nearly all societies, and it is the violation of these ''common rules'' that I would like to emphasize in defining *criminal conduct*.

In considering the issue of crime and society, I am reminded of Cesare Beccaria's concept of a social contract that he presumed exists between a society and its citizenry. Beccaria argued that this social contract gave society permission to develop and enforce laws designed to protect the rights of the individual. Obviously there have been leaders who have abused this contract and violated the public trust. Though unquestionably not a trivial matter, past abuses of the social contract are of less concern at this point in our discussion than is clarifying the rights and responsibilities that come with society's acceptance of this contract. I argue that society has the moral right to establish and sanction certain rules of conduct, provided, of course, these rules are in the best interests of the populace at large. Society, or more precisely, the governing structure of society, is also within its rights to correct persons who knowingly violate these rules—that is, who commit crimes.

The governing structure of society may not have the moral right to establish laws that fail to muster the support of the general populace or that are not in the best interests of its citizenry, yet still have the power to enforce these laws. What the individual must realize is that the governing structure establishes societal rules and to attack the authority of this powerful elite may result in one's own destruction. If, on the other hand, there is sufficient popular dissatisfaction with the governing structure and public support for rebellion, then one's chances of success, in terms of effecting a change in the governing structure, are greatly enhanced. This, in fact, is the substance of the kinds of revolutionary actions that gave birth to not only the United States but to several other modern-day republics. The governing structure of society holds the power and, in many cases, the social contract to make and enforce laws; the individual has the choice to violate these laws and risk reprisal or obey them and live within society's framework.

A society and its governing structure are not one in the same, although the governing structure often expresses the will of the powerful elite and, it is hoped, a substantial portion of the general populace. I therefore define *crime* as violations of societal law that are of sufficient severity and/or frequency to elicit a negative and/or corrective response from the governing structure of that society. This does not necessarily mean that societal laws are "good" or that culturally defined criminals are "bad"; just that the governing structure of society has the power to impose sanctions on behavior that is in violation of its rules and that the individual chooses to either obey or defy these rules. This is a practical rather than moral definition of *crime* and one with which some readers may take issue. Nonetheless, it serves to guide our review of the criminal science field and the questions to which we now turn our attention.

HOW SHOULD CRIME BE MEASURED?

The measurement of crime can be as controversial as its definition. There are, first of all, several schools of thought on how crime might best be appraised. Each system has its own set of individual assumptions, strengths, and weaknesses. However, since a science relies on the vigor of its data base, the issue of measurement has wide-ranging implications for those of us wishing to make the study of criminal behavior more scientific. Although direct observation and the inspection of death certificates and coroner's reports are among the procedures that have been used to catalog crime, the three most popular forms of measurement are official arrest records, self-report inventories, and victimization surveys.

Official arrest records consider the number and type of offenses reported to police authorities. The FBI's Uniform Crime Reports (UCR) are a national compilation of official arrest rates. Although official records have traditionally been the substance of criminal justice research and the foundation for many social and/or governmental policy decisions, they are not without serious shortcomings. For one, half of all crime goes unreported (Eck & Riccio, 1979). More portentously, the "dark figure" of unreported crime obtained with official sources of data (Biderman & Reiss, 1967) is normally inconsistent—(and thus, unpredictable)—across time (Walker, 1971) and jurisdiction (Bottomley & Coleman, 1980). Add to this the realization that arrest records normally only collate certain categories of crime (Index Crimes—murder, aggravated assault, arson, forcible rape, robbery, burglary, larceny, motor vehicle theft—in the case of the UCR) and classify only the most serious crimes in situations where more than one crime has occurred (Bureau of Justice Statistics, 1981a), and we can see that official arrest records, albeit convenient, are subject to potentially serious limitations.

Searching for an alternative to official records, Short and Nye (1957) introduced the self-report method for collecting delinquency data. A researcher utilizing the self-report method will typically provide the subject with a list of delinquent or criminal acts and ask the individual whether he or she has engaged in any of the behaviors on the list, and if so, how often. West and Farrington (1977) found reasonable concordance between the accounts of English youth and arrests documented in official files, while Rutter and Giller (1984) recorded an acceptable level of test-retest stability in self-report measures of delinquency for periods ranging up to several months. Self-report studies have shown that while most persons have committed one or more crimes in their lives, the vast majority of people have never been arrested (Erickson & Empey, 1963).

The primary criticism of self-report data is that they are weighted in the direction of relatively minor and trivial offenses, which would seem to undermine our efforts to study significant criminality. However, as Hindelang, Hirschi, and Weis (1979) observed when they investigated gender, race, and social class as correlates of crime, the conclusion that discrepant outcomes occur for official versus self-report data is unfounded when self-report measures are restricted to those offenses indexed by official sources. A second concern many researchers have expressed about self-report data is the presence of a relatively high rate of nonresponse, which in turn may provide researchers with a distorted picture of specific crime patterns (see Elliott & Ageton, 1980). Even more significant is the fact that persons possessing serious records of prior legal difficulty are less likely to respond to a self-report inventory than persons absent such records (Hirschi & Selvin, 1967). Since self-report studies are normally performed on students in junior and senior high school, and since many career offenders start dropping out of school in the seventh and eighth grades (Walters & White, 1987; Wilson & Herrnstein, 1985), a substantial portion of the more serious offenders are unavailable for inclusion in self-report surveys.

In 1973 the U.S. Bureau of Census began interviewing approximately 128,000 individuals in some 58,000 households for the express purpose of assembling victimization data on six major crime categories: assault, rape, robbery, personal and household larceny, burglary, and motor vehicle theft. Conducted twice a year since that time, the National Crime Survey (NCS) has provided a wealth of information on crime and victimization patterns. It has been consistently demonstrated, for instance, that victimization rates are typically twice that of official reports, a finding which suggests that approximately half of all crimes go unreported (Hindelang, Hirschi, & Weis, 1981). Data from the NCS also reveal that five out of six Americans will become victims of at least one violent crime (rape, robbery, assault) during their lifetime, while approximately half will be so victimized two or more times (Koppel, 1987). Victimization studies further reveal that youthful, black, poor people are more prone to victimization than any other group of individuals (Empey, 1978). Unlike UCR data, which exhibited a sharp incline during the decade of the 1970s and then leveled off after 1980, the NCS suggests that violent crime rose noticeably during the 1970s and then dropped sharply after 1980 (Rand, 1987).

As the last point illustrates, victimization and official arrest rates are often discrepant. Both Nelson (1980) and Messner (1984) report a frustratingly low level of correspondence between the UCR and NCS except for homicide, which experts agree is one of the better estimates of "criminal harm" available to researchers employing aggregate level data (Messner, 1984). The relatively weak level of association between the UCR and NCS is not all that surprising since the NCS considers only personal and household victimization while the UCR catalogs all crimes reported (Wilson & Herrnstein, 1985). A more serious criticism often lodged against victimization studies is that they rely too heavily on a person's memories and are vulnerable to under- and over-reporting (Levine, 1976). Victim reports are particularly unreliable for offenses like rape and assault. Turner (1981) surveyed persons in San Jose, California, who reported assault incidents to police authorities and determined that 52 percent of the sample failed to acknowledge the assault during an interview, the rate being even higher in situations where the alleged assault had been perpetrated by a relative.

Despite the discrepant results often produced when arrest rate, self-report, and victimization studies are compared, they concur in identifying young, urban males as being responsible for a lion's share of all crimes committed. It would be unwise of us to elevate any one data source above the others, however, since each is blessed with certain advantages and plagued by certain handicaps. A more productive approach is to probe and compare the personal strengths and weaknesses of each source since the inter-method discrepancies can sometimes be just as important as the commonalities. We need to keep this in mind as we review Part III of this volume, since the bulk of criminal science research is based on one or more of these three data sources.

WHAT IS A CRIMINAL?

If crime involves violations of societal rules, then a criminal must be an individual who engages in social rule–breaking behavior. It should be noted, however, that strict adherence to such a definition would elevate the prevalence rate of criminality to somewhere in the neighborhood of 100 percent, since self-report studies clearly demonstrate that practically everyone has violated the law at one time or another. Still, the greater portion of the population does not engage in regular violation of societal norms, rules, and mores. Accordingly, the rate or frequency of criminal violation is of central importance as we go about the business of constructing a proper definition of criminality.

Habitual criminal behavior is sometimes marked by greater severity than the crimes committed by others in society. Research on public surveys in which subjects are asked to assess the seriousness of selected criminal acts (Wolfgang et al., 1985) and investigations that have derived monetary estimates of crime severity (Cohen, 1988) have demonstrated a reasonable consensus when the rankings of crime seriousness are considered, although the intervals between rankings may vary (see Cullen, Link, Travis, & Wozniak, 1985). The crimes rated at the upper end of these scales (for example, rape, kidnapping, robbery) tend to be more effective in discriminating between habitual criminals and persons who may engage in an isolated criminal act than offenses achieving lower severity scores on these scales (for example, breaking curfew, gambling, prostitution, public intoxication).

Criminals therefore differ from noncriminal members of society in terms of both the frequency and the severity of their lawbreaking behavior. Although such a statement may be unsettling to the socially minded scholar who views criminality as a function of nefarious social conditions, the approach taken here is interactional in nature. In other words, criminality is neither seated in the individual nor in the environment, but is a function of the complex interaction that occurs between the individual and his or her environment, not to mention the choices the individual makes relative to this interaction. The criminal is therefore a person who engages in criminal acts of sufficient frequency and/or severity to warrant a formal response from the governing structure of society.

HOW CAN CRIMINAL BEHAVIOR BE CONTROLLED?

Control and change are major topics in Volume 2 of this book. As dissatisfaction and skepticism toward psychologically oriented treatment modalities have mounted, we have seen a corollary decrease in scholarly discussion of these methods. In their book *Crime and Human Nature*, Wilson and Herrnstein (1985) devote very little space to intervention strategies. This omission seems based, in large part, on Wilson and Herrnstein's belief that treatment is ineffective in promoting change in habitual or nonhabitual criminal offenders. However, a recent review of the literature by Gendreau and Ross (1987) uncovered evidence supporting the efficacy of juvenile and adult treatment programs, provided, of course, these programs are properly conceived and implemented. The issue then becomes how we might improve the manner in which these programs are developed and administered.

The basis for change as discussed in this text depends heavily on choice and personal responsibility. Until the offender stops blaming his or her criminality on external factors, begins accepting responsibility for his or her actions, and decides to think more rationally, change is highly unlikely (Walters, 1990b). Society is neither blameless nor helpless in the face of crime, for just as it can encourage certain forms of criminality, it can also foster change in individual offenders. Moreover, society has the power to impose external control over those offenders unwilling to curb their antisocial inclinations. As we see when we examine person- and situation-oriented intervention strategies in Volume 2, it is in the best interests of society to find innovative ways to inspire pro-social behavior in its citizenry, just as it is in the best interests of many criminal offenders to find noncriminal solutions to their problems.

WHAT IS CRIMINAL SCIENCE?

Criminal science is the interdisciplinary study of crime and criminals. Though the term *criminal science* may be new, it is based on time-tested ideas that have existed for many centuries. As a matter of fact, criminology and criminal science have similar roots. Criminology, however, seemed to take a turn away from the interdisciplinary study of crime as it became more sociologically affiliated. At present, the majority of criminology departments in U.S. universities and colleges are in schools or departments of sociology and social welfare. Criminal science, on the other hand, is a field unto itself. It borrows liberally from psychology, sociology, criminology, penology, medicine, and law but is subservient to no single field or theory.

The focus of criminal science efforts is, as the name implies, on the individual criminal offender. This does not mean, however, that social and environmental factors are ignored, or that the criminal is viewed as the ''seat of all pathology.'' What it does mean is that the criminal offender serves as a fulcrum, around which investigative efforts might be coordinated. Like the ancient sailors who steered their ships by the stars, we will use the criminal offender as a reference point to develop a scientific approach to the study of antisocial and illegal forms of behavior. Criminal science should therefore be viewed as a tool capable of advancing our understanding of crime and criminals.

The origins of criminal science can be traced to the dawn of civilization, when societies were first forming and deciding what to do with those of their number who violated tribal law. As the Middle Ages came to a close, supernatural and religious explanations for crime diminished in popularity, replaced by more mechanistic and naturalistic interpretations of crime causation (Drapkin, 1983). Humanism became a dominant force around this time and helped stimulate interest in prevention as an alternative to punishment. This vigorous period of artistic and intellectual activity, known today as the Renaissance, breathed new life into the criminal science movement.

Garland (1985) argues that just as the clinic spawned medical science, criminology owes a debt of gratitude to the rise of prisons as a means of social control. Prior to the mid 1800s, criminals were normally disciplined in ways other than through incarceration. However, the prison became increasingly more popular in both Europe and the United States during the latter half of the nineteenth century (Drapkin, 1983) and soon became a kind of primitive laboratory for the study of incarcerated offenders (Garland, 1985). Even more consequential is the fact that the prison served as a springboard for two processes—individualization and differentiation—that would eventually serve as the bulwark of the classical and positivist schools of criminological thought.

Individualization exists as a focus on the person by way of a rudimentary architectural feature of prisons—that is, the individual cell and the individual's inclusion within it (Garland, 1985). Individualization serves as the theoretical base for the classical interpretation of crime. This particular school of thought holds that the individual is free to make choices in life and that the decision to engage in a particular criminal act is all that separates the criminal from the noncriminal. Another physical characteristic of prisons, the prison walls, served as the symbolic framework of a second trend in criminological thought, differentiation. Differentiation involves separating individuals into groups of criminals and noncriminals, which in its simplest form might entail classifying persons inside the prison walls as criminals and those outside the walls as noncriminals (Garland, 1985). According to Garland, differentiation contributed to the development of the positivist school of criminology, which has emphasized categorization, empirical research, and group differences. This demonstrates how the advent of a particular institution—the prison—helped stimulate the evolution of two fundamental branches of criminal science inquiry, classicism and positivism.

The classical school of criminology is beholden to the English philosopher and economist Jeremy Bentham (1748–1832), who advanced the concept of utilitarianism. Bentham hypothesized that the individual seeks to maximize pleasure and minimize pain, and argued that the state should seek to provide a maximum level of happiness to the majority of its citizens. Another classical thinker, Cesare Beccaria (1738–1794) advocated prison reform and, like Bentham, emphasized prevention over punishment. There are signs of Beccaria's pioneering work on deterrence and social control still found in current penological practice. In response to criticism directed at classicism's approach to free will and choice, the neoclassical school was created. Contending that individual behavior could be influenced by certain personal and environmental factors, neoclassical theorists like R. J. Pellegrini and P. H. Rossi introduced such terms as "diminished responsibility" and "extenuating circumstances." Though this modification was implemented in many European countries during the late 1800s, several critics have argued that it actually weakened, rather than strengthened, the basic tenets of classical theory (Garafalo, 1914).

In direct contrast to classicism, the positivist school of criminological thought rejects the notion of free will and sees as the primary goal of criminology investigations into crime causation. Grounded in the philosophical writings of Auguste Comte (1798–1857), positivism took a deterministic approach to the study of human beings. Possibly the most famous of the early positivists was an Italian physician by the name of Cesare Lombroso (1835–1909). Lombroso constructed a biological theory of criminal development after performing several thousand post-mortem studies on criminal offenders confined in late nineteenth-century Italian prisons. Autopsies on two subjects in particular, a highwayman who died in prison and a man who raped, strangled, and dismembered women, were instrumental in revealing the presence of primitive anthropoid characteristics, leading Lombroso to the conclusion that certain criminals were actually throwbacks to an earlier stage of human development (Drapkin, 1983). Lombroso accumulated evidence of cranial abnormalities, facial asymmetries, and digital-glyphic anomalies to support his claim that an atavistic process was responsible for certain forms of criminality, although Charles Goring (1913) later collected data that shed serious doubt on many of Lombroso's conclusions.

Though not necessarily disputing Lombroso's views on the biological correlates of crime, Enrico Ferri (1856–1929) emphasized the socioeconomic and political correlates of lawbreaking behavior. Another champion of positivistic thought, Raffaele Garafalo (1852–1934) devoted much of his life to the study of criminal behavior in an attempt to formulate a sociological definition of crime. Ferri and Garafalo are therefore frequently credited with having founded the sociological school of positivism, an approach to investigating criminal science data that has remained up to the present day. Sociological positivism has, in fact, given rise to a number of influential criminological theories, Merton's (1957) social strain approach, Sutherland's differential association theory (Sutherland & Cressey, 1978), and Hirschi's (1969) social control model, to name just three.

With its emphasis on operationality, verification, and empirical research, positivism would appear to have the inner track in the classical-positivist debate. However, in an article written in 1964, Matza excoriated positivists for adhering to an outmoded theory of crime causation that he argued had lost its vitality and was no longer in keeping with new developments in the philosophy of science. Attempting to effect a rapprochement of these two viewpoints, Gottfredson and Hirschi (1987) have argued that classicism and positivism are not inherently incompatible. They go on to advise the reader that the differences between the positivist and classical viewpoints were originally exaggerated in an effort to provide criminology with greater "scientific" credibility, although arbitrarily excluding a set of findings from consideration simply because they are incongruent with one's hypotheses actually runs counter to the scientific ideal. As I have argued elsewhere (Walters, 1990b), classicism and positivism are but two sides of the same coin, which when combined are more capable of advancing our knowledge than either is separately.

The classical and positivist schools quite naturally grew out of a debate that has raged over many years and across multiple disciplines: namely, do people exert free will over their actions or is their behavior determined by various internal and external conditions? There is no easy answer, although the issue is sure to elicit intense emotional response from proponents of either position. In the evolution of the criminal science field both the classical and positivist perspectives have served a vital function, but for very different reasons. Classicism has proved itself useful to clinicians, policymakers, and others tasked with the responsibility of making decisions about individual offenders. Positivism, on the other hand, has been of benefit to persons empirically investigating crime and its causation. It would seem, however, that the time has come to dispense with the dualistic "either-or" rhetoric that has grown up around the classical-positivist debate and seek a harmonization of these two seemingly incompatible viewpoints.

In attempting to identify a mechanism through which the integration of classicism and positivism might be accomplished, it may well be useful to return to the early eclectic work of Franz von Liszt (1851–1919). Dr. von Liszt believed that it was the interaction between the individual and his or her social environment that accounted for criminal outcomes. He asserted further that criminologists should be familiar not only with sociology but with psychology, penology, criminal anthropology, and statistics as well (Drapkin, 1983). The three *C*'s of conditions, choice, and cognition (Walters, 1990b) might prove particularly useful in translating von Liszt's ideas into action. Using this procedure, I argue that there are certain conditions that limit, but do not determine, one's options. The individual then selects or chooses one or more options and goes about establishing a cognitive system designed to support this decision.

As has been stated several times in this chapter, the defining characteristic of criminal science is the pursuit of knowledge on crime and criminals. Sometimes this search is difficult and fraught with controversy. The criminal scientist must be careful not to overinterpret the data on such controversial issues as gender and crime, yet courageous enough to fully explore all possible avenues of inquiry. We cannot allow our personal beliefs, prejudices, or the possibility that our findings may be poorly received by certain groups interfere with the criminal science effort or distract us from achieving the goal of increased knowledge on crime and criminals. The responsibility incumbent on scientists to guard against misuse of their newly acquired knowledge is a topic of great importance to criminal scientists, and one to which we return in the final chapter of Volume 2.

HOW MIGHT WE PURSUE THE SCIENTIFIC STUDY OF CRIMINAL BEHAVIOR?

A logical question at this juncture is whether a science of criminal behavior is a practical reality or nothing more than an idealistic pipe dream. I have defined criminal science as the systematic application of scientific principles to the interdisciplinary study of criminal behavior, although this tells us nothing about how such an approach might be implemented. In an effort to confront this issue I have taken the liberty of subdividing the criminal science field into five primary areas of investigative inquiry—hence, the reason for the five parts into which this two-volume text has been partitioned. These five parts are, in effect, the five principal foundations of criminal science that encompass the following five general areas of inquiry: the contextual features of crime, the correlates of criminal behavior, theoretical developments in the criminal science field, the use of criminal science data to evaluate current behavior and offer predictions about future behavior, and strategies for intervening with criminal offenders.

The reader should be well aware by now that crime needs to be considered within a societal context. In other words, crime does not exist independent of the society or culture in which it occurs. For this reason, the contextual features of crime is the primary topic of discussion in the second and third chapters of this first volume. First, we examine crime and the behavior of criminals as each has evolved over a period of several hundred years of American history. Next, we survey research on cross-national comparisons of crime with a special emphasis on features that seem responsible for variations in international crime rates. With the aid of information supplied by this first section the reader should be in a better position to comprehend the historical and cultural context of criminal behavior and how this influences the manner in which such behavior is expressed.

Any science requires a solid base of empirical knowledge and understanding, something upon which to rest its theoretical underpinnings and intervention strategies. Research, the second foundation of criminal science, therefore assumes center stage in Part III of Volume 1. In this section we find ourselves probing the correlates of crime, divided into four main categories: person, situation, interactive, and choice variables. Person variables are characteristics of the individual that include heredity, temperament, gender, and intelligence. Situation variables, on the other hand, encompass environmental characteristics—social class, unemployment, drug and/or alcohol abuse, and family atmosphere, among the more popular in this category. The third class of correlates, interactive variables, emerges from person × situation interactions occurring in three primary domains: the physical, the social, and the psychological. Choice and decision making also are discussed as possible correlates of crime.

The fourth part of Volume 1 addresses the third function of criminal science investigation—that of theory. Over the years scientists have come to realize that research data are meaningless unless accompanied by an organizing system of interrelated postulates and theorems. Theories therefore permit us to move beyond the immediate context and apply our knowledge to a wider array of situations. Unfortunately history suggests that there has been a tendency in the past to force criminal science data into preexisting theoretical models (see Gottfredson & Hirschi, 1987). When we allow the tail to wag the dog, as we have done for so long, we court disaster and invite tragedy. This part commences with a review of several existing theories of criminal behavior and concludes with presentation of a multipattern theory of criminal involvement.

Once our data have been collected and arranged into a series of interconnected hypotheses, formulae, or predictions, the next step is to organize this information in ways that facilitate our understanding of individual offenders. Assessment and prediction therefore constitute the fourth function of criminal science investigation, both of which are major topics in Part II of Volume 2. Besides scrutinizing the matter of individual assessment, this section also delves into inmate/offender classification and the alleged connection between mental health difficulties and crime. Prediction, specifically as it pertains to recidivism, institutional adjustment, and estimates of dangerousness, is also explored in this section. The goal of this particular section is to assist the reader in discerning how criminal justice theory and data can augment our ability to manage and understand individual criminal offenders.

Intervention is the fifth and final foundation of criminal science inquiry. Despite the pessimism contained in Martinson's (1974) earlier review, and expressed in Wilson and Herrnstein's (1985) more recent work on criminal behavior, there is abundant evidence to suggest that offenders are capable of change (Czudner, 1985; Gendreau & Ross, 1987; Irwin, 1970; Meisenhelder, 1977; Shover, 1983). Our task, then, is to find ways by which the change process might be facilitated. To this end, we probe person- and situation-oriented approaches to intervention as well as person × situation solutions (as represented by the interaction occurring between the individual offender and criminal justice system through the primary goals of retribution, deterrence, incapacitation, rehabilitation, and restitution). As we proceed through each of these five parts, I believe the reader will become increasingly more cognizant of how the five foundations of criminal science investigation form a unit, around which an ever-increasing body of knowledge, and the application of this knowledge to real-life situations, rotates.

PART II

CONTEXT

2

A Brief History of Crime in America

Many of us can probably recall complaining about having to take history in school. We may have asked ourselves, why should I waste my time learning about events that transpired years ago? The fundamental flaw in this argument, however, is that we can learn a great deal about our present circumstances by taking a look at the past. It is well established, for instance, that crimes of violence were lamentably common during the Middle Ages. Where the rate of violent criminality has steadily declined since that time, the drop in the American crime rate has been less prominent than that witnessed in Europe (Gurr, 1981). The study of history places our current level of knowledge in perspective, without which our scholarly efforts would be devoid of direction, purpose, and meaning. Consequently, if we are to gain a thorough appreciation of the nature of crime in modern-day America we must first examine the historical development of this concept as it relates to the evolving American experience.

Schlesinger, in his book *The Cycles of American History* (1986), muses whether America should be viewed as an experiment or as an unfolding of national destiny. Regardless of which viewpoint one chooses to adopt, violence and crime predate the Declaration of Independence, with roots extending back into sixteenth- and seventeenth-century Europe from whence many of our early ancestors originated. This, in fact, is the primary thesis advanced by Demaris in his book *America the Violent* (1970). Our discussion here will, by necessity, be brief and our focus narrow. However, we need to keep in mind that the goals of this chapter are limited by certain practical considerations. Thus, rather than deriving a formal historical treatise on the American experience, we search for relationships and new information useful in forming various hypotheses relevant to the specific issue of crime in America. This is accomplished by discussing American history within the context of several primary time periods: Colonial America (1607–1775); From Revolution to Republic (1775–1800), Early Industrialization (1800–1860); Westward Expansion (1860–1885); The Age of Internalization (1885–1918); The Rise to World Prominence (1918–1960); and The Modern Era (1960–present).

COLONIAL AMERICA (1607–1775)

Our story begins on an April morning in the year 1607, when several ships under the command of Captain Christopher Newport anchored near the mouth of the Chesapeake Bay. This initial group of colonists settled in an area of modern-day Virginia to be named Jamestown, in honor of the English monarch, King James I. These early settlers faced many hardships in the New World and the death rate was exceedingly high. Some thirteen years later a group of religious outcasts, the Puritans, landed on northern shores in an area known today as Plymouth, Massachusetts. The Jamestown and Plymouth colonies were the first two permanent settlements of Europeans in the New World. These groups brought with them their ideals, values, technology, and a propensity for violence. It was not long before the colonists found themselves in conflict with neighboring Native Americans, adjacent settlements, and each other. This then is the heritage of America, conceived in aggression and signed in blood.

During the first half of the seventeenth century, rule violators were treated rather harshly and the death penalty was meted out regularly. Religious intolerance ran rampant, and groups such as the Quakers were persecuted and eventually banned when they attempted to settle in New England. However, by mid-century justice in colonial America was actually more lenient than it was in England or France. Though there are many reasons for this turn of events, the key may be found in the nature of crime and people in seventeenth-century America. People were a more valuable resource in the sparsely populated New World than they were in Europe. Consequently, fines and whippings took the place of jail and the hangman. In addition, there was simply less crime in America than in Europe. As the noted historian Thomas Jefferson Wertenbaker (1927) once remarked, the incentives for criminality were much weaker in colonial America where food was abundant and unemployment virtually nonexistent.

One commonly held misconception about our American forefathers concerns the belief that many were criminals who had been banished from England or other western European nations. Although many were discontent with conditions, policies, and practices found in Europe, most were law-abiding citizens searching for a better way of life (Wertenbaker, 1927). Laws were written in an effort to promote social order and uphold certain religious principles and teachings, and were, for the most part, obeyed by the vast majority of the population. The elders of the community were responsible for making sure these laws were enforced and for deciding the punishment to be dispensed for a particular transgression. Even though this system of justice was reasonably successful in achieving law and order during colonial times, it did not eliminate crime altogether (Edwards & Fuhrman, 1985).

While the Puritans tended to be rather harsh in punishing religious transgressors, neither the Puritans nor the settlers in Virginia and Maryland were overly severe in their disciplining of persons who violated the civil code. Whippings, fines, the stocks and pillory, and mutilation were the primary forms of punishment administered to offenders during colonial times. The death penalty was applied to a greater number of offenses in New England (heresy, murder, treason, witchcraft) than in Virginia (treason), although neither region relied regularly on this form of retribution (Wertenbaker, 1927). The public embarrassment of whippings and the stocks with minor offenders and the prospect of rapid identification of more serious offenders through mutilation (loss of an ear for an arsonist or burning the letter *B* into the forehead of a burglar) were thought to be sufficient to achieve a sense of social conformity under ordinary circumstances. Under less than ordinary conditions the death penalty or imprisonment might be imposed.

However, long-term incarceration was rarely implemented owing to a general absence of secure facilities. Accordingly, early American prisons were merely places of temporary confinement where conditions were intolerable and escape commonplace. Like the jails found in many present-day Third World countries, the colonial-era prison was a very distasteful place indeed, since little attention was paid to prison reform during this period. Offenders were regularly grouped together irrespective of age, sex, or criminal sophistication and charged for all expenses incurred during their confinement (Adams, 1927). If a prisoner was unable to pay for his or her board the individual was usually sold into servitude for the purposes of reimbursing the jailer.

One interesting feature of colonial law was the regular use of restitution as a means of making reparations to the victims of one's crimes. Part of the burglar's sentence might be to replace stolen items, while the arsonist might be made to pay for damages sustained as a result of antisocial activities. Community service might also be made part of an offender's punishment during the years preceding the American Revolution. Wertenbaker (1927), for instance, discusses the case of a seventeenth-century fornicator who was sentenced to building a ferry for the community in lieu of a more corporal form of discipline. Hence, a number of criminal justice techniques currently in vogue have their roots in colonial American law.

FROM REVOLUTION TO REPUBLIC (1775–1800)

In the war fought for American independence there were atrocities on both sides. The conditions found in most Revolution-era jails and prisons were grossly inadequate and oftentimes inhumane. These adverse conditions existed in part because there was confusion and uncertainty as to who was responsible for the management of jails and prisons during this period. After the Revolution, responsibility for housing serious offenders fell to the individual states, while the punishment of lesser offenders was left to local jurisdictions. Initially, the conditions in most penal institutions were deplorable. However, by 1785 the public had become increasingly concerned with the poor physical repair of these facilities and there was a general outcry for reform.

Stimulated by the third edition of Howard's book *State of Prisons in England and Wales*, published in 1784, and the formation of a society designed to alleviate the miseries of public reformatories, efforts were undertaken to upgrade prison conditions. By 1790 a law was enacted that rectified many of the more obvious abuses to be found in colonial and post-colonial prisons (Greene, 1943). One such development was the construction of separate facilities for men and women. Several jurisdictions also endeavored to segregate adult and juvenile offenders. Such efforts not only produced more humane conditions in American jails and prisons but also paved the way for future developments in the correctional field.

In the last decade of the eighteenth century several significant modifications were made in the American penal code. A committee chaired by Thomas Jefferson recommended that the death penalty be restricted to offenses involving either murder or treason. This recommendation was eventually voted into law several years later. In 1794 a prison was constructed in Philadelphia, Pennsylvania, which served to usher in the era of the penitentiary in America (Lewis, 1922), and it was during this period that the first signs of widespread prison construction began to appear. Barnes (1926) writes that as the end of the eighteenth century neared, jails and prisons were no longer simply sites of detention but were actually starting to be used for the purposes of correction.

As we attempt to form an understanding of crime in post-Revolution America it may be helpful to examine the story of the sociopathic Harpe brothers. Known as Big and Little Harpe, these two early American villains robbed, stole, and murdered their way into the history books. Relatively early in their criminal careers the Harpes, along with two concubines, were arrested and confined. Unfortunately, the brothers subsequently escaped from jail, leaving their female partners to give birth to their progeny at county expense. Big Harpe, the meaner of the two brothers, was said to have been responsible for the deaths of dozens of innocent persons, to include his own infant daughter. However, the brothers' most infamous crime was the massacre of the Trisword family near Clay Lick woods in Tennessee. In all, at least ten men, women, and children were murdered, their bodies stripped, mangled, and hopelessly disfigured (Demaris, 1970). Those of us who find ourselves wondering about the level of senseless criminality in modern-day America might well consider the case of the Harpe brothers, both of whom came to violent ends in the first few years of our next period, early industrialization.

EARLY INDUSTRIALIZATION (1800–1860)

The Industrial Revolution began in Europe around 1760 but did not reach the shores of America until just before the start of the nineteenth century. Sociologists inform us that the industrialization process typically leads to increased levels of urbanization, whereby a large percentage of the population moves into the cities in order to support the expanding industrial complex. Thus, a geographical shift took place at the beginning of the nineteenth century wherein many young adults sought employment in the larger cities. Emancipated prematurely from the supervisory control of their parents, these individuals encountered numerous temptations and associated difficulties, and many of them lived in boarding homes with other young adults (Johnson, 1978). It is not surprising, then, that the crime rate rose abruptly during this period.

In the early nineteenth century, crime was increasing at an alarming rate in cities like New York (Richardson, 1970), Boston (Gurr, 1981), and Philadelphia (Lane, 1980). Crime in New York City was such a problem that a writer for the *New York Herald* proclaimed the "Big Apple" the most crime-ridden city in the entire world. New York's Five Points district, bounded by the Bowery, Broadway, Canal Street, and Park Row, was reputed to have been a haven for drunkards, prostitutes, and malefactors of all types. This environment lent itself to the formation of various criminal gangs, some of the more colorful going by such names as the Dead Rabbits, Bowery Boys, Roach Guards, and Plug Uglies. The heart of the Five Points district, however, was the Old Brewery, where in one room, known as the Den of Thieves, lived 75 men, women, and children without benefit of furniture, beds, or toilet facilities (Demaris, 1970).

In addition to a rise in the overall crime rate, there was also a noticeable increase in the amount of liquor Americans were imbiding. The per capita rate of alcohol consumption rose from 2.5 gallons in 1790 to 7 gallons in 1810, to 10 gallons in 1829 (Clark, 1976). During this time crime and poverty were apparently more intimately linked than they are today. Cole (1934) points out that crime in the first half of the nineteenth century seemed to rise precipitously during the winter months when the cost of living was high and unemployment even higher. As we shall see in Chapter 4, however, a relationship between two or more variables, no matter how strong, is not unequivocal evidence of a causal connection, unless certain other conditions are also present.

The prison reform movement, which had begun during the late eighteenth century, appeared to lose some momentum during the early part of the nineteenth century. As we proceed through this period of high industrialization we find jails becoming increasingly more outdated and inefficient for the purpose of humanely housing criminal offenders. Facilities originally designed to aid in the correctional effort were now overcrowded and antiquated. Philadelphia's Walnut Street Jail, for instance, was a state-of-the-art facility at the time it was constructed in 1790. However, because the jail had never been adequately maintained, in less than 40 years it became a place better known for filth and immorality than sensible, humane correctional treatment (Krout & Fox, 1944).

WESTWARD EXPANSION (1860–1885)

As the Civil War became a reality the humanitarian and prison reform movements were abandoned in favor of more urgent matters. People were more concerned with the progress of the war than with the treatment of prison inmates. Historians have also noted that there was a marked increase in the incidence of violent crime during and shortly after the Civil War (Cole, 1934). This finding is consistent with Archer and Gartner's (1984) observation that many twentieth-century nations experienced augmented homicide rates following major international conflicts like World Wars I and II. It has been noted that the overall crime rate in the United States began to diverge significantly from the rest of the western world shortly after the end of the Civil War. Monkkonen (1989) attributes this to the rising availability of firearms and a growing tolerance for certain forms of homicide.

Shortly after the conclusion of the American Civil War came the bloody Lincoln County War in New Mexico. This violent struggle claimed the lives of many persons and was so intense that President Rutherford B. Hayes had to call in several military units under the command of General William T. Sherman to restore order. It was during the Lincoln County War that William "Billy the Kid" Bonney earned his reputation as a ruthless outlaw and cold-blooded killer. As with the Harpe brothers who preceded him, history suggests that William Bonney was an individual with very little care or concern for others, since he left a trail of bodies strewn over the western plain (Siringo, 1885). When he was finally shot down by a lawman at age 21, William Bonney was said to have killed at least one man for every year he had been alive (Hough, 1907). Other infamous outlaws of the day included Jesse James, Joel Fowler, and the Dalton brothers, their common bond being a reckless disregard for human life and the belief that they were above the law.

It has traditionally been assumed that crime flourished in western frontier towns and that modern-day America's problems with violence can be traced back to the lawlessness of the early American West. However, in a review of criminal statistics for the frontier mining towns of Aurora, Nevada, and Bodie, California, McGrath (1989) of the University of California at Los Angeles uncovered evidence that runs counter to popular lore on the "wild, wild, west." Excluding homicide, crime (juvenile as well as adult) was no more prevalent in the western frontier town than it was in any of the eastern cities in that period and is dwarfed by the crime rate observed in most present-day American small cities. Though homicides were a rather common occurrence in the Old West, they were nearly always the result of gunfights between willing, and often intoxicated, combatants.

McGrath (1989) discusses several factors he believes are responsible for the relatively low rate of crime in frontier America. The control provided by traditional religious teachings, a nearly nonexistent unemployment rate, and a collective sense of optimism were all important in keeping the crime rate low, but possibly the most effective deterrent to crime was the fact that practically everyone carried a firearm that they were willing to use to protect themselves and their property. An important development took place in the mid-1880s, with an increasing number of women moving west and many more men desiring stability and a secure lifestyle. Outside of homicide, crime had never been a major problem on the western frontier, but now it dropped to an even lower rate as the 1880s progressed. In many cases, the farmer's hoe replaced the cowboy's lariat. By the late 1880s Dodge City, notorious for its heavy drinking, promiscuous women, and fast living, lost the primary source of its prosperity, as well as its criminality, when the cattle drives began bypassing that city, which had become increasingly more settled by the decade's end (Schlesinger, 1945).

The crime rate observed in many American cities began to level off and even drop during the later stages of the nineteenth century. This small, but noticeable, curtailment of criminal activity occurred despite the presence of increased industrialization, urbanization, and immigration. Though this ebb was aided by a declining birth rate, the rise of the temperance movement in this country, coupled with religious training which emphasized self-control and the development of responsibility, should not be overlooked as a major contributary factor (Wilson & Herrnstein, 1985). The volume of alcohol use—as well as abuse—declined significantly over the course of the nineteenth century, the per capita rate of alcohol consumption having dropped from 10 gallons in 1829 to 2.1 gallons in 1850 (Clark, 1976). Conversely, the number of adults involved in church and community activities mounted during this period, and the Young Men's Christian Association (YMCA) was formed in an effort to assist young men and women working in the city by cultivating a Christian attitude and sense of self-discipline (Boyer, 1978). In addition, city police departments were becoming increasingly more professional and efficient, and in 1853 New York City became the first municipality to require its police officers to wear uniforms.

Jail conditions were still deplorable during the latter part of the nineteenth century, however there were several bright spots on the horizon. Philanthropists such as E. C. Wines, Franklin B. Sanborn, and Dr. Theodore Dwight stressed reform over retribution and the first national meeting of prison administrators and reformers took place in 1870. This conference stressed treatment over punishment, vocational and/or educational rehabilitation, and the use of indeterminate sentences to encourage better behavioral adjustment in prison (Wines, 1895). In 1877 the state reformatory in Elmira, New York, opened its doors to young male first-time offenders between the ages of 15 and 30 (Winter, 1891). A follow-up evaluation revealed that four out of five graduates remained free of serious legal difficulties ten years after release (Appleton's Annual Cyclopaedia, 1887). It was also during this period that probation was instituted by officials in the state of Massachusetts as an alternative to incarceration.

Despite the good intentions of reformers and a few isolated advances like Elmira, conventional penological practice remained primitive, antiquated, and insufficient for the purposes of correction. Furthermore, one-fifth of all inmates were habitual criminals (Schlesinger, 1945) for whom rehabilitation was viewed as impractical. In many instances separate institutions were constructed for male and female felons but correctional practice and the theory of criminality upon which it was based were fatuous by modern standards. Thus, men's reformatories stressed physical exercise and "manly" activities, while female facilities emphasized domestics and training in "womanly" deportment, based on a theory which held that crime was caused by delayed masculine development in males and a low degree of femininity in females. All in all, however, efforts were being made to improve prison conditions and the crime rate showed signs of decline.

THE AGE OF INTERNALIZATION (1885–1918)

Although national crime data are unavailable for the years prior to 1933, Monkkonen (1981) reports that the arrest records of various large cities reflect a descending crime rate over the course of the nineteenth century. In a detailed analysis of death records for the city of Philadelphia, Lane (1979) determined that the number of murder indictments dropped from 3.3 to 2.1 per capita from the mid- to the late 1800s. Ferdinand (1967) observed a similar decline when he examined homicide rates for the city of Boston collected between 1849 and 1900. There seems little doubt, then, that the rate of serious criminality subsided significantly over the tenor of the nineteenth century. Explaining this downward trend is somewhat more difficult.

One might ask, does the plummeting rate of crime witnessed in cities like Philadelphia and Boston around the turn of the century reflect the more general pattern of the nation as a whole during this time? Of even greater significance, however, is determining the cause of this apparent reduction in crime in major U.S. cities during this period. One possible explanation involves changes in the child-rearing practices followed during the mid- to late 1800s. Sunley (1955) reports that there was a transformation of child-rearing philosophy, if not actual practice, near the mid-nineteenth century that saw greater emphasis placed on moral and religious development and training. In effect, the child was viewed as having been born with certain destructive impulses and it was the parents' responsibility to teach their child the value of curbing antisocial inclinations. Hence, the crux of child-rearing practice during this period may have focused more on self-control than self-expression, and could have been responsible, at least in part, for the changes observed in the crime rate during this time.

By the end of the nineteenth century America was populated by young adults raised under a philosophy that stressed self-control and the value of restraint. Society was also becoming aware of the problems associated with young people leaving home early to work in the cities. Consequently, religious and community programs (for example, YMCA, Boy Scouts) took on added importance as a means of instilling certain moral values. Wilson and Herrnstein (1985), among others, regard this internalization process as one of the primary reasons why the crime rate demonstrated a noticeable dip in the second half of the nineteenth century and remained at a relatively low level well into the twentieth century.

Another possible interpretation for the low rate of criminality in the United States during this period holds that the police were becoming increasingly more effective in their crime control efforts. A proponent of this viewpoint, Gurr (1977) contends that the development of modern policing techniques led to a reduction in crime during the latter decades of the nineteenth century. Wilson and Herrnstein (1985), on the other hand, assert that while an increase in the professionalism of city police forces and the use of modern policing techniques may account for a portion of the general decline in criminality witnessed during this time, they do not explain the bulk of observed change. As a means of establishing support for their position, Wilson and Herrnstein question whether the crime rate could have risen so precipitously during the mid-1960s, when policy technology was reaching new heights, if modern policing techniques have such a powerful deterrent effect.

The correctional system also revealed a number of advances during this stage of American history. Massachusetts had been experimenting with releasing certain inmates on parole since the mid–1800s. Ohio initiated a formal system of parole in the late 1880s, and by 1898, 25 states had provisions for parole in their state charters (Sutherland & Cressey, 1978). Massachusetts was also on the cutting edge in its use of minimum security facilities and prison farms to facilitate correctional reform. The value of prison farms can be found in their ability to provide the offender with the opportunity to learn certain practical skills in an environment that stresses hard work and physical exercise (Schlesinger, 1945). This period also saw expansion of the prison system, which served to ease the problem of overcrowding in many state facilities. However, jails still tended to be overpopulated, understaffed, and in poor physical repair.

Up until this period juvenile offenders had been treated much the same as adults, often housed alongside hardened criminals in jails across the nation. In 1899, Illinois passed a law that required use of special courts for juveniles. Within a decade juvenile courts had been established in all major U.S. cities (Faulkner, 1931). The juvenile justice system not only mandated the use of special court proceedings, but also provided for the development of a network of independent juvenile correctional facilities and probation officers. Juvenile delinquency and adult criminality were no longer conceived of as a singular entity, possibly the most important advance made in the criminal justice field during this period.

One of the most sensationalized cases of the nineteenth century took place in Fall River, Massachusetts, on the morning of August 4, 1892. On that date Andrew Borden and his wife were brutally murdered in their home, each receiving over 20 blows to the head. Mr. Borden's daughter, Lizzie, was the prime suspect in the case but the evidence against her was weak and she was eventually acquitted. What separates this case from similarly brutal crimes of the period was the wide publicity it received from the news media. Lizzie Borden was seemingly tried by the newspapers long before her case ever came to trial. This helped establish the power of the press to influence public opinion on criminal justice matters, a trend which has gained momentum over the past several decades.

THE RISE TO WORLD PROMINENCE (1918–1960)

America's role in World War I did much to enhance its image as a world power. From this point onward the United States saw its influence extend well beyond its borders. However, America's role in world affairs did little to stem the tide of organized criminality, which seemed to be sweeping the nation. Gangsters like Al Capone, Vito Genovese, Charley "Lucky" Luciano, Frank Costello, and Benjamin "Bugsy" Segel violated the law with impunity. In fact, one of the distinguishing characteristics of organized crime is its involvement with legitimate sources of power and control (for example, politics, big business). Consequently, certain judges, politicians, and policemen owed their careers to these mobsters, a sad fact which had, and still has, serious repercussions for society and individual citizens.

One of the more powerful criminal organizations to appear during this time period, the Mafia or La Cosa Nostra, had its roots in the Black Hand criminal organizations originating in Sicily. Salvatore Maranzano is usually credited with organizing the Mafia in America. As was often the case with many of the gangster kingpins of the day, Maranzano was eventually gunned down by the henchmen of one of his own lieutenants, Lucky Luciano (Demaris, 1970). During Prohibition the distribution of illegal alcohol was a major source of income for many criminal organizations. Prostitution rings, murder, illegal gambling houses, political and/or organizational graft, and, at a later period, narcotics were also the bailiwick of organized criminals. The revolver and Thompson machine gun were favorite weapons, not only of the gangster but of many other criminals of the day. In fact, the use of handguns was estimated to have been responsible for approximately three-fourths of all homicides committed during the "roaring twenties" (Kavanagh, 1928).

The violence that seemed to accompany the bootlegging trade of the 1920s and 1930s is attributed to two primary factors—hijackings and competition (Haller, 1989). It was not uncommon for individuals wishing to obtain a piece of the bootlegging pie to hijack someone else's shipment of illegal alcohol. Wholesalers endeavored to minimize such a possibility by arming their drivers. Competition also stimulated violence to the extent that controlling a neighborhood or a cluster of neighborhoods meant lower costs and fewer risks to the wholesaler. Contrasting the midwestern cities of Chicago and Milwaukee, municipalities with high and low rates of bootleg-related violence, respectively, Haller (1989) determined that the political climate also had an influence on the level of violence observed.

Desperadoes and outlaws like Frank Nash, "Pretty Boy" Floyd, "Baby Face" Nelson, "Machine Gun" Kelly, and John Dellinger were also popular during this period in American history. Although they often captured the headlines as well as the imagination of more than one Walter Mitty, these individuals failed to achieve the political influence of the gangster and so typically ended up in a mortuary or penitentiary after a relatively short, but violent, spree of senseless criminality (Demaris, 1970). The more inventive members of this group considered themselves the spiritual descendants of the western outlaw (Demaris, 1970), but the characteristic that most clearly distinguished these individuals from most noncriminals was their seemingly insatiable desire for attention and apparent drive toward self-destruction.

During the 1930s Clyde Barrow and Bonnie Parker were the scourge of the Southwest. Like many of the other highly publicized criminals of the day, the public developed a love-hate relationship with these two individuals, fearing their actions yet admiring them for their bravado. Although their exploits have been immortalized in books and movies, Bonnie and Clyde never pulled off a major bank heist, preferring instead to rob gas stations, grocery stores, and small banks. They were, however, responsible for the deaths of 13 persons before meeting their own violent demise in a hail of police bullets (Demaris, 1970). Once again, we see the importance of the media in shaping attitudes toward crime and criminals, and how these sentiments may have influenced the expression of criminality within the nation itself.

Despite the number of high-profile robbers, murderers, and gangsters active during the early to mid-1900s, the overall rate of criminality did not rise. If anything, crime rates evidenced a decline during this period. National crime statistics, which were first published in 1933, failed to demonstrate an increase until the decade of the 1960s. As was noted earlier, crime and economic conditions appeared to correlate during the nineteenth century, at least when aggregate (large group) data were examined (Thomas, 1925). Yet between 1933 and 1960 we see little change in the crime rate, despite the fact that the Great Depression occurred during the 1930s and a period of unprecedented prosperity took place between 1946 and 1960. It would appear then that the link that may have existed between crime and the economy during the nineteenth century weakened considerably during the twentieth century. Wilson and Herrnstein (1985) speculate that when traditional values are strong, as they were during the nineteenth and early twentieth centuries, property crime will often arise out of necessity, but that when traditional values weaken, as seems to have been the case during the past 30 to 40 years of American history, property crime becomes more a function of opportunity than of necessity.

In a bid to deal more effectively with organized crime, various crime commissions were established in cities throughout the United States. However, this did little to stem the tide of organized criminality that seemed to be inundating the nation. Attempts were also made to stiffen existing laws as a means of keeping dangerous criminals off the streets and away from law-abiding citizens. In 1926 New York State introduced into law a career criminal statute which made life sentences mandatory after an individual's fourth felony conviction

(Slosson, 1931). Over the course of the 1900s clinicians became increasingly more interested in the special problems of the emotionally disturbed offender, particularly as related to the legal issues of competency and criminal responsibility.

Although the penitentiary had been around for more than 100 years, it took on added significance during the time surrounding World War II. It was during this period that the penitentiary became the symbol of American corrections. Names of institutions like Alcatraz, Leavenworth, Stateville, and San Quentin conjure up images that may be both frightening and intriguing to the noncriminal. The actual prison experience was probably pretty much as depicted in the popular movies of the day—hard, cold, and alienating—although efforts were being directed at establishing more humane conditions under which prisoners might live. The reader should realize, however, that deterrence was the philosophy of the day, for it was reasoned that the harshness and regimentation of prison life would deter most people from engaging in crime (Rafter, 1985). As we shall soon see, this was just the first of many attempts to develop a workable theory addressing the mission of corrections in America.

THE MODERN ERA (1960–PRESENT)

Crime began to rise sharply during the mid-1960s, an ascent which did not tapper off until around 1980 (Jamieson & Flanagan, 1989). Whereas juvenile delinquency had been growing since the end of World War II, adult criminality was now also on the rise, and at a fairly substantial rate. There is no doubt that the marked increase in the birth rate following World War II led to a change in the age structure of the United States, and that by the mid–1960s there was a larger cross-section of late adolescents and early adults in American society than had been the case during the early to mid-1900s. Since these age groups have been found to account for a disproportionate share of all crimes committed, it is understandable that a noticeable increase in the number of late adolescents and young adults in the U.S. population would result in a substantial accentuation of criminal activity. However, the crime rate grew even more dramatically than one would predict from changes taking place in the age structure of American society between 1965 and the late 1970s (compare Ferdinand, 1970; Jones, 1976). Factors other than the age structure of the population would therefore appear to be operating to bring about the largest crime surge in American history.

When we explore this issue further we discover that the Racine, Wisconsin, cohort study determined that males born in 1949 were significantly more likely to have been charged with theft, burglary, and assault by age 17 than males born just seven years earlier (Shannon, 1982). Wolfgang (1981), on the other hand, failed to discern a difference in the prevalence of crime when he compared the 1945 and 1958 Philadelphia cohorts (one-third of each group experiencing one or more juvenile arrests). However, the incidence of criminality (the number of arrests per offender) and the severity of crimes committed were much higher in the 1958 cohort. These findings suggest a possible change in the nature of criminality for individuals born after World War II compared to persons born before (or during) the war.

Wilson and Herrnstein (1985) argue that a change in time orientation may help explain the rise in criminality witnessed in 1960s America. As a means of investigating this possibility, Davids and his colleagues (Davids & Falkof, 1975; Davids, Kidder, & Reich, 1962) administered a measure of time orientation to two groups of delinquents, one group tested in 1959 and the other tested in 1974. This research revealed higher rates of selfish concern, impulsive behavior, and a general unwillingness to delay gratification in the group of delinquents tested in 1974. This would seem to support the argument that there has been a shift in the time orientation of delinquents, if not most Americans, over the last 20 to 30 years, with the new focus on immediate gratification.

It seems quite likely that society's lawbreakers have become increasingly more present-oriented and impulsive over the last several decades. How then might we explain this finding? One possible explanation relates to the mobility of American society during this period. Many more Americans exhibited transient lifestyles during the 1960s, 1970s, and 1980s than had been the case just 20 or 30 years earlier. As we saw with the unsettled days of the early Industrial Revolution, it is difficult to maintain strong family ties, and consequently develop effective internal social control, in situations where people are moving about from place to place. Such a state of affairs creates chaos and a loss of community solidarity, both of which are fertile soil for the development of an irresponsible, self-indulgent attitude and an emerging criminal orientation.

It is difficult to say how self-control and discipline are formed, but it appears that early training within the family unit plays a significant role in this regard. Waters and Crandall (1964), for instance, found that there was a gradual decrease in the amount of coercion used in disciplining children between 1940 and 1960. During this 20-year block, the general child-rearing philosophy that espoused self-control, and was so popular during the earlier part of the century, was gradually replaced by a doctrine that extolled the virtues of self-expression. Regardless of how we choose to conceptualize the crime explosion of the mid- to late 1960s, it appears that there was more at work than just a shift in the population age distribution.

One of the more frightening developments occurring during the modern era was an increase in the number of homicides committed by assailants unknown to the victim (Zahn, 1989). This epoch also saw an increase in "motiveless" crime and the appearance of serial killers. In 1966, 6 percent of all homicides were without apparent motive; by 1985 this figure had climbed to 20 percent. Holmes and DeBurger (1985) of the University of Louisville estimate that a significant proportion of all motiveless homicides are actually perpetrated by serial killers. Two other experts in the field, Hazelwood and Douglas (1984) estimate that at least 500 Americans fall victim to serial murders each year. Ted Bundy, the bright, glib, psychopathic law student who had an affinity for young women with long, dark hair parted in the middle, had acknowledged responsibility for the murders of dozens of such young women (Holmes and DeBurger, 1985).

While mass murder (killing a large number of people in one place at one point in time) has its roots in the American experience, dating back to before the Harpe brothers, serial murder is a relatively recent development on the American crime scene. Like many of the European serial killers who preceded them (for example, Jack the Ripper in Victorian England), American serial murderers have received an inordinate amount of attention from the news media. Human predators like Ted Bundy, Wayne Williams, Kenneth Bianchi, and John Wayne Gacy have received the kind of notoriety formerly reserved for international despots and villains like Genghis Khan and Adolph Hitler. It is doubtful that serial murder could be eliminated simply by avoiding the sensationalism found in newspapers, magazines, and movies, although we have no way of knowing for sure since the American mass media have never attempted to test such a hypothesis.

Though prison conditions have improved and the number of correctional facilities grown during the modern era, the criminal justice system still lacks a coherent philosophy by which to guide its own development. The medical model was in vogue during the early years of the modern epoch in which criminals were viewed as disturbed victims requiring treatment and rehabilitation. When half-hearted efforts at remediation met with failure, the philosophy changed to one of incapacitation. Here the criminal offender was viewed as largely intractable and the purpose of corrections was to keep him confined and apart from society (Greenwood, 1983). While there are aspects of the incapacitation perceptive which are valid and meaningful, focusing on this objective to the detriment of other legitimate correctional goals seems both spurious and short-sighted. Though this characterization of the shifting priorities of correctional reform is admittedly oversimplified, it does appear to capture the confusion and lack of direction that has epitomized the American correctional experience since the early 1600s.

CONCLUSION

Now that we have briefly reviewed the history of crime in America it seems appropriate that we attempt to draw some general inferences about crime trends in America from colonial times to the present day. Although national crime statistics were not collected until 1933, a narrative analysis of crime indicates that violations of the civil code were relatively infrequent between 1607 and the early 1800s. With the advent of industrialization, however, came an escalation of the crime rate, which by the mid- to late 1800s began to decline significantly. The crime rate leveled off during the first half of the twentieth century, rose to its highest level between 1965 and 1980, and then began to taper slightly after 1980 (see Figure 2.1). One notable exception to this general pattern has been

Figure 2.1
Percent Change in the Total Crime Index Relative to the Percent Change in the Total Number of Young Adult Males Aged 15 to 29 Residing in the United States between 1960 and 1990

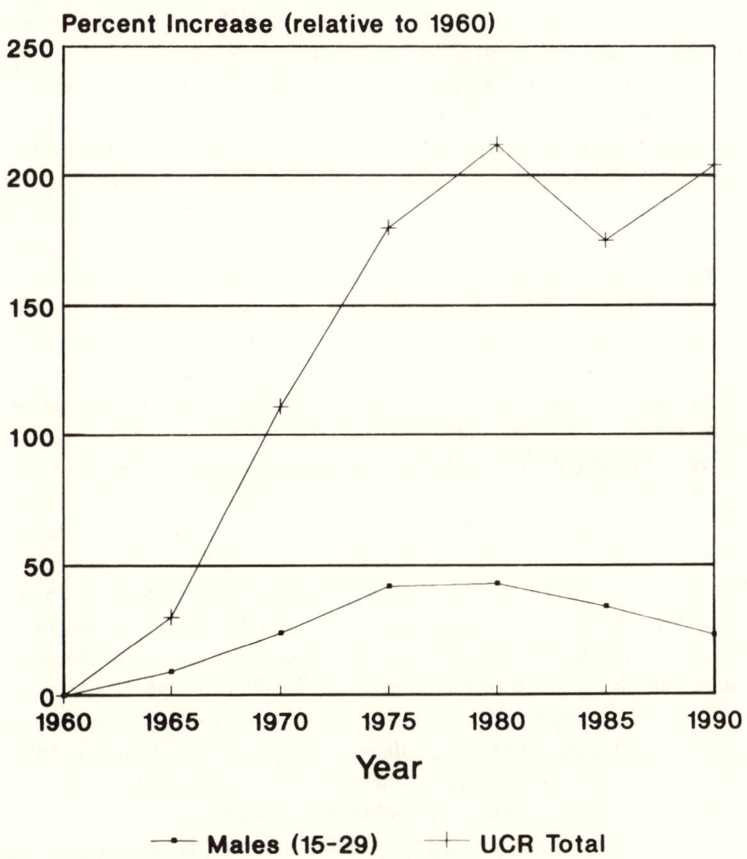

Note: The percent change was calculated relative to 1960. The Total Crime Index was compiled from Federal Bureau of Investigation Uniform Crime Reports, while the population data were derived from U.S. Bureau of Census Reports.

the rate of assault, which demonstrated a noticeably ascending inclination between 1975 and 1985 (Osgood et al., 1989).

Gurr (1989) writes that when historical and contemporary evidence on crime are combined they reveal a distended *U*-shaped curve, with the left vertical arm of the curve symbolizing 1830 to 1840, the right vertical arm of the curve signifying the interval between 1965 and 1980, and the lower portion of the *U* representing the years in between. One explanation for the *U*-curve phenomenon is that it reflects shifts in the age distribution of the population. It is a well-documented fact, for instance, that both the prevalence and incidence of criminality are highest in youth adults. Jamieson and Flanagan (1989) report that persons aged 16 to 34 account for only 32 percent of the total U.S. population but are responsible for 70 percent of all crimes committed. Throughout history there have been alterations in the age distribution of the population of the United States. Thus, in the late 1800s there were fewer high-risk males (ages 15 to 29) in the general population of the United States than there had been some 50 or 60 years earlier. This may help explain the declining crime rate observed during the second half of the nineteenth century.

This same relationship may also help explain increases in the crime rate at various points in history. The post-war baby boom generation, for example, brought about a large increase in the number of ''at-risk'' citizens beginning around 1965 and extending well into the 1970s. Steffensmeier and Harer (1987) determined that a shifting age structure explained approximately 40 percent of the drop witnessed in the American crime rate between 1980 and 1984. That property crimes declined significantly more than person crimes can be attributed to the fact that the age-crime curve is flatter for person crimes than it is for property offenses (Steffensmeier & Harer, 1987). There is little doubt, then, that the changing age structure observed at various times in American history has played a role in the rise and fall of recorded crime rates. However, as Figure 2.1 clearly illustrates, the crime surge observed during the 1960s and 1970s far exceeded the proportion of high-risk males living in the United States at that time.

If a shifting age structure is incapable of explaining American crime trends in toto, then what other factors may be involved? One is urbanization. Gurr (1981) asserts that the transformation from a rural, agricultural nation to an urban, industrialized one in the early 1800s resulted in a disruption of societal control and a corresponding rise in the crime rate. However, once integration into an urban lifestyle has taken place, society moves into a second stage of modernization, according to Gurr, wherein modern cities offer citizens increased economic opportunities that eventually serve to reduce criminality. Moreover, a well-integrated industrial complex demands certain behaviors (for example, self-control, emotional modulation, punctuality) of its citizens that are largely incompatible with violent criminality (Lane, 1979). Gurr explains the right arm of the *U*-curve as reflecting an erosion of many ''second-stage'' values and an attitudinal shift in the ''American psyche'' by which violence has been glamorized and self-indulgence emphasized. Lane (1989) provides data on the homicide rate of Philadelphia between 1899 and 1933 that lend credence to several of Gurr's hypotheses, particularly those addressing the stabilization (second) stage of the modernization sequence.

A third possible explanation for crime trends in American history is the influence of economic conditions on the expression of criminality. It certainly makes good intuitive sense that people tend to engage in more property-oriented crime when faced with financial hardship than when things are going well. In fact, this explanation seems to have merit when applied to property crimes committed prior to 1900. However, during the twentieth century the relationship that had been observed between crime and economics during the eighteenth and nineteenth centuries weakened considerably. Wilson and Herrnstein (1985) surmise that with the loss of a strong internal sense of community, which apparently took place over the course of the twentieth century, property crime became more a function of opportunity than of necessity.

The circumstances under which offenders engage in various criminal acts entail a fourth possible explanation for changing crime rates. Cohen and Felson (1979b) discern that American crime trends between the years 1947 and 1974 were at least partly a function of the amount of time people spent outside the family home, the number of single-adult households, and the supply of portable and movable durables (radios, television sets). These and other findings suggest that we need to consider not only characteristics of the individual (for example, age, proportion of career offenders) but also environmental and situational factors if we are to derive a consummate understanding of historical trends in criminal behavior.

The argument that changes in the social context or person-society bond influence the crime rate is another plausible explanation for the crime rate trends that have been noted. Throughout the colonial period a firm bond was established between the individual and his or her immediate community. This bond worked to keep the crime rate low in the sense that it engendered a desire for social approval and avoidance of embarrassment. The use of stocks and the pillory during this period illustrates the kind of humility the community was capable of instilling in its members. However, this embarrassment was based on a social bond, without which the individual would never have experienced discomfort sufficient to prevent him or her from violating the law in the future.

Over time, the family became an increasingly more important element in the socialization process. However, with the dawn of industrialization and the movement of many young people into the cities where they received minimal supervision from older adults, problems began to arise. This early nineteenth-century surge in crime eventually subsided near the mid-1800s and the crime rate actually began to fall several decades later. It is possible that the increased emphasis placed on moral and religious training in the mid- to late 1800s had something to do with this decline in criminality. However, this focus on self-discipline and internal control gave way to accentuated interest in the value of self-expression just prior to World War II. Even though this trend may have helped some individuals avoid the development of emotional problems, it may also have brought about, or at least encouraged, a rise in the crime rate by virtue of its emphasis on immediacy and verbalization to the detriment of self-restraint, responsibility, and learning to delay gratification.

It would be both naive and farcical to suggest that a return to a Victorian-era philosophy of life would be capable of restoring a state of low criminality in modern-day America. Taking into account numerous technological advances that have occurred over the past 30 to 40 years, it seems highly unlikely that we could ever make life in America as simple as it was around the turn of the century. We could, however, take steps to implement certain facets of this general philosophy in an effort to instill greater responsibility and self-discipline in young Americans. What we need to find is a workable compromise between these two positions so that we teach our children to express and assert themselves responsibly. We must therefore work toward the development of lasting values, but in a way that is reasoned rather than absolute.

A sixth factor that may help explicate the variations observed in the crime rate over nearly 400 years of American history involves a change in the cost of criminality. In other words, crime may have decreased at various points in American history simply because the punishment associated with it was considered sufficient to deter most people from engaging in such behavior. We have already seen that improvements in police technology may have played a role in reducing crime near the end of the nineteenth century, although this theory is incomplete in that it fails to account for the sharp rise in the crime rate that occurred during the mid-1960s, when police technology was also reaching new heights. Incarceration also appears to be much less of a deterrent than was once thought, since the current level of criminality remains high (Jamieson & Flanagan, 1989) despite the fact we continue locking up felons at an ever-increasing rate. Thus, while the differential cost of crime (at least as it has traditionally been measured—for example, confinement) may have an impact on a relatively small percentage of individual offenders (or potential offenders), it cannot be viewed as a viable explanation for crime rate trends across nearly four centuries of American history.

It is somewhat disheartening that despite improved prison conditions, very little progress has been made in the correctional field since the early years of the American Republic. The penitentiary remains the symbol of American corrections, and the warehousing of offenders is unfortunately a penological practice that continues to attract adherents. Lacking an organizing or guiding philosophy, the correctional field has drifted from idea to idea and from fad to fad, but without contributing much substance to our understanding of criminal behavior. At this point the corrections field is at a crossroads. With an ever-increasing number of offenders housed in U.S. prison facilities, the criminal justice and correctional systems will be forced to find workable solutions to their problems or fall even further behind in their efforts to understand and control crime.

It could be argued that changes in the nature of criminality have had an impact on the rate at which crimes have been committed. As was mentioned previously, economic conditions and crime were more strongly correlated during the eighteenth and nineteenth centuries than they are today. This may reflect a fundamental change in the nature of criminality beginning during the early 1900s, when property crime changed from being a crime of necessity to one of opportunity. In a study of males born in Philadelphia in 1945 and 1958, Wolfgang (1981) found the prevalence of crime (number of offenders) to be consistent across the groups but discerned a higher incidence of crime (number of crimes committed) in the later-born group. This would seem to suggest that while general cultural and/or environmental factors may greatly influence the manner in which a criminal predisposition is expressed, these factors have less effect on the criminal predisposition itself.

As history has demonstrated time and again, there is a small percentage of individuals who account for the majority of serious crimes committed regardless of the time period or era referenced. In fact, New York State passed the first habitual offender act in 1797 by mandating a term of life in prison for all two-time felons. Massachusetts followed suit some 20 years later in implementing its own habitual criminal law, and by the mid-1930s nearly half the states in the country had some form of special law for repeat offenders. Over the past ten years there has been renewed interest in crime as a career, and one of the primary goals of the Comprehensive Crime Control Act of 1984 was to find an answer to the career criminal problem.

Whether the Harpe brothers, Jesse James, John Dellinger, or Ted Bundy, the recidivistic offender has been with us from the very beginning. We cannot therefore attribute American crime trends to the presence or absence of career criminals. Though this issue requires further study, I speculate that the principal difference in crime rates over the course of American history has not been with the presence or absence of habitual or lifestyle criminals, but with the number of offenses committed by these lifestyle offenders (subgroup incidence) and the number of non-lifestyle criminals engaged in illegal activity (general prevalence).

In considering crime trends it is important that we are careful not to overlook the impact society may have on expressions of criminality. Perhaps society, in the form of public attitudes or the influence of the mass media, is responsible for some of these trends? As anyone who has read a newspaper or watched a televised news broadcast can attest, the American media have shown a lasting fascination with crimes of violence. Even before the Lizzie Borden case the media seemed to spend excessive amounts of time and effort covering bizarre and shocking cases of rape, murder, and mayhem. Whether this preoccupation has helped create a generation of persons obsessed with crime or simply satisfied an existing interest in such matters, there is little doubt that crime has helped sell newspapers and promote movies. However, to state that American society's apparent preoccupation with crime or the media's treatment of criminal acts is the primary cause of crime is nothing more than speculation in search of facts at this point.

We in the United States have a habit of looking for simple solutions to complex problems. However, in the long run this approach seems to be counterproductive and fraught with many pitfalls. In this chapter we have taken a brief look at the historical aspects of crime in America and found that the issues are certainly more complex than many of us may have initially assumed. Nevertheless, there are several notable trends in these data which are real, potentially predictable, and caused by a wide assortment of factors. Predominant among these variables are a changing age structure and the role of family and/or community values in forming a bond between the individual and his or her social group. However, because very few researchers have divided the crime rate into incidence and prevalence, the factors leading to the rise or fall of criminality at various points in history may differ from period to period. Hence, the crime surge that took place in the early nineteenth century may have been the result of increased incidence, while the crime explosion of the 1960s may have been largely a function of increased prevalence. These and other issues need to be examined further if we hope to achieve a complete understanding of crime trends in American history.

3

Cross-National Comparisons of Crime

Not all nations are as obsessed with crime as the United States appears to be (Adler, 1983). This may be because most countries do not experience the level of criminality presently confronting Americans, or it could simply be a problem of perception. Using data reported to the World Health Organization (WHO), United Nations (UN), and International Police Organization (Interpol), Kalish (1988) estimates that crimes of violence are from four to nine times more prevalent in the United States than in Europe. Furthermore, cross-national research comparing both industrialized and nonindustrialized nations places the United States near the top of the list of countries with high crime rates (Archer & Gartner, 1984). A logical conclusion, then, is that there may be something of value to be learned by examining how other nations and cultures deal with what has become a serious problem in this country.

The noted French sociologist Emile Durkheim once argued that comparative sociology was not merely a subspecialty within the general field of sociology but was actually "sociology itself" (Durkheim, 1938). Much the same could be said of cross-national or comparative research on criminology. What, we might ask, lies beneath the relatively high rate of criminality found in the United States and the relatively low rate observed in many other nations? In an effort to answer this question we inspect crime rates in cross-national research, the salient characteristics of nations with differing levels of industrialization and crime, and identify variables potentially capable of discriminating between high- and low-crime-rate countries.

CRIME RATES IN CROSS-NATIONAL RESEARCH

Researchers interested in investigating crime from a cross-national perspective must learn to deal with a number of hidden obstacles. Paramount among these is finding a reliable estimate of a nation's crime rate. The crime rate is typically expressed as a number representing the proportion of crimes committed annually within a particular locale per 100,000 population. As Wilson and Herrnstein (1985) note, however, this rate is actually composed of two parts—the prevalence and the incidence of crime. The prevalence of crime is the ratio of persons who engage in crime to all persons in a particular city, state, or country; the incidence of crime refers to the number of offenses committed by the average offender. Accordingly, changes could take place in either the prevalence or the incidence of crime and not be reflected in the per capita rate. Unfortunately, very few comparative studies on crime consider prevalence and incidence separately.

Wolfgang (1967) reports that definitions of crime tend to vary from nation to nation. He adds that even if two nations hold a similar definition of a particular offense, the per capita crime rates may still not be fully comparable. This is because nations may assign different degrees of severity to a particular offense, which in turn may influence reporting practices or clearance rates. Research reflects the presence of cross-national variations in the perceived severity of certain offenses, although some categories of crime (for example, robbery) are nearly always rated as more serious than other actions (for example, taking drugs or engaging in public protest) (Newman, 1976). Wolfgang therefore proposes that crime rates be weighted for seriousness as determined by the respective populations of the nations being compared. Bennett and Lynch (1990) compared four definitions or indicators of cross-national crime differences (Interpol, United Nations, World Health Organization, Archer and Gartner's Comparative Crime Data File, or CCDF) and discovered that while crime rates for individual nations varied by data source, consistent results were obtained when temporal, national, and worldwide changes in crime rate were examined. These authors also failed to discern significant variations in the error of measurement across the four data sets.

The crime rate can be deceptive if one does not take into account certain demographic features of the population assessed. This is because certain groups (for example, young urban males) are more inclined to act out criminally than other groups (Wilson & Herrnstein, 1985). Consequently, we might erroneously interpret a crime rate difference as significant when in actuality it reflects nothing more than the presence of more youthful urban offenders in one nation than another. The increased rate of crime observed in the United States between 1965 and 1980, for instance, can be attributed, at least in part, to the entry of the postwar baby boom generation into the crime-prone age group (15 to 29). Likewise, Ireland's lower than average rate of crime can be credited as much to a regular pattern of differential emigration as anything this country has done from a criminal justice standpoint. As a result of emigration, Ireland experienced a 12 percent reduction in the number of males between the ages of 15 to 29 from 1926 to 1971 (Organization for Economic Cooperation and Development, 1980), when the rest of Europe was witnessing increased numbers of males in this crime-prone age group. Although age-corrected crime rates are usually not available, researchers need to be sensitive to the potentially confounding effects of such demographic characteristics as age and gender.

Another criticism often leveled against comparative studies on crime is that they typically rely on cross-sectional rather than longitudinal data. Hence, an investigator who compares two or three nations on a set of measures collected at one particular point in time may overlook vital historical trends in the data. Kalish (1988) argues that if cross-national comparisons are to prove fruitful they need to be conducted using multiple data sets analyzed longitudinally rather than cross-sectionally. Mindful of the general absence of research employing longitudinal or time series designs, Archer and Gartner (1984) created the Comparative Crime Data File (CCDF). The CCDF contains longitudinal (1900–1970) data collected across five crime categories in 110 countries and 44 major cities. Archer and Gartner's approach to cross-national crime research is a recent development worthy of a great deal more attention than it has thus far received.

Although longitudinal studies are usually superior to cross-sectional designs, the longitudinal approach is certainly no panacea. One potential problem is that recordkeeping practices, legal definitions, and arrest patterns sometimes vary over time, even within the same country. Archer and Gartner (1984), for example, report that crime records in Germany differ depending upon whether they were collected before, during, or after World War II. A longitudinal design also does not compensate for the problems encountered when one's measures are missing or inadequate. Archer and Gartner recommend using proxy variables in cases where it can be demonstrated that a known variable correlates reliably with the missing information. A primary consideration, therefore, becomes determining whether the proxy variable is an adequate substitute for the missing measure.

Relative to the issue of missing and proxy variables, it is crucial that we understand that various indicators are more or less useful in comparative research on crime. Thus, the number of offenses is a better estimate of criminality than arrests, while arrests are superior to convictions, which in turn are preferable to the total number of incarcerations (Archer & Gartner, 1984). Since there may be dissimilarities in how many offenses lead to arrest (or conviction) across countries or cultures, a problem arises when we endeavor to contrast two or more nations without the benefit of comparable data (as might be observed in a situation where we have offense data for one nation and arrest rates for another). Different indicators are much less problematic in longitudinal research conducted within the same country since the rate of intranational criminal case mortality (going from one level of data to another; Van Vechten, 1942) tends to be reasonably stable over time.

Irrespective of how one handles the level of data issue, reliance on official crime data can present a problem. This is because official crime statistics routinely underestimate the prevalence and incidence of criminality, particularly in developing countries where recordkeeping policies are much less efficient than they are in developed nations (Clinard & Abbott, 1973). The United Nations Bureau of Social Affairs (1967), for instance, determined that between 45 and 48 percent of all serious crimes in India go unreported. Unreported crime in industrialized nations, on the other hand, tends to be heavily weighted toward minor property offenses (Skogan, 1977) and homicide is characteristically reported at a reasonably high rate in nearly all countries (Archer & Gartner, 1984; Phillipson, 1974). Consequently, Archer and Gartner recommend use of longitudinal designs that focus on the offense rates of such serious crimes as homicide, although even this procedure is not foolproof. Japan, for instance, classifies assaults resulting in death as assaults, and Czechoslovakia reports rapes resulting in death as rapes, whereas the United States tabulates both such offenses as homicides.

A primary aim of criminal science investigators scrutinizing the rate of cross-cultural criminality is making statements of a causal nature about the relationships they observe. Consequently, if *A* and *B* are found to correlate, and our time series analysis reveals that *A* preceded *B*, it may be tempting to conclude that *A* was the cause of *B*. However, in order to make such a statement we must first rule out a variety of alternative explanations that may or may not be causally related to crime. What is important, however, is that such alternative hypotheses be entertained, explored, and evaluated, which in turn adds strength to the validity of our stated position. The ruling out of alternative explanations for a set of findings will be addressed in Chapter 4 of this volume.

In probing the causal issue further, it is well to keep in mind that the majority of cross-national investigations conducted on crime have utilized aggregate or group level data. However, it would be premature to offer causal conclusions on the basis of such findings. Take, for instance, the frequently reported relationship between a nation's crime rate and the number of telephones per household (Clinard & Abbott, 1973). It would be erroneous to conclude that the number of telephones per household causes a rise in the crime rate, or that higher levels of criminality create a greater demand for telephones, without examining this issue at the individual-household level. If we were to plumb this relationship further we would probably find that both the number of telephones and the crime rate correlate with a third variable—urbanization—which may or may not explain both the increased rate of criminality and the augmented number of telephones in industrialized nations (Clinard & Abbott, 1973).

With several of the problems associated with cross-national research on crime delineated, it is now time to direct our attention to specific aspects of comparative criminology. Toward this end we examine crime in four separate nations, two of which display a high rate of criminality and two which exhibit a relatively low rate. After this has been accomplished we discuss certain national characteristics in an effort to ascertain why particular nations seem to experience higher (or lower) crime rates than other countries or principalities.

COMPARATIVE CRIMINOLOGY: A TALE OF FOUR COUNTRIES

Industrialization and crime have been found to correlate, both when a nation is viewed from a historical perspective as well as when various nations are compared cross-sectionally (Clinard & Abbott, 1973). Thus, the more industrialized a nation becomes, the more urbanized its population and the higher its per capita rate of criminality. However, not all of the industrialized countries in the world have high crime rates. Take, for instance, the highly industrialized nations of Japan, Switzerland, and the Netherlands, all of which experience relatively low levels of criminality. This, then, is one factor upon which our present discussion on the crime-related characteristics of four nations is based. The other factor is the relative crime rate (high versus low) experienced by each country.

Being realistic, it is unlikely that we are able to identify all the salient characteristics that likely discriminate between high- and low-crime-rate nations simply by surveying the characteristics of four countries. We can, nonetheless, use this approach to establish certain hypotheses as to what might be important in differentiating between high- and low-crime-rate nations. With this caveat in mind, the Federal Republic of Germany serves as our example of a highly industrialized high-crime-rate nation, and Japan is used to illustrate a highly industrialized country with a low crime rate. Of the low industrialized nations, Uganda is discussed in terms of its high rate of criminality and Peru is examined for the sake of its low crime rate. Each of these nations is perused with an eye toward achieving a clearer understanding of crime from an international standpoint.

High Industrialization–High Crime: The Federal Republic of Germany

Despite the problem of crime in the Federal Republic of Germany (FRG), this nation houses a generally homogeneous population that differs very little from that of its neighbor, the German Democratic Republic (GDR), with which it recently merged in a highly publicized case of reunification. Somewhere between 80 and 85 percent of the population in the FRG resides in urban areas. This is slightly higher than that found in the GDR. With its outstanding system of education, the FRG has given birth to a number of artistic and scientific developments. Furthermore, this nation's literacy rate is nearly 100 percent, while it boasts one of the strongest health-care delivery systems in Europe.

Interesting results surface when we compare the Federal Republic of Germany (FRG) with its sister nation, the German Democratic Republic (GDR). Adler (1983) estimates that the crime rate in the FRG is six times that of the GDR—this, for two nations located in the same general geographical region of the world, with similarly homogeneous populations and roughly equivalent levels of industrialization. While the crime-rate difference between these two nations might be explained by dissimilarities in how they approach police work or report crime, there is something even more fundamental at work here. Consequently, we explore aspects of the criminal justice systems in what were once called East and West Germany.

The criminal justice system in both Germanies has its roots in Roman law.The law in the Federal Republic of Germany is based on two primary codes, the Strafgesetzbuch (criminal code) and the Burgerliches Gesetzbuch (civil code) (Kloss, 1976). Prior to reunification, criminal procedure in the German Democratic Republic was controlled by legal codes that emphasized the collective political will of the working class as the basis for crime control (Adler, 1983), although, as we have come to learn, this system was more politically corrupt than had ever before been imagined. Still, the criminal justice system appears to have received greater popular support in the GDR than has been the case in the FRG (Adler, 1983; Sagel-Grande, 1987). Thus, despite attempts by FRG officials to present the police officer as the citizen's "friend and helper," many fewer crimes are cleared by arrest in the FRG than was once possible in the GDR (Adler, 1983; Kloss, 1976).

The correctional system in the German Democratic Republic also tended to be more popularly supported than its counterpart in the West. It has also been stated that the GDR placed greater emphasis on crime prevention and relied less extensively on incarceration as its primary vehicle for crime control than does the Federal Republic of Germany (Adler, 1983). Touring an FRG prison facility for juveniles, Kulich (1975) remarked that the majority of offenders were poorly educated and lacking in marketable skills. He further observed that there was little apparent interest in providing inmates with the opportunity to advance their education or learn various work skills in this particular juvenile facility. While drawing conclusions on the basis of a single observation is not justified from a scientific standpoint, there is some evidence that the focus of the criminal justice system in the GDR, despite the corruption, was geared more toward rehabilitation than is presently the case with its counterpart in the FRG (Kloss, 1976; Sagel-Grande, 1987).

Although the family has always been important to Germans, the state seemed to play a more active role in promoting informal social control by way of family and neighborhood solidarity in the German Democratic Republic before reunification than is presently the case in the Federal Republic of Germany (Sagel-Grande, 1987). Of course, the greater restrictions on personal freedom in the GDR, or the fact that the GDR was less well off financially than the FRG (and thus presented fewer opportunities for economically oriented crime), may account for some of the crime-based differences between the two Germanies. Nevertheless, industrialization, perhaps because it took place more rapidly in West Germany, did not appear to have as devastating an effect on informal sources of social control (particularly the family) in the GDR than in its sister nation. In conclusion, the FRG and GDR appear to differ along several salient dimensions potentially capable of explaining the wide disparities observed in the national crime rates of each. It will be interesting to monitor the crime problems of these two areas as reunification brings them to be a single nation once again.

High Industrialization–Low Crime: Japan

As with most industrialized nations, Japan has experienced an increase in its urban population during the last several decades. Nearly three-quarters of its population is urbanized and the literacy rate is virtually 100 percent. Since ancient times Japan's society has been structured, ordered, and hierarchical (Clifford, 1976). This appears to have aided the Japanese in their efforts to control crime despite the negative effects of rapid industrialization. Japan also appears to have benefited from the fact that its population is fairly homogeneous, with just a small percentage of indigenous Caucasoid people and 600,000 Koreans compared to a large number of individuals of Japanese heritage (Adler, 1983).

The Japanese criminal justice system is spearheaded by a highly trained and well-motivated police force. Like Japanese society, this force is hierarchically organized (Ministry of Justice, 1970). In contrast to what is oftentimes found in the United States, the Japanese police officer is treated with respect and honor rather than fear and apprehension (Vogel, 1979). Toward a goal of public support for their police force, Japanese authorities rely on a concept known as the "police box" where the police officer and his or her family live. The officer assigned to a community "box" not only handles criminal matters but also helps search for runaways, mediate family disputes, and assist with various routine tasks such as helping a neighbor apply for a driver's license or escorting an elderly woman to and from the market (Adler, 1983). Owing to the rather high level of popular involvement in Japan's criminal justice system the clearance rate for serious crimes is three times that of the United States (Vogel, 1979). Conviction rates are also much higher in Japan than they are in the United States.

Incarceration is viewed as a last resort in Japan. An individual is much more likely to receive diversion, a fine, or a suspended sentence than confinement under the Japanese system of criminal justice. If confined, the Japanese offender can expect to be treated fairly, firmly, and consistently. The correctional system in Japan is composed of 67 prisons and is viewed as humane and effective by at least one commentator (Suzuki, 1977). Suzuki adds that inmate classification is based on the vocational and training needs of the individual and that prisoners typically receive remuneration for any work done while confined. The prison population in Japan has remained remarkably stable since the early 1980s, with approximately 30,000 new admissions and 30,000 releases each year (Cripe, 1990).

Despite the significance of the formal criminal justice system in achieving crime control, informal networks of control have even more powerful social influence in Japan. The Japanese take their obligations to family, community, and nation very seriously. Group harmony is more important to the Japanese than individual achievement or personal rights, and this has led to a greater internalization of cultural values than is typically observed in most Western countries (Wilson & Herrnstein, 1985). Moreover, despite the large number of social changes that characteristically accompany industrialization, the Japanese have been successful in affirming the strength of the nuclear family (Adler, 1983). In fact, they appear to have preserved the atmosphere of community, so much a part of village life, in making their transition to the city. The industrialized complex itself has played a monumental role in promoting this transition by establishing the company as a surrogate extended family through higher salaries, better security, and active employee assistance programs (Hazama, 1976).

Low Industrialization–High Crime: Uganda

The crime rate in Uganda began climbing several decades ago when this nation first entered the initial stages of industrialization. The sharp rise in crime that accompanied industrialization in Uganda was enough to cause one Ugandan official to assert that his country's crime rate was among the highest in the world (*New York Times*, 1971). Between the years 1948 and 1968, for instance, the crime rate in Uganda nearly tripled and there was an increase of about 80 percent over the final four years of this period (Clinard & Abbott, 1973). These findings unquestionably suggest the presence of a serious crime problem in Uganda despite a relatively low degree of industrialization.

Besides being largely nonindustrialized, the major portion of Uganda's population resides in rural rather than urban areas. Recent estimates place less than 10 percent of the Ugandan population in cities and urban areas. As is the case with developed countries, however, the majority of Ugandan crime occurs in the cities. Clinard and Abbott (1973), for instance, report that one-fourth of the crime in Uganda is committed in the capital city of Kampala. While it has been speculated that homogeneous populations lend themselves to less crime (Wilson & Herrnstein, 1985), Uganda's population is extremely homogeneous. It would seem, then, that there are factors other than population homogeneity that separate high-crime nations like Uganda and the Federal Republic of Germany from low-crime countries like Japan.

Variations in the criminal justice systems of certain nations may be one explanation for the crime-rate differences. The Ugandan legal system is based on the Colonial Office Model Codes (Clinard & Abbott, 1973). In contrast to the situation in Japan, the Ugandan police are typically underpaid, understaffed, undertrained, and underequipped. In Kampala (population 450,000), the capital city of Uganda, there are only 30 to 40 officers, most of whom patrol the city on foot, and the few police cars that do exist rarely come with radios. The Ugandan court system is equally antiquated; the jails are packed with individuals awaiting trial; and the vast majority of offenders, as is the case with many nations, derive from the lower socioeconomic strata of society (Clinard & Abbott, 1973).

One of the primary reasons given for the military coup in 1971 that eventually led to General Idi Amin's rise to power was a concern on the part of the populace with a sudden increase in a form of robbery known as *kondoism* (Clinard & Abbott, 1973). Kondoism characteristically involves a gang of individuals armed with guns or knives who rob an isolated store, domicile, or person; unfortunately, the victims in these attacks are often killed or seriously injured. The problem of crime in Uganda is not easily explained, although it does appear to coincide with a movement toward greater industrialization, despite the fact this African nation remains largely agricultural in nature.

Why Uganda has experienced such serious crime problems with only modest levels of industrialization, when Japan has done so well in the face of fervent urbanization is a question that has plagued Uganda's leaders as well as its scientists. The answer may rest with the different systems of informal control exercised by these two countries. When it was primarily a nation of small villages, Uganda had no crime problem. However, the rise of industrialization led to increased migration and the development of the first urban centers in this nation of 15 million people (Clinard & Abbott, 1973). Uganda did not approach urbanization as did Japan, and so the village-based atmosphere of community and obligation, which the Japanese brought with them when they moved to the city, was replaced by individualism and impersonality (Clinard & Abbott, 1973). Consequently, the more urban regions of Uganda began to rely nearly exclusively on formal measures of social control, a practice which is appreciably less effective in curtailing crime than is a solid system of informal social control (Adler, 1983; Archer & Gartner, 1984; Clifford, 1967; Clinard & Abbott, 1973).

Low Industrialization–Low Crime: Peru

The population of Peru is made up of two general classes of individuals: a small upper class and a much larger lower class. The small upper class, from which the more powerful members of Peruvian society originate (Weil et al., 1972), is composed largely of the descendants of Spanish colonists. The lower class, on the other hand, contains the Peruvian Indians, descendants of the Incas, and a racially mixed group (*mestizos*). There has been a migration of between 1 and 2 million Peruvians into urban areas over the past 30 years. However, cities are not the only targets of migration in Peru. Oftentimes these individuals settle in a provincial town before moving to the city. This appears to have eased the transition from rural to city living and may be partly responsible for the low rate of non-drug trade-related criminality enjoyed by this nation of 20 million people (Adler, 1983).

The Peruvian penal code is based on the Continental—Latin American model which was adopted in 1924 (Levene & Zeffaroni, 1978). On paper, this system is as good as any found in Latin America. In practice, however, Peruvian law is complicated, conflictual, and capricious (Adler, 1983). Criminal proceedings are marked by long delays and it is not uncommon for an individual to spend three to four years in pretrial confinement (Cooper, 1975). Another problem with Peru's criminal justice system is the unsatisfactory manner in which certain types of sex offenses are handled. As of January 1967, any adult male convicted of having a sexual encounter with a female under the age of 16 can anticipate a minimum sentence of five years (Cooper, 1971). Cooper adds that there is no room for judicial discretion in these cases, even if extenuating circumstances exist. One of the more positive aspects of the Peruvian legal system is that decisions are typically handled at the local level. Unfortunately, the average citizen remains largely ignorant of the law and very few ever get actively involved in the workings of the system.

On paper, the goal of the Peruvian correctional system is rehabilitation (Cooper, 1971). In reality, however, very little rehabilitation takes place. Peruvian prisons are overcrowded, inadequately staffed, and controlled largely by the more powerful inmates in the prison population. Consequently, the strong prey on the weak and the weak capitulate to the demands of the strong in order to survive. To make matters worse, the correctional system itself is largely corrupt as exemplified by the fact one can purchase various privileges, to include being transferred to a more desirable location (hospital) in exchange for money or services (Cooper, 1971).

What Peru is lacking in its formal system of criminal justice it more than makes up for in an outstanding system of informal social control. Most Peruvians—Spanish and Indian alike—continue to hold to strong family values. The Spanish segment of the population focuses on family tradition and group loyalty while the Peruvian Indians rely on the traditional tribal and extended family values handed down from generation to generation (Adler, 1983). Either way, informal social control seems to be an important factor in keeping Peru's crime rate low. Actually, the majority of crime in Peru is committed by a very small portion of the population. These individuals reside in urban areas and have had regular contact with the legal and correctional systems from an early age (Cooper, 1971). Thus, while the substance of informal social control differs for the Spanish and Indian segments of Peruvian society, the end result is the same—a low rate of crime for Peru.

The crime rates for the Federal Republic of Germany, Japan, Uganda, Peru, and the United States can be found in Table 3.1. As this table clearly suggests, the rate of robbery and property crime is higher in the industrialized nations (Germany, Japan, United States) than it is in the developing countries (Uganda, Peru). However, as we saw with both Japan (high industrialization, low crime) and Uganda (low industrialization, high crime) the correlation between industrialization and/or urbanization and crime is far from perfect. Nonetheless, the urbanization hypothesis continues to be a popular way of explaining the crime rate differences that clearly exist among various nations. For this reason we discuss this issue in greater detail in the next section of this chapter.

DISCRIMINATING BETWEEN HIGH- AND LOW-CRIME-RATE NATIONS

In this section we discuss five factors that have been implicated as potentially important in discriminating between high- and low-crime-rate nations. As we saw earlier, urbanization appears to be associated with criminality from a developmental (within nations) as well as cross-sectional (between nations) standpoint. Accordingly, urbanization is one topic examined in this section. The other

Table 3.1
Crime Rates of Five Nations Over a Period of Ten Years (per 100,000)

		Offense Type				
Nation	Year	Assault	Homicide	Rape	Robbery	Theft
Federal Republic of Germany	1962	51.29	0.70	11.33	11.26	1594.79
	1972	63.59	1.26	11.35	30.46	2760.65
Japan	1960	89.53	3.05	-	5.97	557.86
	1970	59.57	2.07	-	2.75	450.73
Uganda	1958	33.70	-	3.79	149.21	176.07
	1968	87.00	-	15.77	213.14	230.27
Peru	1961	-	-	18.27	79.71	41.86
	1969	-	-	14.81	9.48	63.51
United States	1960	85.10	5.00	9.50	59.90	976.70
	1970	163.00	7.80	18.50	171.40	2391.10

Sources: Crime rates were derived from information provided by Archer & Gartner (1984), except for the Ugandan assault data, which were derived from Clinard & Abbott (1973).

four factors discussed are formal social control, informal social control, the death penalty, and the career criminal.

Urbanization

Economist Wilbert Moore (1963) has noted that industrialization typically leads to a population shift whereby more people move to urban areas in order to support the expanding industrial complex. Urbanization has become an explanatory concept for theorists attempting to understand why certain countries experience higher rates of criminality than others. There is solid research evidence to suggest that a climbing rate of antisociality often accompanies a rise in industrialization and urbanization (compare Adler, 1983; Archer & Gartner, 1984; Wolf, 1971). This increase in crime is typically specific to property-related and economically oriented categories of offense. In exploring the rate of criminality within the Soviet Union, for instance, Shelley (1981) discovered that more developed regions had higher rates of property crime, while less developed areas experienced higher rates of violent crime. A developmental shift in the percentage of violent to property crimes committed in a particular country has also been reported in studies conducted by Wolf (1971) and a United Nations task force (United Nations, 1977).

Regardless of how developed or underdeveloped a nation is, most crime takes place in the city. This has not only been documented in industrialized nations like the United States, Japan, and Soviet Russia (Wilson & Herrnstein, 1985) but also in less developed countries like India (U.N. Bureau of Social Affairs, 1967), Morocco (El Bacha, 1962), Mexico (Quiroga, 1957), Tunis (Bouhdiba, 1965), South Korea (Ro, 1971), and Uganda (Clinard & Abbott, 1973). Cross-sectional comparative research on crime suggests that there is a higher per capita rate of criminality in larger as opposed to smaller cities. However, longitudinal research, such as that conducted by Archer and Gartner (1984), indicates that the rate of serious criminality does not necessarily expand as a city grows. Archer and Gartner speculate that it is the size of the city relative to the rest of the nation (urban versus nonurban), rather than the absolute size of the city, which is most reliably correlated with crime.

Clinard and Abbott (1973) remark that the deleterious effects of urbanization can be mollified somewhat by approaching modernization in a more graduated, orderly manner. Consequently, a nation might be able to control some of the negative effects of urbanization by decentralizing new industry, implementing a more organized plan of migration, and educating its citizenry on the potential problems it is likely to encounter upon moving into the city. Whereas this may help explain the low crime rates of nations like Switzerland and Ireland, for whom industrialization occurred gradually and over an extended period of time, it fails to account for the low rate of criminality experienced by Japan and Saudi Arabia, both of whom underwent rapid industrialization (Adler, 1983).

As we saw in the previous section, Japan is just as industrialized as the United States but suffers only a fraction of the crime America does. Japan's cities are three times as densely packed as those in the United States, yet the chances of being robbed are 208 times greater for those of us living in the United States (Bayley, 1976). Hence, industrialization alone cannot explain crime-rate differences among nations. There are, however, several factors that may play a moderating role in the relationship that seems to exist between crime and urbanization. Although several variables could exert such an effect, the primary candidates are reduced social cohesion, economic inequality, increased criminal opportunity, racial and/or cultural heterogeneity, and the development of a criminal subculture.

In preindustrialized societies cities are nothing more than large clusters of individualized villages. While the population of the preindustrialized city is large, a strong sense of community, permanence, and cohesion still runs through them because of the villagelike atmosphere. The industrialized city, on the other hand, is characterized by transience, impersonality, and change. The Japanese appear to have retained a strong attitude of group solidarity within their highly industrialized society, in part by bringing to the city a group-oriented attitude (Adler, 1983). Clinard and Abbott (1973) established that low-crime slum areas in Uganda were distinguished by a greater sense of solidarity and family cohesion than high-crime slum areas. Thus, one explanation for the urbanization-crime connection is that urbanization brings about a state of social alienation and incohesion that lends itself to increased criminal activity on the part of persons predisposed to such acts. A society can attenuate these effects, however, by reinforcing existing avenues of informal social control.

A second explanation for the apparent association between urbanization and crime is that the industrial complex, which facilitates the process of urbanization, also precipitates gross social and economic inequities, which, in turn, contribute to a growing state of dissatisfaction and unrest on the part of the average citizen. An increased rate of criminal behavior may therefore be an expression of this discontent. Krohn (1976), for example, observed a relationship between inequality and homicide, although inequality did not appear to correlate with property crime. More recently, Hansmann and Quigley (1979) found that both affluence and inequality corresponded with augmented rates of criminality in several nations, while Braithwaite and Braithwaite (1980) ascertained the presence of a link between crime and inequality but not affluence. Despite the outward appearance of a relationship between inequality and crime, Wilson and Herrnstein (1985) conclude that a causal connection has not yet been established.

A third explanation for the proposed nexus between urbanization and crime is that urban areas provide greater opportunity for crime and less chance of detection owing to the impersonal nature of the environment. One of the effects of industrialization is that greater value is placed on material goods. Thus, when Busia (1966) conducted a study on delinquency in a major Ghanian city he noted that theft was motivated more by a desire to secure material goods than to avoid starvation. This may help explain why urbanization leads to an increase in the rate of property-oriented offenses but usually does not effect the rate of murder and homicide (Wolf, 1971).

A fourth possibility is that the racial and/or cultural heterogeneity found in most large urban areas helps create a climate that encourages criminality. Owing to their cosmopolitan nature, most cities attract individuals from diverse ethnic, cultural, educational, and political backgrounds. This cultural divergency may lend itself to increased violence, conflict, and possibly crime. Wilson and Herrnstein (1985) point to the homogeneity of the Japanese population and the cultural heterogeneity of people in nations like the United States and Chile as corroborating the importance of cultural and/or racial similarity in cultivating a low crime rate. However, in the previous section we encountered one culturally heterogeneous nation (Peru) with a low crime rate and two high-crime-rate nations (Federal Republic of Germany, Uganda) with fairly homogeneous populations. Therefore, while cultural or ethnic heterogeneity may help promote certain forms of conflict, it is not viewed as a viable explanation for the link that apparently exists between urbanization and crime.

It also seems plausible that the urbanization-crime relationship may owe its existence to the fact that urban areas facilitate the development of various criminal subcultures. This subculture approach to urbanization rests on research that suggests crime is often learned from others. Clinard and Abbott (1973), for instance, ascertained that Sutherland's differential association theory of criminality explained the process of crime acquisition in a number of developing countries. It might therefore be that urbanization fosters the type of associations necessary to learn particular criminal attitudes and skills. As we shall see later, where the development of a subculture of crime may help explain certain criminological features of urbanization, this factor normally fails to discriminate between high- and low-crime-rate nations.

Formal Social Control

The relative inequality of a society or nation is often reflected in its system of criminal justice. Toward this end we discuss the potential criminogenic effects of different systems of formal social control. In China, the police, in addition to enforcing the law, play an important role in educating the public about legal matters (Allen, 1987). Use of the "police box" in Japan has not only engendered a great deal of community support for the Japanese policeman but also aided this nation's crime prevention efforts (Vogel, 1979). The Japanese policeman generally is bestowed greater respect, admiration, and prestige than his counterpart in the United States. The popular support of police officers in the German Democratic Republic has also been used to explicate how this nation was able to get through industrialization without suffering the side effect of a high crime rate (Adler, 1983).

The court systems of the low-crime countries also tend to be oriented to the populace. The Chinese, for instance, prefer informal to formal resolution of various legal disputes, and the law has purposely been kept simple so as to make it understandable to the vast majority of Chinese (Allen, 1987). Court proceedings in Japan are less adversarial than they are in many Western nations, and public confession is much more common in Japan than it is in the United States (Vogel, 1979). Community involvement in the Swiss courts has been achieved through reliance on a system of justice that decentralizes power and allows more decisions to be made at the local level (Hauser, 1978).

Many of the low-crime nations studied by Adler (1983) accentuated prevention and rehabilitation and deemphasized punishment in their approach to corrections. Low-crime-rate nations like China, Japan, and Switzerland, for example, view incarceration as a last resort. When these countries do incarcerate someone they typically dedicate a higher portion of their resources to re-education than does the United States and other higher crime nations. Work is often an important element in the rehabilitation process and many low-crime countries compensate their incarcerates for work done. The general philosophy of corrections in these countries is to reestablish the person-society bond that has been severed and that normally keeps crime at a relatively low level.

Lest we be deceived into believing that there is a simple relationship between crime and the popularity of a nation's criminal justice system, let us direct our attention to several very important exceptions to this general rule. The nation of Peru, for instance, has one of the most unpopular, ineffective systems of formal social control in the entire world and yet its crime rate is among the lowest in Latin America (Adler, 1983). Great Britain's criminal justice system, on the other hand, is reasonably popular with the general populace, yet this nation experiences a higher rate of violation than many of its neighbors whose criminal justice systems are not as popular. While there is more popular support for the police, more publicly oriented court systems, and greater emphasis on prevention than punishment in low-crime countries, criminal justice system factors do not fully explain why certain nations suffer from higher crime rates than others.

Informal Social Control

Examining the characteristics of ten low-crime nations, Adler (1983) uncovered one general factor that all ten countries appeared to have in common. This was an effective system of informal social control that supplemented the formal control exercised by each nation's criminal justice superstructure. By relating this to urbanization, it has been proposed that one of the primary effects of industrialization is a heightened reliance upon formal means of social control (Clifford, 1967). The question then becomes, how did states like Japan and Switzerland retain their strong attitude of informal control despite the deleterious effects of industrialization?

In explaining this phenomenon it is important that we consider the personality and value structure of the societies in question. As we saw earlier, the Japanese value group solidarity and social obligation over personal goals and individual rights. They have internalized values and ideals that have controlled social behavior for centuries. When the Japanese began migrating to the cities they brought these values and ideas with them (Adler, 1983). To the south and across the East China Sea, we find the Chinese, a culture which also places great stock in the family and community as informal sources of social control. Accordingly, the citizens of China typically abide by the rules of their society for the good of the group rather than out of a fear of punishment (Allen, 1987). Nations like Costa Rica, Algeria, and Saudi Arabia also attribute their relatively low crime rates to the fact that the family is still a very strong source of social control.

For many developing nations the village serves as a form of informal social control, and such mechanisms as familiarity, social bonding, and gossip help keep the crime rate reasonably low (Clinard & Abbott, 1973). In the previous section we discussed how Peru's low crime rate exists despite widespread poverty and marked inequality (Adler, 1983). One can only wonder whether the premium this nation places on kinship and family cohesion has created this seeming paradox. However, Peru is largely underdeveloped; what of the more industrialized countries and nations?

With more industrialized nations the government will sometimes step in and assist in the development of strong informal bonds. The Bulgarian government, for example, insists that parents provide a healthy home environment for their children, the intent being to establish a strong sense of social responsibility in its younger citizens (Stefanov & Naumov, 1974). It therefore seems likely that the breakdown in family and/or community cohesiveness, often seen when a nation moves in the direction of industrialization, may be an essential link in the relationship between urbanization and crime. It may also be possible for a nation to avoid many of the criminological effects of urbanization by working to retain a strong sentiment of informal social control, which is oftentimes lost during the early stages of industrialization.

The Death Penalty

The death penalty has always attracted a great deal of attention and is frequently the topic of heated debate. The argument against the death penalty is that it is inhumane, expensive, and ineffective. Proponents of the death penalty, on the other hand, maintain that it can serve as a deterrent to certain types of crime. While the death penalty can be found in most regions of the globe, it is used with the highest degree of frequency in less developed nations (UN Economic & Social Council, 1971). This is not to say, however, that certain industrialized nations like the United States, Japan, and Saudi Arabia will not also employ the death penalty under special circumstances.

Sellin (1967), in reviewing early research on the death penalty, concluded that there was no evidence that this form of punishment influenced the rate of homicide in various jurisdictions. While this conclusion has been criticized from a number of different vantage points (Ehrlich, 1975), the bulk of recent evidence on this issue (compare Bailey, 1979; Brier & Fienberg, 1980; Loftin, 1980) is generally supportive of Sellin's position. Taking a cross-national approach to the question of deterrence and the death penalty, Archer and Gartner (1984) studied 12 nations that had abolished the death penalty. The results of their investigation revealed that of the 12 nations studied, 7 recorded a reduced number of homicides and 5 reported an increased rate of homicide following abolition. The deterrence hypothesis was further disconfirmed by the fact that the reduced number of homicides that occurred subsequent to abolition of the death penalty was customarily associated with an increase in the number of offenses other than homicide.

Although the results of cross-national research on the death penalty argue against its use as a deterrent for serious criminality, there is no evidence that it is necessarily affiliated with increased rates of per capita criminality either. Five of the ten low-crime countries studied by Adler (1983) were using the death penalty around the time Archer and Gartner (1984) were conducting their study on crime and violence in cross-national perspective. In addition, there are nations who have no death penalty yet still have a problem with crime (for example, Federal Republic of Germany, Great Britain). Hence, the presence or absence of capital punishment statutes does not appear to differentiate meaningfully between high- and low-crime nations.

The Career Criminal

It is clear that crime exists to some extent in all nations of the world. As long as there are laws there will be those individuals who will try to circumvent them. As was argued earlier, urbanization may facilitate criminality by creating a subculture of crime. For one, gangs are more commonly found in urban areas (Clinard & Abbott, 1973) and, for another, the gang is frequently a spawning ground for new criminal ideas. With the advent of industrialization several decades ago, the nation of Thailand began experiencing a large increase in the incidence of gang robberies although there was very little change in the frequency of single robber offenses (Nagel, 1967). These results suggest that there may be a connection between urbanization and the development of a subculture of crime.

Examining crime rates for a large cohort of individuals growing up in Philadelphia, Wolfgang, Figlio, and Sellin (1972) determined that 6 percent of their sample accounted for 52 percent of the offenses. Hamparian, Schuster, Dinitz, and Conrad (1978) observed similar outcomes in a sample of adolescents living in the Columbus, Ohio, area. Mednick, Gabrielli, and Hutchings (1984) acknowledge that a very small percentage of their sample of Danish adoptees (1%) were responsible for 30 percent of all cohort convictions, while Stattin, Magnusson, and Reichel (1989) note that 10 percent of the males in their Swedish cohort study accounted for 66 percent of the crimes committed by members of this particular Swedish cohort. Corresponding results have been reported in Ireland (Russel, 1964), Peru (Cooper, 1971), Uganda (Clinard & Abbott, 1973), Japan (Kobayashi et al., 1982), and the United Kingdom (West and Farrington, 1977).

There appears to be some truth in the notion that urbanization helps promote a subculture of crime. Gangs tend to conglomerate in the larger cities and peer associations are a fairly common means through which one learns about crime. However, the subculture of crime seems to exist in industrialized (United Kingdom) as well as nonindustrialized (Peru) nations, irrespective of whether the crime rate is high (United States) or low (Ireland). Therefore, while this research supports the cross-national validity of the career criminal concept, the subculture of crime explanation for the relationship between crime and urbanization is weak.

CONCLUSION

As this chapter clearly illustrates, comparative criminology holds great promise of furthering our understanding of crime and criminals. Unfortunately, a number of methodological problems seriously limit the utility of this area of research. Kalish (1988), for instance, compared international crime rates collected by three different agencies: the United Nations (UN), World Health Organization (WHO), and International Police Organization (Interpol). Though there were a number of commonalties in these data, there were also several notable differences based on variations in sampling technique, dissimilar inclusion criteria, and divergent methods of calculation. Furthermore, Kalish discerned that crime rates for specific offenses vary by as much as 50 to 100 percent from one year to the next. Such findings demonstrate how hard it is to draw firm conclusions about cross-national issues in crime.

While we need to be ever cognizant of the flaws extant in cross-national research on crime, several general summations can still be offered. One conclusion that has been reasonably well established from cross-national studies on crime is that urbanization and criminality are meaningfully correlated. This does not signify the inevitability of increased criminality with industrialization or urbanization, since several nations have shown that it is possible to avoid a major increase in crime despite rapid urbanization (for example, Japan, Switzerland). Such an outcome suggests the presence of a third factor that links urbanization and crime by means of its common association with both variables.

There are several factors that could potentially moderate the crime-urbanization relationship. The formal characteristics of the criminal justice system and the informal aspects of the social environment are among the factors demonstrating the strongest moderating effects. Low-crime nations tend to have a wider base of popular support for and involvement in their criminal justice systems compared to high-crime countries. However, as we discussed earlier, there are several conspicuous exceptions to this general pattern that cast doubt on the utility of formal social control as the primary variable linking urbanization to crime. Turning our attention to the informal aspects of the social environment we find that low-crime nations place greater importance on informal sources of social control than do high-crime countries (Adler, 1983). It is therefore speculated that urbanization might achieve its criminological effect by disrupting families. neighborhoods, and other forms of informal social control. However, this general conclusion awaits further empirical verification since it has never been tested directly using stringent research criteria.

A second general conclusion is that longitudinal designs are to be preferred over cross-sectional designs and that data should be measured at the offense, rather than arrest or conviction, level. As Archer and Gartner's (1984) research on violence in cross-national perspective indicates, restricting our definition of crime to serious offenses like homicide and armed robbery provides us with an avenue through which we might learn to control common methodological problems like underreporting and inadequate recordkeeping. Although homicide data provide an accurate reading of the amount of violence experienced by a nation, they may be misleading as an indicator of criminality, since many homicides are committed against family or friends by individuals most of us would not consider hardened criminals. Still, it is recommended that cross-national research on crime combine longitudinal and cross-sectional methodologies to study the rate for offenses falling at the upper end of the crime severity continuum (for example, aggravated assault, burglary, armed robbery).

Comparing this chapter on cross-national criminology with the previous one on the historical development of crime in America, two general trends come to the forefront. One concerns the authority of social bonding to control the criminal inclinations of people worldwide. With an emphasis on material success, personal goals, and the rights of the individual, American culture has bought itself a multiplicity of trouble in the form of increased criminality. Nations like Japan and Switzerland, which are just as industrialized as the United States but which place a premium on loyalty, commitment, and group cohesion, enjoy lower crime rates. Thus, while I do not necessarily agree with Sellin's (1983, p. xvii) statement that the United States suffers from "the criminality it deserves," it is obvious that a nation's general attitude toward crime greatly influences the rate of criminality it experiences.

The second trend noted in this and the previous chapter is that a relatively small number of individuals account for a lion's share of the serious offenses committed in a particular nation, culture, or state. As we saw in Chapter 2, since time immemorial there has been a small band of individuals who are responsible for the majority of serious crimes committed in the United States each year. We also find this pattern in countries outside North America. Furthermore, the pattern appears to bear no resemblance to a nation's developmental status or crime rate. The presence of career or habitual criminals, independent of the historical or cultural context, is what served as a foundation for Walters' (1990b) work on the criminal lifestyle.

Those of us in the criminal justice field have often taken a rather parochial approach in our work with criminals. The present chapter suggests that cross-national research is capable of providing us with information that might significantly expand the boundaries of our current knowledge on crime and criminals. However, this will require that we abandon certain of our pet theories and preconceived notions about criminal behavior. Accordingly, while the results reviewed in this and the previous chapter suggest that understanding the contextual features of crime might well open up potentially important doors to new knowledge and information on this subject, we must first demonstrate that we are willing to explore what is behind those doors.

PART III

RESEARCH

4

Research Methodology

The nature of science is often expressed in its methodology. Implemented appropriately, scientific methodology provides us with a conduit through which we can investigate the natural relationships that surround us. In the best of all worlds sound research methodology contributes to our general fund of knowledge by revealing the underlying associations among selected social behaviors. Absent a program of sound methodology, however, our research efforts would be fragmented, our findings spurious, and our conclusions faulty. It follows then that research methodology is vital to the development and cultivation of knowledge.

In some ways science is very much like common sense. Kerlinger (1973, p. 3), in fact, defines science as the "systematic and controlled extension of common sense." According to Kerlinger, it is the systematic and controlled nature of science that separates it from everyday experience and common sense. Thus, science is concerned with the systematic application of certain principles in an attempt to further our understanding of a particular topic. As a method of information gathering, common sense is normally an efficient means of accumulating knowledge. However, overreliance on this method can mislead us into concluding that certain chance relationships are meaningful when, in fact, they are not. Science provides us with a means of methodically probing these assumptions in ways that are less subject to error than is common sense.

Kerlinger (1973) maintains that randomization and control are at the heart of scientific inquiry. Hence, if we can randomly assign subjects to conditions, at least one of which controls for factors other than those being investigated, we can be reasonably confident in the veracity of our findings. Unfortunately, it is often the case that we are unable to achieve randomization in studies on crime owing to certain practical and ethical considerations. It is also sometimes difficult to find an adequate control or comparison group in conducting such investigations. In this chapter we examine a general strategy that we hope will make studies on crime more comprehensible, mindful of the fact that there are many research situations in which maximal experimental control is not possible. First, however, we turn our attention to the issue of variance as it relates to the study of criminal behavior.

THE ROLE OF VARIANCE IN RESEARCH

Variance is the statistical deviation of data around a mean or central point. As researchers, we are concerned with two primary categories of variation: systematic and random. Systematic variance concerns vicissitudes of data points in a coordinated pattern, although we may not always be able to properly label or understand this pattern. Between-group variance is a special form of systematic variance in which the pattern is identified and controlled through our methodology. Thus, if we employ the Galvanic Skin Response (GSR) as a measure of general anxiety in groups of criminals and noncriminals exposed to a particular situation (for example, prisoner's dilemma), the variation in scores between the two groups would form the systematic between-group variance. The variation of scores within groups, on the other hand, would constitute the random or error variance.

There are many reasons why error variance exists, but predominant are the unreliability of our measures, subject characteristics unrelated to the research problem, and erroneous conceptualizations by the researcher. In short, error variance involves random fluctuations of data that are not controlled or taken into account by the design of our research. Returning once again to our contrived research study on anxiety and decision making, we find that error variance is introduced into the design because: (1) the GSR is not a perfect measure of skin conductance; (2) skin conductance is only one aspect of the wider concept known as anxiety; and (3) each subject has a slightly different physical or psychological constitution. All of these influences, plus several additional factors, may interject unsystematic variation into our contrived research situation.

Borrowing two terms from the field of audiometry, we might conceptualize between-group variance as the signal and error variance as the noise in a signal: noise decision matrix. As with audiometry, the object of behavioral research is to maximize the signal and minimize the noise. In determining whether the variations observed in a particular data set are sufficiently systematic to be considered significant, we must compare the between-group variance with the error variance. Such a comparison determines whether the signal can be heard above the noise created by random fluctuations in our data set. This is accomplished by contrasting the between-group variance with an estimate of error variance derived through consideration of within-group sources of variation. Figure 4.1 illustrates the relationship between systematic (between-group) and error (within-group) variance in statistical tests of comparison.

If the ratio of systematic (between-group) to error (within-group) variance exceeds a certain level, then the results are said to be statistically significant. If, on the other hand, this ratio does not achieve statistical significance, then the

Figure 4.1
Comparing Systematic and Error Variance

$$S = \frac{V_b}{V_w}$$

S = statistical comparison
V_b = between group variance
V_w = within group variance

null hypothesis of no difference or relationship cannot be rejected. This does not mean, however, that no difference or relationship exists; it just means that we are unable to demonstrate such an association in this particular research situation. Although the signal: noise analogy clearly captures the nature of procedures like analysis of variance and the univariate *T*-test, it also applies to linear regression and multivariate techniques like factor analysis. It is well to keep in mind that all statistical procedures are designed to examine the signal: noise ratio as a means of determining if the level of systematic variation exceeds the level of error variance to a statistically significant degree.

A GENERAL RESEARCH STRATEGY

When outlining an approach to research it is important that certain factors be taken into account. We must understand the background of the problem, derive testable hypotheses, implement a cogent research design, define the independent and dependent variables, select appropriate statistical procedures, meaningfully interpret the results, and consider various ethical issues before our research effects can be expected to yield much in the way of clinically useful information. Each of these areas will be discussed in turn, but first, we will consider three general categories of criminal science research.

One form of research investigation with relevance to the science of criminal behavior is termed basic research. Basic research is characteristically conducted in controlled experiments where the researcher manipulates one or more independent variables in an effort to gauge their effect on a dependent variable or set of variables. Investigating the influence of a particular drug (versus placebo) on a concentration task using a group of chronic offenders randomly assigned to the experimental and placebo control conditions would constitute a basic research paradigm. Of the three research categories discussed in this section, basic research provides the best prospects for experimental control.

Clinical research, on the other hand, is normally administered in clinical settings, to include prisons, hospitals, and outpatient drug or mental health clinics. Consequently, experimental controls are often not as stringent as those found in basic research designs, although clinical research frequently provides us with valuable practical information not accessible to investigators following a basic research approach to the question of crime. A research psychologist investigating the predictive value of a battery of pencil-and-paper tests in a group of parolees would be utilizing a clinical research design.

A third form or category of criminal science research encompasses program evaluation. Although experimental control is usually less of a concern in conducting program evaluations than it is with either basic or clinical research, the design of our evaluation should be sufficiently stringent so that we can obtain the most reliable results possible. Consequently, if we wished to survey a chemical-abuse treatment program for white-collar probationers we would want some assurance that our results reflect what is actually going on in the program. Regardless of our reasons for conducting research in the criminal sciences—basic research, clinical research, or program evaluation—the research methodology should be implemented systematically, commencing with a clear statement as to purpose of our research investigation.

The Problem

The initial stage in the criminal science investigative progression is defining the research problem. When addressing this issue it is vital that we define the purpose of our study and what we hope to learn from the results. In formulating a specific plan of action investigators sometimes fail to provide a statement of the problem that is lucid, understandable, comprehensive, and testable. Any study administered without benefit of a well-defined plan will most assuredly fall short of providing us with useful information. Kerlinger (1973), in fact, remarks that the research problem is the single most important step in the research progression, for without a clearly defined purpose subsequent stages in the research sequence weaken considerably.

Hypotheses are an integral part of the research problem. These hypotheses, which are actually theoretical or conjectural statements addressing the proposed relationship between two or more variables, direct the flow of the entire research sequence. These statements should be defined in operational terms that tie in with clear behavioral referents (Kerlinger, 1973). If not, they will inspire confusion and distance us further from our research goals. It is also crucial that researchers clearly discriminate between theoretical and statistical hypotheses. Without such an understanding one might falsely interpret a statistical effect as bona fide evidence of a significant theoretical outcome when in fact the theoretical hypothesis is spurious. Neale and Liebert (1973) offer the example of a drug study in which the influence of a placebo is mistaken for a genuine treatment effect in arguing that theoretical and statistical hypotheses need to be treated separately.

The research problem is sometimes phrased as a null hypothesis. The null hypothesis presupposes that no relationship exists between the variables under investigation, the object of our research being to determine whether the null hypothesis can be rejected. Ergo, if our research problem is to determine the relationship between socioeconomic status and crime, the null hypothesis might postulate the absence of any differences in criminality between high- and low-status adolescents. If, on the other hand, a significant difference were to be found between these two groups, then we would be justified in rejecting the null hypothesis. However, we would also need to examine the relevant issues further in order to determine whether socioeconomic status was, in fact, the cause of the higher level of criminality witnessed in the low-status group. This suggests that the proper role of science is to reject hypotheses, null or otherwise, and that validity is gauged by the absence of negative findings rather than the presence of positive outcomes.

Variables

The second step in our research sequence is selecting the variables to be investigated. The selection of variables will follow directly from the statement of the research problem, and as with the delineation of hypotheses, the variables should be clearly specified and operationalized. Variables assume several different forms, the most common perhaps being the categorical-continuous dichotomy. Categorical variables embody a finite number of categories or groupings (for example, high-, middle-, or low-income home of origin), while continuous variables encompass a range of scores (for example, age). The nature of the research problem, as well as certain practical considerations, will determine which form is most appropriate under which specific set of investigative circumstances.

In executing a particular program of research it is imperative that investigators clearly identify the dependent and independent variables in their studies. Whereas the independent variable is either manipulated by the researcher or thought to have been previously manipulated (by heredity, the environment, or certain experiences), we estimate the impact of these manipulations on the dependent or measured variable. Consequently, if we were to scrutinize the effect of financial assistance on the subsequent community adjustment (job stability, absence of legal difficulties) of released prison inmates, then the financial aid payments would be our independent variable, since this is the variable we are manipulating (some releasees would receive financial aid payments and others would not), while measures of community adjustment would constitute our dependent measure.

Research Design

The research design of an investigation is the actual strategy one follows in testing the hypotheses generated during stage one of our research sequence. The design provides us with the opportunity to address the research problem in an organized and systematic manner. Technically, the research design controls variance, without which our results would be subject to a number of confounding influences. The research design should be engineered in such a way as to maximize between-group variance, minimize error variance, and control extraneous sources of variance that might interfere with our interpretation of the results (Kerlinger, 1973).

The maximization of between-group variance can best be realized by creating a research scenario in which our conditions, hypotheses, and variables are adequately defined. The minimization of within-group or error variance can be accomplished through use of standardized procedures, reliable measures, and homogeneous samples (Neale & Liebert, 1973). Extraneous variables can be controlled through matching, blocking, or integrating these variables into our research design (Kerlinger, 1973). Although these three goals are never fully realized, they serve as useful guides to researchers interested in pursuing knowledge in nearly all fields of inquiry.

Many factors need to be taken into account when selecting a research design. Campbell and Stanley (1966) discuss three primary categories of research design: pre-experimental, experimental, and quasi-experimental. Pre-experimental designs, like the case study method, typically fail to exert sufficient control over the independent and dependent measures to be of much scientific value, although they may be useful in the initial stages of theory and hypothesis building, when one is simply searching for possible connections between variables. Experimental designs, on the other hand, exert maximal control over the variance observed in one's dependent measure and offer the best opportunity for robust, reliable results. Since maximal research control is not always possible, quasi-experimental designs (Campbell & Stanley, 1966) were developed. Such designs achieve optimal experimental control in situations where the research questions do not lend themselves to experimental manipulation.

Time is also a factor that needs to be considered in selecting a research design. Designs can either be cross-sectional or longitudinal. A cross-sectional design compares two or more groups at a single point in time, whereas a longitudinal design focuses on the same group of subjects followed over time. Although cross-sectional designs are more commonly seen in criminal science research, longitudinal designs are an invaluable source of information, particularly when it comes to investigating the developmental features of criminal behavior (Farrington, 1988). Menard and Elliott (1990) compared longitudinal and cross-sectional data and found large discrepancies in the correlates and predictive models generated by each. The issue of longitudinal versus cross-sectional designs will be elaborated upon further when we survey research on the early childhood correlates of criminal behavior.

Analysis

Once the research data have been collected, the next step in the investigative sequence is to analyze one's findings. In most cases the statistical analyses follow from the design. Therefore, if our design involves a cross-tabulation of several different categorical variables we would probably want to analyze our data with a nonparametric procedure like the chi-square statistic or phi coefficient. If, on the other hand, we implement a more sophisticated design with a continuously measured dependent variable, we would be justified in utilizing a parametric technique like analysis of variance or multiple regression. It is also worthy of note that since calculating a large number of separate analyses increases the chances of one erroneously rejecting the null hypothesis, multivariate techniques should be used in situations where multiple comparisons are made. For a more detailed examination of these and other statistical issues relevant to research in the behavioral sciences the reader is referred to Harris' (1975) book on multivariate statistics.

Multivariate techniques are normally preferable to univariate procedures since they more adequately represent the complex interactive nature of human experience. However, multivariate techniques have their own set of limitations. Multiple linear regression, for instance, can give rise to collinearity if the regressors in one's equation are strongly correlated. This collinearity has been shown to produce wide variations in the estimated regression coefficients when variables are added to or deleted from the regression equation. It also introduces instability into regression estimates measured over time or across samples. Statistical experts recommend that under conditions of collinearity a principal-components analysis be used to simplify the dimensionality of the structured covariate space for the purpose of developing a more stable estimate of one's results (Land, McCall, & Cohen, 1990).

After selecting a statistical technique, one must choose the level at which the results should be considered statistically significant. An important consideration in deriving this alpha or significance level is weighing the cost of making a Type I error against that of making a Type II error. The Type I error rate concerns the probability of rejecting a valid null hypothesis, while the Type II error rate measures the probability of failing to reject a null hypothesis that is false. Setting the alpha level at the .05 level indicates that there is a 1 in 20 chance that the results obtained were a function of chance fluctuations in the data. Lowering the alpha level to .01 would decrease our chances of making a Type I error but at the cost of an increase in the rate of Type II errors. It follows, then, that in conducting a research study we want to maximize the internal validity of our design (by minimizing Type I errors) without sacrificing the external validity or power of the design (by minimizing Type II errors). This is unfortunately easier said than done since internal validity and power are at cross purposes; a decrease in one often resulting in a corresponding increase in the other. Consequently, we must consider the relative costs of Type I and Type II errors in selecting an alpha level by which to evaluate the statistical significance of our results.

Interpretation

Once the research data have been analyzed, the next step is to make sense of the results. In addition to examining possible limitations in methodology, we want to interpret our findings in light of the research problem. Oftentimes this research problem is couched in terms that reflect the desire to assess the validity of a particular theory or model of human behavior. However, a theory's vitality is not determined by how it fares in a single research study but by how it fits within a wider nomological net. In other words, research is never conducted independent of its context. A single study simply strengthens or weakens certain facets of a theory. A series of studies, on the other hand, provides us with a rich sense of continuity, meaning, and purpose. As such, an organized program of research is a necessity if we wish to engage in meaningful theory building.

When interpreting the results of research investigations it is vital that we consider the internal and external validity of our methodology and design. Internal validity reflects the degree to which one can be confident in the outcome attained in a given research investigation. Stated somewhat differently, can observed changes in the dependent variable be attributed to the influence of the independent variable? External validity, on the other hand, helps establish the generalizability of outcomes achieved in one study to subjects in other settings and situations. As was remarked earlier, however, a problem arises for behavioral scientists to the extent that internal and external validity are based on antagonistic foundations, an increase in one normally leading to a decrease in the other.

Campbell and Stanley (1966) state that internal validity is the sine qua non of sound research, and while this position is certainly defensible, external validity should never be sacrificed in the process. A finding devoid of general applicability, no matter how eloquent, seems to have very little to offer a science of criminal behavior. For this reason, both internal and external validity should be taken into account when designing research programs since a single study is incapable of solving the internal-external validity conundrum. The precise order of studies is less important than making sure both internal and external threats to validity are considered. Therefore, we might choose to employ an in-out strategy, establishing our model through work in the laboratory and then moving into the more generalizable clinical studies, or an out-in strategy, exploring certain relationships in naturalistic settings first and then validating the model through rigorous experimentation. What is being proposed here is not an indictment of experimental research but a call for greater balance in how we administer investigative programs so that our theories are as externally useful as they are internally consistent.

Ethical Considerations

In conducting research on selected criminal science topics we need to be cognizant of certain ethical issues. The researcher must consider the future benefit of a particular study against the potential risks or hazards created by one's involvement in the investigation. Even if it is determined that the potential benefits outweigh the possible risks, subjects should understand that they are participating in a research study, that their participation is voluntary, and that they can withdraw from the study at any time without suffering adverse consequences. Thus, informed consent is a necessary feature of research conducted with human subjects.

Although full disclosure as to the purpose of a study may not always be feasible, researchers should make an effort to discuss the purpose of the investigation with potential subjects in a manner that does not vitiate the integrity of the research design. Should full disclosure not be a realistic alternative prior to a subject's participation in a study, then full disclosure should be made once all the data have been collected or the subject voluntarily drops out of the study. Such an approach is not only good ethical practice but also helps assure greater cooperation on the part of subjects who may be asked to participate in future research investigations.

Information concerning subjects who have taken part in a research study should be kept confidential. This can best be accomplished by removing all idiomorphic information, with the exception of a randomly generated identification number, from one's research files. This random number can then be paired with the identifying information on a separate sheet of paper, the "master sheet" being in a locked area. Once all the data have been collected, this master sheet should be destroyed. To protect subject anonymity even further, information should typically be presented in a group data format (for example, means and standard deviations). If, per chance, individual case histories are desired, such information should be kept general so as to protect the identity of the participating subject. Wolfgang (1981) argues that ethics and scientific research are inextricably linked and that we must address the problems this association brings about if we are to advance as a science.

COMMON METHODOLOGICAL PROBLEMS IN RESEARCH ON CRIME

There are a number of factors that serve to confound the results of many research investigations. These factors threaten the integrity of our designs as well as the validity of our conclusions. In this section we discuss ten factors regularly encountered in research on crime that can have a detrimental effect on the results of our investigations.

Definitional Problems

A fundamental issue confronting all researchers is the manner in which the variables are defined. This is particularly true of the criminal science field, where we must decide how to define such diverse, elusive, and complicated terms as *criminality*, *choice*, and *change*. Whether conceptualized as an independent or dependent variable, attempts to define *criminality* are replete with unknowns. For instance, should our definition of *crime* consider all arrests or just arrests for "serious" offenses? Should an arrest leading to conviction and confinement be treated the same as one for which a conviction was not obtained? Should adult offenses receive more attention than juvenile ones? These and other questions need to be answered before we can offer an adequate definition of *crime*. One possible solution is to focus on subcategories of crime, rather than allowing our research efforts to be guided by a general (and many times trivial) definition of *offending*.

There can also be problems with the way in which variables other than crime are defined for the purposes of research. Complications that arise when inadequate operationalization of terms becomes an issue may not only interfere with the internal validity of our design but may also detract from the generalizability of our findings. This can occur with such seemingly straightforward variables as race and ethnic status. Take, as a case in point, Leibrich's (1986) observation that arrest and prison records for the Maoris of New Zealand are incomparable because the police and justice systems in New Zealand employ different definitions of *Maori*. Such definitional problems must be resolved before we can be confident in any inferences we may draw from our results.

History

Science does not operate in a vacuum. Rather, it must be considered within the wider context of the environment in which it takes place, an environment which is continually undergoing change, revision, and modification. Thus, if over the course of a longitudinal study on rape, certain changes take place in the laws governing the definition and punishment of certain forms of sexual transgression, we may obtain results that are more a function of history (changes in the law) than of the variable under investigation (for example, a particular treatment program). The use of a comparison group that does not receive sex-offender treatment but is nonetheless exposed to the same historical influences as our treatment group might help control for this particular threat to the integrity of our research design.

Maturation

Change takes place not only in the environment but also in the individual. Therefore, another source of invalidity is the maturational changes that occur in subjects over time (Campbell & Stanley, 1966). If we follow the criminal careers of 100 burglars from, say, 1970 to 1990 (a time period when neighborhood watch programs became increasingly more popular) we would likely observe a noticeable decrease in the rate of offending. However, this decline in the burglary rate may have more to do with maturational changes occurring in our subjects (offenders commit fewer crimes as they grow older) than with the efficacy of the neighborhood watch program.

Biased Sampling

When our subjects are not randomly sampled from the population of individuals to which we wish to generalize our findings, we are flirting with the problem of biased sampling. If we ask for volunteers to participate in a study on paranoia in the penitentiary, we will likely end up with a biased sample since the more paranoid and mistrustful individuals in our population would tend to avoid speaking with the research staff. Moreover, as Leibrich (1986) points out, volunteers are often better motivated, more psychologically minded, and less negative in their attitude toward authority than nonvolunteers. Accordingly, our penitentiary study will probably underestimate the level of paranoia to be found in this particular correctional facility because of certain selection factors. We must therefore attempt to design our studies in ways that minimize selection bias.

Even if certain subjects agree to participate in our research project, several will drop out before the study is completed. The level of attrition witnessed in a particular study is a function of the demands placed on subjects in terms of both time and effort. The mortality of subjects from a research study can have a profound effect on the results obtained, particularly when it comes to psychotherapy research. Walters, Solomon, and Walden (1982), for example, found several notable differences between individuals who remained in counseling versus those who dropped out prematurely. Thus, if we are examining personality change as a function of participation in group therapy but record an attrition rate of 50 percent, it is important that we address the issue and realize that our sample is less than fully representative of the general population of inmates who initially entered group therapy. Attrition is particularly problematic in cases where our groups differ substantially in the rate at which they drop out of treatment. This, then, is the problem of differential mortality (Campbell & Stanley, 1966).

Nonresponse may also introduce bias into our results. If in conducting a telephone interview we were to ask respondents to recount any past instances of victimization, we could anticipate less than a full accounting of all victimization experiences. Some individuals may be unwilling to cooperate in the interview altogether, while others may participate but fail to report certain victimization experiences because of fear, embarrassment, or forgetfulness. Needless to say, nonresponse will tend to limit the generalizability of our findings. Whether it is the result of volunteerism, mortality, or nonresponse, sampling bias can play havoc with our research findings and, when it occurs, should be addressed during the interpretive stage of the research process.

Instrumentation and Testing

In directing a research investigation on crime we have available to us a plethora of measures. Thus, a study using interview data may differ from one in which self-report personality measures are employed, and both may differ from the results obtained using behavioral outcome measures. Debate continues to rage over whether self-report measures, official records, or victimization surveys provide the most accurate crime-rate reading. Whereas self-report measures tend to overrepresent minor offenses, not to mention the fact that they are susceptible to a variety of response biases, official sources of data often underestimate the incidence of crime and can be distorted by bias in the arrest practices of law enforcement officials (Wilson & Herrnstein, 1985). Victimization surveys, on the other hand, control for many of these limitations, although the results of such surveys can be highly misleading if the interviews are not conducted properly.

Messner (1984) compared crime indices from two alternative sources, the Uniform Crime Reports (official data) and the National Crime Survey (victimization data). Like Nelson (1980) before him, Messner found low levels of correlation between the UCR and NCS. However, when a multivariate composite heavily weighted for homicide offenses was implemented, Messner observed a much stronger relationship between these two sources of criminal science information. The ideal solution to the problem of differential measurement is to employ multiple indicators of criminality in addressing pertinent criminal science concerns, although this is not always practical or even possible.

A related concern involves the loss of information on subjects that occurs when we go from a direct measure of criminality (crimes committed) to one which is highly indirect (convictions leading to incarceration). As students of crime statistics will attest, not all crimes are reported and a significant proportion of reported crimes are not cleared by arrest. The numbers shrink even further when we consider conviction and incarceration rates. As Figure 4.2 illustrates, of every 100 rapes, an average of only 18 will lead to conviction, while only 1 out of every 100 larcenies will result in confinement. These facts need to be considered in selecting our measure of criminality as well as in interpreting the results of our analyses.

Certain measures may change with time or vary as a function of previous testing. If, for some reason, we wish to ask a group of observers to rate inmate behavior over a period of several days, we might notice a change in ratings unrelated to our manipulation of variables. This is because observers can become increasingly more sensitive, skilled, or careless in their ratings over time. Furthermore, if a measure is administered before we introduce the independent variable, this may affect how the subject responds on the posttest. Under such circumstances we cannot rule out the possibility that our posttest results were largely influenced by the subject's exposure to the pretest. Because of this, many researchers avoid administering a pretest altogether.

Sample Size

Methodological problems may arise as a function of the number of subjects employed in a particular research design. Important differences may be obscured if the sample size is too small, while trivial results may become magnified in

Figure 4.2
The Sequence of Crimes Committed to Convictions Leading to Confinement for Rape and Household Larceny

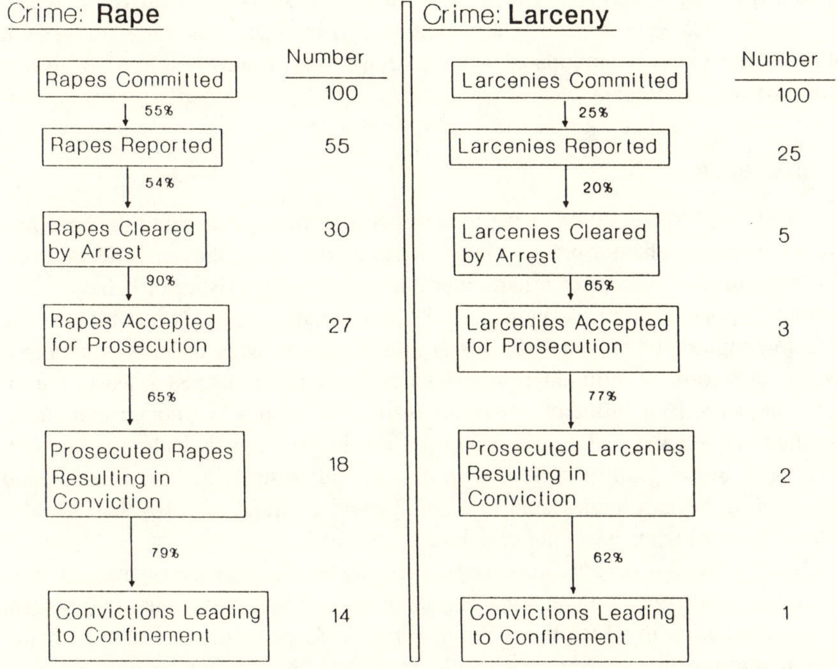

Source: Percentages were derived from the Bureau of Justice Statistics *Report to the Nation on Crime and Justice* (1988c).

situations where the sample size is exceedingly large. Hence, a 15 *T*-score mean group difference on Scale 4 of the Minnesota Multiphasic Personality Inventory (MMPI) may fail to achieve statistical significance in a study with only ten subjects per group. Likewise, MMPI mean score differences as small as 2 *T*-score points may attain statistical significance in a study with 500 subjects per research cell. One way to determine whether the proposed sample size is sufficient for the purposes of our investigation is to conduct a power analysis (Cohen, 1969) using data previously collected on similar groups of criminal offenders.

Statistical Regression

It is a well-known statistical fact that extreme scores tend to gravitate toward the mean as a function of repeated testing (Campbell & Stanley, 1966). Therefore, higher scoring subjects demonstrate a tendency to score lower on a second testing and lower scoring subjects typically score higher the second time around because of statistical regression. If we inspect the level of criminality for the two cities with the highest crime rates in 1981 (New York and Los Angeles), we discover that the rate of offending actually declined by 17 and 3 percent, respectively, from 1981 to 1985. However, the national crime rate during this same time period rose by 4 percent. This is an example of statistical regression, where because of the error present in any measure, to include crime rates, movement toward the mean is anticipated when extreme scores are considered from one time period to the next.

Base Rates

Meehl and Rosen (1955) have argued that one must understand the base rate of a particular behavior before attempting to predict that behavior. The base rate is the natural incidence of a particular attribute, characteristic, or behavior in a group or population of individuals. Take as an example a study in which we set out to compare the criminal records of individuals growing up in broken homes with the records of individuals whose parents remained married at least up until the subject's 16th birthday. After analyzing our results we notice that males outnumber females in the first group but not in the second. Unless we control for these initial group differences in gender, our results may be spurious and misleading because males tend to commit more criminal offenses than females (they have a higher base rate of criminal activity).

Base rates also help us understand the clinical significance of our findings. If, for instance, we find that a measure predicts recidivism at a rate of 60 percent for a population in which the recidivism rate is 75 percent, we would be better off predicting that all inmates would reoffend than relying on our measure. Coupled with additional sources of information, however, our measure might achieve clinical significance if it were included as part of a successive sieves scheme in which several different predictors are considered. However, this scheme would need to exceed the 75 percent natural recidivism rate before we could have any confidence in its practical value.

The base-rate issue also comes into play when we discuss the use of cutting scores. There are four possible outcomes in any classification matrix: true positives, true negatives, false positives (incorrectly identifying an attribute which is absent), and false negatives (failing to identify an attribute which is present). Our goal is to locate a cutting score that maximizes the true positives and true negatives while minimizing the false positives and false negatives. However, just as there are different weights attached to Type I and Type II errors, false positives and false negatives may not be of equal significance. In addition to the possibility of differential base rates for a specific behavior or test score, one type error may be viewed as more serious than the other in any particular research situation.

Assume for the moment we have developed a hypothetical measure of lifestyle criminality capable of generating scores of between 0 and 20. We will presume further that it is our intent to identify as many true lifestyle criminals as possible

Figure 4.3
Use of a Low Cutting Score

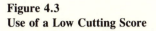

Non-lifestyle Criminals

Lifestyle Criminals

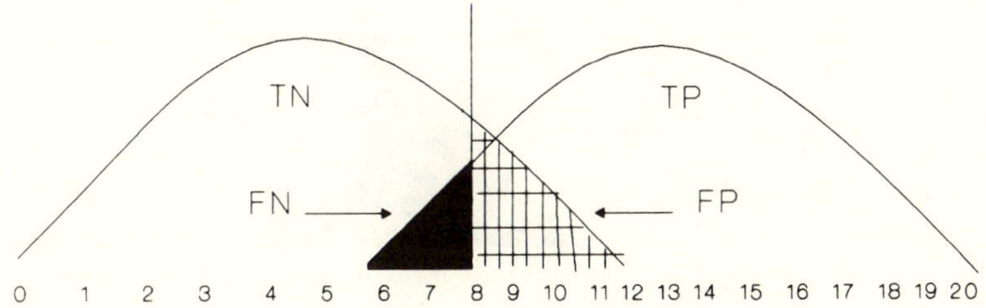

Lifestyle Criminality Scale Score

TP = True Positives
TN = True Negatives
FP = False Positive
FN = False Negative
Cutting Score = 8

with only minor concern for the number of false positives our scale may promulgate. Under such circumstances we would likely select a low cutting score that, as Figure 4.3 clearly delineates, will tend to enhance the sensitivity of our measure (true positives/true positives + false negatives) but at the expense of its specificity (true negatives/true negatives + false positives). If, on the other hand, we desire a sample composed of offenders who are most assuredly lifestyle criminals and are willing to accept a certain percentage of false negatives we would select a higher cutting score. Such a procedure would inspire a relatively high rate of specificity but lower the sensitivity of our putative measure of lifestyle criminality (see Figure 4.4).

Extraneous Variables

Extraneous variables are sources of systematic variance other than those which are the focus of investigation. Thus, age, sex, education, or IQ may interact with our design in a manner that confounds our findings and complicates our discussion. Major sources of extraneous variance can be controlled methodologically, by matching, blocking, or incorporating the variable into our design, or statistically, such as might be achieved with an analysis of covariance or partial correlation. Unless the effects of these extraneous variables are adequately controlled, a study's internal validity will suffer.

Figure 4.4
Use of a High Cutting Score

Non-lifestyle Criminals Lifestyle Criminals

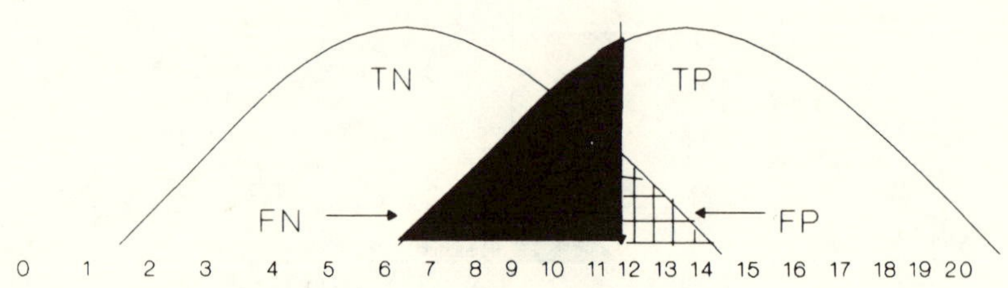

Lifestyle Criminality Scale Score

TP = True Positives
TN = True Negatives
FP = False Positive
FN = False Negative
Cutting Score = 12

Adequate Control and Comparison Groups

Many of the methodological problems discussed in this section could be remedied through use of an adequate control group. The control group permits us an opportunity to limit the effect of factors other than those that have been manipulated by the investigator. Although many criminal science studies contain comparison groups, very few of these control for major sources of extraneous variance. This is because it is difficult to find two or more naturally occurring groups that differ only on the dimensions we are attempting to investigate. Randomly assigning subjects to conditions offers the best prospect of achieving equivalence between one's experimental and control groups, but this is not always possible.

Therapy research is one area of criminal science research in which randomization of subjects to conditions is a distinct possibility. However, even here there may be problems if we rely exclusively on no-contact control groups. This is because we have no surety that these groups are equivalent on all relevant dimensions. In other words, the effects we observe may be a function of the amount of attention awarded treated subjects relative to that provided no-contact control subjects; such phenomena as the placebo and Hawthorn effects may account for a significant portion of the systematic variance between the treatment and no-contact control groups in therapy outcome studies. For this reason it is recommended that researchers conducting therapy research consider employing placebo control groups in which control subjects receive the same amount of attention as subjects enrolled in therapy, but in a different form. The advantage of having a placebo control group is that it provides us with the opportunity to approximate, and perhaps control, the nonspecific effects of contact with a therapist.

CAUSE AND EFFECT

The issue of cause and effect is one of the most misunderstood subjects in the entire field of scientific endeavor. It is difficult to pick up a magazine, newspaper, or professional journal and not read about the causes of this or that behavior. However, if we examine these topics in greater detail what we often discover is that the authors of these papers and articles have failed to adequately address the issue of cause and effect relative to three prerequisite conditions. In a now-classic position paper, Selltiz, Jahoda, Deutch, and Cook (1959) discussed three criteria that they stated must be substantiated before one is justified in making statements of a causal nature.

The first criterion is that the putative cause-and-effect variables should correlate or covary. In other words, these two variables should demonstrate a positive, negative, or curvilinear relationship. If we postulate that certain learning difficulties are a primary cause of behavioral problems and later criminality, then these two variables should correlate. The presence of a substantial positive correlation between measures of school achievement and subsequent criminal behavior is not sufficient evidence of a causal nexus, however. To investigate the causal nature of such a relationship, two additional conditions must first be satisfied—that is, directionality and the absence of alternative explanations.

The second criterion is directionality. In other words, the putative cause should precede the putative effect chronologically. Examining once again the association between learning disabilities and crime, we must establish that these learning difficulties preceded the behavioral problems as a condition of the second rule of cause and effect. If our data indicate that learning anomalies often do in fact antedate behavioral and criminal problems, then we move to the third and final rule of causality.

The third condition to be satisfied as part of the law of cause and effect is that reasonable alternative explanations of the particular relationships observed should be evaluated and preferably eliminated scientifically. Hence, we need to determine whether a third variable—such as intelligence, early home environment, or choice behavior—may be mediating the apparent association between learning disabilities and behavioral and/or criminal outcomes. If such viable alternative explanations can be ruled out, then we can be more confident that a causal connection actually exists between learning disabilities and subsequent criminality.

CONCLUSION

In this chapter we have examined the nature of criminal science inquiry. We discussed the composition of scientific research and how in directing investigations we are, in actuality, comparing the variance obtained through a manipulation of certain variables (between-group variance) with an estimate of the random error (within-group) variance. If the between group:within group ratio exceeds a certain level, then we are justified in rejecting the null hypothesis of no difference or relationship. If, on the other hand, this ratio fails to achieve significance, then the null hypothesis cannot be rejected. In this chapter we also discussed several common methodological problems confronting researchers wishing to investigate a variety of different criminal science questions. With an eye toward helping researchers deal more effectively with some of these methodological limitations, a general research strategy was introduced. Lastly, we explored the issue of cause and effect in terms of the conditions that must be satisfied before one is justified in making causal-type statements.

Now that we have examined the pertinent issues, it is time we move into a discussion of the primary areas of research on the correlates of criminal behavior. This discourse on criminal science research is presented in the next four chapters. Chapter 5 considers criminal science research on person variables; person variables being characteristics of the individual—for example, heredity, intelligence, and personality. Chapter 6 encompasses a survey of research addressing the role of the environment in crime genesis, most notably factors like early home environment, peers, and substance abuse. Consequently, the influences discussed in this section will be referred to as situation variables. In Chapter 7 we probe the person by situation interaction, while our discussion in Chapter 8 centers on choice as an explanation for criminal outcomes.

An important lesson to be learned from this chapter is that we cannot accept a research finding at face value. Accordingly, we must utilize available research tools to critically evaluate the relationships observed in our research investigations. Systematic application of the scientific method to criminal science data would do much to make crime less mysterious and more intelligible. Unfortunately, empirical findings have often taken a back seat to certain personal, political, or guild interests. Without a healthy sense of skepticism we are handicapped in our efforts to find meaningful answers to the questions posed by criminal science. As we proceed through the next several chapters we maintain a critical yet realistic perspective, dedicated to identifying and examining putative correlates and causes of crime.

5

Correlates of Crime: Person Variables

The field of criminology, with its sociological bias, has been largely remiss in examining individual differences as part of its investigation of criminal behavior. With an almost exclusive emphasis on social structure, criminological investigators have seemingly ignored the individual. Two social scientists, Hirschi and Hindelang (1977), in fact, have taken the field to task for failing to consider individual differences, such as might be found with intelligence, in its approach to research. One explanation for the tacit rejection of individual differences by sociologically minded criminologists is the moral belief that deviants are "as good as anyone else" (Liazos, 1972). Hirschi and Hindelang argue, however, that criminologists have confused the moral "as good as" with the empirical "the same as," and that this has led them to unjustifiably reject findings that denote the presence of individual differences.

Psychologists have taken a path very different from that of sociologists in their study of crime. Emphasizing the person rather than the situation, this group of social scientists has displayed an enduring interest in the differences among individuals on such variables as intelligence, temperament, and personality. Instead of focusing on the social characteristics that groups of individuals share, the psychologist's major concern is with the differences among individuals. This perspective has led to a number of important discoveries but is not without its own limitations (Mischel, 1969). Regardless, it is a viewpoint worthy of further investigation. In short, I believe it is shortsighted and neglectful of us to enter into the scientific study of crime without taking into account the divergent nature of human behavior.

Along the lines of research on individual differences, person variables are characteristics of the individual. That these characteristics are important in the development of significant patterns of criminal conduct will become increasingly evident as we proceed through this chapter. In the absence of a psychology of individual differences, we are left with only a portion of the equation we will use to explain criminal behavior. This equation will be presented in Chapter 7, but unless person variables are incorporated into this equation we will most assuredly fail in our efforts to fully understand the nature of crime and the behavior of criminals. The present chapter is subdivided into six primary categories of person variables—heredity, neurological factors, physical attributes, intelligence, features of personality, demographic characteristics—all of which will be discussed in the pages that follow.

Before proceeding it is important that we examine the similarities and dissimilarities between criminals and psychopaths. In his now-classic book on psychopathy, *The Mask of Sanity*, noted psychiatrist Harvey Cleckly (1976) characterized the psychopath as superficially charming, unreliable, impulsive, free of anxiety and guilt, and prone to engage in repetitive antisocial acts. It is easy to see that while psychopathy and criminality are related, they are far from interchangeable. In this section, research on psychopathy will be reviewed alongside research on criminality for two basic reasons. First, much of the research on person variables has been conducted using groups of "psychopaths." Second, what researchers commonly refer to as psychopathy seemingly reflects a pattern of antisocial behavior capable of capturing the irresponsibility, self-indulgence, interpersonal intrusiveness, and chronic rule breaking associated with serious criminality (Walters, 1990b).

HEREDITY

Social scientists have traditionally been unreceptive, if not outwardly hostile, to genetic interpretations of human behavior. This has done little to retard research on heredity and crime, however. As of this writing there were nearly 100 research investigations addressing the general issue of heredity and crime, beginning with Dugdale's (1877) examination of the Juke family. In fact, what genetic research on crime has lacked in quality (see Walters & White's [1989a] review), it seems to have more than made up for in quantity. Genetic studies on crime are often organized into three general categories of investigation: family or pedigree studies, twin studies, and adoption studies.

Family studies focus on the criminal patterns found in families or groups of biologically related persons. Glueck and Glueck (1974), for instance, recorded a higher rate of delinquency and/or criminality in the relatives of delinquent boys than in the relatives of nondelinquent boys (40% vs. 32% in the case of paternal relatives, and 55% vs. 36% in the case of maternal relatives). Robins, West, and Herjanic (1975) and Cloninger and Guze (1973) witnessed similar results. Examining family data in some detail, Cloninger, Reich, and Guze (1975a, 1975b) observed a cross-generational link for sociopathy and concluded that if this link is inherited it is more likely to be polygenetic than unigenetic.

The problem with family or pedigree studies is that they are incapable of distinguishing between a genetic effect and an environmental effect, since family members share not only a common genetic background but numerous environ-

Table 5.1
Twin Studies of Criminal Behavior

Study	Location	Monozygotic		Dizygotic	
		Pairs	Concord	Pairs	Concord
Lange (1930)	Germany	13	76.9%	17	11.8%
LeGras (1934)	Holland	4	100.0%	5	0.0%
Rosanoff et al. (1934)	United States	37	67.6%	28	17.9%
Kranz (1936)	Germany	31	64.5%	43	53.5%
Stumpfl (1936)	Germany	18	61.1%	19	36.8%
Borgstrom (1939)	Finland	4	75.0%	5	40.0%
Slater (1953)	England	2	50.0%	10	30.0%
Yoshimasu (1961)	Japan	28	60.7%	18	11.1%
Tienari (1963)	Finland	5	60.0%	-	-
Christiansen (1970, 1974)	Denmark	81	33.3%	137	10.9%
Dalgard & Kringlen (1976)	Norway	49	22.4%	89	18.0%
Rowe (1983)	United States	61(M) 107(F)	.66 .74	38(M) 59(F)	.48 .47

Notes: Monozygotic = identical twins; dyzygotic = same-sexed fraternal twins; pairs = number of twin pairs; concord = concordance of twin pairs criminality. In the D. C. Rowe (1983) study concordance was measured in terms of the intraclass correlation between twin pairs on a 25-item Antisocial Behavior Scale.

mental experiences as well. This has led some researchers to consider twin studies whereby monozygotic (single-egg) and dizygotic (dual-egg) twins are compared in an effort to disentangle the individual contributions of nature and nurture. Since monozygotic twins have all of their genes in common, compared to dizygotic twins who share only 50 percent of their genetic inheritance, we would anticipate greater similarity in the behavior of monozygotic, as opposed to dizygotic, twins if the behavior in question is genetically based.

As Table 5.1 illustrates, from the early pioneering work of Lange (1930) to the more recent treatment of this subject by Rowe (1983), monozygotic twins characteristically exhibit greater concordance for criminality than do same-sex dizygotic twins. However, these differences have not always been conceptually meaningful and there is a trend wherefore the better designed studies (Christiansen, 1970, 1974; Dalgard & Kringlen, 1976; Rowe, 1983) demonstrate less of a monozygotic-dizygotic difference than do several of the earlier, more methodologically flawed, investigations.

One frequently cited criticism of twin-research is that it does not always control for important environmental factors. Research, for instance, demonstrates that monozygotic twins spend more time together and are often treated more similarly than dizygotic twins. Dalgard and Kringlen (1976) determined that when monozygotic and dizygotic twins were matched for closeness and mutual identity, the already small relationship they observed between zygosity and crime all but disappeared. In a similar vein, Rosenthal (1975) notes that adults tend to treat monozygotic or identical twins more alike than dizygotic or fraternal twins, a phenomenon known as twinning. It would appear, then, that twin studies are less than ideal for the purpose of teasing out the individual contributions of genetic and environmental influence toward the development of significant criminality.

Although the results of family and twin studies suggest that crime does in fact follow along family lines, it is difficult to determine whether genetic or environment factors are responsible. Adoption studies, on the other hand, offer a more precise test of the genetic hypothesis by affording investigators the opportunity to examine the behavior of individuals adopted away from their biological parents at an early age. Hutchings and Mednick (1975), for instance, performed a cross-foster analysis of 1,145 Danish adoptees listed in a Copenhagen birth registry. Results revealed the presence of criminal convictions in 10 percent of the adoptees whose biological and adoptive parents had no history of prior criminality, 11 percent of the adoptees with at least one criminal adoptive parent but no criminal biological parent, 21 percent of the adoptees with at least one criminal biological parent but no criminal adoptive parent, and 36 percent of the adoptees with at least one criminal biological and one criminal adoptive parent. In an analysis of 14,427 Danish adoptees (to include the 1,145 subjects who constituted the original Copenhagen study), Mednick, Gabrielli, and Hutchings (1984) obtained percentages of 13.5 percent, 14.7 percent, 20.0 percent, and 24.5 percent, respectively—outcomes which are consistent with the genetic hypothesis but which demonstrate a somewhat weaker genetic link than the earlier study.

In 1978, Bohman examined the level of criminality in groups of Swedish adoptees. Although he observed a relationship between biological parentage and adoptee alcohol abuse, there was no effect for criminal behavior. In analyzing these data further, Bohman, Cloninger, Sigvardsson, and von Knorring (1982) discovered a cross-generational link for petty criminality in cases where there was no evidence of past alcohol abuse. Besides it being difficult to fathom a genetic predisposition specific for petty criminality, the Bohman and associates' (1982) study is hampered by a host of serious methodological flaws, not the least of which was a written presentation which defies meaningful interpretation and obfuscates the reader's ability to understand which analyses were performed on which subset of subjects (see Walters & White, 1989a).

Crowe (1972, 1974) employed the adoptive methodology to examine the criminal records of a sample of Iowan adoptees separated from their mothers at an early age. The mothers of these adoptees were inmates at a woman's reformatory or state training school who had given their babies up for adoption at a fairly early age (usually within the first year). A control group was selected from the state adoption agency and individual cases were matched with probands (adoptees with criminal mothers) on age, sex, race, and approximate age at time of adoption. In analyzing these data, Crowe determined that significantly more proband (15.4%) than control (3.8%) adoptees had police records. Using a larger sample of Iowan adoptees, Cadoret (1978) obtained results that showed that the biological offspring of parents previously diagnosed as antisocial personalities were significantly more likely than adoptees whose biological parents were without such diagnoses to receive a diagnosis of antisocial personality themselves.

A common outcome of adoption research has been that the relationship between heredity and crime is stronger for persons charged with property crimes than for persons arrested for violent offenses (Mednick, Brennan, & Kandel, 1988; Mednick et al., 1984; Bohman et al., 1982). Utilizing data from the Mednick and associates' (1984) study, Moffitt (1987) ascertained that recidivistic criminality correlated positively with biological parent criminality and psychological diagnoses of personality disorder and substance abuse but negatively with biological parent diagnoses of psychosis. There was also a nonsignificant trend that found violent antisocial behavior in adoptees corresponding with biological parent criminality and personality disorder and/or substance abuse diagnoses.

Although adoption studies on crime appear to support a partial genetic explanation of criminal behavior, they are not without serious problems and limitations. In a review of the genetic research on crime, Walters and White (1989a) cataloged the relative weaknesses of adoption studies designed to examine the proposed link between heredity and crime. Such methodological problems include the use of proband and control subjects who differed in terms of their base rate for criminality (Mednick), age at which they were separated from their mothers (Bohman, Crowe), and amount of time they spent in an orphanage (Crowe). In addition, a number of definitional and statistical issues limit the utility of adoption studies on crime. The interested reader is referred to a recent exchange in the journal *Criminology* for both sides of a debate on the methodological rigor of genetic research on crime (Brennan & Mednick, 1990; Walters, 1990a).

Conceding for the moment the methodological limitations of genetic research on crime, there does nonetheless appear to be some validity to the genetic hypothesis. In point of fact, it does not seem imponderable that many forms of social behavior are influenced by heredity. One way researchers gauge the degree to which a particular trait or behavior is genetically transmitted is by calculating a heritability ratio or index. The heritability index contrasts the biological concordance of a particular behavior with the base rate concordance of the behavior, and while it frequently overestimates the contributions of heredity by confounding genetic and environmental influences, the outcome of the majority of these studies suggests the presence of a fairly consistent relationship between heredity (defined globally) and assorted indices of criminal involvement (see Table 5.2).

The results obtained in genetic studies on crime clearly suggest that inherited

Table 5.2
Heritability of Criminal Conduct

Heritablity Index	Family Studies	Twin Studies	Adoption Studies
Minimal (.00 to .25)			Bohman (1971, 1978) Mednick et al. (1984)
Low-Moderate (.26 to .50)	Guze et al. (1967)		Cadoret (1978) Hutchings & Mednick (1975) Schulsinger (1972)
High-Moderate (.51 to .75)		Christiansen (1970) Dalgard & Kringlen (1976) Slater (1953)	Cadoret et al. (1985) Cloninger et al. (1982) Crowe (1974)
High (.79 to .99)	Cloninger & Guze (1973) Cloninger et al. (1975)	Borgstrom (1939) Kranz (1936) Lange (1930) Stumpfl (1936) Rosanoff et al. (1934) Yoshimasu (1961)	

Note: See Walters & White (1989a) for a more complete explanation of how these figures were derived.

features are part of the equation we use to explain significant criminality. Where genetic research on crime appears to have floundered is by failing to identify which specific attributes are inherited and how they aid in the development of later criminality. Scrutinizing genetic investigations on crime in greater detail we find that they seem to treat heredity as a global attribute, thereby seriously limiting the theoretical and practical value of any research findings that do surface in support of the genetic hypothesis. As we search for a link between heredity and behavior, such person characteristics as temperament, intelligence, and physical stature loom in importance. Unfortunately, few investigations have addressed these or related issues. In this chapter we explore several additional person variables, some of which may assist us in our efforts to understand the nexus thought to exist between heredity and certain forms of criminal behavior.

It is also important that we consider a second major limitation of genetic research on crime. It appears that several of the investigators in this area have underestimated the influence of sundry environmental conditions on criminal development. An exception to this general rule is found in a recent study by Rowe and Osgood (1984). Rowe and Osgood examined the impact of both genetic (twin status) and environmental (association with delinquent peers) variables on a measure of antisocial behavior and learned that the causal sequence responsible for delinquent involvement accommodated both individual differences in genes and various environmental influences—in this case, associating with delinquent peers. Several other studies also highlight the importance of considering the person-environment interaction (Cadoret, Cain, & Crowe, 1983; Van Dusen et al., 1983), an issue which will receive greater attention in Chapter 7. First, however, we must consider several other classes of person variables.

NEUROLOGICAL FACTORS

In formulating possible explanations for the manner in which heredity impacts on criminal behavior, neurological factors come to mind immediately. After all, it is hard to conceive of any behavior operating independently of the central nervous system. From a simple knee jerk to reasoning out a complex arithmetic problem, the human nervous system is central to our behavior. It follows, then, that since individual differences in neurology are often the result of inherited influences (Carlsson, 1977), such differences may help forge a link between genetics and criminal behavior, though they may also be important in their own right. To this end we discuss studies on general brain activity, frontal lobe dysfunction, autonomic nervous system reactivity, neuroendocrinological levels, and perceptual asymmetries.

General Brain Activity

Initial attempts to study the neurological correlates of crime frequently employed the electroencephalogram (EEG). The EEG is an instrument designed to measure brain-wave activity by way of sensors attached to the scalp. EEG research on criminal and psychopathic subjects dates back to the early 1940s and demonstrates a fairly consistent relationship between EEG abnormality and criminal behavior. Post–1960 research studies scrutinizing the EEG patterns of criminals and psychopaths are outlined in Table 5.3. Even though the percentages obtained in EEG research on offender populations hint at the prospect of a link between EEG-measured abnormalities and criminality, caution needs to be exercised in interpreting these findings since they are confounded by a number of serious methodological flaws and shortcomings.

Several of the more noteworthy limitations found in EEG research on crime include inadequate criterion diagnoses (Mark & Ervin, 1970), apparent disregard for the potential impact of anxiety and arousal on EEG results (Syndulko, 1978), and frequent failure to age-correct one's data (Mark & Ervin, 1970). As can be seen in Table 5.3, many of the studies failed to include a control group. Moreover, for studies in which a comparison group was included, "control" subjects were

Table 5.3
EEG Studies on Psychopaths and Criminals

Study	Index Subjects	Controls	EEG Abnormalities (%) Index	Control
Craft et al. (1962)	Psychopaths	None	24.0%	-
Arthurs & Cahoon (1964)	Psychopaths	None	44.0%	-
Small (1966)	Sociopathic Felons	None	33.0%	-
Monroe & Mickle (1967)	Psychopaths	Normal Volunteers	70.0%	21.7%
Sayed et al. (1969)	Insane Murderers	Medical Staff	65.6%	15.6%
Williams (1969)	Repeat Violent Offenders	Single Violent Offense	57.0%	12.0%
Ohlesen et al. (1970)	State Prisoners	Normal Controls	47.0*	3.0*
Harper et al. (1972)	Psychopaths	None	53.0%	-
Murdoch (1972)	Prisoners	Normal Controls	89.0%	83.0%
Driver et al. (1974)	Prisoners Charged with Murder	Normal Controls	10.0%	10.0%
Okasha et al. (1975)	Prisoners Charged with Murder	Normal Controls	43.5%	-
Krynicki (1978)	Assaultive Delinquents	Nonassaultive Delinquents	42.8%	0.0%

Note: Sleep EEGs are reported here. Waking EEGs evidenced no group differences, although Ohlesen et al. (1970) fail to provide the percentages.

often inadequate for the purposes of making a valid comparison. Part of the problem appears to be that the EEG itself produces a large number of false positive and false negative readings. Filskov and Goldstein (1974) report that the EEG is only about 60 percent accurate, while a study conducted by staff at the Mayo Clinic (1976) in Rochester, Minnesota, reveals that between 15 and 20 percent of all individuals without apparent neurological dysfunction produce abnormal EEGs.

Although the research in this area has been poorly designed, it is difficult to argue with Syndulko's (1978, p. 149) general conclusion ''that a subset of subjects labelled sociopaths do show an excessive incidence of EEG abnormalities.'' However, whether these abnormalities are the cause of criminal and/or sociopathic behavior or reflect the fact that the individual has chosen a lifestyle in which drug abuse and head injury are more common than they are in the general population is of even greater importance. With an eye toward answering this question, Petersen, Matousek, Mednick, Volavka, and Pollock (1982) conducted EEG evaluations on 571 Danish adoptees before any of them showed signs of criminality. After removing subjects exhibiting symptoms of an overt neurological disorder, these authors found evidence of significant alpha wave slowing on the EEGs of future thieves ($N = 20$) relative to others in their sample ($N = 517$). Further analysis of these data revealed that adoptees convicted of more than one theft displayed even more alpha slowing than thieves possessing a single conviction.

The results of EEG studies on criminals and psychopaths indicate that criminals may, in fact, demonstrate greater levels of disturbance in general brain activity than noncriminals. However, as with the research on heredity, most EEG studies on crime are methodologically flawed and offer only the prospect of a generalized deficit that at this point seems devoid of theoretical and practical significance. Furthermore, there is some research to suggest that the EEGs of criminal offenders are oftentimes indistinguishable from those achieved by other deviant groups (psychiatric patients; Syndulko, 1978). With these problems in mind, we move into a discussion of several other putative neurological correlates of criminal behavior.

Frontal Lobe Anomalies

Attention, planning, impulse control, and voluntary action are some of the functions controlled by the left frontal lobe of the brain. It is not surprising, then, that frontal lobe dysfunction has been implicated in the development of criminal and psychopathic forms of behavior owing to the fact that inattention, poor planning, and weak impulse control are commonly found in criminals and psychopaths. Pontius (1972) goes so far as to speculate that frontal lobe difficulties actually cause certain categories of juvenile delinquency, an argument for which there is circumscribed research support. As such, delinquents have been found to achieve lower scores than nondelinquents on the Halstead-Reitan Trailmaking and Category tests (Yeudall, Fromm-Auch, & Davies, 1982), Knox Cubes (Gilbert & Gravier, 1982), and Raven Progressive Matrices (Yeudall et al., 1982), all of which are thought to measure frontal lobe function. On the other hand, no delinquent-nondelinquent differences were noted on these same measures in several other investigations (Andrew, 1982; Tarter, Hegedus, Alterman, & Katz-Garris, 1983).

Extending the frontal lobe argument to cases of adult criminality, Schalling (1978) states that frontal lobe dysfunction may be instrumental in the behavior of adult offenders and psychopaths. However, unlike the equivocality of research on delinquency and frontal lobe abnormality, studies investigating frontal lobe dysfunction and adult criminality have met with largely negative results. Even though Gorenstein (1982) ascertained that psychopathic patients performed more poorly on certain putative measures of frontal lobe ability, subsequent research has failed to replicate these findings, whether subjects were prison inmates (Hare, 1984) or inpatients enrolled in a V.A. drug abuse program (Hoffman, Hall, & Bartsch, 1987). Research conducted by a group from the Veterans Administration Medical Center in New Orleans (Sutker, Moan, & Allain, 1983) also failed to identify a link between psychopathy and various measures of frontal lobe dysfunction. In sum, there appears to be little solid empirical support for the supposition that frontal lobe deficits play a leading role in criminal and psychopathic development.

Autonomic Nervous System Reactivity

The autonomic nervous system (ANS), which is involved in the regulation of smooth muscles, glands, and cardiac functions, is composed of two anatomically distinct divisions commonly referred to as the sympathetic and parasympathetic subdivisions. The sympathetic branch of the ANS comes into play when stored energy is released—the so-called fight or flight response. The parasympathetic branch, on the other hand, is dedicated to conserving the body's reservoir of stored energy. Accordingly, with sympathetic activation comes increased heart rate, a rise in the blood sugar level, elevated sweat gland activity, and secretion of epinephrine from the adrenal glands located above each kidney. The parasympathetic branch of the ANS brings about a general state of body relaxation, reduced heart rate, and increased salivation, and augments the mobility of the digestive tract.

A commonly employed measure of autonomic reactivity is the heart rate. Raine and Venables (1981) observed slower heart rates in higher socioeconomic-status students rated as undersocialized by their teachers but not in a group of lower socioeconomic students. In an effort to find a genetic link between autonomic response and criminality, Venables (1987) examined a Danish birth cohort and discovered that the children (mean age = 11) of criminal biological fathers evidenced significantly lower resting heart rates than adoptees born to noncriminal fathers. Employing a prospective design in which he measured the tonic heart rates of 5,000 English schoolchildren and then followed them up several years later, Wadsworth (1976) discovered that future delinquents possessed significantly lower heart rates than nondelinquents (83.9 vs. 85.9 bpm) and that individuals eventually convicted of violent offenses had recorded even lower resting heart rates (81.7 bpm) as children. After reviewing the research on cardiac measures, Hare (1978) concluded that phasic heart rate (in response to stimulation) is largely ineffective in discriminating between psychopaths (or criminals) and normal controls, although tonic (resting) heart rate may be capable of identifying potential criminal-noncriminal variations in autonomic response.

While research utilizing heart rate as a measure of autonomic reactivity has produced interesting hypotheses, it is far from conclusive in establishing the presence or absence of autonomic deficits in offenders because it is only a very gross index of autonomic response. Conversely, electrodermal activity or electrical skin conductance is a more reliable measure of the responsiveness of one's autonomic nervous system. Acknowledging the lack of uniformity in prior research outcomes, Hare (1978) concluded that skin conductance, particularly in response to stimulation or threat of punishment, tends to be lower in criminals and psychopaths than comparable groups of noncriminals and nonpsychopathic offenders. Combining the results of eight separate studies, Hare observed a highly significant inverse correlation between psychopathy and tonic skin response. Siddle (1977), on the other hand, reports that tonic or resting skin conductance frequently fails to discriminate between criminals and/or psychopaths and normal individuals, although phasic skin conductance (in response to stimulation) may yield more positive outcomes. In support of Siddle's position, Raine (1982) failed to find a consistent relationship between various ratings of socialization and resting skin conductance. Additionally, Venables et al. (1978) found no difference in tonic skin conductance for lower socioeconomic delinquents and nondelinquents, but did witness a higher resting electrodermal level in higher socioeconomic delinquents when contrasted with higher socioeconomic nondelinquents (contrary to predictions).

Whereas the results of research on tonic or resting skin conductance have been equivocal, investigations on phasic conductance in response to stimulation have been much more encouraging. In research which is now two decades old, Borkovec (1970) and Siddle, Nicol, and Foggitt (1973) observed reduced electrodermal reactions in psychopathic subjects exposed to a series of tones. Examining prison inmates rated high, medium, and low on a measure of psychopathy, Hare (1982) witnessed fewer skin conductance responses in the high psychopathic group for situations in which an aversive stimulus could be avoided but no differences when the aversive stimulus could not be avoided. Utilizing a median split procedure, Ogloff and Wong (1990) discerned that high psychopathic inmates displayed lower skin conductance levels (SCL) response compared to nonpsychopathic inmates when both groups were exposed to a countdown task.

Hare and Quinn (1971) used a classical conditioning paradigm to demonstrate that psychopathic subjects experience difficulty forming autonomic responses, as measured by skin conductance, to a conditioned stimulus. Similarly, Levander, Schalling, Lidberg, Bartfai, and Lidberg (1980) note that a group of 25 criminal offenders were less electrodermally responsive to aversive stimuli than has been documented in nondeviant samples. Although Raine and Venables (1988) failed to identify autonomic underarousal in psychopathic offenders compared to nonpsychopathic offenders, they did note abnormal levels of linguistic processing on the part of subjects in the psychopathic group. In related fashion, Raine, Venables, and Williams (1990) note that male subjects achieving lower heart rate and skin conductance autonomic orienting results at age 15 were significantly more likely to own a record of criminal conviction at age 24 than subjects who at age 15 were functioning within normal limits on these measures of autonomic response.

It is not outside the realm of possibility that the results of these autonomic studies reveal idiosyncrasies in the learning styles of criminals and psychopaths. Examining electrodermal response to a conditioning task, Loeb and Mednick (1977) deduced that children later convicted of various crimes displayed smaller autonomic reactions than control children. Venables (1987) reports that the SCL responses of subjects in a longitudinal investigation measured at age 10 were significantly lower in subjects rated by teachers, employers, and other adults as suffering from conduct disorder problems at ages 17 or 18. Earlier, Hare (1975) had recorded evidence of slowed electrodermal recovery in psychopathic subjects and had speculated that this may interfere with these individuals' ability to learn to avoid certain negative consequences. These findings have been integrated into a theory whose main hypothesis is that criminals and psychopaths fail to learn prosocial behaviors like rule following and responsibility because of an inadequate level of fear and weak avoidance conditioning (see Hare, 1978; Mednick, 1977).

Neuroendocrinological Levels

The neuroendocrinology of criminal behavior is concerned mostly with gonadal hormones like estrogen, progesterone, and testosterone. Testosterone, which stimulates growth of the testes in men and is commonly referred to as the male sex hormone, has received a fair amount of attention from researchers concerned with identifying the neurological correlates of violence and criminal behavior. In a series of animal studies, Goy (1968; Goy, Wolf, & Eisele, 1977) determined that administration of androgenic steroids like testosterone to prepubescent female rhesus monkeys resulted in an increased level of adult aggressiveness. The bulk of research on human subjects indicates that more violent male offenders display higher testosterone levels than less violent offenders and noncriminal controls (Ehrenkranz, Bliss, & Sheard, 1974; Rada, Laws, and Kellner, 1976). Since the sample sizes in many of these investigations were small, it is difficult to attach much credence to the results. As such, the possibility of a relationship between testosterone and violent criminality remains ambiguous (compare Matthews, 1979).

If increased levels of testosterone are a cause of criminal violence, then we should expect to find decreased levels of aggressiveness when testosterone is reduced and increased levels when this hormone is augmented. Money et al. (1975) ascertained that administration of an antiandrogenic agent designed to reduce testosterone led to a decline in the level of erotic imagery and behavior present in a group of sexual offenders. Conversely, the administration of estrogen (a female hormone) has been found to correspond with decreased levels of violence in aggressive male sex offenders (Chatz, 1972; Field & Williams, 1970).

Whether reduced levels of estrogen or augmented levels of testosterone actually cause criminal violence cannot be determined from the results of these studies. Several studies, however, have found that the administration of steroid testosterone will produce increased masculine body type and heterosexual interest in persons with low natural levels of the male sex hormone, although there are no reports of increased violence or antisocial behavior on the part of these individuals (Davidson, Camargo, & Smith, 1979).

Rubin (1987) remarks that we could learn a great deal more about the role of testosterone in criminal violence by measuring testosterone action at the receptor site level. However, research to date has been equivocal as to the relationship between testosterone and criminal violence. Therefore, while it may be that testosterone is high in persons prone to behavioral violence, there is no convincing evidence at this point that enhanced levels of testosterone are a prime cause of this behavior.

Several studies have examined the relationship between the neurotransmitter serotonin and habitual violent behavior. Preliminary findings obtained by a group of U.S. and Finnish scientists suggested that a lower than normal level of serotonin was found in arsonists to a significantly greater degree than a group of controls without any history of violence (Virkkunen et al., 1987). However, these conclusions need to be tempered with the realization that the serotonin–violent crime relationship recorded by Virkkunen and his colleagues may have been an artifact of arsonists having spent an average of six months in confinement before being tested, since research has shown that serotonin levels tend to drop in response to the stress and isolation of incarceration (DeFeudis & Schauss, 1987).

Perceptual Asymmetries

The most recent trend in research on neurological correlates of criminal involvement concerns perceptual asymmetries, or the relative strength of the two cerebral hemispheres. In most people the left cerebral hemisphere is involved with the comprehension and production of speech, while the right hemisphere takes care of spatial relations and various artistic expressions. In their efforts to measure lateral preference, researchers have examined sinistrality (dominance of one side of the body over the other), visual field organization, and relative performance on dichotic listening tasks.

Most of the research on sinistrality has been conducted on small samples and has yielded mixed outcomes, some studies showing an association between delinquency and left-handedness (Andrew, 1978; Fitzhugh, 1973) and other studies demonstrating no such relationship (Yeudall et al., 1982). A prospective study of 129 high-risk male children revealed that subjects favoring their left hand or foot were more likely than subjects displaying a right-side preference to have been charged with a criminal offense during a six-year period of follow-up (Gabrielli & Mednick, 1980). However, in a more extensive examination of male prison inmates and normal controls, Hare and Forth (1985) discerned that criminals were more likely to be right-side dominant than noncriminals. These results led Hare and Forth to conclude that sinistrality is an inadequate measure of cerebral dominance, at least where research on crime and delinquency is concerned.

Another means of evaluating lateral dominance is to examine the relative pattern of visual field dominance, the right visual field attaching to the left cerebral hemisphere and the left visual field networking with the right cerebral hemisphere. Hare (1979) presented a series of words tachistoscopically (40 to 80 msec exposure) to groups of prison inmates recording high, medium, and low scores on a measure of psychopathy. Results indicated that the high-psychopathic group achieved more accurate outcomes with the right visual field than with the left visual field, a finding which is similar to patterns observed in normal subjects. However, such comparisons may be an inadequate test of the perceptual asymmetry hypothesis in the sense that the right hemisphere is dyslexic.

Switching methodologies, Hare and McPherson (1984) compared 146 male prison inmates and 159 male noncriminals on a dichotic listening task. The noncriminals exhibited significantly better performance than criminals but no differences were noted in terms of left versus right ear preference. The authors interpret this finding as reflecting lowered attention and motivation on the part of the criminal subjects in their study. Comparing offenders high and low on a measure of psychopathy, Hare and McPherson determined that the high-psychopathic group recalled more words presented to the left ear (right hemisphere) and fewer words presented to the right ear (left hemisphere) than the low-psychopathic group. Such a finding suggests that psychopathy may be associated with decreased efficiency of the left cerebral hemisphere.

In a series of investigations conducted by Hare and Jutai (reported in Hare & Connolly, 1987), criminals and noncriminals were compared in terms of their ability to process simple and complex semantic material. Whereas noncriminals demonstrated no hemispheric preference on the simple task, there was a shift in the direction of greater reliance on the left hemisphere when the semantic demands of the task were increased. Criminals, on the other hand, evidenced a left hemisphere advantage on the simple task and a right hemisphere advantage on the more complex task. This shift was even more pronounced in criminals classified as highly psychopathic. Interestingly, Kosson and Newman (1986) report that psychopaths have problems shifting their attention between processing tasks. These findings could be interpreted as lending support to the hypothesis that the left cerebral hemisphere of criminals and psychopaths is less strongly specialized for linguistic operations, which, in turn, makes it more difficult for them to process certain kinds of information and switch their attention from one processing task to another.

Crime and Neurological Disorder

In summary, while EEG studies apparently suggest that criminals and psychopaths are at increased risk for certain forms of cortical abnormality, the meaningfulness and direction of this relationship cannot be determined from the data available. The frontal lobe and testosterone explanations of violent criminality make good theoretical sense but have amassed very little empirical support to date. We are therefore left with autonomic nervous system reactivity and perceptual asymmetry as the sole neurological explanations of criminal behavior with any degree of theoretical and/or empirical validity. In this regard, Hare and Connolly (1987) speculate that criminal offenders, particularly those high on measures of psychopathy, evidence greater right than left hemisphere arousal compared to noncriminals. Consequently, criminals may tend to rely more extensively on imagery than linguistic operations in dealing with people and situations. The fact that neurological markers of inferior autonomic response are more strongly associated with delinquency in higher as opposed to lower socioeconomic subjects suggests that the antisocial behavior displayed by persons with lower socioeconomic origins is more heavily influenced by environmental and non-neurologic person factors than may be the case with persons raised in higher socioeconomic status homes.

In a review of neuropsychological studies on delinquency, Miller (1988) concludes that most delinquents are probably not "brain damaged" in a traditional neurological sense. Rather, they display patterns of neuropsychological dysfunction in which their response regulation, verbal and linguistic reasoning skills, and complex problem-solving abilities are disturbed. Miller goes on to draw a parallel between delinquencv and Attention Deficit Disorder/Hyperactivity, a syndrome which has been observed in a relatively large number of psychopaths and adolescent conduct disorders (Hinshaw, 1987; Loeber, 1990; Prinz, Conner, & Wilson, 1981; Shapiro & Garinkel, 1986). Both, according to Miller, can be traced to delayed neurologic development and maturation. Although we can only speculate about the validity of this hypothesis given the paucity of data currently available, it certainly holds interesting possibilities for a science of criminal behavior.

PHYSICAL ATTRIBUTES

Lombroso, in proposing his atavistic theory of criminal behavior, conducted several thousand postmortem studies on criminals confined in Italian prisons during the later decades of the nineteenth century. He reportedly observed a number of unusual physical characteristics during the course of his investigations. Specifically, he discerned an increased incidence of slanting foreheads, protruding jaws, protracted ear lobes, and sundry facial asymmetries. Lombroso (1911) used these findings to advance his theory that criminals were biological anomalies, throwbacks to a more primitive stage of human development. Although contesting Lombroso's position on atavism and crime, Hootin (1939) argued that his survey of over 17,000 American prisoners revealed a general constitutional deficiency in many of his subjects.

Findings such as those recorded by Lombroso and Hootin were vehemently attacked by individuals taking a sociological approach to the question of crime

(Barnes & Teeters, 1943). This unfortunately led to a backlash in which this line of research was nearly abandoned. Studies have shown, for instance, that compared to nonoffenders, criminals often exhibit a significantly greater number of correctable facial defects (Masters & Greaves, 1967) and that facially abnormal children and adolescents have fewer friends, suffer lower self-esteem, and are more likely to react with aggression than more physically attractive children (Lowenstein, 1978; Waldrop & Halverson, 1971). The Masters and Greaves study revealed the presence of facial deformity in criminal offenders that was two to three times that observed in general population subjects.

A series of investigations surveying the physical characteristics of criminal offenders in Denmark revealed an association between minor physical anomalies (for example, wide-set eyes, low-seated ears, high-steeped plate, curved fifth finger) and criminal convictions, but only for adoptees raised in unstable home environments (Mednick & Kandel, 1988). The latter finding once again points out the importance of understanding the interaction between the individual and his or her environment. Further analysis of these data revealed that minor physical anomalies measured at ages 11 to 13 were more prominent in subjects subsequently arrested for two or more violent crimes than subjects possessing no more than one subsequent arrest for a violent offense (Kandel et al., 1989).

Perhaps the most famous attempt to find a connection between physical characteristics and criminality was initiated nearly a half-century ago by the noted American psychologist, William Sheldon. In proposing a theory that linked body type with temperament (personality), Sheldon (1954) introduced three basic body types: endomorphy (obesity), ectomorphy (linearity), and mesomorphy (muscularity). Sheldon postulated that features of delinquency and criminality are most common in persons exhibiting mesomorphic body types, a premise which subsequent research has tended to bear out. Hence, in a study of 500 delinquent and 500 nondelinquent subjects carefully matched on several pertinent dimensions, Glueck and Glueck (1950) surmised that primary mesomorphy was twice as prevalent in delinquent, as opposed to control, subjects (60% vs. 30%). Shasby and Kingsley (1978) report that a group of behaviorally disordered male adolescents not only demonstrated increased levels of mesomorphy but also carried significantly less body fat than a group of nondelinquent junior and senior high school students. Similar findings have been recorded in studies of adult criminals (Nielsen & Tsuboi, 1970), British delinquents (Gibbens, 1963), and female offenders (Epps & Parnell, 1952).

The presence of tattoos is a crime-linked physical attribute that is self-inflicted rather than derived prenatally. Body graffiti has been observed with a high degree of regularity in delinquent (DeRen, Diligent, & Petiet, 1973), adult offender (Yamamoto, Seeman, & Lester, 1963), and chronic heroin addict (Bennahum, 1971) populations. Newman (1982) determined that assaultive felons sported a significantly greater number of tattoos than nonassaultive felons. It would seem likely, however, that instead of causing crime, tattoos simply reflect a preexisting identification with a criminal subgroup and antisocial ideal. There is evidence, nonetheless, that tattooing represents an attempt by certain individuals to overcome feelings of inadequacy, and in one recent study it was determined that low self-esteem and self-mutilative behavior were both more prominent in the minds and histories of tattooed inmates than nontattoed prisoners (Harry, 1987).

There is ample evidence to suggest that certain physical characteristics (facial features, height, eye color, general body type) are inherited, or at least greatly influenced by genetic factors (Lefton, 1985). Accordingly, physical characteristics provide a possible avenue through which heredity and criminal behavior might be linked. Just because certain physical features are found more frequently in criminals, however, even if such characteristics precede the initial stages of criminality, is not unequivocal evidence that such physical features cause crime (Bull, 1982). It may simply be that a child born with certain minor physical anomalies experiences a greater sense of social alienation than a child unfettered by such personal defects, or that an adolescent with a mesomorphic physique learns he can get his way by bullying weaker peers, an opportunity which may not be available to a scrawny, asthenic ectomorph or fat, pudgy endomorph. Rather than being forced into a life of crime, a mesomorphic child could just as easily become a construction worker, professional athlete, or politician. Moreover, while it is likely that some of the physical characteristics known to correlate with criminality are genetically influenced, the effect these characteristics have on criminal behavior is, at best, indirect.

INTELLIGENCE

In 1905, Alfred Binet and Theodore Simon, in an effort to find a measure which identified children of subnormal intelligence, developed the first reliable measure of intellectual ability. Since that time such luminaries as Lewis Terman (1877–1956), David Wechsler (1896–1981), and Alan Kaufman have refined both the definition and the assessment of intelligence. Intelligence tests normally yield one or more Intelligence Quotient (IQ) scores with a mean of 100 and standard deviation of 15 or 16. Hence, most investigations on intelligence utilize IQ scores as the criterion measure. While there is more to intelligence than IQ, there is sufficient documentation to suggest that intelligence tests are reasonably stable measures of cognitive ability, capable of predicting such outcomes as school performance and later occupational achievement (Anastasi, 1982).

In an early attempt to assess the intellectual ability of criminal offenders, Goddard (1914) concluded that between 25 and 50 percent of the prison inmates of that period were mentally defective as measured by an English translation of the Binet test. A decade later, Murchison (1926) wrote in his book *Criminal Intelligence* that a group of federal prisoners achieved higher IQ scores than their guards. Furthermore, inmate performance exceeded that attained by enlisted men tested during World War I. Whereas Murchison's study was superior to Goddard's earlier investigation, which suffered from inadequate sampling and testing procedures, Murchison apparently overlooked the fact that federal prisoners may not be representative of American inmates.

Since both the Goddard and the Murchison studies were methodologically flawed, it is interesting that sociologists have chosen to focus on the foibles of the former while ignoring the failings of the latter. One of the early patriarchs of American criminological thought, Edwin Sutherland (1931) concluded that the deficiency was with the research rather than with the intellectual ability of offenders. Unfortunately, this conclusion has been uncritically accepted by the authors of many criminology textbooks (Haskell & Yablonsky, 1978; Reid, 1982). In this section we explore whether Sutherland was justified in summarily dismissing the influence of intelligence on criminality.

General Intelligence

Using official court records, Reiss and Rhodes (1961) determined that the rate of legal adjudication for their low IQ group was twice that of their high IQ group. Hirschi (1969) observed correlations of −.31 for white males and −.16 for black males in comparing IQ with official delinquency in a group of 3,600 male adolescents. Several prospective studies provide even more positive evidence of a relationship between intelligence and later criminal and/or delinquent outcomes. Based on the results of the Philadelphia Verbal Ability Test, Wolfgang et al. (1972) surmised that the chronic offenders in their sample achieved a mean IQ score ten points below that attained by nondelinquents. West and Farrington (1973), on the other hand, observed that only one-fourth of their high IQ group (IQ > 109) wound up with police records as compared to one-half of their low IQ group (IQ < 91). In addition, while only 1 out of 50 boys in the high IQ group was a recidivist, fully 20 percent of the low IQ group could be so classified.

Longitudinal investigations, such as those conducted by Wolfgang et al. and West and Farrington, provide us with the best opportunity to explore the link between delinquency and/or crime and IQ. In a prospective study of high- and low-risk Danish families, Kierkegaard-Sorensen and Mednick (1977) discovered that the childhood IQs of future felons were significantly lower than the childhood IQs of other subjects in their sample. In a follow-up investigation of these same data, Moffitt, Gabrielli, Mednick, and Schulsinger (1981) observed a relationship between delinquency and IQ scores that was independent of socioeconomic status.

The outcome of studies employing self-report measures, rather than official data, also points to the presence of a relationship between intelligence and crime and/or delinquency. Hirschi's (1969) study, for instance, reveals that nearly twice as many of the white low IQ subjects reported having engaged in two or more (out of a total of six) delinquent acts compared to the highest IQ group. For black subjects the ratio was 3 to 2 in favor of low IQ subjects reporting greater delinquent involvement. Consistent with the results achieved in their previously reviewed study on official data, West and Farrington (1973) determined that 28.4 percent of that fourth of their sample with the lowest IQ scores reported delinquent acts compared to 16.6 percent of the other three-fourths of their sample. Nearly twice as many lower IQ (< 110) as higher IQ (110 or higher) subjects scored above average on a self-report measure of property offending and general deviance in an investigation of 255 male and female eleventh-grade students living in a white upper-middle-class suburb of San Francisco (Weis, 1973). These data seem to support the positive results of research probing the relationship between intelligence and official indices of crime and delinquency.

One argument against the meaningfulness of observed differences in the intelligence scores of criminals and noncriminals has been that these findings can be explained by variations in such factors as social class and race. However, in a review of the literature on intelligence and delinquency, two well-respected sociologists, Hirschi and Hindelang (1977), concluded that the relationship between crime and intelligence is at least as strong as is the association between social class or race and official indices of criminal involvement, and stronger than the connection between social class or race and self-report measures of criminality. Hence, we find that intelligence exerts an influence over criminality that is independent of social class, whether it is measured by the father's educational level (Hirschi, 1969), parental socioeconomic status (Reiss & Rhodes, 1961), family income (West & Farrington, 1973), or general socioeconomic status (Toby & Toby, 1961).

This finding of invariability in the relationship between crime and intelligence across social class has also been reported in research on adult criminals. Consequently, Wolfgang and his colleagues observed IQ score differences between chronic offenders and nondelinquents in his sample of Philadelphians independent of social class. In fact, the largest offender-nondelinquent difference in intelligence (14 IQ points) was observed in a group of low-socioeconomic-status white subjects. Research therefore intimates that while matching on socioeconomic status may in some cases reduce the intelligence score differentials between offenders and nonoffenders (Woodward, 1955), it does not eliminate the differences altogether.

A second argument often leveled against intelligence testing in general and the intelligence-delinquency relationship in particular is that intelligence tests are biased against minority and lower-income respondents (Chamblis & Ryther, 1975). In order to demonstrate that intelligence tests are biased against a certain group of individuals, however, one must show that the discriminative validity or power of these measures differs across groups. However, available research suggests that individual tests of intelligence predict as well for blacks and minorities as they do for white respondents (Jensen, 1980; Miele, 1979; Sattler, 1982). This equivalence of discriminative power across racial groups has also been observed in research on criminals and delinquents (Hirschi, 1969; Short & Strodtbeck, 1965; Williams & Gold, 1972; Wolfgang et al., 1972). Hence, while individual tests of intelligence are rarely culture free, they yield results that seem capable of discriminating between offenders and nonoffenders regardless of race or socioeconomic status.

A third argument challenging the relationship between crime and intelligence is that arrested or incarcerated offenders, the subject of nearly all studies on crime and IQ, may not adequately represent the pool of criminals present in society. It could be argued, then, that the less successful or less intelligent offender has a greater chance of being arrested, confined, and participating in a study on the IQ patterns of criminal offenders. In fact, this is exactly what one group of researchers witnessed in a now-classic study on delinquency (McCord, McCord, & Zola, 1959). However, noninstitutionalized delinquents, such as gang members not currently in trouble with the law, also tend to record lower IQ scores than nondelinquents (Gordon, 1975; Short & Strodtbeck, 1965). These findings suggest that, like race and socioeconomic status, the manner of one's recruitment into a study (inmate versus unconfined criminal) does not explain the significant IQ differences between offenders and nonoffenders.

Verbal-Performance Split

Several individually administered intelligence tests, such as the Wechsler (1967, 1974, 1981) scales, not only provide an overall IQ score but also yield scores on several subscales. The Wechsler subscales can be grouped into two general categories: verbal (VIQ: understanding and using verbal concepts) and performance (PIQ: understanding and manipulating spatial relations). Research suggests that a significant discrepancy between VIQ and PIQ in favor of the latter not only predicts delinquent involvement (Andrew, 1982; Glueck & Glueck, 1950; Walsh & Beyer, 1986) but also portends poorer prognosis as measured by an increased rate of recidivism in tested delinquents (Haynes & Bensch, 1981; Lueger & Cadman, 1982). Wilson and Herrnstein (1985) assembled data on 21 separate investigations and found that the mean PIQ exceeded the mean VIQ by eight points and that the PIQ transcended the VIQ in 20 of 21 comparisons.

Despite the apparent significance of the verbal-performance split in understanding criminal forms of behavior, one could argue that this finding might be artifactual in nature, a consequence of the lower total IQ scores obtained by criminal offenders. In addressing themselves to this issue, a group of researchers from the Patuxent Institute in Maryland discerned that the PIQ > VIQ discrepancy actually widened when offenders achieving higher full-scale IQs were examined (Manne, Kandel, & Rosenthal, 1962). Several studies have failed to identify a connection between the verbal-performance split and delinquency (Gibbs, 1982; Sacuzzo & Lewandowski, 1976), although an important consideration in research on this index is the number of murderers included in one's sample, for as DeWolfe and Ryan (1984) have shown, the PIQ > VIQ differential is largely ineffective for the purposes of identifying murderers, though it is much more useful in classifying persons convicted of violent offenses other than murder. Such a finding is understandable in light of the fact that most homicides and murders are committed by nonhabitual offenders against friends, relatives, and family members.

The results of a recent study administered by Walsh, Petee, and Beyer (1987) insinuate that it may be the presence of a verbal-performance split, and not the direction of this split, that is responsible for the association between intelligence and delinquency. Controlling for social class and race, Walsh et al. determined that despite the fact that intellectual imbalance (a difference of at least nine IQ points) was three times more likely to be in favor of the performance IQ (37% versus 11%), it was imbalance regardless of the direction (VIQ > PIQ or VIQ < PIQ) that was most strongly associated with delinquent involvement. While this study presents certain interesting possibilities, it awaits replication and further examination.

Crime and Intelligence

Research suggests that most samples of delinquents and criminals achieve mean full-scale IQs in the low 90s (Caplan, 1965; Gordon, 1975; Wilson & Herrnstein, 1985). This is certainly lower than the scores achieved by members of the general population, although when we compare an average IQ of 92 (which is one of the numbers most commonly cited for criminal populations) with the mean IQ score achieved by a comparable group of nondelinquents who have been matched with our offenders on social class and race, we perceive a difference of only four or five IQ points. This is because the mean IQ of the nondelinquent group would be slightly less than 100 (Matarazzo, 1972). Even though full-scale IQ differences between delinquent and/or criminal samples and comparable groups of nondelinquent controls may not be clinically meaningful, they still may hold theoretical significance.

In discussing the meaning of the link between intelligence and crime, it is important that we examine the role of school performance. Hirschi and Hindelang (1977) believe that school failure is what binds intelligence to delinquency, and they cite research that suggests that when factors like highest grade completed (Wolfgang et al., 1972) and teacher ratings of "troublesomeness" (West, 1973) are controlled, the relationship between IQ and delinquency fades into obscurity. If we consider the fact that failure in school tends to predict failure in later life (Jencks, 1979) we can see how lowered intelligence and lack of success in school might lead to increased frustration and a sense of inferiority. This could then impact on the individual's subsequent life adjustment.

Intelligence may interface with crime in a number of ways. First, intelligence may moderate the effect other variables have on crime. Accordingly, Kandel and associates (1988) observed that high IQ scores served a protective function in persons predisposed to antisocial involvement in a sample of high-risk Danish males. The protective role of high IQ has also been documented in a study of New Zealander males, although there was no such protective effect for females in this particular study (White, Moffitt, & Silva, 1989). Heilbrun (1982) and Walsh (1987), on the other hand, note that below-average intelligence and low verbal IQ, respectively, accentuate violent tendencies in persons criminally predisposed. Intelligence may also play a moderating role in its effect on other classes of person variables, to include race, learning, and cognitive style.

Possibly of even greater significance than delinquent-nondelinquent variations in IQ is the verbal-performance split that apparently characterizes the intelligence-test performance of many delinquents and criminals. Despite the presence of recent research challenging the performance over verbal discrepancy as a useful marker of delinquency (Walsh et al., 1987), the bulk of evidence on this subject substantiates the presence of a meaningful connection between such a discrepancy and significant criminal involvement. Since verbal tasks tend to be mediated by left cerebral hemisphere activity and spatial organizational skills can be lateralized to the right cerebral hemisphere (Bornstein & Matarazzo, 1982), the PIQ > VIA pattern seemingly lends support to neurological studies implicating right hemisphere dominance as a major correlate of criminality. On the other hand, this verbal-performance split may simply reflect the problems many criminals and delinquents have had with school and other academic pursuits. Regardless of which interpretation one chooses to adopt, there is sufficient evidence of a relationship between intelligence (particularly a verbal-performance split) and delinquency and/or crime to reject the pessimistic conclusions of Murchison (1926) and Sutherland (1931), whose views have too long served as the final word on intelligence and crime.

FEATURES OF PERSONALITY

Personality has been defined in different and sundry ways. To Freud (1922) personality involved the study of unconscious factors and intrapsychic conflict; to Adler (1927) personality was the conscious decisions an individual makes to compensate for feelings of inferiority; to Allport (1961) personality focused on the dynamic interplay of personal characteristics and traits; and to Bandura (1969) personality concerns the manner in which one learns within a social or interpersonal context. As part of their review of psychological theories of human personality, Hall and Lindzey (1970) partitioned the science of personality investigation into three functions. First, the study of personality should lead to the collection of data on empirical relationships, some of which may not always be directly observable. Second, personality investigations should focus on incorporating these empirical findings into a logically coherent theoretical framework. Finally, personality theory should help explain natural events in a manner that is important, parsimonious, and empirically valid.

The motif of relatively enduring personality traits or characteristics is difficult for some theorists to swallow, although even Mischel (1969), an inveterate critic of personality trait theory, acknowledges the salience of certain individual characteristics. It is therefore essential that personality factors not be ignored if we intend to form a comprehensive understanding of crime and criminal behavior. As we shall soon see, personality factors not only help explain certain genetic and neurological findings already cited but are probably valuable in and of themselves. With this in mind, we turn our attention to five personality characteristics of potential significance to criminal scientists: temperament, arousal level, learning and conditionability, cognitive style, and aggressiveness.

Temperament

There are aspects of one's personality that appear to be innate, if not genetic. Freedman (1979), for instance, found Chinese-American newborns to be more adaptable and less easily annoyed than Caucasian or black American newborns when prenatal care, birth sequence, and socioeconomic background were controlled. Additional research suggests that at six months Chinese-American infants are less extroverted, more inhibited, and exhibit significantly more stable pulse rates than Caucasian American infants (Kagan, Kearsley, & Zelazo, 1978). Based on interviews with the parents of neonates, Thomas, Chess, and Birch (1963) found nine personality characteristics on which newborns regularly differed: activity level, rhythmicity or regularity of cycles, approach-withdrawal, adaptability, intensity of reactions, threshold of responsiveness, quality of mood, distractability, and attention span. More recently, Buss and Plomin (1984) identified three fundamental dimensions of temperament—activity level, emotionality, and sociability—that may be useful in understanding future criminal involvement.

Least we overestimate the importance of these initial differences in temperament, the research of Thomas and Chess (1977) reminds us that many of these early characteristics change as the child ages. In fact, Murphy and Moriarity (1976) contend that it is nearly impossible to predict later adjustment from a child's temperament over the course of the first several weeks of life. This is because many additional factors interact to alter and modify this early predisposition. As such, a child born with a difficult temperament may become increasingly more adaptable if raised in a nurturing, supportive home environment.

While early temperament may correspond only weakly with later personality, it is still important in the sense that it forms a context in which the child and caretaker interact. Most mothers find a happy, adaptable baby easier to respond to than one who frequently cries and rarely cuddles. More to the point, child temperament is at least as important as various maternal attributes and characteristics (for example, experience, general mood, attitude toward the child) in the formation of a social bond between infant and caregiver (Goldsmith & Campos, 1982; Rothbart & Derryberry, 1981; Thomas, Chess, & Korn, 1982). Tarter (1988) argues for a connection between temperament and substance abuse that is mediated by personality. It does not take a developmental psychologist to see the potential implications of Tarter's ideas for a science of criminal behavior.

Thus far, few investigators have entered the study of temperament as a predictor of later criminality. However, preliminary findings suggest that a link may, in fact, exist between these two variables. Differences in male and female temperament may actually aid in our efforts to explain the surprisingly strong relationship that occurs when gender and criminal involvement are correlated. Thus, compared to the female newborn, the male neonate is more irritable (Moss, 1967), active (Thomas, Chess, & Birch, 1968), and independent (Kagan, 1978). While purely speculative at this point, there are data to suggest that the boys in one prospective study who eventually engaged in delinquent behavior were more restless during infancy and early childhood than subjects failing to engage in future delinquent behavior (Taylor & Watt, 1977). In a more direct test of the proposed nexus between temperament and crime, Kellam, Adams, Brown, and Ensminger (1982) found that temperamentally aggressive boys were more prone to delinquent behavior during adolescence than tempermentally nonaggressive boys. Olweus (1980) also determined that mother-generated retrospective accounts of a child's early temperament corresponded with the level of antisocial behavior displayed by their child during adolescence.

Arousal Level

As we saw in the section on neurological correlates of criminality, psychopaths and criminals frequently display lower levels of electrodermal activity, less variation in heart rate, and lowered autonomic reactivity compared to normal controls and nonpsychopathic offenders. In proposing a stimulation-seeking theory of criminality, Quay (1965) argued that criminals require greater amounts of sensory input than noncriminals in order to achieve an optimal level of cortical arousal. Goldman (1977) speculates that this occurs because of a diminution in the level of catecholamine available at various receptor sites in the brain. Although this catecholamine theory of crime is not without its detractors, there is some evidence to suggest that a significant portion of the criminal population endeavors to maximize sensory input, perhaps because its normal level of brain activity does not provide a satisfactory level of arousal (Hare, 1978).

Research indicates that all humans require minimal levels of stimulation in order to survive (Zuckerman, Persky, Link, & Basu, 1968). However, there are important individual differences in the level of stimulation viewed by the subject as optimal (Quay, 1965). Therefore, while some children avoid even moderate amounts of stimulation and excitement, others seek out excessive sums of mental and/or physical excitation. Farley (1986) refers to these tendencies as aspects of the Type T (thrill seeking) personality and adds that the emphasis can either be on physical or mental sensation seeking and risk taking. The stability of these characteristics is something that has not yet been adequately probed, although of the research presently available the consensus is that sensation-seeking patterns are established relatively early in life and persist well into adulthood (Zuckerman, 1979).

With the intent of developing an adult measure of sensation-seeking activity, Zuckerman, Kolin, Price, and Zoob (1964) constructed the Sensation Seeking Scale (SSS). Persons scoring high on this measure have been described by those familiar with their everyday behavior as active, impulsive, thrill seeking, and antisocial and nonconforming. Investigations have highlighted the relationship between high SSS scores and drug usage in college students (Jaffe & Archer, 1987; Zuckerman, Tushup, & Finner, 1976), polydrug abuse in military veterans (Kilpatrick, Sutker, & Smith, 1976), drug use levels in heroin addicts (Sutker, Archer, & Allain, 1978), and alcohol intake in college populations (Zuckerman et al., 1976). In addition, SSS scores have been found to correspond with sexual experience (Zuckerman et al., 1976), risk taking (Waters & Kirk, 1968), and lowered cortical arousal (Zuckerman, Murtaugh, & Siegel, 1974). The thrust of this research, while certainly not definitive, suggests that many criminally related activities and characteristics tend to be associated with elevated SSS scores.

Studying sensation-seeking tendencies in criminal populations, Kipnis and Wagner (1967) acknowledge having uncovered a positive association between SSS scores and a measure of impulsive, psychopathic tendencies. Farley and Farley (1972) scrutinized the relationship between SSS scores and disruptive behavior in a group of confined delinquent females and found higher SSS girls engaging in more disruptive behavior (for example, fighting, general disobedience, escape attempts) than lower SSS girls. Farley and Sewell (1976) compared 32 black delinquents and 32 black nondelinquents matched on age, sex, and socioeconomic status (SES) and discerned that the delinquent group earned significantly higher SSS scores than subjects in the nondelinquent group. Though Stewart and Hemsley (1984) failed to find offender-nonoffender differences on the SSS, subjects in the offender group were slightly older than subjects in the control condition. Thus, while stimulation seeking may not be a universal characteristic of criminality, there is evidence to suggest that a substantial portion of society's lawbreakers strive to achieve above-average levels of stimulation and excitement, possibly as a means of compensating for an underresponsive autonomic nervous system.

Learning and Conditionability

In 1927, Ivan Pavlov, a Russian physiologist, introduced classical conditioning to the world through a series of ingenious experiments. Presenting a neutral stimulus (bell) paired with an unconditioned stimulus (meat), Pavlov studied their effect on the salivatory response of dogs. The meat, of course, would elicit the salivation response, but after several trials so would the bell, even though the meat was no longer presented. Pavlov referred to salivation in the presence of the meat as the unconditioned response and salivation in reaction to the bell as the conditioned response. Since Pavlov, classical conditioning theory has been advanced by such researchers as Rescorla and Wagner (1972), although pairing a neutral stimulus with an unconditioned stimulus in order to produce a conditioned response remains fundamental to this approach.

In an early study employing a classical conditioning paradigm, Lykken (1957) coupled a buzzer with electrical shock in an effort to determine their effect on a subject's galvanic skin response (GSR). Psychopathic criminals evidenced significantly smaller GSR-based conditioned responses than subjects in the nonpsychopathic criminal group. Discrepancies in the reaction of subjects to the buzzer were even wider when the psychopathic group was contrasted with normal controls. Since Lykken's classic study on inadequate conditioned emotional responses in criminals and psychopaths, there have been several additional investigations on this issue. Hare and Quinn (1971), for instance, witnessed a diminished conditioned GSR in psychopathic offenders exposed to a tone paired with electrical shock. Ziskind (1978) observed similar results in a group of "sociopathic" offenders.

Instrumental or operant conditioning is a second general approach to learning. Skinner (1938) is probably the most famous proponent of this particular model of learning. According to operant theory, learning takes place as a function of the consequences accompanying a particular behavioral response. Hence, reinforcement tends to increase the future occurrence of a specific behavioral outcome, while punishment normally serves to decrease the future likelihood of a particular behavior being emitted. Therefore, if we were to reward a laboratory rat with food pellets every time it discharged a response lever, we would anticipate an increase in this behavior over time, just as we would expect a decrease in a behavior that is followed by a painful electrical shock to the animal's paw.

In one of the few studies entertaining the possibility of a deficit in operant learning in criminally oriented individuals, Sarbin, Allen, and Rutherford (1965) ascertained that male adolescents scoring low on the Socialization scale of the California Personality Inventory (a reasonably strong correlate of delinquent and criminal mentation) exhibited weaker motivation for social approval in a laboratory situation than male adolescents achieving higher scores on this scale. There is also evidence of a deficit in the future time orientations of many offenders. Mischel (1974), for example, discerned that delinquent children were more inclined to bypass a large, delayed reward in favor of a small, immediate reward than was the case with nonbehaviorally disordered children. Criminals, too, have shown a preference for immediate gratification over consideration of the long-term consequences of a particular act or behavior (Black & Gregson, 1973).

Because criminals and psychopaths tend to develop conditioned emotional responses more slowly than nonoffenders, it seems logical that they may also be less responsive to operant-style punishment. In a sense this is exactly what has been observed. Siegel (1978) found psychopathic criminals and controls to be equally responsive to various penalties when the probability of punishment was high. However, when the prospect of punishment was uncertain or remote, as is often the case with crime, psychopaths produced the least amount of suppression and the lowest winnings on a probability-learning card game. Criminals may have even greater difficulty balancing the anticipated rewards and potential punishments of a particular behavior when confronted with competing contingencies. Thus, Newman and others (Kosson & Newman, 1986; Newman & Kosson, 1986; Newman, Widom, & Nathan, 1985) discovered that psychopathic offenders performed as well as nonpsychopathic offenders when they only had to avoid punishment. However, when passive avoidance was paired with competing reward contingencies, or subjects had to shift their attention from one contingency to another, the performance of psychopaths revealed obvious deficits.

Modeling, or social learning, is the newest of the major learning theories. While not insensitive to the role reinforcement plays in human behavior, Bandura (1969) introduced the notion of observational learning and argued that certain behaviors could be more rapidly acquired by observing the actions of others. Cognitive factors are given priority in Bandura's scheme and a study by Camp (1977) demonstrates that a deficiency in "internal speech" and the improper use of language to mediate and control behavior were primary factors in the aggressive-conduct problems of a subsample of elementary school-age children. Platt, Spivak, and Shure (1976) further discerned that adolescents who failed to internalize their actions through effective self-talk exhibited inadequate interpersonal problem-solving behaviors and were at increased risk for antisocial and delinquent outcomes. Grier (1988), on the other hand, failed to identify problem-solving skill deficits in a group of incarcerated sexual offenders, although she did note that the sexual offenders generated fewer ideas for solving problems in heterosexual relationships than a group of nonoffender control subjects. An independent group of investigators determined that by second grade, future delinquents already displayed distinctive learning styles that not only made it more difficult for them to be successful in school but also more likely to seek negative forms of attention (Meltzer et al., 1984).

This favorable review of learning problems and crime should in no way be taken as support for the related argument that many criminals suffer from formal learning disabilities (Dalby, Schneider, & Arboleda-Florez, 1982). Two independent reviews of the literature in this area (Murray, 1976; Coons, 1981) have arrived at the general conclusion that there is no concrete proof of a meaningful link between learning disabilities and crime. While a third review (Brier, 1989) identified higher levels of learning disability in delinquent groups, the author concedes that there is no firm support for the argument that learning disabilities cause delinquent outcomes. Several studies have shown, however, that learning-disabled youth are more apt to be labeled by the courts as delinquent relative to nonlearning-disabled youth (Broder, Dunivant, Smith, & Sutton, 1981; Dunivant, 1982). Consequently, while learning-disabled youth may be more readily labeled delinquent, there is no convincing evidence that these individuals engage in a greater amount of delinquent activity than their nonlearning-disabled peers.

Research on the learning and conditionability of criminals, psychopaths, and delinquents denotes that these individuals encounter difficulty when it comes to learning law-abiding behavior. Whether this flaw in the learning histories of criminal offenders is a function of specific genetic factors or environmental experiences (for example, school), two things are certain: the flaw is real and it has important implications for a science of criminal behavior. The deficit seems most pronounced in the offender's response to punishment or in situations when he or she must weigh conflicting and varied contingencies. The learning problems of the habitual and semihabitual offender would appear to have some relevance to our next personality characteristic, cognitive style, as well.

Cognitive Style

In a review of the literature on personality correlates of crime for studies spanning the years 1950 through 1965, Waldo and Dinitz (1967) observed significant differences between criminals and noncriminal controls in 80 percent of the investigations, even after the groups were matched on such demographic characteristics as age, gender, and social class. Tennenbaum (1977) observed similar results (80% of studies revealing significant criminal-noncriminal differences) in studies conducted between 1966 and 1975. In that a number of these personality divergencies may reflect discrepancies in one's style of thought, there may be cognitive factors other than intelligence that play a role in the behavior of criminal offenders.

Several longitudinal studies reveal the presence of a meaningful relationship between cognitive factors and criminality. Robins (1978), for instance, determined that deviance during childhood, to include impulsivity and a general absence of guilt, was strongly associated with adult deviance and criminality. As part of their research on youthful male Londoners, West and Farrington (1977) ascertained that classroom aggressiveness and its cognitive affiliates correlated convincingly with subsequent juvenile delinquency and later adult criminality. Utilizing a retrospective design, Conger and Miller (1966) matched 184 male delinquents with 184 nondelinquent males on age, race, IQ, socioeconomic status, and school environment for the purpose of studying the past school records and psychological test results of subjects in both groups. Findings from both the testing and records review revealed greater impulsivity, hostility, egocentricity, and irresponsibility on the part of delinquent subjects. In addition, the delinquents displayed a more negative attitude toward authority and appeared to suffer from a general sense of dissatisfaction and unhappiness.

Formal personality test results also tend to differentiate between criminals and noncriminals. Greene (1980) reports that criminals characteristically elevate the Psychopathic Deviate (*Pd*) and Hypomania (*Ma*) scales of the Minnesota Multiphasic Personality Inventory (MMPI) relative to both the MMPI normative sample and noncriminal controls. Megargee (1972) relates that the Socialization (*So*) scale of the California Personality Inventory (CPI) has been known to effectively discriminate between groups of criminal and noncriminal respondents.

A series of 18 separate comparisons of criminals and noncriminals in ten individual nations produced significant differences on the Socialization scale that were in the predicted direction for all 18 comparisons (Gough, 1965).

Although impressive, it is uncertain whether these findings reflect actual differences in cognitive style. Taking a somewhat more direct approach to the study of cognitive style and criminality, Kipper (1977) administered the Kahn Test of Symbol Arrangement (KTSA) to groups of habitual offenders. In the end, the KTSA proved effective in discriminating between habitual criminals and a group of control subjects, the precise pattern of results indicating that the thinking of the offender group was more stereotypical, repetitive, and concrete than that witnessed in control subjects. Kipper noted further that while offenders experienced minimal difficulty understanding abstract conceptualizations, forming their own concepts was much more troublesome. It seems noteworthy that Newman, Patterson, and Kosson (1987) found perseveration, frequently observed in persons lacking the ability to think abstractly, to be characteristic of the behavioral adjustment of incarcerated psychopaths required to perform a card-sorting task.

Justification and rationalization are aspects of everyday human behavior. Criminals utilize these cognitive-defense strategies with remarkable regularity. This has been observed in juvenile delinquents (Sykes & Matza, 1970), violent maximum security offenders (Henderson & Hewstone, 1984), rapists (Burt, 1983), and white-collar criminals (Benson, 1985). Besides attempting to justify and rationalize their rule-breaking actions, many criminals are adept at deceiving even themselves. Several studies, for instance, suggest that criminals approach some situations as if they were impervious to detection and arrest, and that chronic offenders are much worse than infrequent offenders in terms of holding to an attitude of invulnerability (compare Henshel & Carey, 1975; Kraut, 1976). Likewise, research studies on the decision-making abilities of robbers (Feeney, 1986), burglars (D. Walsh, 1986), and professional shoplifters (Carroll & Weaver, 1986) point to a characteristic cognitive style that differs greatly from the thinking of the average citizen.

In their book *Time to Change*, Ross and Fabiano (1985) not only provide a cognitive model of treatment for use with juvenile delinquents but also discuss certain cognitive-skill deficits that they propose interfere with adult and juvenile offenders' ability to function responsibility in the community. Such persons are said to exhibit inadequate self-control in addition to lacking such basic cognitive skills as social perspective taking, critical thinking, interpersonal problem solving, and empathy and/or role taking. Moreover, their thinking is characteristically rigid, concrete, and externally oriented. Ross and Fabiano argue that these cognitive-skill deficits are even more pronounced in the chronic, recidivistic offender, and they support their claim with a fair amount of evidence (Ellis, 1982; Jurkovic & Prentice, 1977). This would seem to suggest that cognitive skills training may be an effective weapon in the war against crime and juvenile delinquency.

The cognitive features of criminality discussed in this section may, in part, be genetically influenced, although there is currently no reliable evidence by which to evaluate this hypothesis. Consequently, the concrete, perseverative quality of criminal thinking could just as easily be a product of cognitive immaturity as a reflection of neurological dysfunction. It is also uncertain whether these cognitive characteristics are a cause of criminal behavior or simply a long-term effect of one's involvement in a life of crime. There is little doubt, however, that cognitive style is a meaningful and potentially important correlate of criminal conduct. As such, it deserves a great deal more attention than was possible in this admittedly brief exposition (see Walters 1990b for a discussion of the cognitive features of serious criminal conduct).

Aggressiveness

It makes good intuitive sense that childhood aggressiveness should correlate with later criminality, a supposition which finds support in available research data. Univariate correlations of between .24 and .31 have been recorded when peer- and teacher-generated ratings of aggression are cross-lagged with subsequent levels of criminal involvement (Huesmann et al., 1984; Pulkkinen, 1982). The results of several additional studies insinuate that approximately half the criminals studied had been previously nominated as highly aggressive, whereas only one out of every six noncriminals had been so nominated (Mitchell & Rosa, 1981; West & Farrington, 1973). Utilizing a large New Zealand birth cohort, White et al. (1990) determined that early antisocial behavior was the best predictor of later antisocial behavior. Finally, two psychologists from the University of Stockholm pooled the rates of registered criminality through age 26 for a group of 1,027 Swedish subjects and discovered that teacher ratings of aggressiveness taken at ages 10 to 13 predicted later criminal outcomes for both males and females in a way that was largely independent of a subject's intelligence and family educational background (Stattin & Magnusson, 1989).

DEMOGRAPHIC CHARACTERISTICS

Demographic characteristics are the final category of person variable to be discussed in this chapter. Recent research suggests that certain demographic features of the individual may do a better job of predicting criminal science outcomes than more commonly studied variables like social class and peer associations (Hirschi & Gottfredson, 1983). Accordingly, it has been noted that the typical predatory criminal is a young, black, male (Wilson & Herrnstein, 1985). In this section we probe the validity of this seemingly speculative statement by examining the three variables upon which Wilson and Herrnstein's statement is based, namely age, gender, and race.

Figure 5.1
Age Distribution and Patterns of Arrest for Violent and Property Crimes in the United States

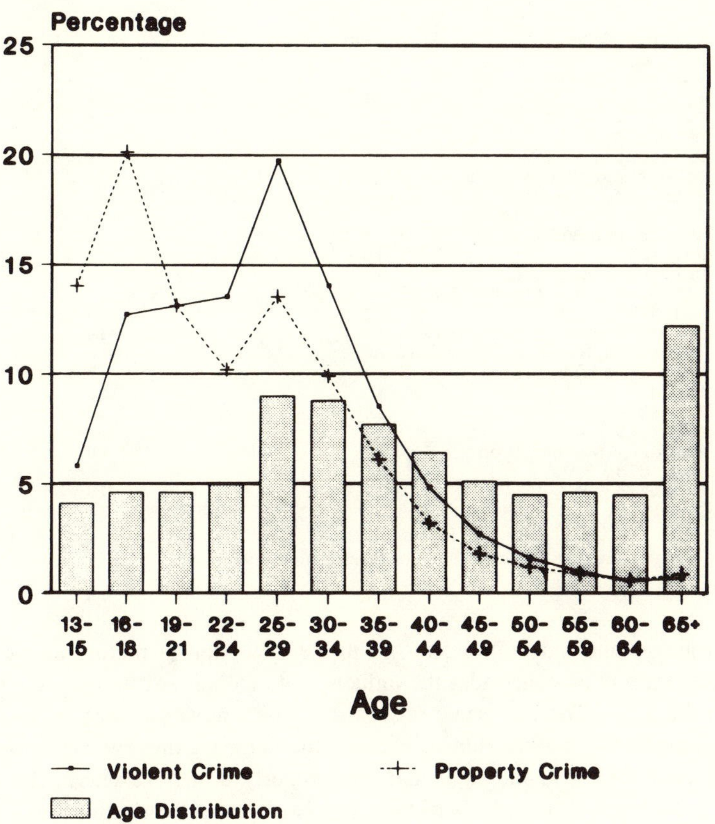

Source: Federal Bureau of Investigation (1988).

Age

Hirschi and Gottfredson (1983) argue that the relationship between age and crime is one of the "brute facts" of criminology. Age seems to possess the ability to predict criminality in and of itself. Take for instance a study by Rowe and Tittle (1977) in which it was demonstrated that even after controlling for initial differences in education, occupation, and family size, age retained much of its predictive power relative to the question of crime. As Figure 5.1 clearly implies, crime peaks in the late teens or early twenties and displays a rapidly declining slope from here. Actually, when offense rather than arrest data are considered, the apex of criminal involvement shifts left by several years (mid to late teens). On the other hand, the specific types of crime that are most popular

Table 5.4
Arrest Rate Rankings for Persons Under Age 18 and 18 Years of Age and Older for 20 Selected Crimes

Offense Category	Ranking: Under Age 18	Ranking: Age 18 or Older
Larceny-theft	1	2
Burglary	2	8
Other Assaults	3	4
Vandalism	4	9
Disorderly Conduct	5	5
Drug Abuse Violations	6	3
Motor Vehicle Theft	7	13
Aggravated Assault	8	6
Stolen Property	9	12
Robbery	10	11
Driving Under the Influence of Alcohol	11	1
Fraud	12	7
Sex Offenses (except forcible rape, prostitution)	13	14
Forgery/counterfeiting	14	15
Arson	15	20
Forcible Rape	16	16
Prostitution	17	10
Murder & Nonnegligent Homicide	18	18
Embezzlement	19	19
Gambling	20	17

Source: Derived from the Federal Bureau of Investigation (1988).

with younger and older offenders—with the exception of motor vehicle theft, prostitution, and driving under the influence of alcohol—differ only slightly by age (Table 5.4). The age-crime relationship does, however, vary according to general crime categories. Hence, because the person crime-age curve is flatter and pushed further to the right than the property crime-age curve, the modal crime category for individuals in their late twenties and early thirties is person crimes while the modal category for adolescents and young adults is property crimes.

An interesting relationship is uncovered when official and self-report data on crime are compared. Official data show property offenses peaking during the mid-teens and person crimes cresting between late adolescence and early adulthood (see Figure 5.1). Self-report studies, on the other hand, show both property offenses and person crimes peaking during the middle teenage years (14–16). Hirschi and Gottfredson (1983) speculate that self-report data more accurately reflect the true nature of the relationship between age and crime, since many personal injury offenses involving juveniles (such as school-yard fights) may not be reported to the police. This pattern of differential reporting of offenses to the police would have the effect of masking the true age distribution of person crimes by shifting the person crime curve to the right by several years.

Victimization studies have also been administered as part of an effort to achieve a better understanding of the age-crime relationship. Hindelang and McDermott

(1981; Hindelang, 1981; McDermott & Hindelang, 1981) collected victimization data for 26 major American cities and found that offenses greatly outnumbered arrests. Though this finding is hardly noteworthy in and of itself, what is of interest here is that younger offenders (as estimated by the victim) were overrepresented and older offenders underrepresented in a manner consistent with the age-distribution pattern witnessed in studies employing official and self-report sources of criminal justice information.

The cross-sectional data presented in Figure 5.1 need to be considered relative to the outcome of longitudinal research as represented by the West and Farrington (1977), Shannon (1982), and Wolfgang et al. (1972) studies, if we are to obtain an accurate estimate of the association between age and crime. Blumstein and Cohen (1979) used a combined cross-sectional–longitudinal design containing over 5,000 adult offenders arrested in Washington, D.C., to argue that the nexus observed to exist between age and crime in cross-sectional analyses was due, at least in part, to the higher rates of arrest achieved by more recently born cohorts (turned 18 in 1966, as opposed to 1963). While these findings do not necessarily invalidate traditional views on the age-crime relationship, they do point to the limitations of cross-sectional studies, although in the best of all worlds longitudinal research and the less expensive cross-sectional design should not be made to stand alone but should be studied in combination.

Longitudinal investigations reveal that there may be several different age-crime patterns. It has, for instance, been fairly well established that most serious adult criminals began offending at a relatively early age, but that most juvenile lawbreakers do not go on to become serious adult offenders. Longitudinal analyses of population data for persons born in Racine, Wisconsin (Shannon, 1982), and Philadelphia, Pennsylvania (Wolfgang et al., 1972), have shown that a disproportionate percentage of the offenses committed by these groups can be traced back to a relatively small portion of the total offender population. As a group, these chronic offenders enter crime at an earlier age, peak later (mid-twenties), and exit crime at a slower rate and later age than other persons. Despite the fact there may be two or more distinct age-crime patterns, Hirschi and Gottfredson (1983) argue that variables central to the thesis that there is more than one age distribution (for example, age of onset, age of desistance, life-course changes) are only weakly correlated with relevant criminal-science criteria.

Hirschi and Gottfredson (1983) touched off a debate of sorts with their statement that the age-crime relationship is invariant across time, culture, race, gender, and crime category. They provide reasonably impressive documentation in support of their claim, although not all of the data are entirely consistent with their position (for example, Christie, 1974; Hartjen & Priyadarsini, 1984). Greenberg (1985) has severely criticized Hirschi and Gottfredson's thesis, although a careful reading of his argument reveals a number of theoretical and conceptual oversights (Hirschi & Gottfredson, 1985). In short, there is no solid evidence with which to attack Hirschi and Gottfredson's (1983) hypothesis that the age-crime relationship is largely impervious to the influence of a number of environmental (culture, history, socioeconomic status) and personal (race, sex) variables.

Loeber and Snyder (1990) recently corroborated Hirschi and Gottfredson's premise that the age-crime curve is invariant over selected "criminal career" conditions. These investigators determined that offending was largely a function of chronological age and generally unrelated to the onset of one's "criminal career." Shavit and Rattner (1988) provide cross-national support for the Hirschi and Gottfredson position by virtue of their inability to identify ethnic, religious, or socioeconomic variations in the age distribution of delinquent behavior for a large sample of Israeli males studied longitudinally. In opposition to Hirschi and Gottfredson's postulations, Steffensmeier, Allan, Harer, and Streifel (1989) witnessed oscillation in the crime-age relationship measured between 1940 and 1960 and offense type using data gathered from the FBI's Uniform Crime Reports.

Hirschi and Gottfredson (1983) asseverate that the age-crime relationship cannot be explained by theories and variables currently available to researchers in the field. Again, it is difficult to dispute Hirschi and Gottfredson's argument since it is based on a solid empirical foundation. It has been speculated that the age-crime association is a function of changes in social contingencies (Jolin & Gibbons, 1987), a decline in the stimulus-seeking motive (Baldwin, 1984), variations in testosterone level (Faiman & Winter, 1974), and exclusion of youth from viable employment opportunities coupled with increased social integration over time (Greenberg, 1979). As Hirschi and Gottfredson (1983), point out, the plausibility of these explanations is vitiated by the fact that the relationship between age and crime remains invariable over time, across cultures, and between various social conditions. This does not mean, however, that the age-crime relationship is inexplicable; it just means that it cannot be construed, according to Hirschi and Gottfredson, using theoretical concepts and models presently available to criminologists.

After reading this section the reader might be left with an empty feeling in the pit of his or her stomach, similar perhaps to the one I experienced following my review of this area of research. It is as if something important is missing. After all, age is not only a robust correlate of crime but also one of its most potent predictors, at least where aggregate-level data are concerned. What's more, Cohen and Land (1987) note that the age-crime association is symmetric to the extent that the connections are unidirectional rather than bidirectional, and simple rather than complex. Hence, while Hirschi and Gottfredson (1983) are correct in asserting that no current theory is capable of clearly explicating the age-crime connection, several possibilities nonetheless exist.

One possible explanation for the age-crime relationship is that it reflects developmental changes, not only in sensation seeking (Baldwin, 1984) but in what is valued by the individual (Levinson et al., 1978). Whereas a young felon may place excitement and personal gain high on his or her list of priorities, personal freedom and social relations may take on added significance as he or she grows older.

As we discussed earlier, most chronic offenders commenced their rule-violating careers in adolescence but most juvenile delinquents do not become serious adult offenders (Shannon, 1982; Wolfgang et al., 1972). Choice, cognitive development and maturity, and the ability to balance alternative contingencies therefore serve as possible explanatory intermediaries in our search to find a solution to the mystery behind the relationship between age and crime. A third consideration is that the age-crime association feeds off natural attrition. Thus, for persons who continue offending once they have passed through the period of high risk (mid-twenties), there are certain environmental impediments to their continued violation of society's laws (for example, death, serious injury, imprisonment). Although these observations may not provide a "true explanation" of the nexus between age and crime, they certainly warrant further investigation.

Gender

Like the age-crime relationship, the association between gender (sex) and antisocial forms of behavior is rarely disputed by investigators in the field of criminology. This is because it is well documented that many more males than females engage in criminal activity. This difference persists whether the prevalence (percentage of offenders) or incidence (number of offenses per offender) of crime serves as the criterion measure (Hindelang, Hirschi, & Weis, 1981). In a survey of 25 nations, Simon and Sharma (1979) denote that the proportion of arrestees who were female ranged between 2.02 (Brunei) and 20.90 (West Indies) percent. The median value for the 25 nations was 11.53 percent and the rate for the United States was 13.66 percent. This general ratio of 8 or 9 to 1 is reflected in nearly all offenses known to investigators (see Figure 5.2) except, of course, for those crimes traditionally associated with females (for example, prostitution).

As Figure 5.2 illustrates, there are wide variations in the rates at which males and females are arrested for most categories of crime. Since official sources of data do not measure offense-prevalence rates, there is always the possibility that male-female differences in arrest over-dramatize the gender disparity of offense rates because of certain discrepancies in how law enforcement officials deal with the two sexes. The results of self-report (Datesman & Scarpitti, 1980) and victimization (Hindelang, 1979) studies, however, support the conclusions of research drawn from official sources. Pooling data from 44 separate studies, Smith and Visher (1980) surmised that sex is a robust correlate of criminal conduct, although it is strongest when data come from official police sources, the subjects are Caucasians above the age of 18, the crime falls into the property-offense category, and the violation severity is moderate to high.

Figure 5.2
Percent Distribution of Male and Female Arrests for Six Offenses

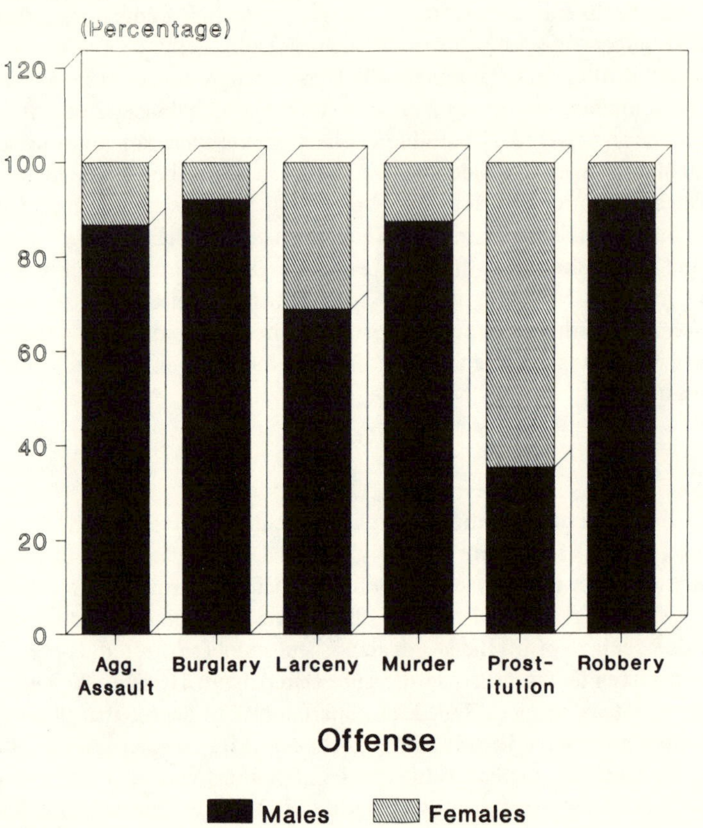

Source: Federal Bureau of Investigation (1988).

Despite the results of Smith and Visher's (1980) analysis, the invariability of gender across the other major demographic characteristics and several selected social factors is nearly as robust as the immutability of the age-crime relationship. Even though several studies have recorded smaller sex differentials in blacks than in whites (Forslund, 1970; Giordano & Cernkovich, 1979), other studies have produced outcomes that intimate that male-female divergencies in criminality cut across racial and ethnic lines (Hindelang, Hirschi, & Weis, 1981). Gender differences in crime also appear to be reasonably resistant to the effects of age (Rowe & Tittle, 1977), geography (Canter, 1982; Laub, 1983), and the intactness of one's home of origin (Canter, 1982).

History tells us that there was a sharp increase in the rate of female criminality during the 1960s and 1970s that surpassed even the rate of crime witnessed in males during this same time period. Whereas female involvement in violent crime rose slowly between 1934 and 1977, there was a much sharper increase in the number of females arrested for larceny, fraud, and forgery during this period (Steffensmeier & Cobb, 1981). One explanation for this rise in female criminality is that as women attained greater status and equality in the 1960s and 1970s, traditional barriers that may have previously kept female criminality low became less effective (Adler, 1977). Hence, the sharp rise in female property crime coupled with a reasonably stable rate of female person violations may have been due to augmentation of criminal opportunities for women. However, research findings in this area have tended not to corroborate this supposition (Datesman & Scarpitti, 1980; Giordano & Cernkovich, 1979; Renzetti & Curran, 1981).

Steffensmeier and Allan (1988) examined the gender equality–crime hypothesis that predicts the disappearance of the male-female discrepancy in crime as the social roles of the sexes become more equivalent (Sutherland & Cressey, 1978). Not only did the results of the Steffensmeier and Allan study fail to verify the gender equality–crime hypothesis, but they were also unable to identify significant variations in the gender-crime relationship across age, race (black, white), or geography (urban, rural). Similar results were recorded in a cross-sectional study directed by Simon and Baxter (1989). There is also evidence to indicate that serious female delinquency declined significantly between 1976 and 1980, even though there was no corollary decline in the woman's movement (Ageton, 1983). Berger (1989) asserts that the strain inherent in women's efforts to traverse ambiguous and contradictory gender roles may explain contemporary patterns of female criminality, although Sarri (1983) responds that the only real change in the female criminality picture in recent years has been an increase in the harshness with which society treats its female offenders.

While female criminality may be on the rise, a large gender gap continues to exist in both the prevalence and incidence of serious criminality. How might we explain this difference? One common observation is that male and female criminality are as different qualitatively as they are quantitatively. Ward, Jackson, and Ward (1969) report that the female felons in their study rarely displayed violence against strangers even if their offense was classified as violent. Thus, they may have been involved in a robbery but normally played a supporting (for example, driving the getaway car) rather than a central role. In cases where a murder or assault was committed, the victim was almost always a friend or family member and the context a personal or domestic dispute. Similarly, female offenders are less likely to own a record of juvenile arrest compared to male offenders (Sarri, 1987) and more likely to be saddled with intellectual deficits than their male counterparts (Cowie, Cowie, & Slater, 1968).

Warren and Rosenbaum (1987) conducted a longitudinal study of 159 women committed to the California Youth Authority (CYA) during the 1960s, the mean follow-up period lasting 16 years (range = 12 to 20 years). Results indicated that a large percentage of the women in Warren and Rosenbaum's sample (96%)

were arrested at least once during adulthood. Ninety percent of the sample had been apprehended for an offense of moderate severity, while nearly half had been arrested for an offense in the high-severity range. Warren and Rosenbaum found that a fourth of their sample had recorded ten or more arrests as adults and 60 percent had experienced adult confinement (although the majority of these incarcerations were in county jails rather than in state prisons). Consequently, while the patterns of male and female criminality may differ, the results of studies such as the one directed by Warren and Rosenbaum are consistent with studies conducted using male offenders as subjects (Petersilia et al., 1978; Shannon, 1982; Wolfgang et al., 1972). In a similar vein, Smith and Paternoster (1987) observed minimal variation in the ability of popular criminologic theories to explain marijuana usage in male and female adolescents.

If an explanation of the apparent rise in female criminality over the past several decades and a demonstration of significant qualitative differences between male and female offenders elude us, then it is also likely that we will have difficulty clarifying the quantitative differences in criminality noted between males and females. One possible explication concerns the biological differences that exist between males and females. The greater degree of aggressiveness noted in males, for instance, has been credited, at least in part, to differences in the level of certain sex-linked hormones, particularly testosterone (Maccoby & Jacklin, 1974). As of yet, however, there is very little convincing evidence that hormonal differences account for male-female discrepancies in aggression (Dixson, 1980). Gender differences in temperament have also been noted (Moss, 1967; Thomas et al., 1968). It is thus significant that males typically lag behind females in terms of fine motor skill development (Laosa & Brophy, 1972), a relationship which may reflect noteworthy variations in the neurological maturity levels of male and female infants and toddlers.

A second possibility is that certain social learning experiences play a major role in the crime divergencies noted between male and female subjects. For one, little girls are often exposed to less aggressive role models than little boys (Bandura, 1977); for another, boys are more likely to be reinforced for rough and active play while girls are taught to prize emotional expression and affiliative relationships (Janis et al., 1969). These hypotheses await further appraisal, and of course there is always the possibility that biological and social learning variables interact in bringing about an association between gender and crime.

Race

The study of racial differences is difficult because of the emotional nature of some of the comparisons. However, a science of human behavior will most certainly fail to be effective if it disregards certain areas of legitimate inquiry for fear of offending one group or another. The study of race is complicated further by the fact that, unlike age and gender, race is a more arbitrary classification. Do we classify a dark-skinned Cuban as black or Hispanic? Should an individual born of a black mother and white father be considered black or white? Consequently, the study of race and crime is fraught with more difficult questions than studies investigating the relationship between crime and other demographic characteristics (for example, age, gender). This, however, should not deter us from trying to make sense of the information currently available on this subject.

All of the major investigations of black-white differences employing official crime data have found that crime is overrepresented in blacks (Bureau of Justice Statistics, 1988a; Wolfgang et al., 1972). Note, however, that black male criminals tend to be, on the average, seven years younger than white males, although if we restrict our analyses to black and white men under the age of 18, we still find a higher rate in the black group (Wilson & Herrnstein, 1985). Self-report studies, on the other hand, are more equivocal in showing black-white differences in crime. Therefore, while Elliott and Ageton (1980) uncovered racial variations in self-reported delinquent behavior, particularly when predatory forms of crime were considered, a number of other studies have recorded only diminutive black-white discrepancies in self-reported criminality (Gold & Reimer, 1975; Hirschi, 1969). Chambliss and Nagasawa (1969) compared black and white adolescent males attending high schools in areas populated by low-SES families. While black subjects experienced higher rates of arrest than white subjects, there were no significant black-white variations when self-reported delinquency was examined.

In discussing the divergent outcomes generated by official and self-report data-based studies, Hindelang, Hirschi, and Weis (1979) remark that if self-report measures are confined to offenses falling into a moderate to high level category of severity and/or violence, significant black-white effects similar to the ones found with official sources of data surface. Victim surveys base their conclusions on the observation that most perpetrators of violent crime are of the same race as the victim. While this assumption may not always hold true, particularly with crimes like robbery, the results of the few victimization studies addressing the issue of race and crime typically confirm the results obtained with official data (Bureau of Justice Statistics, 1988a; Hindelang, 1978; McGhee, 1984). In an ecological survey of the 125 largest metropolitan areas in the United States, moreover, Blau and Blau (1982) observed a positive correlation between the proportion of blacks in a particular area and the rate of several classes of violent criminality.

The possibility of an interaction between race and gender has been probed in several investigations on ethnic status and crime. Williams and Gold (1972), for instance, determined that while black girls were no more likely to be delinquent than white girls, white male juveniles were less frequently, but no less seriously, delinquent relative to black male youth. Ageton (1983) recorded black-white differences in the prevalence but not the incidence of female delinquency. Although not as fixed in the face of other variables as either age or gender, a black-white disparity has been noted in the rate of crime at all levels of age considered and for females as well as males (Bureau of Justice Statistics, 1988a). Besides, in studies in which social class has been controlled, blacks continue to display higher rates of criminal arrest than whites (Bee et al., 1969; Wolfgang & Weiner, 1982).

Several theories attempting to explain the apparent connection between race and crime have been entertained. Wilson and Herrnstein (1985), for instance, have advanced a constitutional theory of black-white differences in crime, while Rushton (1987) has proposed a genetically based theory of race and crime. In presenting their constitutional explanation of black-white discrepancies and crime, Wilson and Herrnstein point to research showing a higher percentage of young black males fitting the mesomorphic body type than young white males (Malina, 1973). McCandless, Persons, and Roberts (1972), however, failed to discern a relationship between mesomorphy and either official or self-reported incidents of criminality when they restricted themselves to black male delinquents. Rushton's genetic theory of black-white differences in crime and other behaviors, on the other hand, has been attacked on both conceptual and empirical grounds (Roberts & Gabor, 1990). Although blacks tend to record lower scores on most individually administered measures of intelligence (Osborne & McGurk, 1982), a finding which some researchers have enlisted in support of a genetic (Jensen, 1980) or prenatal (Fuchs, 1983) interpretation of the data on racial effects and behavior, a more parsimonious explanation is that important early environmental differences between blacks and whites account for these variations in IQ (Brody & Brody, 1976).

In the absence of a solid biological or constitutional explanation for the observed link between race and criminal involvement, we turn our attention to sociocultural explanations. It might be that social class differences between blacks and whites in America explain much of the variation in crime displayed by these two groups. Wolfgang et al. (1972), however, observed that arrest rates were two times higher in lower-class black youth than in lower-class white youth. This does not necessarily rule out the influence of class-related environmental factors, however, since a lower-class black home may have little in common with a lower-class white home. For one, three times as many blacks as whites are raised in father-absent homes (Darity & Myers, 1983), a condition sometimes found to be associated with later delinquency (see Kellam et al., 1982). Likewise, racial variations in crime have been attributed to the high rate of marital instability present in many lower class black homes (McCord, 1982). There may also be black-white discrepancies in certain important relationship factors; the results of a laboratory-based problem-solving scenario revealed that lower-class black mothers provided fewer comments, less support, and looser structure for their children than did lower-class white mothers (Bee et al., 1969).

Another sociocultural explanation for the differential crime patterns of blacks and whites concerns the anger and resentment many blacks may harbor toward American society for years of racial prejudice and inequality (compare Silberman, 1978). However, in conducting a participant observer study of black men patronizing a popular bar in a lower-class section of South Chicago, Anderson

(1978) observed that his subjects spent more time admiring ''successful'' black criminals than expressing hatred for powerful whites. In a study carried out in a New Jersey correctional facility, Harris and Lewis (1974) determined that blacks viewed crime as enhancing their self-worth, while whites evidenced a converse pattern in which crime was seen as detracting from their self-esteem. Harris and Lewis interpreted their results as confirmation of a differential relationship between black and white crime based on varied associations with self-esteem: in other words, white males may need to traverse more psychological barriers than blacks in directing themselves toward a life of crime. Another possible means of support for the differential role of self-esteem in crimes committed by black and white offenders can be found in research that shows that offending is more strongly correlated with unemployment in blacks than in whites (Sviridoff & McElroy, 1984).

Black-white variations in crime may also reflect the fact that the police patrol black neighborhoods more frequently or are more apt to arrest blacks than they are whites who engage in the same behavior. Smith, Visher, and Davidson (1984) discerned racial variations in the arrest practices of police officers which found black subjects being arrested significantly more often than white suspects. Once certain contextual factors, like the poverty level of the neighborhood, were controlled, however, these racial disparities in arrest practices all but disappeared. On the other hand, Smith et al. (1984) did record an independent racial effect in which the police were more prone to respond to a white victim than to a black victim. Huizinga and Elliott (1987) discovered a potential racial bias in American criminal justice practice in the form of black youth being charged with more serious offenses and being incarcerated at a higher rate than white youth engaging in a comparable level of delinquent behavior.

Though the research in this area is plagued by several major methodological problems (Pope, 1979), support for the presence of a meaningful connection between crime and race nevertheless exists. Such a conclusion does not, however, eliminate the fact that there are variables, to include employment opportunities (Duster, 1987) and economic inequality (Joe, 1987), which moderate, and to a certain extent control, the relationship between race and crime. Nor should we close our minds to other possibilities and explanations of the findings observed on the subject of black-white differences in crime.

This review of the demographic correlates of serious criminality reveals the presence of high (age, gender) to moderate (race) associations between crime and certain demographic features of the individual. We should remain ever vigilant, however, to overinterpretations of the relationship between these variables and criminal involvement, for while young black males may be at increased risk for criminal involvement, the majority of such persons never engage in a single incident of serious adult criminality. The next logical step in our research on the demographic correlates of crime might be to more clearly examine the hows and why of the strong to moderate connections found to exist between criminal status and such variables as age, gender, and race.

CONCLUSION

This completes the first leg of our journey through the correlates of criminal behavior. Though it is not always an easy route to travel, we have observed a number of interesting connections along the way. Several of these associations suggest the possibility of causal links, although the majority of studies lack the methodological rigor and sophistication necessary to adequately address the issue of causality. In this final section we discuss two general conclusions, to be followed by several more specific points on the relationship presumed to exist between crime and selected person variables.

The first general conclusion I draw from the results of this review is that genetic factors do indeed appear to play a role in the behavior of criminals, psychopaths, and delinquents. This, despite the methodological lassitude inherent in this area of research endeavor (Walters and White, 1989a). It should be kept in mind, however, that the relationship between crime and heredity is probably indirect and relatively weak in comparison to some of the other effects discussed in this chapter. Therefore, while certain physical, neurological, and psychological factors may be influenced by heredity, these in turn being somewhat more strongly correlated with criminal behavior, the connection between crime and heredity is once, twice, even three times removed. For instance, facial deformities may have a strong genetic component and may also be reasonably robust predictors of later criminality (once removed), but then again, they may be linked to crime because of their effect on a person's self-image (twice removed) or how an individual makes certain life choices relative to his or her self-image (three times removed).

The second general conclusion I offer is that the practice of neglecting individual differences, or person variables as we have come to call them in his chapter, for the purposes of understanding crime and criminal behavior is unwarranted, unjustified, and unscientific. Parochial concerns and poorly concealed displays of self-interest have at times taken precedence over the pursuit of knowledge. The ostracization of thoughts, concepts, and ideas inconsistent with our own views, while understandable, has no place in the scientific study of crime and criminals. It is difficult to dismiss the consistency and replicability of research on several of the person variables discussed in this chapter. It therefore seems appropriate that we reject the argument that individual differences do not contribute to our understanding of criminal behavior and work to construct an integrated program of research designed to answer many of the questions raised by contemporary research on person-variable issues.

A topic that seems to have received a fair amount of empirical attention, if not support, concerns the hypoarousability of the central nervous systems of many criminals and psychopaths. Most studies investigating the autonomic reactivity of criminal offenders report that these individuals tend to be underaroused. This may help explain why so many criminals seek out stimulation and excitement. In other words, because the central nervous system is underaroused the criminal or psychopath views higher than normal levels of environmental stimulation as optimal. In a related sense, criminals develop conditioned emotional responses more slowly and less efficiently than noncriminals. As was pointed out by Hare (1970) some 20 years ago, this may help explain why criminals appear to have trouble learning certain pro-social behaviors. This would appear an intriguing possibility that will be examined in some detail in Chapter 9 of this volume.

Not only does the criminal or psychopath likely possess an underaroused central nervous system, he or she may also exhibit abnormalities of cerebral response. In contrast to noncriminals, who are primarily left-hemisphere (or verbal) problem solvers, many criminals and psychopaths exhibit a right-hemisphere dominance which becomes more apparent in response to increased environmental stress (Hare & Connolly, 1987). Underdeveloped linguistic problem-solving and verbal-reasoning skills have also been documented in research investigations on delinquents and criminals (Andrew, 1982; Miller, 1988) and may help explain why many criminal offenders have trouble solving everyday tasks.

A third specific conclusion is that personal characteristics that affect self-image also interact with criminality. Individuals exhibiting certain physical features (anomalies or a muscular body build), intellectual limitations, or a peculiar style of thinking take a different approach to life than most other people. It follows, then, that individuals possessing such characteristics may be at increased risk for expressing a pattern of serious criminality by virtue of the perspective they adopt toward their environment. After all, Harris and Lewis (1974) identified important discrepancies in the relationship between crime and self-image for black and white inmates. The avenues for research inquiry into these questions would seem limitless.

A fourth person variable of potential value to the scientific study of criminal behavior is the manner in which an individual interacts with his or her social environment. Interpersonal style may have its foundation in early temperament, general learning style, or physique (all of which may be genetically based to one degree or another), but it is modified by certain environmental and contextual considerations. It should be clear to anyone who has ever worked with criminals that their interpersonal styles differ substantially from those observed in noncriminals and also tend to vary as a function of certain environmental contingencies. What is less clear is whether this is the cause or simply an effect of a criminal lifestyle. Research on temperament and crime (compare Kellam et al., 1982) suggests that some of these features may predate criminality. However, offenders, at least the more sophisticated ones, will respond very differently to a parole board than to a correctional officer who has just confiscated their radio. The interrelated nature of interpersonal style as both a cause and effect of criminality deserves further empirical attention.

It is worthy of note that many of the relationships witnessed between selected person variables and crime were strongest when chronic, serious, and recidivistic offenders served as the subject of investigation. This not only occurred in several of the genetic and neurological studies but also surfaced in research focusing on intelligence, thinking style, and other cognitive correlates of criminal conduct. It does not seem out of the question, then, that we might be better off studying offenders grouped according to criminal career pattern, at least one of which is the lifestyle pattern. This is an issue to which we will return in the final chapter of this volume.

In this chapter we have discussed only a portion of the equation we will use to explain criminal behavior. In the chapter that follows we probe a second general group of correlates—environmental or situation variables. This research should also provide us with valuable insight into certain aspects of antisociality on our way to constructing a useful model of criminal science inquiry. As our journey continues, however, we would do well not to lose sight of the practical significance of the person variables and individual differences discussed in this chapter, for it is a topic to which I refer liberally as we make our way through the labyrinth of research studies, theoretical notions, and practical applications that are criminal science.

6

Correlates of Crime: Situation Variables

Environmental or situational correlates of crime have received far greater attention from criminologists than have person variables. This is not all that surprising in light of the sociological bent of many present-day criminologists. Other professions also place sociocultural factors high on the list of factors responsible for significant criminality. Psychologist Harrison Gough (1948), for instance, has studied the role of early socialization in the development of later criminal behavior. However, we concern ourselves with more than just the socialization process in our review of situational correlates of crime. Though the socialization process will be a primary topic of discussion in sections on familial and extrafamilial sources of social control, we also entertain such agents of situational influence as adverse social conditions, substance abuse, stress-related experiences, and physical environment features like ambient temperature.

As we saw in Chapter 5, studies utilizing psychopathic offenders as subjects are a major source of information on person correlates of criminality. In the present chapter we find that studies focusing on delinquent populations contribute greatly to our understanding of situational correlates of crime. While there are problems associated with the practice of employing delinquency research to understand adult criminality, it is imperative that we not summarily dismiss the pertinent delinquency research, since several of the issues reviewed in this chapter have not been adequately investigated in research utilizing adult samples. Furthermore, studies suggest that a certain percentage of the conduct-disordered population continues violating the law well into adulthood (Kazdin, 1987; Loeber, 1982). With this in mind, we commence our discussion of situational correlates of criminal conduct by considering research on adverse social conditions.

ADVERSE SOCIAL CONDITIONS

In the opening sentence of their paper on crime and poverty in California, Rauma and Berk (1982, p. 318) assert that "common sense suggests that poverty

Table 6.1
Prevalence and Incidence of Self-Reported Delinquency by Social Class

	Middle (N=349)	Working (N=442)	Lower (N=628)
Aggravated Assault			
Prevalence	2%	5%	6%
Incidence	.03	.09	.10
Damage to Property			
Prevalence	3%	5%	4%
Incidence	.05	.28	.10
Drug Sales ("Hard" Drugs)			
Prevalence	2%	3%	2%
Incidence	.08	.31	1.99
Felony Theft (over $50)			
Prevalence	1%	2%	2%
Incidence	.14	.16	.06
Strong-armed Robbery (excluding teachers and fellow students)			
Prevalence	0%	1%	0%
Incidence	.00	.12	.04

Source: D. S. Elliott et al. (1983). Data were collected in 1983 and based on interviews using a stratified sample of 18- to 24-year-olds. The social class measure is based on the status of the principal wage earner in each youth's family.

leads to crime.'' Such a statement seems to reflect the general attitude of many social scientists toward the prospect of a causal link between poverty and crime. However, the fact that many persons arrested for common street crimes are poor, unemployed, and derive from lower socioeconomic circumstances is not unequivocal proof that such adverse social conditions cause crime. In this section we focus our attention on four expressions of social condition of potential significance in explaining the development of subsequent criminality: social class, poverty, inequality, and unemployment.

Social Class

Although there is little consensus as to the proposed nature of the connection between social class and crime (Hirschi, 1972), it has traditionally been assumed that an inverse causative relationship exists between these two variables (compare Cohen, 1955; Merton, 1957; Miller, 1958). A belief in such a relationship is strong in many camps (Cressey, 1966) and finds support in several early studies examining the proposed nexus between crime and social class (compare Kvaraceus, 1945; Little & Ntsekhe, 1959; Reiss & Rhodes, 1961). However, more recent investigations delving into this issue, particularly when self-report measures have been utilized, demonstrate a much smaller crime-social class relationship. As depicted in the results displayed in Table 6.1, the connection between social class and self-reported criminality in a sample of 18- to 24-year-olds is appreciably lower than that recorded by studies relying on official arrest records (Kvaraceus, 1945; Reiss & Rhodes, 1961).

Reviewing the results of 35 studies with information of relevance to the crime-social class controversy, Tittle, Villemez, and Smith (1978) observed an overall gamma (mean correlation) for 363 separate comparisons of only −.09. In addition, these authors found the crime-social class relationship to be strongest when official (−.25), as opposed to self-report (−.06), data were considered. Tittle et al. further estimate that the relationship between crime and social class has declined steadily over the course of the past several decades, with the mean correlation falling from −.73 to −.31 to −.13 to −.03 when the relationship was measured by decade from 1940 through the late 1970s. Incidentally, this finding corresponds with a temporal decline in the officially measured association between social class and crime, rather than being the sole function of increased reliance on self-report studies in research addressing the proposed nexus between these two variables. Tittle et al. conclude that self-report studies reveal the true relationship between social class and crime, and attest on the basis of their data that once the biases contained in official statistics are corrected, the crime-social class connection depreciates significantly. This conclusion finds further support in the work of Hindelang, Hirschi, and Weis (1979).

Despite the significance of Tittle et al.'s (1978) contribution, it has not gone unchallenged. Elliott and Ageton (1980), for example, argue that self-report data, which are the cornerstone of Tittle et al.'s research approach, tend to accentuate nonserious violations and underrepresent more serious crimes. Furthermore, the reliability and replicability of many of these self-report measures tend to be weak. With the development of a more formalized self-report measure, Elliott and Ageton discovered important differences between lower- and middle-class youth in terms of their propensity for self-reported delinquent behavior. Though there were no social-class differences for public disorder, drug usage, or status offenses, lower-class youth were reportedly involved in nearly four times as many aggressive and predatory-type crimes and twice as many property offenses as middle-class youth.

In a reanalysis of the original Elliott and Ageton study, Elliott, Knowles, and Canter (1981) found somewhat smaller social-class differentials than those obtained in the earlier study. Moreover, an investigation that delved into the proposed association between financial resources and delinquency showed that adolescents possessing greater personal financial independence (monetary resources) were more rather than less likely to engage in delinquent acts (Cullen, Larson, & Mathers, 1985). This finding was interpreted by the authors of this report as reflecting the possibility that financial resources provide youth with greater freedom from parental control and, in the end, may actually exacerbate rather than mitigate lawbreaking tendencies. The results of a study conducted by Agnew (1990) show that resources correlate positively with criminal outcomes in adolescent populations predisposed to delinquency.

Clelland and Carter (1980) argue that Tittle et al. (1978) failed to adequately operationalize their terms and that this may have confounded their results. They contend further that Tittle et al. inappropriately used such terms as *class*, *status*, and *SES* interchangeably, and that this too many explain the lack of significant findings in the Tittle et al. meta-analysis. There is the additional issue of comprehensiveness, since Clelland and Carter (1980) maintain that Tittle et al. failed to consider all of the available evidence on socioeconomic status and crime. In a more exhaustive review of the literature on social class and crime, Braithwaite (1981) uncovered a moderate correlation between social class and official measures of crime and delinquency and a modest, but significant, coalition between these two variables when self-report measures were employed.

One of the primary disparities between the Tittle et al. (1978) and Braithwaite (1981) studies is that Braithwaite included ecological studies on crime (where neighborhoods, cities, or states rather than individuals are the subjects of investigation). Whereas the results of most ecological studies witness the presence of a moderately strong relationship between social class and crime (Braithwaite, 1979, 1981; Nettler, 1978), Tittle et al. did not include these studies in their review for the following reasons: (1) criminals residing in a low-status area may not be of low status themselves; (2) many crimes committed in low-status areas may be perpetrated by outsiders; and (3) a high ecological rate of officially recorded criminality may be a function of increased police presence in specifically targeted neighborhoods. Tittle et al.'s concerns notwithstanding, it is critical that we not reject ecological studies out of hand, although we do need to be aware of their limitations.

Victimization studies are a second source of information not considered in the Tittle et al. (1978) review and meta-analysis. Hindelang, Gottfredson, and Garofalo (1978) observed a negative relationship between victim income level and victimization rates for such serious crimes as assault, rape, robbery, and burglary. If we assume that most offenders are of the same general social status as their victims, this finding would seem to portend the presence of an inverse association between social class and crime. In a study combining the ecological and victimization methodologies, Sampson and Castellano (1982) determined that social class and urbanization had an interactive effect on crime. Consequently, while a strong inverse relationship was observed between neighborhood economic status and personal victimization in urban precincts, the correlation in suburban areas was moderate and the correlation in rural regions weak.

While in general accord with the conclusions and viewpoints espoused by Tittle et al. (1978), Stark (1979) contends that a prominent crime–social class connection does, in fact, exist when current social status and indices of delinquency and/or crime are correlated. Examining data from the Philadelphia birth cohort (Wolfgang et al., 1972), Thornberry and Farnworth (1982) found support for Stark's argument. Besides noting greater concordance between social status and crime for blacks than whites and for official, as opposed to self-report, data, these authors found a connection between current social status and crime but no relationship when family status and crime were correlated. Hence, while the social status of one's family of origin, as measured by the father's occupation and the socioeconomic status of the area of youthful residence, was largely unrelated to adult criminality, estimates of an individual's own social position, as measured by educational attainment, occupation, and job stability, were moderately correlated with adult criminality. In the words of Travis Hirschi (1969, p. 82), "the 'class' of the father may be unimportant, but the 'class' of the child is most decidedly not."

One of the primary failings of social class research on crime has been a paucity of information on the delinquency patterns of individuals raised in middle- and upper-middle-class home environments. Are individuals growing up under such conditions any less likely to engage in delinquent behavior, or are they just better equipped financially to avoid arrest, prosecution, and imprisonment? Buikhuisen et al. (1984) examined 82 middle- and upper-middle-class students matriculating at a university in the Netherlands (modal age = 20 to 21 years). Ninety-three percent of the sample reported having had engaged in at least one offense that could have resulted in imprisonment under the Dutch penal code, and 12 percent of the sample admitted to having committed more than 30 such offenses. Correlates of criminality in this group included low anxiety, high impulsivity, increased hostility, and an external locus of control. Both the prevalence of self-reported criminality and correlates of delinquent behavior were similar to outcomes obtained in an earlier study of lower-social-class subjects (Buikhuisen & Meijs, 1983).

The results of this review suggest the possibility of a connection between social class and crime, although the actual magnitude of the association appears to be relatively weak. In addition, the relationship that appears to exist between crime and a person's own social status may not extend to the status of one's home of origin (the usual focus of crime–social class theorizing). This certainly brings into question the causal status of social class relative to crime and delinquency. Of even greater significance, however, is explaining the mechanism that underlies the crime-class relationship, for as Tittle (1983) points out, each of the theories predicting an inverse class-crime association do so with the aid of numerous external assumptions. Because poverty, by definition, is restricted to the lower social classes, this is one possible explanation for the proposed link between social class and crime.

Poverty

In an early study examining the crime-poverty connection, Shaw and McKay (1942) found that impoverished neighborhoods displayed higher rates of delinquency than nonimpoverished communities. These authors add that observed crime-poverty patterns remain reasonably stable over time, even though the ethnic composition in several of the areas they studied changed dramatically over the course of several decades. There are several possible interpretations of these findings. Banfield (1974), for one, speculates that impoverished persons have an inherent proclivity for criminal activity, while Kornhauser (1978) argues that poverty creates social disorganization that, in turn, leads to increased levels of delinquent behavior, and Miller (1958) refers to the subculture of poverty wherein potentially criminogenic characteristics like toughness, excitement, and action are valued above sensitivity, tranquillity, and patience. Regardless of which explanation one chooses to adopt, there is ample evidence to suggest that crime is not only more prevalent in poverty-stricken areas (Curtis, 1974; Quinney, 1966), but exists more prominently in less affluent, as opposed to more affluent, cities (Humphries & Wallace, 1980).

Loftin and Hill (1974) recorded a positive association between state homicide rates in 1960 and the Structural Poverty Index. In corroboratory fashion, Parker and Smith (1979) uncovered similar results when they examined state homicide rates for 1970. However, Messner (1982) criticized Loftin and Hill's Structural Poverty Index on the basis that it contains a large number of noneconomic factors and only one economic indicator (percentage of families with annual incomes under $1,000). Taking a more direct approach to the question of poverty and crime, Messner discovered, first, that income inequality was unrelated to homicide rates in a sample of 204 major metropolitan areas and, second, that the percentage of families living in abject poverty actually correlated negatively (opposite to what would be expected if poverty were the cause of crime) with the homicide rate. This points to an obvious problem with the crime-poverty hypothesis. However, when cities rather than metropolitan areas become the units of analysis, a small but statistically significant positive correlation surfaces between serious criminality and poverty (Bailey, 1984; Loftin & Parker, 1985).

When considering the limitations of the poverty approach to crime it is well to keep in mind that most poor people do not engage in serious criminal activity, most criminal offenders did not grow up in abject poverty, and the crime-poverty relationship varies according to the particular criminal offense being examined. Hence, Tagaki and Platt (1978) state that Chinatown during the 1960s not only sported one of the highest rates of poverty in the city of San Francisco but also enjoyed a relatively low crime rate. In a study where the files of 516 maximum security prison inmates were carefully examined, Walters and White (1987) observed that the majority of inmates hailed from working- and lower-class home environments, but only one in five had been raised in impoverished social conditions. Lastly, DeFronzo (1983) ascertained that while public assistance to poor families was associated with a declining rate of homicide, rape, and burglary, it had very little impact on the rate of robbery, larceny, and auto theft.

Loftin, McDowall, and Boudouris (1989) used the infant mortality rate to estimate the poverty level in an investigation of the homicide rate in Detroit, Michigan, between 1926 and 1979. Multivariate analyses of the data revealed that infant mortality was meaningfully associated with domestic and criminal transaction homicides. These findings would seem to imply that crime and poverty are meaningfully linked, although it is important to consider that even though the infant mortality rate has been shown to correlate inversely with socioeconomic status (Stockwell, Wicks, & Adamchak, 1978), it is questionable whether it accurately measures the level of poverty in an established urban area. Moreover, the presence of a significant correlation between various indicators of poverty and crime is not bona fide proof of a causal affiliation, for as Stewart (1986) so aptly points out, crime may be as much a cause of poverty by lowering property values, stimulating resident fear, reducing opportunities for legitimate business, and suffocating extralegal sources of social control, as it is an effect.

Blau and Blau (1982) examined the hypothesis that variations in the rate of urban criminal violence were a function of racial inequality in the socioeconomic conditions of a particular community. In this study, the 125 largest metropolitan areas in the United States served as the independent variable and violent criminality (murder, forcible rape, robbery, aggravated assault) served as the dependent measure. The outcome of this investigation revealed that once economic inequality was controlled, the relationship between crime and poverty disappeared. The Blaus interpreted their findings as lending credence to the hypothesis that economic inequality is central in the chain of events that give rise to violent criminality. Sampson (1985), on the other hand, writes that the effects of poverty and income inequality differ as a function of race, poverty being correlated with juvenile delinquency in white youth and income inequality being correlated with juvenile delinquency in black youth.

Inequality

Findings from the Blau and Blau (1982) study insinuate that inequality, rather than poverty, is what links crime to adverse social conditions. Marxist theory (Quinney, 1966) has long held that inequality is one of the root causes of crime. Even Wilson and Herrnstein (1985) seem drawn to the possibility that inequality may help explain certain categories of criminal offense. They reason that the individual who perceives his or her efforts as producing fewer rewards than the next person's may react in a number of ways, one of which might involve taking the other individual's accumulated rewards. Such a possibility is also suggested in the results of studies conducted with aggregate or ecological data. Consequently, a relationship has been observed between inequality and crime, regardless of whether metropolitan areas (Braithwaite, 1979), individual states (Loftin & Hill, 1974), or entire nations (Messner, 1980) are compared. These findings appear to hold true for crimes like robbery, homicide, and assault but are much more equivocal when applied to rape. Maume (1989), on the other hand, provides data that suggest inequality may influence rape indirectly through a person's lifestyle and routine activities.

As with the social class and poverty explanations of crime, the inequality hypothesis is not without its drawbacks. Though Danziger and Wheeler (1975) ascertained that criminality, measured both cross-sectionally and longitudinally, rose as economic inequality widened, the results of their study are open to a number of alternative explanations, not all of which are congruent with the inequality hypothesis (Wilson & Herrnstein, 1985). In a study investigating inequality and homicide in 26 Manhattan (New York) neighborhoods, Messner and Tardiff (1986) failed to identify a meaningful connection between these two variables. Earlier, Messner (1982) had been unable to establish a link between inequality and crime in an investigation of 204 U.S. metropolitan areas. What's more, as we saw in Chapter 3, the association between inequality and crime, even though it may look strong on the surface, frequently varies when scrutinized from a cross-national perspective (Stack, 1982).

Individual-level comparisons directed at the inequality hypothesis are precluded by the very nature of this theorem. We must therefore rely upon aggregate-level data (organized by neighborhood, city, state, nation) with all of their inherent complications. Besides the methodological failings previously noted (criminals living in low-income areas may not be low income themselves; offenders from another neighborhood may be responsible for the crimes committed in the target neighborhood), aggressive police patrols also have been found to impact directly on the aggregate rate of arrest observed for such crimes as robbery, theft, assault, and disturbing the peace (Reiss, 1971; Wilson & Boland, 1978). It is therefore difficult to assert with any degree of confidence that inequality is a major cause of criminality, since even the aggregate studies fail to fully support this hypothesis.

Unemployment

Few scholars would dispute the fact that most criminals are less than fully successful in maintaining legitimate employment. This is because research clearly reveals the sparse, spotty, flaccid work records of most criminal offenders (Chaiken & Chaiken, 1982; Peterson & Braiker, 1980; Walters & White, 1987). Brenner (1976), however, takes this argument one step further by contending that a person's inability to secure a certain standard of living is a primary cause of criminal behavior. Backing his position with data, Brenner uncovered positive correlations between unemployment and homicide and between unemployment and state prison admissions. Before we begin rejoicing in the knowledge that we can solve the crime problem by assigning jobs to offenders, we should realize that Brenner's research has been challenged on several counts, from failure to consider noneconomic factors like the age structure of one's sample (Cohen & Felson, 1979a) to use of inadequate and faulty measures of criminality (Wilson & Herrnstein, 1985).

Research on unemployment and crime can be subdivided into three general categories: aggregate studies, individual-level studies, and experimental programs. Aggregate studies entertain aggregate or group data in the form of cities, states, or countries. Gillespie (1975) assessed aggregate crime-unemployment studies conducted between 1959 and 1975 and discerned that three of the studies displayed a positive relationship, seven of the studies showed no relationship between crime and unemployment, and four of the studies produced equivocal findings. Reviews of aggregate-level studies conducted since Gillespie's contribution have derived even less support for the crime-unemployment argument (Long & Witte, 1981; Orsagh & Witte, 1981). More positive results were obtained in a review by Chiricos (1987), who concludes that a small, but oftentimes significant relationship can be observed between crime and unemployment when male subjects are studied. There is, however, little evidence of such a relationship when female samples are considered (Naffine & Gale, 1989).

Probing the possibility of a crime-unemployment connection with longitudinal data, Freeman (1983) surmised that a 50 percent reduction in the unemployment rate would attenuate crime by no more than 5 percent. While such an outcome appears to cast serious doubt on the meaningfulness of the crime-unemployment hypothesis, Sampson and Castellano (1982) unearthed evidence of a connection between neighborhood unemployment and victim reports of violent crime, a relationship which was stronger in black as compared to white neighborhoods, and urban as opposed to rural areas. More recently, Devine, Sheley, and Smith (1988) established a link between unemployment and crime in a time-series analysis of employment status and Uniform Crime Report estimates of homicide, robbery, and burglary rates measured between 1948 and 1985. These mixed findings may reflect the influences of gender (Naffine & Gale, 1989) or age (Allan & Steffensmeier, 1989). Concerning the moderating role of age, Allan and Steffensmeier remark that unemployment was more important in explaining juvenile crime while the quality of employment was more vital in explicating crimes committed by young adults.

Regardless of the results achieved with aggregate studies, this research is limited by factors previously discussed. As such, we need to consider studies that center on individuals rather than neighborhoods. Where Witte (1980) failed to identify a relationship between job availability and recidivism in a study conducted on individual subjects, a link between unemployment and criminal outcome has been implied in several other nonaggregate studies (Cook, 1975; Davis, 1983; Sickles, Schmidt, & Witte, 1979). Berk, Lenihan, and Rossi (1980) report that ex-offenders released from prisons in Georgia and Texas, who maintained steady employment for a period of one year, committed approximately one and one-half times fewer property offenses than ex-convicts bearing no such work record. Though these findings suggest that unemployment and criminality may be correlated, at least where released offenders are concerned, the results of several longitudinal studies imply that unemployment and crime may be linked, but not causally related.

In one such longitudinal study, Bachman, O'Malley, and Johnston (1978) interviewed 2,000 young boys entering high school and then followed them for a period of eight years. It was determined at follow-up that the subjects who had dropped out of high school were twice as likely to be unemployed at the time of the follow-up interview and significantly more likely to have a history of adult criminality than subjects owning a high school diploma. Bachman et al. conclude that unemployment and later criminality both reflect early delinquent and behavioral problems. West and Farrington (1977) arrived at a similar conclusion in their analysis of longitudinal data collected on a sample of male London youth; that is, boys with early behavioral problems were less likely to remain in school, exhibit steady employment, and refrain from later criminality. Further examination of these outcomes, however, unearthed a link between unemployment and crimes committed for material gain, particularly in the case of youthful offenders (ages 15–16) and persons strongly predisposed to criminality (Farrington et al., 1986).

Experimental studies are a third research paradigm by which the relationship between crime and unemployment has been explored. In the typical experimental investigation offenders are provided with funds, jobs, or training in an effort to determine whether these factors effect future rates of criminal recidivism. As part of the Transitional Aid Research Project (TARP), randomly sampled groups of offenders received unemployment compensation while they searched for jobs (Rossi, Berk, & Lenihan, 1980). This project revealed mixed outcomes, although offenders, whether or not they received compensation, were slow to investigate legitimate avenues of employment. While Rauma and Berk (1982) estimate that projects such as TARP could save taxpayers as much as $2,000 a year per participant and reduce recidivism by 34 percent, their analyses were based on a quasi-experimental design in which compensated offenders very likely received more attention, feedback, and supervisory structure than noncompensated offenders.

Wiederanders (1981) argues that parolees encounter problems not in landing a job but in retaining it for any reasonable length of time. In a sample of 145 California parolees, Wiederanders observed that 90 percent were working a regular job within four months of their release and 96 percent had found employment within a year. However, the modal length of employment was only two months and the mean length of employment was less than three months. The Manpower Demonstration Research Corporation (MDRC) set out to provide job training and experience to certain target groups, to include delinquents and ex-convicts. Although the project seemed to assist some ex-addicts and women on welfare in their efforts to find and retain employment, there was very little effect for ex-convicts and delinquents (Piliavin & Gartner, 1981).

Part of the problem with unemployment research on crime may be that the relationship between unemployment and crime is neither simple nor unidirectional. Chiricos (1987) reviewed 63 studies of unemployment and crime, and ascertained a conditional relationship between these two variables, subnational aggregate studies on property crime conducted since 1970 yielding the most impressive outcomes. Cantor and Land (1985) argue that the criminal opportunity and criminal-motivation effects of unemployment need to be considered independently since they exert converse effects on crime rates. When Cantor and Land considered these factors separately they found that there was a negative (criminal opportunity) as well as positive (criminal motivation) relationship between major index crimes and unemployment. Though both effects were small, they were nonetheless statistically significant. Thornberry and Christenson (1984) further determined that a reciprocal model of causality (unemployment causing crime and crime causing unemployment) produced more positive results than the more traditional unidirectional model (unemployment causing crime).

Adverse Social Conditions and Crime

The major problem in attempting to forge a link between crime and adverse social conditions is the apparent complexity of the relationship between such conditions and traditional measures of criminality. There are a number of factors in addition to social class and economic conditions that impact on crime, and there are factors that influence these adverse economic conditions in a manner that may be similar or antagonistic to the effect these variables have on criminality. Untangling these influences is often difficult, although studies such as those conducted by Cantor and Land (1985) and Thornberry and Christenson (1984) are certainly steps in the right direction. Actually, the status of social condition as a correlate of criminal involvement is reminiscent of the heredity-crime link discussed in the previous chapter; that is, there seems to be a mild but consistent connection between certain markers of social condition (for example, social class, poverty, unemployment) and criminal outcome. However, unlike the connections noted to occur between age and crime or gender and crime, the social condition–crime association is moderated by a number of other variables. Thus, the social condition–crime affiliation appears to be stronger in blacks than whites (Blau & Blau, 1982; Thornberrry & Farnworth, 1982) and more clearly accounts for offenses like burglary than person crimes like murder, rape, or assault property (Wilson & Cook, 1985).

SUBSTANCE ABUSE

Many a political campaign has been conducted on the strength of a candidate's resolve to crack down on drugs. This argument is based in part on the belief that drugs are a primary cause of criminality, an attitude which seems deeply embedded in the American psyche. The connection between crime and drugs has been presumed from the early decades of the twentieth century (Reasons, 1975). In fact, the primary driving force behind passage of the Harrison Act of 1914 was the assumption that a meaningful link existed between drugs and crime (McBride, 1981). However, we need to look past the zeitgeist of a significant drug-crime connection and determine for ourselves whether there is any substance to this proposed nexus.

First, there is little doubt that criminals exceed the population base rates for alcohol and drug use and abuse. In a national survey of state prison inmates it was determined that one in three reported having been drunk just prior to committing the instant offense and one in five admitted to having abused alcohol daily for a period of at least one year prior to entering prison (Bureau of Justice Statistics, 1983a). Drug usage was also widespread in this sample, and one out of every three inmates reported having been under the influence of an illegal substance at the time of the instant offense and 40 percent had used an illegal substance on a daily basis for at least one month prior to coming to prison (Bureau of Justice Statistics, 1983b). Since prisoners who committed offenses under the influence of an illegal substance were much less likely than other inmates to have abused alcohol, a large majority of the subjects in this population abused either alcohol, drugs, or both.

The results of the 1979 survey (Bureau of Justice Statistics, 1983a, 1983b) were subsequently replicated in a 1986 survey of inmates also confined in state correctional facilities (Bureau of Justice Statistics, 1988b). Extending this methodology to male delinquents confined in a Texas youth facility, Watts and Wright (1990) noted that the use of tobacco, alcohol, marijuana, and other illegal substances accounted for between 40 and 47 percent of the variance in minor delinquency and between 34 and 59 percent of the variance in violent delinquency for groups of black, white, and Hispanic youth. It should be noted, however, that in at least one study (Wish, Cuadrado, & Martorana, 1986) offenders greatly underreported their drug usage patterns. Thus, while 25 percent of the probationers interviewed by Wish et al. reported ingesting a drug within 24 to 48 hours of their interview with a probation officer, 68 percent produced urinanalyses positive for at least one illegal substance. Be this as it may, the self-reported alcohol and drug use patterns of subjects in the 1979 Bureau of Census survey of state-prison inmates can be found in Tables 6.2 and 6.3, respectively.

Conceding for the moment that prison inmates possess a more extensive history of alcohol and drug misuse than comparable groups of nonoffenders (Bureau of Justice Statistics, 1983a, 1983b), we must examine the data further to determine whether a causal nexus actually exists between substance abuse and criminal behavior. To this end, there are at least six interpretations of the interface that clearly exists between drugs and crime. First, drugs may stimulate violence or aggression in users as might be found in cases of severe alcohol or phencyclidine (PCP) intoxication. Second, by virtue of the fact that many of the drugs we discuss in this section are illegal, their usage brings one into closer contact with the criminal element and may, in turn, contribute to a subtle breakdown of the subject's moral code, whereby he or she finds themselves engaging in behaviors he or she would have avoided previously.

A third possible interpretation of the crime-drug association is that because the cost of certain drugs is prohibitive, the individual engages in criminal activity in order to secure funds for the purchase of illegal drugs through black market sources. Johnson et al. (1985) estimate that the average street heroin user will engage in nondrug crimes (theft, burglary, robbery) that result in an economic loss to victims of $14,000 per annum. A fourth possibility is that drugs and crime exert a bidirectional or reciprocal effect whereby each is a cause and effect of the other (Hammersley et al., 1989). In a related vein, it is interesting that

Table 6.2
Drinking Patterns of State Prison Inmates One Year Prior to Instant Offense

Frequency	
Abstain	18.1%
< once a month	4.4%
once a month	3.1%
3-4 times a month	4.5%
1-2 times a week	21.8%
3-4 times a week	9.8%
nearly every day	5.2%
every day	32.7%
no data	0.3%

Amount[1]	
Abstain	18.1%
less than 4 oz.	45.3%
4 oz. or more	36.3%
no data	0.3%

[1]Amount of ethanol (pure alcohol) consumed in a typical drinking session.

Source: Survey based on the responses of 274,564 state prison inmates. Bureau of Justice Statistics (1983a).

Table 6.3
Drug Use Patterns of State Prison Inmates

Drug	Ever Used	Recently Used[1]
Marijuana	75%	48%
Amphetamines	37%	10%
Cocaine	37%	13%
Barbiturates	35%	10%
Heroin	30%	12%
LSD	24%	4%
PCP	19%	5%

[1]Within past month.

Source: Survey based on the responses of 274,564 state prison inmates. Bureau of Justice Statistics (1983b).

heavy involvement in property crime or drug dealing frequently retards the process of ''maturing out'' of a drug lifestyle (Anglin et al., 1986). A fifth possible explanation for the crime-drug nexus is that just as there is a criminal lifestyle (Walters, 1990b), there are also several drug lifestyles (Faupel, 1987) with features and correlates similar to, but not identical with, the criminal lifestyle.

A final denotation of the relationship presumed to exist between substance abuse and crime is that the two are not causally connected, but correlate simply because of their common association with a third variable. This third variable, which might involve general deviance, social policy, or self-indulgence, could be the cause of both substance abuse and crime. Bean and Wilkinson (1988), for instance, propose that contact with the illicit supply system is the third variable that links crime to drug usage. Taking an analogous approach to explaining the observed association between drugs and crime, Fagan and his colleagues (1990) argue that drug use and delinquency are spuriously related in the sense that while they may operate along parallel dimensions, these dimensions are not causally connected.

As we proceed with our discussion of drugs and crime, we are well advised to keep these six possible explanations for the proposed crime-substance abuse relationship in mind. We now turn our attention to the proposed relationship between crime and six specific categories of drug: alcohol, marijuana, heroin, cocaine, amphetamines, and PCP.

Alcohol

Alcohol is a colorless liquid produced from the fermentation of sugar by yeast. Alcohol is normally classified as a central nervous system depressant; the active ingredient in alcohol, ethanol, affects the body by gradually dulling the reactions of the brain and nervous system. Most Americans are light drinkers, with only 11 percent of the population consuming an average of at least one ounce of ethanol a day (American Psychiatric Association, 1987). Some estimates place the number of adult abusers of alcohol in the United States at 9 million, a figure which is nearly 9 percent of the entire adult population. Conservative estimates note that alcohol abuse costs the nation several billion dollars a year, is involved in at least half of all fatal auto accidents and a third of all suicides, and may shorten the life expectancy of the average abuser by 10 to 12 years (National Institute on Alcohol Abuse and Alcoholism, 1978). What, however, is the relationship between alcohol and crime?

Research clearly indicates that criminal offenders abuse alcohol more frequently than nonoffenders (Bureau of Justice Statistics, 1983a; Petersilia, Greenwood, & Lavin, 1978; Roizen & Schneberk, 1977). Guze et al. (1962) discovered that 43 percent of their sample of 223 male probationers satisfied criteria for a diagnosis of alcoholism. Alcohol-abusing criminals in this study also exhibited significantly higher rates of arrest than non–alcohol-abusing offenders, although a majority of these arrests were for drinking, disturbing the peace, traffic violations, and fighting. There is also some evidence to suggest that problem drinkers are at increased risk for antisocial behavior (Goodwin, Crane, & Guze, 1971). Again, however, the majority of crimes committed by this group of individuals center on such offenses as public intoxication, indecent exposure, and disorderly conduct, although assault and battery is also quite common (Bacon, 1963).

Despite the apparent relationship between alcohol abuse and crime, there is very little evidence that the former causes the latter. If the abuse of alcohol is an important cause of criminality we would expect to find a regular pattern of alcohol usage to precede significant criminality. However, most studies report the exact opposite: criminality normally antedates regular use of alcohol (Guze et al., 1962; Roizen & Schneberk, 1977). Moreover, a review of the literature on the personality correlates of alcoholism by Nathan (1988) denotes that antisocial behaviors occurring in childhood and adolescence are one of the more consistent precursors of adulthood alcoholism. These results imply that a predisposition to criminality may predate a regular pattern of alcohol usage and that alcohol abuse may be a reflection of a criminal predisposition rather than its cause. A notable exception to this general pattern can be found in a study administered by Newcomb and McGee (1989). Reviewing the responses of a group of 847 high school students to a substance-abuse questionnaire, these authors found greater support for the supposition that early alcohol abuse causes deviance than for the counterargument that early delinquent behavior encourages heavy alcohol consumption.

The biographical accounts of various criminals seem to indicate that while many of them have engaged in excessive drinking, most view their use of alcohol as etiologically unrelated to their criminal activities (Collins, 1981). Bennett and Wright (1984) interviewed 91 burglars and found that nearly all of their subjects acknowledged alcohol consumption prior to at least several of their offenses, and one out of three had reportedly ingested alcohol before nearly every one of their crimes. However, the vast majority of subjects in this study failed to see a causal connection between their use of alcohol and criminal conduct. Many of these individuals reasoned that since they imbibed alcohol on a regular basis there was little need for them to change this pattern simply because they were contemplating, planning, or engaging in a particular criminal act. We must keep in mind, however, that many criminal offenders have less than maximal insight into their actions and behaviors.

Even if alcohol is not a predominant cause of criminality, it may still give rise to specific criminal events. It has been argued that since two of the primary effects of alcohol intoxication are the release of impulses and the reduction of inhibitions (Kaplan, 1984), alcohol may therefore stimulate reactions that the individual normally suppresses when sober (Plaut, 1967). In one laboratory study, Taylor and Gammon (1975) observed greater aggression on the part of intoxicated subjects compared to a group of nonintoxicated subjects. Greene (1981) obtained results that imply alcoholics are more violent than other drug users.

It has also been stated that alcohol reduces the efficiency with which one might accomplish a particular criminal task (Bacon, 1963). In a review of the research on alcohol abuse and crime, Berry and Boland (1977) concluded that there is evidence of a link between alcohol and crimes of violence, particularly murder, assault, and rape. Researchers from the New York State Division of Alcoholism and Alcohol Abuse, however, were unable to unearth support for the disinhibition theory of alcohol-related violence when they compared the alcohol consumption patterns of persons confined for violent and property crimes, to the extent that they were unable to identify significant alcohol use differences between the subjects in these two offense categories.

An issue often raised when the relationship between two variables is being investigated is the potential impact of moderator variables. Three moderator variables that have been considered in juxtaposition to the connection between crime and alcohol are age, social class, and race. Petersilia et al. (1978) ascertained that alcohol and drugs were viewed by a group of career offenders as more etiologically significant during the latter stages of their criminal careers than during the earlier stages. Collins (1981) contends that while alcohol may produce more serious behavioral effects in young men, the alcohol-crime connection is probably strongest in middle-aged as compared to younger offenders. Conversely, Temple and Ladouceur (1986) determined that while crime and alcohol use were moderately correlated during adolescence, these two variables were unrelated by the time subjects had turned 31. These authors conclude that traditional beliefs concerning the causal nexus between alcohol abuse and crime are age-specific, if they exist at all.

There are some data to suggest that social class also plays a moderating role in the relationship between crime and alcohol misuse. Hence, the crime-alcohol connection is strongest in lower-class samples, a group which commonly reports a high number of specific problems relative to their use of alcohol (Cahalan, 1970; Cahalan & Room, 1972). Roizen (1981), in fact, found little evidence of significant black-white variations in the crime-alcohol nexus when he controlled for preexisting differences in social class.

Research studies examining the crime-alcohol nexus have been criticized for their lack of methodological rigor. Investigators in this area of inquiry have thus been excoriated for relying on amorphously defined criterion measures and utilizing outdated bivariate statistical models that fail to capture the complexity of the relationship presumed to exist between drug use and crime (Greenberg, 1981). Greenberg adds that dependence upon designs composed only of incarcerated offenders may lead one to overestimate the magnitude of the alcohol-crime connection.

In conducting his own review of the alcohol-crime literature, Collins (1981) concludes that the evidence does not provide a clear picture of the causal status of the apparent association between alcohol and crime. This is particularly true in the case of career or lifestyle criminals. Consequently, while "it does not seem accurate to characterize drinking as an important influence in the etiology of a criminal career . . . drinking does appear to contribute to the occurrence of particular criminal events" (1981, p. 198). Future research, however, should concentrate on how drinking contributes to specific criminal acts in certain individuals under a given set of circumstances.

Marijuana

Marijuana grows in the form of a plant known as *Cannabis sativa*. The leaves and flowering top of this plant are dried and then smoked in a pipe or rolled cigarette (commonly referred to as a joint). The immediate effects of marijuana intoxication include a distorted sense of space and time, decreased inhibitions, heightened sensations, and a general feeling of well-being. While there are those who view marijuana as a reasonably safe, innocuous substance (Grinspoon, 1977), others argue that the negative long-term effects of prolonged marijuana usage come upon the individual gradually (Schwartz, 1984). Some of these effects include an insidious change in mood and personality (Nahas, 1973), serious damage to the respiratory-pulmonary system (Wu et al., 1988), and the appearance of sundry attention, memory, and learning sequelae to heavy abuse (Nicholi, 1983).

Although marijuana is the illegal substance most often abused by criminal offenders (Table 6.3), there is a paucity of data on the connection between marijuana smoking and crime. Opinion, however, has been abundant. Hence, Williams (1967, p. 141) argues that marijuana "is the immediate and direct cause of the crime committed" while Grinspoon (1977, p. 323) takes the opposite position; that is, that marijuana "is not addicting [and] is not criminogenic." In partial support of Williams' thesis, there is evidence to suggest that marijuana users tend to be more violent than nonusers (Robins, Darvish, & Murphy, 1970). However, this may simply reflect the fact that aggressive, criminally oriented individuals are more inclined to use marijuana than less criminally involved persons. In fact, if marijuana has any direct effect on aggression at all, it tends to be inhibitory rather than excitatory (Kaplan, 1970).

Were there to be a connection between crime and marijuana it would appear to be indirect. As related by Yochelson and Samenow (1986), the current view of marijuana holds that this substance may release certain antisocial or criminologic tendencies, though these tendencies probably existed long before the individual began smoking marijuana. While there are data which support the release of criminogenic tendencies hypothesis (MacDonald, 1976; Winick, 1971), there is just as much evidence to corroborate the position that criminally oriented individuals use marijuana as a means of expressing antisocial inclinations or achieving self-indulgent ends (McGlothlin & West, 1968). In short, there is little solid empirical evidence to support the presence of a causal connection between the use of marijuana and subsequent criminal behavior.

Heroin

First synthesized from morphine in 1874, heroin is an opiate that produces a warm, pleasurable sensation most intensely localized in the stomach, skin, and genitals. As is the case with all opiates, heroin has analgesic or pain-killing qualities. Pure heroin is a white powdery substance that can easily be identified by its bitter taste. However, most street heroin contains dilutents and is only about 5 percent pure. The normal route of entry is either through the nose (snorting), skin (subcutaneous injection), or vein (intravenous injection). A highly addictive substance, the primary risks associated with heroin usage include overdose, contamination, and infection. Overdose deaths are particularly common, and it has been estimated that heroin overdose is responsible for 1,000 to 1,500 deaths per year in New York City alone (Wurmser, 1978).

Heroin has been at the center of the drug-crime controversy from the very beginning. This is because we find a large amount of crime in neighborhoods where heroin use runs rampant (Speckart & Anglin, 1985). Eckerman, Bates, Rachal, and Poole (1971) determined that 80 percent of the arrests for robbery in New York City and 45 percent of the arrests for robbery in Washington, D.C., were committed by heroin addicts and users. A Miami, Florida, sample of 356 heroin users acknowledged involvement in a sum total of 118,134 criminal offenses over a one-year period (Inciardi, 1979). Results such as these have led Nurco (1987, p. 7) to conclude that "there is no longer any serious controversy about the relationship between narcotic drug use and crime in the United States" and that "evidence of a causal link" between these two variables clearly exists. In assessing the validity of Nurco's statements we inspect pre-post addiction designs, pre-during treatment studies, aggregate investigations, and longitudinal analyses.

The results of pre-post addiction studies indicate that there is a substantial increase in the number of arrests and incidents of self-reported criminality with the onset of heroin addiction (Hayim, 1973; Voss & Stephens, 1973). Similarly, the majority of pre-during treatment studies demonstrate that with the advent of methadone maintenance there is a significant drop in the amount of criminality engaged in by addicts (Demaree & Neman, 1976; Edwards & Goldner, 1975; Simpson & Sells, 1982). However, not all of the pre-during treatment research confirms the presence of a meaningful heroin-crime association (Alexander & McCaslin, 1974; Kleinman & Lukoff, 1975). There are also a number of serious methodological deficiencies found in the designs of pre-post addiction and pre-during treatment studies scrutinizing the proposed crime-heroin addiction link.

Greenberg and Adler (1974) argue that pre-post addiction designs suffer from a lack of specificity to the extent that the onset of heroin addiction and criminality often occur within the same general time period owing to their common age-risk distributions. Consequently, the rise of crime in a pre-post addiction study may be more a function of age than of heroin addiction. Pre-during treatment studies, on the other hand, have been criticized for being biased in their selection of subjects (McGlothin, Anglin, & Wilson, 1978). First, many persons referred to substance-abuse programs regularly display high levels of both criminality and addiction, factors which may have stimulated the referral in the first place. There is also the problem of differential mortality if the investigators restricted their analyses to subjects who completed the program, since such individuals are not representative of substance abusers in general. These methodological issues need to be kept in mind when interpreting the results of pre-post addiction and pre-during treatment studies of the crime-heroin question.

Aggregate studies examine the relationship between heroin use and crime from a community or neighborhood perspective. Silverman and his colleagues (1977, 1975) ascertained that aggregate property crimes varied according to the street market value of heroin, while there was no such relationship between nonfinancially oriented violent offenses and the price of heroin. During a period in which efforts were made to reduce the amount of heroin available to addicts in the Washington, D.C., area there was a corresponding decrease in the rate of property crime (DuPont & Greene, 1973). In corollary fashion, it was determined that the property crime rate dropped during the 1972 East Coast heroin shortage (Research Triangle Institute, 1976).

Maddux and Desmond (1979) report that the crime rate in San Antonio, Texas, has been known to fluctuate with the availability of methadone maintenance as a treatment for heroin addiction, the crime rate increasing during periods of decreased methadone availability. Despite the seeming credence these findings lend the crime-heroin hypothesis, aggregate studies are less than ideal for the purposes of testing a causal theorem. In addition to the problems noted earlier, aggregate studies are limited by the fact that narcotics addicts and persons who commit property crimes are often located in the same census tract (McBride & McCoy, 1982). Moreover, high-addiction tracts are normally afflicted with a wide variety of problems, which include disrupted families and impoverished living conditions (Chein et al., 1964).

In an effort to overcome some of the problems associated with the use of pre-post addiction, pre-during treatment, and aggregate methodologies, McGlothin, Anglin, and Wilson (1978) longitudinally examined the criminal and drug use patterns of 690 admissions to the California Civil Addict Program. The results of this longitudinal analysis not only revealed the presence of a prominent increase in economically oriented crimes like burglary, theft, and drug sales in subjects addicted to heroin, but also showed substantial decrements in these offenses during periods of voluntary abstinence or less than daily usage. Subjects were arrested two to three times more often when addicted than when abstinent or using less than every day. These differences were even larger when self-reported criminality was considered.

Ball and associates (1981, 1983) conducted a similar set of studies using an East Coast sample. A group of 354 male heroin addicts randomly sampled from 7,500 known addicts in the Baltimore metropolitan area were interviewed and followed for a period of several years. Basing their analyses on crime-days (a 24-hour period in which one or more crimes of a specific nature are committed by a given individual), Ball and his colleagues discovered that there was a marked increase in criminality with the onset of addiction and that the level of criminality remained high over successive periods of addiction. Conversely, the first period of nonaddiction was accompanied by a dramatic decrease in criminality (82 composite crime-days per year versus 255 composite crime-days per year observed with the onset of addiction), a rate which continued to diminish over successive nonaddiction periods. Similar to the results obtained by McGlothin et al. (1978), Ball and his colleagues found a strong relationship between addiction and property crimes but very little connection between addiction and crimes of violence.

Implementing an equally sophisticated design, several different dependent measures, and a multivariate statistical analysis, Anglin and Speckart (1988) studied 671 male Anglo and Chicano heroin addicts residing in California. Consistent with the results obtained in the McGlothlin and Ball studies, Anglin and Speckart discovered that during periods in which narcotics were used sparingly (including the time before and after the addictive career), the rate of property crimes and drug dealing decreased substantially while legitimate employment and alcohol usage rose to their highest levels. These authors also found that while the more extreme, threatening offenses like robbery were not normally a part of these offenders' repertoire, they were most prevalent during peak periods of heroin addiction and usage. Anglin and Speckart reason that robbery may be viewed by heroin addicts as a last resort in obtaining money to support their drug habit. Similar outcomes were obtained in a sample of British heroin addicts (Jarvis & Parker, 1989).

As was mentioned in our section on alcohol and crime, it is essential that we consider the temporal order of our variables in attempting to establish a causal nexus between these variables. A number of early studies found very little criminality in the behavior of heroin addicts prior to the onset of addiction (Kolb, 1925; Terry & Pellens, 1928). More recent investigations, however, indicate that between 50 and 70 percent of the samples surveyed had engaged in criminal activity prior to becoming involved with heroin (Jacoby et al., 1973; McGlothlin et al., 1978; Nurco, Cisin, & Balter, 1981; Voss & Stephens, 1973). This finding brings into question the causal nature of the relationship between heroin and crime. It is important to note, however, that when we turn our attention to self-reported crimes of a serious nature, the proportion of subjects involved in pre-heroin criminality falls to a level slightly below 50 percent (Nurco & DuPont, 1977; Voss & Stephens, 1973).

Similar to research conducted on alcohol and crime, the literature on heroin and crime has considered the potential impact of various moderator variables. In general, there have been very few significant differences noted in the crime-heroin relationship as a function of either gender or race. Thus, while Inciardi (1979) reports that male heroin addicts demonstrate a stronger propensity for crime than female addicts, increased levels of criminality were found in both groups. Examining the role of race in the crime-heroin relationship, Anglin and Speckart (1988) observed a similar crime-drug pattern in groups of Anglo and Chicano heroin abusers enrolled in a methadone maintenance program in California. Time, however, may play a moderating role, in the sense that post-1950 samples have typically displayed more criminality prior to the onset of addiction than had been the case in samples studied before 1950 (Speckart & Anglin, 1985). In fact, the results of two investigations suggest that more recent cohorts of heroin addicts are more violent than addicts who began their addictive careers prior to 1970 (Stephens & Ellis, 1975; Zahn & Bencivengo, 1974). Finally, social policy may play a moderating role in the crime-heroin relationship, since Mott (1981) determined that heroin usage and criminality in Great Britain (where heroin use has been decriminalized) correspond less than they appear to in the United States, where it is illegal.

Where the results of recent studies suggest the presence of a strong connection between heroin addiction and property-type crimes, there are several additional facts that need to be considered. First, even when not using heroin the rate of criminality found in most samples of heroin addicts is still rather high (Anglin & Speckart, 1988; Ball et al., 1983; McGlothlin et al., 1978). Additionally, Shaffer, Nurco, and Kinlock (1984) ascertained that some addicts commit a large number of crimes regardless of whether they are actively using heroin. This same group of investigators also determined that juvenile criminality and family pathology were more strongly correlated with crimes committed during nonaddictive periods than with crimes committed during addictive periods (Shaffer et al., 1987). These authors speculate that during nonaddictive periods an individual's true criminologic tendencies surface since the confounding influence of addiction has been removed. It has been suggested by Faupel and Klockars (1987) that the causal relationship between crime and heroin addiction varies as a function of the stage in the addictive career, a possibility which warrants further study.

In reflecting upon research on crime and heroin it is critical that we realize predatory criminality is only one of several options available to someone intent on supporting a drug habit. After interviewing 54 heroin addicts in the East Harlem section of New York City, Goldstein (1981) arrived at the conclusion that while many of these addicts engaged in predatory forms of criminality, other means of support were also available. Among these alternative avenues of support, all of which at least a portion of the sample had used to sustain their heroin habit at one time, were the commission of nonpredatory crimes (for example, selling drugs), involvement in legitimate employment, and dependence on public relief, hustling, or financial assistance from friends and family. Though Nurco, Cisin, and Ball (1985) observed a moderately strong association between heroin addiction and crime, fully 10 to 15 percent of their sample eschewed criminality altogether, even during periods of heavy narcotic addiction. There was a much larger group of addicts in the Nurco et al. study who were minimally dependent on income accrued illegally.

A final consideration is that despite the rather sophisticated nature of research studies recently conducted on the proposed crime-heroin nexus, there are still several methodological questions that need to be answered. We might query whether sampling bias had anything to do with the obtained results or whether inadequate operationalization of terms and use of simplistic statistical models may account for some of the findings (Speckart & Anglin, 1985). In addition, many of the studies investigating the crime-heroin connection have been conducted using incarcerated offenders, despite Pottieger's (1981) caveat that outcomes obtained on captive drug-crime samples cannot be readily generalized to drug-crime samples living in the community.

Even though the longitudinal studies conducted on samples of heroin addicts in California (Anglin & Speckart, 1988; McGlothlin et al., 1978) and Maryland (Ball et al., 1983; Shaffer et al., 1987) are a significant improvement over earlier studies, there are still several issues that need to be explored further. One such issue is whether the results of these longitudinal studies may have been colored by the fact that the addicts were often more likely to be under some form of supervision (either parole or probation) during their low-drug periods. Although purely speculative at this point in time, it does not seem unreasonable to argue that supervision may have suppressed both the usage of drugs and involvement in crime for this sample and thus artifically accentuated the relationship between crime and drugs.

Cocaine

Cultivated in the Andean highlands of South America, cocaine is derived from the leaves of the coca plant. Cocaine is distributed as a white, crystalline powder and can either be snorted, injected, or smoked (free-based). The acute effects of cocaine intoxication include a rush of energy, hypervigilence (which with regular use can metastasize into paranoia), and a general state of well-being and euphoria. The use of cocaine in America, while not reaching the near-epidemic proportions suggested by the media, has significantly increased over the past several decades. In fact, a threefold increase in the number of cocaine-related emergency room visits and a fivefold increase in the number of admissions to drug-treatment programs for cocaine abuse took place between 1976 and 1980 (Morbidity and Mortality Weekly Reports, 1982). Moreover, the physical, social, and psychological toll levied on cocaine abusers and their families is especially frightening. In short, there is increasing evidence that cocaine is a truly dangerous drug that can produce tolerance, withdrawal, and other signs of dependency (Busch & Schnoll, 1985).

The outcome of research assessing the relationship between cocaine and crime is mixed. Thus, while Ewing (1967) and Siegel (1982) observed that violence often accompanies consumption of high dosages of this substance, Williams (1974) argued that some criminals may use cocaine to stimulate their temerity before engaging in a particular criminal act. Carr and Meyers (1980, p. 186) conclude that the proposed link between cocaine and violence "derives more from fears and long-standing biases against the drug than from any empirical data." This conclusion may be overstated, however, particularly in light of a recent study that discerned escalating levels of cocaine ingestion that corresponded with a rising rate of criminal activity in methadone maintenance patients (Hunt et al., 1987). Still, the proposed nexus between cocaine utilization and violent criminality remains unclear.

Inspecting the presumed association between criminal behavior and cocaine usage, Helfrich et al. (1982) discovered that 15 percent of the subjects they interviewed who were seeking treatment for cocaine dependency reported legal problems stemming from their use of cocaine. Washton and Gold (1984) note that a substantial proportion of a group of heavy cocaine users were dealing cocaine to support their habits (39%), 12 percent had experienced arrest for dealing or possessing cocaine, and nearly one-third (29%) had stolen from friends, family, or work as a means of supporting their use of this substance. Finally, Sanchez and Johnson (1987) studied cocaine and/or heroin abuse and criminal activity in a sample of female jail detainees. Though these findings allude to the possibility of a link between cocaine and crime, they are far from conclusive. The use of more representative samples surveyed over time, as Ball et al. (1981) have done with heroin addicts, will be required if we are to determine whether cocaine and crime are meaningfully connected.

Amphetamines

A second class of stimulants, the amphetamines, have also been investigated relative to the crime-drug hypothesis. Asnis and Smith (1978), for instance, discerned a relationship between violence and amphetamine usage, while Ellinwood (1971) entertained the possibility of a causal connection between violence and amphetamine intoxication on the basis of interviews conducted with 13 felons serving time for homicides committed while under the influence of stimulant drugs. Greenberg (1976) has severely criticized researchers examining the proposed nexus between amphetamines and crime for offering conclusions on the basis of studies that are of questionable methodological rigor and sophistication. She argues that without better designed, large-scale investigations little can be inferred about the proposed link between crime and amphetamines.

Phencyclidine (PCP)

Phencyclidine became available as an anesthetic for animals during the 1960s, but the manufacturer halted production in 1978 in response to federal legislation outlawing this substance. However, this has done little to stem the tide of PCP, which is now regularly manufactured in clandestine laboratories throughout the United States. PCP, also known as Angel Dust, Crystal, Killer Weed, and Embalming Fluid, is typically sold in liquid form and applied to cigarettes or joints of marijuana for the purposes of smoking. Effects range anywhere from a sense of detachment and slurred speech to loss of coordination, vivid auditory hallucinations, paranoia, and uncontrolled bursts of violent activity. In fact, it may be the unpredictable nature of PCP that makes it so attractive to youthful consumers (Schroeder, 1980).

Violence, in the form of self-injury and assaultive behavior, by individuals under the influence of PCP has been reported in the popular press (Fauman and Fauman, 1982) as well as in several clinical observation studies (Burns & Lerner, 1978; Wright, 1980). Fauman and Fauman state further that persons who commit crimes while under the influence of PCP are often incapable of recalling the crime in question. Simonds and Kashani (1980) observed that PCP-abusing boys in a training school owned a more extensive history of person-oriented criminality than boys who abused other drugs. However, it is difficult to draw a connection between PCP and person crimes based on the results of this study. First, the majority of PCP-abusing youth who took part in Simonds and Kashani's study had a history of poly-drug abuse. Second, only 17 percent of the person crimes committed by subjects in this sample were perpetrated within 24 hours of having used an illicit substance. Of related interest, a group of investigators reviewed 81 clinical toxicity reports on incidents involving the use of PCP and found little support for the common notion that PCP stimulates violence in persons not predisposed to such behavior (Brecher et al., 1988).

Research suggests that PCP usage is concentrated in groups of youthful offenders (Wish, 1986). Nonetheless, 30 percent of a large group of arrestees in Washington, D.C., tested positive for PCP (Wish, Klumpp, Moorer, & Brady, 1980), while 12 percent of a large group of arrestees in New York City produced urine samples positive for PCP (Wish, 1986). Contrary to what would be predicted if PCP were a primary cause of violent crime, however, persons in the New York City sample who tested positive for PCP were more likely to have been arrested for robbery and larceny than for violent transgressions like murder, rape, or assault. Davis (1982) concludes that the media have exaggerated the connection between PCP and violence because such accounts sell newspapers and attract television audiences. However, when one examines the entire spectrum of PCP users it becomes apparent that the vast majority experience no such adverse reactions.

Crime-Drug Patterns

There is little question that substance abuse and criminality are strongly correlated and that intoxication and drug usage are a regular part of many offenders' lives. This does not mean, however, that substance abuse causes crime. In fact, as we saw in research conducted on alcohol, marijuana, and heroin, antisocial activity often predates heavy drug usage. In a large-scale study of recalcitrant offenders, Walters and White (1987) discovered that arrest preceded the onset of drug usage in approximately 60 percent of the cases. Inciardi (1986) reports that the nonnarcotic drug users in his study began ingesting drugs and engaging in crime around the same time, while narcotics addicts began using drugs first but were involved in crime long before they ever became addicted to heroin. Parker, Newcombe, and Bakx (1986) discerned that two-thirds of the 196 offending opiate abusers in a sample of British subjects possessed a prior record of arrest, and that one-third had been of "good character" before becoming involved with drugs. The outcome of a somewhat better controlled investigation of British addicts denotes that heroin use is an extension, rather than a cause, of delinquent activity (Burr, 1987). The contradictory findings connote that the relationship between crime and drugs is formidably complex.

In summarizing the results of several ongoing research projects, Speckart and

Anglin (1986) comment that there is at least a qualified causal connection between crime and drug usage. They go on to argue, however, that since drug abuse and addiction-induced criminality represent a "choice" on the part of the individual, both are amenable to intervention. Consequently, methadone maintenance has a predictable, suppressing effect on both heroin usage and criminality (Anglin & Speckart, 1986) while parole supervision with urine surveillance for drug usage has been found to be effective in interrupting addiction periods and concomitant criminality (Anglin, McGlothlin, & Speckart, 1981). Rather than taking a "nothing works" approach to the question of drug interventions and crime, Speckart and Anglin (1986) ask "what works for which types of addicts, at what point in the addiction career, and for how long."

McBride and McCoy (1982) contend that persons prone to criminal activity and drug abuse have become increasingly likely to be drawn from the same population, and Kaplan (1980) refers to a generalized deviancy that expresses itself in both criminal activity and substance abuse. Such speculation is supported by data that show that the onset of marijuana and other drug usage can be reasonably well predicted from prior behavioral and personality deviancy (Jessor & Jessor, 1977; Smith & Fogg, 1978) and that the single best predictor of subsequent alcohol abuse is early antisocial activity (Nathan, 1988). Moreover, in an innovative study administered by Shaffer et al. (1987) it was determined that a high rate of juvenile criminality was strongly associated with a high rate of adult criminality, that both were linked to heroin usage, and that both normally preceded the onset of addiction.

With these findings in mind I suggest that a parsimonious but accurate interpretation of the research on crime and drugs supports the proposition that certain substances play a facilitative role in the development of later criminality. Therefore, while drugs do not appear to cause crime per se, they do seem to accelerate, exacerbate, and stimulate preexisting criminologic tendencies. Heroin, because of its high cost, and alcohol and PCP, because they occasionally lead to violent reactions, are the strongest candidates for links in the crime-drug chain. However, we should not lose sight of the fact that typologies need to be developed so that we can differentiate between offenders for whom substance abuse is simply a reflection of an underlying criminal lifestyle and drug abusers who engage in criminality as a consequence or facilitation of their drug-oriented lifestyles.

SOCIALIZATION AND THE FAMILY

We have already noted the presence of a deficit in the process of criminologic thought (see Chapter 5), particularly when it comes to conditioning, learning, and problem solving. However, there are important differences between criminals and noncriminals in the content of their thinking as well. When considering the content of criminological thought and learning, socialization invariably comes to the forefront. It is hard to imagine human development in the absence of human contact and socialization experiences. Save for a handful of persons raised by animals (so-called feral children), we have all learned, by way of socialization, the values and expectations of others. Socialization experiences, which typically commence early in life, provide a child with an opportunity to learn about him or herself, the outside world, and his or her place in that world. These experiences would therefore appear to hold great value for a science of criminal behavior.

One of the primary agents of socialization is the family. The family is normally the first social constituent with which the child interacts. This particular aspect of socialization can be a rich source of role models and early learning experiences that serve to provide a framework for later behavior. Through such interactions the child acquires information relevant to self-identity, relationship-building, frustration tolerance, and self-control. In this section we probe the evolution of the self-identity function by examining research on paternal attitude and crime, the relationship function by inspecting research on parental absence and crime, the frustration tolerance function by scrutinizing research on child abuse and crime, and the self-control function by reviewing research on parental disciplinary style and crime.

Parental Attitude

In an early study investigating the relationship between parental attitude and delinquency, Glueck and Glueck (1950) learned that the parents of delinquents were more hostile and/or rejecting and less affectionate than the parents of nondelinquents. Subsequent research has been largely supportive of the Gluecks' initial findings. The parents of delinquents frequently receive ratings that indicate that they are hostile, indifferent, and emotionally constricted (Ferreira & Winter, 1968; Hetherington, Stouwie, & Ridberg, 1971; West & Farrington, 1977). Furthermore, Eisenberg, Langner, and Gersten (1975) located the existence of an association between delinquency and a factor they labeled "parental coldness." It could be, however, that delinquents have as much of an effect on the attitude of their parents as parental attitude has on the development of later delinquency. Addressing this possibility, Simons and colleagues conducted a multivariate path analysis and discovered that the direction of the relationship between parental attitude and crime flowed from parental rejection to delinquency rather than from delinquency to parental rejection (Simons, Robertson, & Downs, 1989).

A question often raised but rarely researched asks about the differential impact of maternal versus paternal attitude in the development of later criminality. Analyzing information first collected in 1937, McCord and McCord (1958) noted that maternal rejection and deviant paternal role modeling were instrumental in later crime genesis and that these two variables had a synergistic effect on delinquency. Further inspection of these data by the McCords and Zola (1959) revealed that while maternal rejection was associated with offspring delinquency, the correlation between delinquency and paternal attitude was even stronger. Crime rates were highest when the father was indifferent, unconcerned, or neglectful and lowest when the father was either warm or passive. Buikhuisen, van der Plas-Korenhoff, and Bontekoe (1985) also unearthed a connection between problematic father-child interactions and delinquency in support of an earlier study that found tacit parental reinforcement of antisocial behavior, particularly by the father, to be predictive of subsequent aggressive delinquent behavior on the part of their male offspring (Johnson & Burke, 1955). Ergo, paternal attitude seems just as important as maternal attitude in understanding the evolution of criminality in affected offspring.

Though these results confirm the importance of parental attitude in the development of delinquency and criminality, it needs to be understood that parents do not interact in the same manner with each of their progeny. Consequently, parental attitude may be criminogenic for some children but not for others. As far back as 1945, Kvaraceus had recorded outcomes that indicated nine out of ten delinquents were the only members of their immediate families with any history of lawlessness. Furthermore, only 9 percent of the families in the Kvaraceus study had produced two or more delinquent adolescent members, even though the average family contained five children. Fifty-eight percent of the recidivistic offenders in the Leavenworth 500 sample were the only members of their immediate families with criminal records (Walters & White, 1987). Such a finding suggests the possibility that parental attitude may vary across children within the same family, for as Weinstein and Sackhoff (1987) discerned, first- and last-born children were over-represented in a sample of jail inmates. The issue of differential parental attitudes and criminality is taken up again when we consider the issue of person × situation interaction.

Parental Absence

A home might be broken by divorce, death, abandonment, or prolonged illness. In the Leavenworth 500 sample it was deduced that 58 percent of the 500 plus federal inmates studied had experienced one or more of these losses before the age of 16 (Walters & White, 1987). However, the results of research on broken homes are influenced by how parental absence is defined and the age at which loss occurs. Thus, a relationship between delinquency and loss is more likely to be evident if the parent left the home when the subject was six or seven than when the subject was an adolescent (Kellam et al., 1982) and when separation was due to divorce or desertion rather than death or prolonged hospitalization (West and Farrington, 1973). However, a study carried out by investigators from the University of Southern California failed to generate support for an age-mediated moderator effect when the child's age at the time of parental divorce was correlated with subsequent criminal activity (B. Mednick et al., 1987).

Early research on parental absence and crime pointed to the presence of a fairly strong association. Glueck and Glueck (1950) found parental absence to be common in the backgrounds of delinquent boys, Monahan (1957) ascertained greater recidivism on the part of delinquents hailing from broken homes, and

Greer (1964) discovered that sociopaths were more likely to have lost a parent within the first four years of life than neurotic patients. In their review of the literature on parental absence and crime, Peterson and Becker (1965) concluded that there was a one-and-one-half to twofold increase in the rate of delinquency for adolescents raised in a broken home relative to adolescents originating in two-parent homes. Several more recent studies also support the crime–broken home connection (Wadsworth, 1980; Wilkinson, 1980), although not all of the outcomes have been confirmatory (compare Robins, 1966; Tennyson, 1967). In fact, a survey of 18 investigations on this subject uncovered seven studies confirming, four disavowing, and seven providing mixed support for the crime-parental absence hypothesis (Herzog & Sudia, 1973).

One possible explanation for the lack of congruence in outcomes examining the proposed broken home–crime and/or delinquency nexus concerns the potential role of moderator variables. Rosenquist and Megargee (1969), along with several other investigators (Berger & Simon, 1974; Tennyson, 1967), have failed to identify significant variations in the crime–parental absence relationship according to such factors as race and ethnic status. Rosen, Lalli, and Savitz (1975), on the other hand, witnessed a stronger crime-parental absence bond in blacks than whites, while Austin (1978) and Hamparian et al. (1978) observed a converse relationship in which whites more clearly demonstrated a crime-parental absence bond than blacks. Matsueda and Heimer (1987) acknowledge finding a stronger crime–broken home connection in black as opposed to white youth, but go on to state that the process was similar for both groups. Given the mixed nature of outcomes on race as a moderator of the crime–broken home relationship, it is likely that the effect of race on this relationship is a function of additional factors. Two such factors might be social class and gender. Farnworth (1984), for one, observed minimal relationship between parental absence and delinquency in a group of 15-year-old lower socioeconomic status males and females, although the connection was slightly stronger in males than females.

The meaningfulness of the nexus presumed to exist between broken homes and crime is brought into question by data originating out of the Cambridge-Somerville project. McCord, McCord, and Zola (1959) argue that conflict within the home is more critical than loss of a parent in the genesis of subsequent patterns of criminal conduct. These authors go on to state that intact families characterized by conflict and neglect were two times more likely to produce delinquent offspring than homes broken by divorce or death. Nevertheless, parental absence may exacerbate a bad home situation, as McCord, McCord, and Thurber (1963) observed in a group of delinquents hailing from conflict-ridden families in which the mother worked outside the home. A wealth of additional research supports the McCords' claims that it is family conflict, and not parental absence, that is responsible for the bulk of variance observed in family studies on crime and delinquency (compare Hetherington, Cox, & Cox, 1979; Laub & Sampson, 1988; Robins, 1966; Van Voorhis et al., 1988). Interestingly, Rutter and Giller (1984) note that family conflict tends to affect male children more than it does female children. A broken home or parental absence may owe its place in the criminal-science scenario to its common association with parental and family turmoil.

The Abusive Home

It has been clearly established that many abused children grow up to be physically abusive themselves (Allan, 1978; Spinetta & Rigler, 1972). Straus, Gelles, and Steinmetz (1980) determined that persons who had been subjected to regular doses of physical abuse during their formative years were significantly more likely to utilize physical force in their own relationships, particularly those involving spouses and children, than persons not exposed to physical abuse. Likewise, investigators have established the presence of a coalition involving physical abuse during childhood and later displays of physical aggression (George & Main, 1980), although not all of the evidence is consistent with the supposition that exposure to physical abuse as a youngster leads one to be abusive as an adult (Elmer, 1977). This area of research also suffers from a number of serious methodological shortcomings, not the least of which is the nearly exclusive reliance on official arrest records (Widom, 1989). Hence, while there are data to suggest that early socialization experiences influence the manner in which one deals with conflict and frustration in later life, there is no clear indication of an association between early physical abuse and later criminality. Maternal neglect has also been shown to be largely unrelated to later criminality (Henggeler, McKee, & Borduin, 1989).

As was previously indicated, research linking crime and early abuse has produced equivocal outcomes. Reid, Taplin, and Loeber (1981), for instance, report that approximately one out of every three antisocial boys referred for treatment had been physically abused by a caretaker at some point in his life. However, Langevin et al. (1983) failed to locate a more extensive history of physical abuse in the backgrounds of 109 convicted murderers compared to what was identified in the histories of a sample of nonviolent offenders. In a study of adults admitted to the Boston City Hospital, Climent and Ervin (1972) determined that relative to a group of nonviolent control patients, violent and criminally assaultive patients were more likely to have been raised in physically abuse homes. Although findings such as those reported by Reid et al. and Climent and Ervin are interesting, they are limited by faulty research designs. Utilizing a more methodologically rigorous design, Widom (1989) noticed slightly higher rates of juvenile (26 vs. 17%) and adult (29 vs. 21%) criminal arrest in the backgrounds of abused and neglected children compared to a group of matched controls, although even this study does not confirm the presence of a causal connection between crime and childhood abuse.

Owing to the flawed methodological-conceptual state of the research on abusive homes and crime, a number of alternative explanations of the abuse-crime relationship come to mind. Accordingly, physical abuse may simply reflect the presence of inadequate parent-child bonding, a feature which may be more strongly tied to later criminality than an abusive home. Furthermore, without condoning child abuse we can see how it may reflect the misguided attempts of a frustrated parent to exert control over a child who is already well down the road to a life of serious criminal involvement. All in all, however, we can deduce very little about the proposed affiliation between physical abuse and crime since the few studies that have been conducted on this issue have been marred by methodological oversights and mixed outcomes.

Parenting Style

The manner in which a parent disciplines his or her child is often a barometer of the quality of the relationship between parent and child. It also likely contributes to the eventual development (or lack of development) of self-control in the child. We might well ask why the child in our discussion on physical abuse and crime is so far down the road toward antisociality. The answer may be found in the approach the child's parents took in disciplining him or her for transgressions of parental rules and dictates. Parenting or disciplinary style therefore entails a fourth possible avenue by which family socialization may impact on later criminal outcomes.

Baumrind (1978) observed the play of a group of bright, middle-class children in nursery school and laboratory settings and found that one group of children came across as content, curious, and self-reliant while another group presented as sad, withdrawn, and poorly controlled. Analyzing the disciplinary approach exercised by the parents of children in these two groups, Baumrind determined that a parenting style characterized by control and support or nurturance was found to a much higher degree in the parents of the better adjusted children. Shore (1971) argues that parental discipline varies along three dimensions—intensity, consistency, and quality—and that parents who are moderate, consistent, and inductive (who rely on explanation and withdrawal of affection rather than physical punishment) tend to produce children who are better able to internalize the prohibitions of their parents. We see, then, that discipline and parenting style correspond with internalization of parental values, something which may be lacking in many criminal offenders.

What forms of parenting are most criminals likely to have been exposed to as they were growing up? McCord, McCord, and Zola (1959) discuss the importance of lax and erratic models of discipline in the early backgrounds of delinquents and criminal offenders, and note that delinquency is quite uncommon in situations where fathers are consistent in their approach to discipline. Bennett (1960) adds that inconsistent, erratic forms of discipline are a robust correlate of later delinquency. Along similar lines, Hirschi (1969) states that many of the delinquents in his sample of older adolescents reported a lack of close parental supervision and complained that the rules were often never fully explained.

Results analogous to these have been authenticated in English (West & Farrington, 1973), Finish (Pulkkinnen, 1980), and Swedish (Olweus, 1980) samples. A group of researchers operating out of Tel Aviv University in Israel and headed by Shlomo Giora Shoham (Shoham et al., 1987) ascertained that attachment to family members served to inhibit impulsive violence, while parental impunativeness facilitated planned violence in a group of incarcerated Israeli offenders. Studies on the intergenerational transmission of antisocial behavior suggest that aggressive families tend to produce aggressive, and in some cases criminal, offspring (Huesmann & Eron, 1985; McCord, 1988).

Conducting a meta-analysis of early predictors of delinquency, Loeber and Dishion (1983) found a composite measure of family management technique to be the single best predictor of subsequent delinquency. In a study of British youth, Wilson (1980) ascertained that the level of parental supervision was more strongly associated with later delinquency than any of the other variables he investigated. Kazdin (1985) adds that the parents of delinquents are often lacking in family management skills, a finding which may help identify ways by which the criminological effect of parenting style might be ameliorated. Attempting to forge a theoretical link between crime and family management techniques, Patterson (1986) argues that inept parenting leads to a pattern of peer rejection, school failure, and low self-esteem, which then places the individual at increased risk for subsequent delinquency. Patterson contends further that poor parenting skills are often passed on from one generation to the next, as evidenced by his observation that the inferior parenting practices of grandparents tend to correlate with the antisocial behavior of both their offspring and grandchildren (Elder, Caspi, & Downey, 1983; Huesmann et al., 1984).

Poor parenting seems particularly pertinent to our investigation of serious criminality, given that research indicates lax parental discipline and inadequate supervision are quite common in the families of repeat delinquent offenders (Wilson, 1980) and adult recidivists (McCord, 1979). Exactly how one's style of parenting contributes to the unfolding of a criminal lifestyle is largely unknown at this point, but it may have something to do with the process of internalization. Authoritarian and lax forms of discipline make it difficult for children to internalize parental attitudes, values, and beliefs. There is also the corollary finding that exposeure to rigid, "position-oriented" approaches to discipline lead to the development of ineffective cognitive problem-solving strategies on the part of the affected child (Bearison & Cassel, 1975). Whatever the explanation, there seems to be little doubt that parenting style plays a significant role in the generation of criminal forms of adjustment across a wide spectrum of specific family situations.

Control theories of criminological thought have examined crime in light of the socializing effects of the parent-child social bond (Hirschi, 1969). In contrast to this emphasis on indirect or informal social control, direct controls have been largely ignored by many criminal-science investigators. Wells and Rankin (1988) argue that part of the problem with past research on direct social control is the manner in which it has been defined. When these two investigators reconceptualized direct control in terms of three specific behaviors—normative regulation, monitoring, punishment—they observed a reasonably strong relationship between direct parental control and delinquency. Utilizing data from the Youth in Transition project, Rankin and Wells (1990) investigated the relationship between direct (discipline) and indirect (attachment) forms of social control and found them to be independent. They also correlated strictness, contingency of punishment, and strength of punishment with delinquent outcome, and ascertained that these features of parental disciplinary style were differentially linked to crime: medium strictness, greater contingency, and decreased punishment strength corresponding with lower levels of delinquency.

Crime and the Family

An article by Schulman (1987) ponders why there isn't more street crime in light of the many temptations available to disaffected, urban youth. He answers his own question with the assertion that parents who teach their children to be kind, just, and responsible account for this outcome. In an investigation of young men and women originating in disadvantaged homes yet leading law-abiding lives, Lee (1985) found a pattern of close-knit families in which discipline was moderately strict and consistent and where parents insisted that their children meet their obligations in school as well as at home. This helps explain why some homes produce more delinquents than other homes (Loeber & Dishion, 1983). As the present review attests, parental attitude and parenting style appear to be particularly influential in the development of subsequent patterns of significant criminal involvement.

Despite the role the family obviously plays in the evolution of criminal behavior, offenders still tend to be in the minority when it comes to regular law-violating conduct within their families of origin. In fact, research has consistently shown that many offenders are the sole members of their families with a history of delinquent and/or criminal behavior (Farrington, 1979; Kvaraceus, 1945; Walters & White, 1987). After interviewing a group of violent delinquents, Fagan and Wexler (1987) surmised that family environment seemed to be less important than outside social influences (school, peers) in shaping future delinquent behavior. Though we might take issue with Fagan and Wexler's conclusions, it would be foolhardy of us to overlook extra-familial agents of socialization in our review of situational correlates of criminal behavior.

EXTRA-FAMILIAL SOURCES OF SOCIALIZATION

It has been noted for some time now that communities lacking social integration are often afflicted with higher-than-average levels of delinquency and crime (Maccoby, Johnson, & Church, 1958). Without a clear sense of community or network of friends and relatives, the neighborhood becomes a haven for crooks, thieves, and drug dealers. On the other hand, a community characterized by solidarity and cohesion should provide a positive socialization experience that might then compensate for other criminogenic factors. This may explain why Tagaki and Platt (1978) found such low levels of crime in San Francisco's Chinatown district despite a high rate of both poverty and unemployment. This may also explain why urbanization is so much more strongly associated with crime on the aggregate than on the individual level. In this section we examine three sources of extrafamilial socialization: peers, schools, and the mass media.

Peers

Peers are important agents of socialization in that they are a source of emotional support and provide the adolescent with specific behavioral norms (Panella, Cooper, & Henggeler, 1982). Moreover, aggressiveness has been found to correlate with the level of peer rejection (Hartup, 1983). McCord, McCord, and Zola (1959) discovered that 75 percent of their subjects who associated with delinquent peers wound up with criminal records, while only 30 percent of the subjects who had not associated with delinquent peers encountered legal difficulties. In advancing their differential association theory of criminality, Sutherland and Cressey (1978) presumed that criminal behavior was learned through association with those already involved in crime, particularly peers. Despite evidence that differential association is an important factor in delinquency development, it should not be considered independent of various family influences (compare Rutter & Giller, 1984). Accordingly, Rohrer and Edmonson (1960) determined that black youth in New Orleans were strongly influenced by significant adults in the home, but that when such role models were absent these youth frequently joined juvenile gangs as a means of filling this void. Similar results were recorded in a sample of Oregon youth (Patterson & Dishion, 1985).

Comparing peer associations with parental associations and the pro-social definitions provided by parents and friends, Johnson and his colleagues (1987) discovered that associations with drug-using friends had, by far, the strongest effect on whether a subject eventually used drugs himself. Similarly, Fagan and Wexler (1987) ascertained that the effect of peer associations superceded the influence of family factors in predicting the criminal activities of 99 violent delinquents. Peer relationships, like child-parent bonding, temperament, and intelligence, can also serve a protective function for otherwise vulnerable youth. Feldman, Caplinger, and Wodarski (1983), for example, determined that high-risk adolescents with higher levels of exposure to pro-social peers were significantly less likely to engage in delinquent acts than high-risk youth exhibiting low levels of exposure to pro-social peers. It would seem, then, that peer relationships might serve either a criminogenic or protective function, depending upon the peer group with which one associates.

There is ample evidence to indicate that juveniles are encouraged by peers to commit various crimes. Scott (1966), for one, determined that a large majority of the crimes perpetrated by juveniles are committed in the company of other youth. In a more recent study it was ascertained that loyalty to and regular participation in a delinquent peer group were the most powerful predictors of serious and repetitive criminality, accounting for between 10 and 31 percent of the variance in the dependent measures (Hanson et al., 1984). Likewise, Elliott, Huizinga, and Ageton (1985) found delinquent friends to be the strongest correlate of subsequent offending in a longitudinal investigation of delinquency outcomes. There are also data sufficient to suggest that an individual enhances his or her prospects of remaining crime free by disengaging from certain peer groups. Hence, West (1982) reports that by age 18 or 19, 95 percent of his group of ''persistent'' recidivists were still associating with an all-male peer group in comparison to only 62 percent of his ''temporary'' recidivists.

When we speak of the influence of peers on delinquency and crime, the topic of juvenile gangs comes up almost naturally. In a now-classic study on adolescent gangs, Thrasher (1927) discussed how leaders, planned action, and group loyalty gave rise to these gangs. Cloward and Ohlin (1960) added further to our knowledge by proposing that juvenile gangs serve several functions, but are most notably a means by which the individual deals with alienation from society, derives collective sources of deviant solutions to everyday problems, and finds ways to justify and rationalize his or her antisocial behavior. Yablonsky (1966), however, asserts that most juvenile gangs are best conceptualized as loosely organized near-groups whose constituency changes regularly and with whom only the most disturbed, violent members actively identify. Likewise, it may be inappropriate to refer to juvenile gangs as criminal subcultures, in that there is little commonality in the criminal activities of group members except for smaller cliques within the gang (Short, Tennyson, & Howard, 1966). Short et al. add that conflict with authority and retreat from responsible society are the ties that bind most juvenile gangs.

Since lower-socioeconomic-status juveniles are more likely to associate with delinquent peers than middle-class youth (Cloward & Ohlin, 1960), there is always the possibility that social class may play a moderating role in the crime-peer relationship. Nonetheless, middle-class adolescent gangs also exist (Myerhoff & Myerhoff, 1966). Moreover, Erickson and Empey (1965) were unable to discern an interaction between social class and peer identification in their study on the correlates of delinquent behavior. These authors add that the relatively small social class effect observed in their study may have been entirely a result of the social-class variable's affiliation with peer identification and/or association. Whereas these results highlight the potential influence of peers on the development of delinquent behavior, the degree to which these findings tell us anything about serious adult criminality is largely unknown at this point in time.

School

The first few weeks of school can be a traumatic experience for a young child. This is probably the first time the child has had demands placed upon him or her from outside the family. School is also where the child is first exposed to the rules of outside authorities. Some children seem better able to make the adjustment than others. Research conducted since the mid-1930s suggests that delinquents characteristically experience social, academic, and disciplinary adjustment problems at school (Gottfredson, 1981). These problems normally begin early in the future delinquent's school career, often before the child is midway through the primary school years, and continue until the individual eventually drops out of school (compare Glueck & Glueck, 1950, 1968). The Gluecks (1968) report that only 2 percent of their sample of delinquents graduated from high school in comparison to 22 percent of the control subjects. In an era where high school graduation has become more commonplace, Walters and White (1987) note that only 12 percent of their sample of recidivistic federal offenders graduated from high school, although many more had acquired their General Equivalency Diplomas, often while in prison.

Even though there is little doubt that delinquents and criminals are largely unsuccessful in school, there is a great deal more uncertainty as to the nature of this relationship. Polk and Schafer (1972) argue that schools cause crime and delinquency by labeling or stigmatizing certain students. Comparing college-preparatory and noncollege track students in two high schools, these investigators determined that the rates of misconduct and official accounts of delinquency were higher in the noncollege track students. However, this study suffers from the fact that subjects were not randomly assigned to conditions (college-preparatory track vs. noncollege track) and so factors involved in the selection process, such as interest patterns, intelligence, and socioeconomic status, may have actually produced the results observed. In fact, Bachman, Green, and Wirtanen (1971) discovered that by holding social class and ability constant, any relationship that may have existed between delinquency and tracking in their sample of high school students disappeared entirely.

The possibility exists that some children enter school with certain characteristics that interfere with their ability to succeed in this environment, but which encourage their continued involvement in crime. Analyzing data from the Cambridge-Somerville longitudinal project, Powers and Witmer (1951) discovered that boys who later became delinquent were often described by their teachers in the primary school years as impulsive, distractible, aggressive, and troublesome. West (1983) witnessed a fairly strong relationship between early teacher ratings of troublesomeness and subsequent delinquency in a longitudinal analysis of data collected on a group of working-class British male youth. Although this "common cause" explanation for the link presumed to exist between crime and school difficulties is not without certain limitations, it would appear to have more merit than Polk and Schafer's (1972) overly simplistic causative explanation.

The characteristics of schools have also been investigated in relationship to their potential impact on delinquency. One fairly common observation is that the delinquency rate found in a particular school tends to correlate with the percentage of working-class youth in that school (Kratcoski & Kratcoski, 1977). Rutter et al. (1979) found socioeconomic status and intelligence to be more salient correlates of delinquency than school variables, although the latter did tend to moderate the effect of socioeconomic status and intelligence slightly. As with the results of an earlier study (Coleman et al., 1966), Rutter and his colleagues were unable to discern a relationship between delinquency and such characteristics as the physical plant or teacher-pupil ratio. They did, however, notice a connection between delinquency and a school's intellectual balance (a healthy proportion of gifted students who demonstrate a positive attitude toward school and set a good example for other students) and general ethos (an attitude in which good performance is reinforced and disciplinary problems are handled in a firm but fair manner) to the advantage of schools displaying such characteristics. An association has also been observed between decreased levels of delinquency and clear and consistent, rather than authoritarian, models of school disciplinary practice (Finlayson & Loughran, 1976; Gottfredson, 1983).

Some parents reason that placing a troublesome adolescent in a private or parochial school, where discipline is adhered to more stringently than in many public schools, may provide the structure this youth so sorely needs. In a survey of nearly 60,000 students attending over 1,000 public, private, and parochial schools in 1980, Coleman, Hoffer, and Kilgore (1982) witnessed more problems with fighting, vandalism, substance abuse, and verbal assaults on teachers in public as compared to private and parochial schools. Even though Coleman et al. attempted to control for certain subject characteristics in order to eliminate the possibility of a "third-variable" explanation of their results, the feasibility of such third-variable inferences remains strong. Consequently, while private and parochial schools tend to have fewer problems with serious delinquency than many public schools, this may be partly because it is normally easier for private and/or parochial schools to discharge students who continue engaging in disruptive behavior despite warnings from school officials.

Based on the belief that school variables are important in the eventual development of delinquent involvement, several experimental programs have been implemented. In a large-scale study of 400 male youth with serious maladjustment problems and below-average academic ability, Ahlstrom and Havighurst (1971) randomly assigned subjects to a special work-study program or regular school milieu. Although youth in the experimental group gave the program positive marks, they were no less likely to be in trouble with the law six years later than students in the control group. Reckless and Dinitz (1972) took a group of troublesome juveniles about to enter junior high school and randomly assigned half to a experimental school program that emphasized remedial reading, the rights of others, and positive role models, and the other half to a traditional junior high classroom. Four years later there were no significant differences between the two groups in terms of either the frequency or severity of delinquent behavior.

Schweinhart and Weikart (1983) studied high-risk three- and four-year-olds in one of the poorest neighborhoods in Ypsilanti, Michigan. The children in this study were randomly assigned to one of two groups: an experimental group that participated in a special preschool program 12 hours a week for a period of one to two years, and a control group that received no special attention. As teenagers, the experimental-group participants were significantly less likely to have been arrested or report involvement in one or more arrestable crimes compared to a group of control subjects. Thus, while interventions aimed at adolescents may be ineffective in changing trends in delinquent behavior, interventions taking place at the preschool level may be more successful.

There are two general explanations of the apparent interface between delinquency and school adjustment. Strain theory argues that the middle-class school environment creates delinquent behavior because of the frustration it engenders in lower-class students. This theory predicts that the rate of criminality should fall once high-delinquency students drop out of school (Cloward & Ohlin, 1960). Control theorists, on the other hand, maintain that since school provides youth with a sense of institutional control we should witness increased levels of criminality once delinquents drop out of school (Hirschi, 1969). Studies conducted prior to 1980 tended to support the strain theory interpretation of the crime-school nexus (Elliott, 1966; Elliott & Voss, 1974; LeBlanc, Biron, & Pronovost, 1979). However, more recent investigations provide increased confirmation of the predictions of social control theorists (Bachman et al., 1971, 1978; Polk et al., 1981; Shavit & Rattner, 1988). Moreover, Farrington et al. (1986) were unable to identify meaningful differences in the crime rate of fully employed subjects before and after they dropped out of school, although a post-dropout rise in crime was noted in unemployed subjects. In what is perhaps the most methodologically sound study thus far conducted on this subject, Thornberry, Moore, and Christenson (1985) examined the short- and long-term effects of school dropout on subsequent delinquent patterns in a sample of 10,000 male Philadelphians. Controlling for the effects of age and postschool experience, Thornberry et al. determined that dropping out of school was followed by increased short- and long-term patterns of delinquent involvement.

Mass Media

In modern society we experience more than ever the effects of television, movies, newspapers, and books. It is said that the average household watches a total of several hours of television each day (Comstock, 1980). This is more time than the average child spends with a parent, teacher, or close friend. Consequently, television and other mass media have assumed increased importance as agents of socialization over the past several decades. It is no wonder, then, that many persons have raised concerns about the content of many modern films and television programs. In fact, a National Institute of Mental Health update (1962, p. 89) announced the presence of "a causal relationship between viewing televised violence and later aggressive behavior."

Although the conclusions offered in this NIMH update have been criticized (Freedman, 1984), they are not without their proponents, public as well as scientific. Aggregate studies, for one, are generally supportive of the crime–media violence hypothesis. After such highly publicized events as the assassination of President John F. Kennedy in 1963 and the murder of eight nurses by Richard Speck in 1966, the rate of violent criminality rose across the nation (Berkowitz & Macaulay, 1971). Phillips (1983) conducted several time-series regression analyses of championship heavyweight prize fights between 1973 and 1978, and found a 12 percent increase in the aggregate homicide rate following each of the fights. The effect was strongest for the more highly publicized matches, peaked three days after the fights, and was found to be independent of various seasonal effects. Phillips (1983) also denotes a temporary, but significant, decline in homicides in London, England, following public executions, the magnitude of the effect being positively correlated with the amount of media attention paid each execution. However, this relationship may have been based on a spurious empirical foundation, in that Milavsky (n.d.) uncovered several errors in the data analyses that when corrected resulted in nonsignificant findings.

Examining long-range trends in the relationship between violent television content and national crime statistics, Clark and Blackenburg (1972) failed to identify an association between these two variables. Although Hennigan and her colleagues (1982) determined that larceny rates increased with the introduction of television in the early to mid-1950s, there was no media effect for burglary, auto theft, or violent criminality. Messner (1986) examined the relationship between levels of televised violence and assault, rape, and robbery rates and ascertained that the association was negative (greater exposure to violent television programming correlating with lower rates of violent criminality). Messner interpreted these findings as supporting a "criminal subculture/routine activities" explanation of the relationship between crime and the mass media. In other words, television shows not only actively discourage association with the criminal subculture through negative portrayals of crime and criminals but also promote certain behaviors (such as staying at home and watching TV) that are incompatible with a criminal lifestyle.

One of the primary criticisms leveled against aggregate studies is that they fail to control for the effects of such influences as history and maturation. The television viewing habits of incarcerated violent and property offenders failed to differ in one micro-level (nonaggregate) study of violence in inmates' choices of programs (Menzies, 1971). Analysis of micro-level, cross-sectional data by Friedman and Johnson (1972) revealed that aggressive eighth and ninth graders not only watched more television but were also more likely to list violent programs among their favorite television shows than nonaggressive eighth and ninth graders. On the other hand, McCarthy et al. (1975) observed a small association between television viewing and aggressiveness but no relationship between violent television viewing and delinquency, fighting, or conflict with one's parents.

Heath, Kruttschnitt, and Ward (1986) set out to investigate the impact of television violence and physical abuse on subsequent criminality, and discovered that watching violent television shows only correlated with violent criminality when accompanied by parental abuse within the home. Therefore, the presence of a live role model of aggressiveness may be a necessary condition if television violence is to have an effect on subsequent behavior. Being cross-sectional in nature, however, studies such as these suffer from a number of serious methodological defects; longitudinal designs, since they provide one with the opportunity to examine a subject's behavior over time, may yield more reliable results.

In one longitudinal investigation, researchers studied the connection between the television viewing habits of a large group of third graders and peer ratings of aggressiveness. Initial outcomes revealed that boys who preferred violent shows were more frequently rated as aggressive by their peers than boys who preferred less violent television programs (Eron et al., 1972; Lefkowitz et al., 1977). Ten years later, when these boys were 18 and 19 years of age, the relationship between television watching habits at age 8 or 9 and peer ratings of aggressiveness at age 18 or 19 was still significant. In fact, Lefkowitz et al. (1977) determined that initial television watching preferences and follow-up aggressiveness correlated .31 while initial aggressiveness and follow-up television watching preferences correlated only .01. They then used this to support their conclusion that watching violent television programs was the "cause" of later aggressive behavior. Ten years after the first follow-up, a second follow-up revealed that aggressiveness and criminality both corresponded with the television viewing habits of subjects 20 years earlier (Huesmann et al., 1984).

Despite the obvious advantages of this study over aggregate and cross-sectional investigations, several methodological problems nevertheless exist. For one, Eron and his colleagues were not able to randomly assign subjects to conditions. Consequently, there is always the possibility that preexisting characteristics (which led violence-prone children to select violent TV programs in the first place) were responsible for the results attained by this group of investigators. Second, Eron et al. failed to account for the differential role of gender, since an aggression–television viewing relationship was noted only for male subjects (Kay, 1972). Third, the level of exposure to television violence was not measured, just a report by the mothers as to their child's favorite TV program (Wilson & Herrnstein, 1985). Lastly, a host of statistical problems limit the validity of the results obtained (Rogosa, 1980).

Two longitudinal studies conducted within the past decade have had as one of their primary goals methodologically rigorous examination of the crime–mass media connection. Milavsky et al. (1982) ascertained that compared to children whose taste in television programs favored nonviolent shows, children who preferred violent television programs were more prone to exhibit aggressive behavior three years later. However, the effect was relatively small (accounting for only 1% of the variance in aggressiveness) and disappeared nearly entirely when the individual contributions of social class and race were partialed out. Huesmann, Lagerspetz, and Eron (1984) examined the relationship between violent-television-viewing habits and aggressiveness, again using a three-year follow-up, in one sample of children attending elementary school in a Chicago suburb and another sample of children in public school in Turku, Finland. Though the outcome of this study demonstrates the presence of a relationship between aggressiveness and exposure to violent television programming, independent of preexisting tendencies for aggressive behavior, the level of concordance was somewhat weaker than that observed in the earlier New York studies (Eron et al., 1972). Furthermore, the crime–television violence connection tends to be stronger in younger children (Milavsky et al., 1982) and those who identify with violent fictional characters (Huesmann et al., 1984).

Although more methodologically sound than Eron et al.'s original investigation, the Milavsky and Huesmann studies still suffer from the fact that subjects were not randomly assigned to conditions. In fact, this limitation applies to all aggregate, cross-sectional, and longitudinal studies conducted in this area of research. Laboratory studies, on the other hand, provide a more exact test of the crime-media hypothesis. The impact of exposure to various aspects of the mass media on aggressive behavior has been found in young children (Bandura, Ross, & Ross, 1963), adolescents (Hartman, 1969), and college students (Berkowitz & Rawlings, 1963) using such diverse definitions of violence as punching a Bobo doll (Bandura et al., 1963), shocking a confederate (Berkowitz & Geen, 1966), and engaging in minor delinquent acts (Belson, 1978). However, the principal strength of laboratory studies is also their greatest weakness. Because such designs require maximal experimental control over extraneous variables, laboratory studies often produce modest effects that are difficult to generalize to real-life situations, specifically because of the artificiality of the experimental manipulations (Cook, Kendzierski, & Thomas, 1983).

A series of naturalistic experiments were devised in an effort to overcome the limited external validity of laboratory studies while still retaining a certain degree of experimental control. In an early naturalistic investigation, Feshback and Singer (1971) randomly assigned dormitories of boys to two groups, one of which viewed violent television shows (for example, "Batman") and the other of which viewed nonviolent shows (for example, "Lassie") for a period of six weeks. Contrary to predictions, boys in the nonviolent condition engaged in more violent activity than boys exposed to the violent television programs. However, there is always the possibility that this unanticipated outcome was largely a result of the frustration experienced by boys in the nonviolent condition at having been deprived of their favorite television shows.

A second set of studies verified that preschool children exposed to violent programming displayed higher levels of interpersonal aggression provided they were predisposed to such behavior (Friedrich & Stein, 1973; Stein & Friedrich, 1972). In this same study it was reported that pro-social programs like "Mr. Rogers' Neighborhood" seemed to produce positive outcomes in some children by teaching them important moral lessons and social skills that, in turn, might aid them in learning how to delay gratification or get along with peers.

Several cottages of troublesome male youth enrolled in a Belgian school were randomly divided into two groups, one which viewed violent films each evening for one week and one which watched nonviolent films each evening for one week (Leyens et al., 1975). Though there was a small increase in aggressiveness for boys in one of the cottages exposed to violent films, the significance of these findings was mitigated by the fact that this study contained serious methodological and statistical oversights (Freedman, 1984). Assessing the influence of violent films on aggression in an American sample, Parke et al. (1977) note that a cottage of boys exposed to violent films for five days was more likely to engage in aggressive behavior than those enrolled in a nonviolent film condition. However, the effect was relatively minor and tended to dissipate over time. Similar to the results of the Stein and Friedrich (1972) study, Parke et al. discerned that the effect of violent film content on aggressiveness was most persistent in high-risk boys (those subjects high in aggression before the onset of the study).

Utilizing "mentally disabled" offenders housed in a maximum security state hospital, Dietz and Rada (1982) discovered a peak in the number of battery incidents taking place on the wards on days movies were shown. Unfortunately, their design did not allow for an analysis of the relationship between film content and violent behavior. Consequently, Harry (1983) directed a study in which the relationship between film content (adventure vs. nonadventure) and ward behavior in this same state hospital was examined. Subsequent analyses of the data obtained by Harry revealed a small but statistically significant increase in the number of assault and battery incidents following the presentation of adventure films but no such increase after nonadventure films were shown. However, the adventure-nonadventure variable seemed to have little effect on disorderly conduct incidents.

The majority of studies examining the association between television viewing habits and behavior have focused on aggressiveness in general rather than on criminality specifically. Milgram and Shotland (1973), however, scrutinized the crime–mass media hypothesis more directly in a rather ingenuous though highly deceptive naturalistic investigation. Randomly assigning subjects to conditions, Milgram and Shotland showed each group a different version of the same film. In one version a charity box is broken into and the perpetrator caught and punished; in a second version the perpetrator gets away with the crime; and in still yet another version the charity box scene is deleted altogether. Subjects were later apprised that they had won a free radio and instructed to pick their prize up at a local store. However, when they arrived at the store a clerk informed them that there were no more radios in stock. Although several charity boxes, strategically placed throughout the store, were broken into, there was no correlation between this behavior and the version of the film to which subjects were exposed.

Pornography has also been implicated as a potential mass-media correlate of criminality, with particular reference to sex crimes. In an interview held just prior to his execution on January 24, 1989, serial killer Ted Bundy informed psychologist James Dobson that his murderous behavior had been largely the result of alcohol and his interest in hard-core pornography. Bundy cited as support for his argument, an FBI study (1985) that showed that 35 incarcerated serial killers ranked pornography as their primary sexual interest, followed by compulsive masturbation, fetishism, and voyeurism. Most research, however, has failed to uncover a meaningful link between pornography and crime. Several laboratory investigations note an acceleration of rape fantasies, reduced sensitivity to the harmfulness of rape, and increased acceptance of common rape myths in male college students exposed to aggressive pornography (Donnerstein, 1984), but reviews of data collected under more naturalistic circumstances fail to support the argument that pornography promotes sexual violence (Kupperstein & Wilson, 1971; U.S. Commission on Obscenity & Pornography, 1970). In fact, one study has recorded results that suggest the presence of a negative or inverse relationship between exposure to pornography and the proclivity to offend sexually (Cook, Fosen, & Pacht, 1971).

Aggregate-level investigations tend to show a positive correlation between the availability of pornography and the frequency of reported rapes (Baron & Straus, 1987; Scott & Schwalm, 1988). However, this may indicate nothing more than that more permissive jurisdictions experience augmented levels of both pornography and sexual assault, a prospect supported by the outcome of a study administered by Chappell et al. (1971). Kutchinsky (1983) denotes that the incidence of rape has been found to decline slightly when aggressive pornography was made readily available in nations like the United States, Great Britain, West Germany, and Denmark. Hence, the majority of research studies in this area have yielded results largely inconsistent with the crime-pornography hypothesis, although in certain specific cases aggressive pornography may provide already deviant individuals with a focus for their perverse sexual attitudes and beliefs.

There are several possible interpretations of the apparent connection between crime and the mass media. Social learning theory, for instance, argues that a child imitates the behavior of aggressive television and mass-media role models. While the results of laboratory studies tend to confirm this explanation, support for the social learning hypothesis becomes more equivocal when we move from the laboratory into real-life situations (Freedman, 1984). Proponents of the catharsis approach, on the other hand, assert that media violence and pornography provide an outlet for the vicarious release of pent-up aggressive and sexual impulses, respectively, thereby making it less likely that such impulses will be expressed overtly. However, while there is evidence of a mild cathartic effect for pornography (Kutchinsky, 1983), there is very little empirical support for a cathartic interpretation of the aggression-media nexus, even in studies that show an inverse relationship between television violence and aggression and/or crime (Messner, 1986).

A third possibility is that television sells a lifestyle, as represented by such shows as "Dynasty" and "Lifestyles of the Rich and Famous," which is beyond most people's means and which generates frustration and possibly motivates the individual to explore illegal avenues through which this lifestyle might be obtained (Edgar, 1977). While the results of one study tend to support this supposition (Hennigan et al., 1982), the outcomes obtained in a second study failed to corroborate the frustrated lifestyle hypothesis (Messner, 1986). A variation on the aforementioned frustration hypothesis is that television teaches one that problems can be solved over the course of an hour or half-hour show and may retard the development of adequate frustration tolerance and problem-solving skills in young children confronted with the harsh reality that most problems take much longer than an hour to resolve. While this may be an intriguing possibility, the validity of such an assertion is vitiated somewhat by the fact that most studies denote that the effects of television on aggressive behavior are usually mild and short-lived (Freedman, 1984).

A final possibility is that there is no causal connection between mass-media violence and behavioral displays of aggressiveness and/or crime. In other words, media violence and aggressiveness may be linked by a variable that is common to both (that is, the third-variable hypothesis). Wilson and Herrnstein (1985), for example, contend that children who are predisposed to violent alternatives often feel alienated from their peers and so many find refuge in violent television programs or pornographic magazines. This explanation rests on a fairly stable empirical foundation, since several studies suggest that an individual must be predisposed to aggressiveness before television viewing will have a significant impact on his or her behavior (compare Friedrich & Stein, 1973; Parke et al., 1977). This third-variable explanation will be explored in greater depth in the conclusion of this chapter.

STRESS-RELATED FACTORS

Stress is a part of everyday life. Handled properly it can motivate and direct one's behavior toward constructive goals. Handled improperly it can induce ulcers, promote headaches, contribute to family conflict, and lead to a general state of malaise and discomfort. It seems logical, then, that stress may also invoke certain aggressive and criminological reactions in persons with limited coping ability. In this section we inquire into the possibility that a meaningful interface may exist between crime and one particular form of ineffective coping—that is, post-traumatic stress disorder (PTSD).

Although PTSD occurs in persons exposed to a wide variety of environmental stressors, Vietnam veterans are thought to display these symptoms more frequently and intensely than most others for several reasons, including the nature of the Vietnam War, the relative youthfulness of the U.S. fighting force in Vietnam, and the negative reactions veterans typically encountered upon their return from Southeast Asia (Marciniak, 1986). A November 1979 Bureau of Justice Statistics survey (1981b) revealed that approximately one-fourth of all state prisoners were veterans of military service. However, less than 5 percent of the total sample had ever served in Southeast Asia during the Vietnam conflict. In fact, Vietnam-era veterans were less likely to be confined in state facilities than nonveterans.

Studies administered in California (Pentland & Rothman, 1982), Massachusetts (*Trial* magazine, 1977), and Pennsylvania (Kehrer & Mittra, 1978) show that 25 percent of the prison populations in these states were veterans, approximately half of whom were Vietnam-era vets. Wilson and Zigelbaum (1983) contend that PTSD in Vietnam veterans is linked to the onset of criminal behavior through the survivor mode of behavioral functioning, although the data they summon in support of their argument is correlational in nature and subject to a variety of alternative interpretations.

If the PTSD explanation of crime were valid, we would expect to see a positive relationship between the level of combat exposure and PTSD symptoms. This is exactly what was observed in two studies in which Vietnam veterans served as subjects. In one study, PTSD was twice as prevalent in high- as opposed to low-combat exposure groups (Engendorf et al., 1981). According to the results of a second study (Yager, Laufer, & Gallops, 1984), high exposure to combat was associated with more crime (26.1 vs. 6.3%) and a greater number of violent offenses (4.9 vs. 0.6%) than low combat exposure. Shaw et al. (1987), on the other hand, denote that they were unable to discriminate between Vietnam veteran inmates and noncriminal Vietnam veterans on the basis of PTSD symptomatology. The incarcerated veterans did, however, present a larger number of antisocial personality diagnoses.

Time-series analyses of Bureau of Justice Statistics data reveal that 36 percent of the Vietnam veterans in that sample had been on probation at least once prior to age 20, and one-fourth had served time in a correctional facility previous to entering the military. Walters and White (1987) determined that 45 percent of the Vietnam veterans in their sample of habitual offenders had at least one documented arrest prior to entering the military. Very few of the 1,000 Vietnam veterans surveyed by Card (1983) had been arrested before or during their involvement in the conflict in Southeast Asia, and there were no differences in the rates of arrest obtained by Vietnam veterans, other veterans, and nonveterans from 1960 on (although the Vietnam vets had a higher conviction rate than persons falling into the other two categories). Shaw et al. (1987) note that a number of characteristics, among them authority conflict, dropping out of school, and incarceration, were more prominent in the premilitary lives of criminal as compared to noncriminal veterans. Drug usage, a possible third-variable explanation for the relationship observed between certain indicators of stress and crime, demonstrates an ambiguous relationship with PTSD—several studies showing an increased incidence (for example, Landolfi & Leclair, 1976) and other studies demonstrating a decreased incidence (Pentland & Rothman, 1982) of alcohol and drug abuse problems in Vietnam veterans.

Psychologist John Wilson (1978) estimates that between 30 and 70 percent of all veterans of Vietnam are currently suffering from signs of PTSD and that many of these individuals have experienced serious legal trouble as a result. In fact, Schultz (1982) estimates that one-fourth of all Vietnam veterans with heavy combat experience have been charged with a criminal offense since leaving the Southeast Asian theatre of operation. Likewise, Boulanger (1986) observed increased criminal violence and stress-related problems in veterans with higher levels of combat exposure. However, this study is hampered by a considerable number of methodological flaws and conceptual oversights (Beckerman & Fontana, 1989).

All in all, the fact that U.S. prisons are not overflowing with Vietnam veterans suggests that there are problems with the crime-PTSD hypothesis. Moreover, accepting such a proposition in the absence of convincing empirical support does a grave disservice to the thousands of U.S. servicemen who may have encountered problems in Vietnam but who chose to deal with those problems in ways other than by violating the law. Whereas there is some indication that stress-related factors, as represented by research linking PTSD with law-violating behavior, may play a role in crime genesis, this would appear to be rather minor compared to the effect drugs, peers, and family relations apparently exert on criminal outcomes.

THE PHYSICAL ENVIRONMENT

The physical environment is often overlooked by sociologists investigating situational correlates of crime. As far back as the mid-nineteenth century, Adolphe Quetelet observed that person crimes were more prevalent during the summer months and property crimes more common during the winter months (Lab & Hirschel, 1988). More to the point, the seasonality of criminal behavior has been consistently demonstrated, whether the data source is based on official, self-report, or victimization statistics (Block, 1984). A recent analysis of victimization data collected as part of the National Crime Survey (NCS), for instance, uncovered evidence that household larceny, unlawful entry, and rape display high levels of seasonality compared to robbery, motor vehicle theft, and simple assault (Bureau of Justice Statistics, 1988d). Since the general pattern appears to be for highly seasonal crimes to peak during the summer months, the possibility of a link between increased temperature and crime has been proposed.

In examining the influence of temperature on behavior, the results of several laboratory studies hint at a connection between uncomfortably warm temperatures and negative subject reactions (Bell, Garnand, & Heath, 1984; Griffitt & Veitch, 1971). Laboratory studies attempting to investigate the relationship between ambient temperature and aggression, on the other hand, have generated mixed outcomes, the association being positive in some instances and negative in others (Baron, 1972; Bell & Baron, 1976). This has led some investigators to speculate that the relationship between negative affect and temperature is curvilinear. In essence, proponents of the curvilinear hypothesis contend that rising temperatures contribute to a heightened level of agitation and possibly aggression up to the point where discomfort becomes so great that the behaviors that are emitted in an effort to seek relief from the high temperatures become increasingly incompatible with aggression. The results of at least one laboratory study provide support for this curvilinear theory of the ambient temperature–behavioral agitation relationship (Bell & Baron, 1976).

Baron and Ransberger (1978) were the first researchers to test the curvilinear hypothesis outside a laboratory setting. The results of this initial study identified an inverse relationship (inverted *U*) between 102 instances of collective violence (riots) and daily ambient temperatures. However, Carlsmith and Anderson (1979) have contested the authenticity of these findings by arguing that they were, in truth, artifactual given that there were significantly more days in the 80 to 85 degree temperature range than any of the other temperature range groups. After controlling for the prevalence of daily temperature, Carlsmith and Anderson unearthed a linear rather than curvilinear relationship between ambient temperature and occurrences of collective violence. Bell and Fusco (1986) nevertheless argue for more research on the prospect of a curvilinear association between temperature and aggression and the mediational nature of negative affect in the development of such a relationship.

Anderson and Anderson (1984) scrutinized the concordance of ambient temperature and crime rates in Chicago and Houston, and discovered a linear relationship between temperature and crimes like rape and murder even after adjustments were made for the level of nonviolent crime. Much the same outcome was observed when ambient temperature and violent criminality were examined in Dallas (Harries, Stadler, & Zdorkowski, 1984) and Des Moines (Cotton, 1986). Using crime and weather data from Indianapolis, Cotton (1986) found evidence of a curvilinear relationship between temperature and violent crime. However, this may simply reflect the fact that the rate of increase dropped once the ambient temperature climbed into the nineties, not that the pattern approached the shape of an inverted *U*. A composite graph of the crime-temperature relationship can be found in Figure 6.1.

By comparing aggregate rates of more (murder, rape, assault) and less (burglary, larceny-theft, robbery) violent crimes between the years 1971 and 1980, Anderson (1987) discovered that hot days (maximum temperature ≥ 90 degrees), hotter quarters of the year (April through September), and hotter years all correlated monotonically with violent criminality after the rate of nonviolent crime was partialed out. Anderson estimates that a year with ten more hot days than

Figure 6.1
Composite Graph of the Relationship between Violent Crime and Ambient Temperature

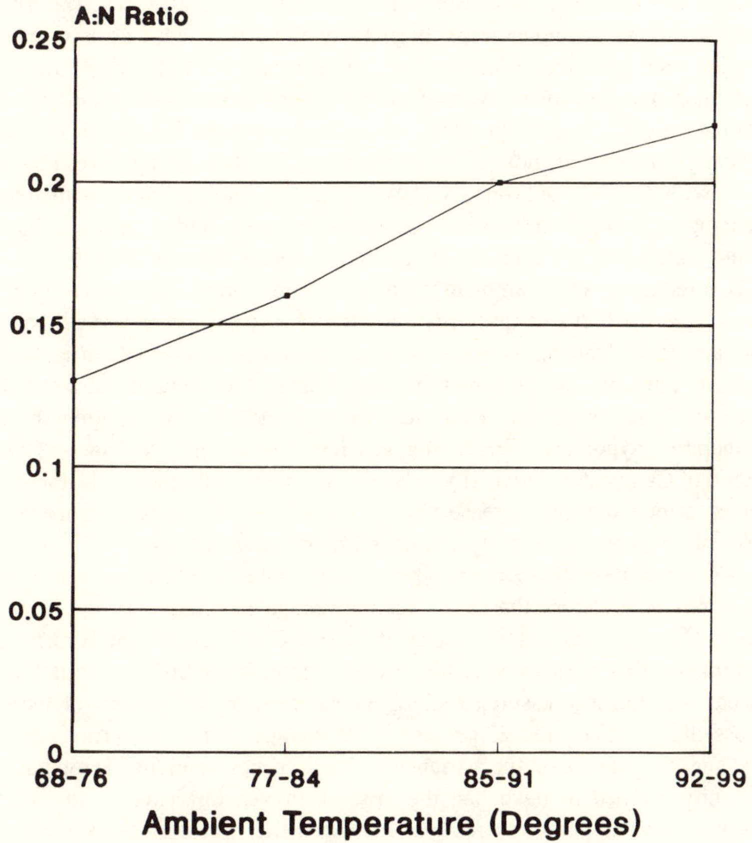

Note: A:N ratio is ratio of aggressive to nonaggressive crime in three cities.
Source: Data collected from Des Moines, Iowa (Cotton, 1986), Houston, Texas (Anderson & Anderson, 1984), and Indianapolis, Indiana (Cotton, 1986).

normal will produce a 7 percent increase in the rate of violent criminality. These results were found to be independent of various seasonal and time cycle effects, thereby eroding the alternative hypothesis that the outcome was simply a function of increased opportunity for interpersonal violence during the warmer months of the year. Although these findings tend to support the presence of a positive relationship between ambient temperature and violent crime, they fail to corroborate the curvilinear hypothesis.

Not all of the research on ambient temperature and violent crime has been positive. DeFronzo (1984) analyzed the proposed connection between three climatic factors and crime (violent, property) in the 142 largest metropolitan areas in the United States. The relationship between crime and these climatic variables was dwarfed by the much stronger association between crime and such nonclimatic variables as age, gender, family income, and unemployment. In only one instance did a climatic variable enter into a regression equation when both climatic and nonclimatic variables were correlated with various index crimes; that is, the burglary rate and number of hot days (temperature ≥ 90 degrees) suffered by a particular city. DeFronzo interprets this outcome as evidence of an opportunity-facilitation effect for temperature, since homes located in warmer climates are typically unoccupied more often than cooler climate housing developments.

Notwithstanding DeFronzo's (1984) negative findings, there still may be a meaningful connection between ambient temperature and violent criminality. In a study similar to the one conducted by DeFronzo, Michael and Zumpe (1987) discovered that average ambient temperature and crime failed to correspond when cities were the focus of investigation. However, they also observed that assault and rape peaked during the summer months and robbery crested during the winter months. This hints at the possibility that the mean temperature of a city may be too gross and inaccurate a measure to be useful in investigating the crime-temperature hypothesis. Reviewing research studies conducted since 1950, Cohn (1990) of Cambridge University in England concluded that while the more violent person crimes tend to increase linearly with higher temperatures, there is little association between property crime and temperature change.

Besides ambient temperature, there are a number of other meteorological and environmental factors that have been investigated relative to the question of crime. Using data collected in Charlotte, North Carolina, Lab and Hirschel (1988) determined that weather variables (temperature, humidity, precipitation, wind speed, barometric pressure, visibility) accounted for 25 percent of the change in assaultive crimes and 22 percent of the change in property crimes during the day and 13 percent of the variance in both crimes at night. Temperature and humidity seemed to have had the greatest impact on crime in this particular study, higher temperatures being associated with increased rates of violent crime and greater humidity corresponding with lower levels of both violent and property crime. Walters and Walters (1991) witnessed a moderately strong correlation between airborne pollen levels and 911 calls to police assessed during a four-year period, although this association appears to have been largely a consequence of the third-variable effect of ambient temperature.

Less well understood meterologic and environmental factors like nuclear fallout, air pollution, and lunar phase have also been studied as possible correlates of aggregate-level criminal involvement. Pellegrini (1987), for instance, found affirmation of a link between toxic radiation fallout levels in early childhood and data from the FBI's Uniform Crime Reports. These results are confounded, however, by the fact that the age distribution of the U.S. population around the time nuclear fallout levels were rising was skewed toward adolescents and adults, age groups known for above-average rates of rule-violating behavior. Rotton and Frey (1985) correlated crime rates with measures of air pollution, high temperature, low winds, and breakdowns in the ozone layer and discovered that all of these meterologic conditions evidenced a direct link with family disturbances and assaults against persons. However, there appears to be little support for the presence of an association between lunar phase and crime (Pupura, 1979; Wagner & Almeida, 1987). Population density and overcrowding have also been scrutinized as possible correlates of crime and/or delinquency, but the outcome of such research has been inconsistent and inconclusive (Baron & Needel, 1980; Schmidt & Keating, 1979).

Emile Durkheim (1951) attributed seasonal effects to cultural factors like the frequency and intensity of social contact. While this most assuredly plays a role in the results reviewed in this section, there is preliminary evidence to suggest that ambient temperature has a more direct effect on human behavior, aggression and violent criminality in particular. The issue then becomes whether such physical features as ambient temperature cause crime or simply exacerbate preexisting tendencies. Of even greater significance, however, is the question of intervention. If we find schools to be a cause of crime, then we can strive to make them less criminogenic; if we find parents to be a critical causal factor in crime genesis, then we can teach them to be more effective disciplinarians. But as any meteorologist can attest, we can do very little about the weather. Possibly all we can hope for is further investigation into how local modifications (for example, air-conditioning a prison cell house or opening up a fire hydrant in a ghetto neighborhood during a heat wave) may help alleviate some of the criminogenic and noncriminogenic problems associated with changes in the physical environment.

CONCLUSION

With the second leg of our journey through the correlates of criminality complete, one thing is clear: social scientists have invested a great deal of time and effort in examining the situational features of crime. The fact that the literature on situational correlates of crime could easily fill several volumes is living testimony of the significance scholars in the criminal science field assign this area of research endeavor. Drawing on the research reviewed in this chapter, it is evident that a great deal more work needs to be accomplished, although several preliminary conclusions can still be offered. If nothing else, the literature on situational correlates demonstrates that crime and situation variables correspond along a continuum that ranges from minimal relationship to a moderately strong association.

Commencing with variables at the lower end of the continuum (parental absence, poverty, social class, stress), we find factors that either fail to correlate with criminality or whose connection with crime appears to be the result of their common association with one or more third variables. Research conducted by McCord, McCord, and Zola (1959), and corroborated in several later investigations (Hetherington et al., 1979; Robins, 1966), suggests that conflict within the home is more vital than parental absence in the genesis of criminal behavior.

It may therefore be that a broken home corresponds with criminality largely because of its common association with family conflict and the fact that it is often more difficult to provide adequate supervision and discipline in a one-parent home than in a two-parent home. Poverty and social class also fail to explain criminality other than through their common association with parenting style, ethnic attitude, and such community factors as urbanization and peers. Although research on stress and crime is sparse, stress-related factors appear to hold very little for a science of criminal behavior at this juncture.

A second group of variables, while failing to explain crime from a causal standpoint, are quite effective identifiers of crime and delinquency. Consequently, a history of disciplinary problems in school or a spotty work record during one's adult years may be fairly reliable indicators of a possible criminal orientation, although they fail to answer causal questions, in part because their effect seems to be largely a function of third variables. This issue will be discussed in greater detail when we examine criminality from a theoretical standpoint, but suffice it to say at this point that providing jobs to ex-felons or switching a trouble-making juvenile from one school to another will be ineffective in controlling crime under ordinary circumstances. It should be noted, however, that if intervention takes place early, such as at the preschool level (see Schweinhart & Weikart, 1983), it may effect a change in the socialization process and actually help curb future criminality.

Third level variables, although they do not cause crime directly, tend to excite, stimulate, and exacerbate preexisting criminal tendencies. Included in this category are mass-media violence, ambient temperature, and substance abuse. Media accounts of violence may impact on criminal behavior by providing role models who display aggressive solutions to interpersonal problems. However, it is probably more accurate to state that television and media violence satisfy a modeling function only in children predisposed to aggressive behavior through inadequate socialization (Brody, 1977), violence in the home (Heath et al., 1986), or a particular mental state (Milavsky et al., 1982). Save a handful of laboratory studies, the preponderance of research on crime and ambient temperature has focused on aggregate data. As such, it is difficult to address the causal status of the apparent relationship between aggressive crime and increased ambient temperatures. In the absence of any solid evidence to the contrary, I speculate that high temperatures exert their effect on violent crime by lowering the tolerance threshold of persons predisposed to aggressive behavior.

Substance abuse appears to be a more meaningful and robust correlate of criminality than either media violence or ambient temperature. However, time-series analyses reveal that many offenders began offending long before they ever started using drugs or abusing alcohol. Consequently, while substance abuse is a powerful correlate of criminal involvement, one clearly capable of stimulating specific criminal events, it is much less consequential in explicating this involvement. In other words, instead of being a major cause of criminal conduct, substance abuse is just as much a reflection of criminal involvement as it is a stimulator of such activity. However, unlike employment and poor school adjustment, drugs do play a contributory role in certain specific criminal acts. Therefore, while eradicating the drug problem in the United States should theoretically lead to a noticeable drop in the crime rate, there is sufficient evidence to suggest that drugs are largely superfluous to the development of a significant number of criminal careers (Tuchfeld, Clayton, & Logan, 1982).

Finally, there are several variables linked to crime in such a manner that they betray the possible presence of a causal nexus. Though we are light years away from clearly delineating the specific causes of crime, two situation variables come to mind when the issue of cause is introduced: peers and family. Peers are important in the early evolution of a delinquent identity, while parental attitude and general style of discipline seem to have a noticeable effect on a wide number of factors, but most prominently on frustration tolerance, self-discipline, and empathy. The possibility that peers and family members assume a major etiological role in the flow of events that define the research foundation of criminal science is supported further by the fact that these elements often serve as the third variable in the noncausal relationships observed to exist between crime and factors like social class, school, and media violence.

The salience of peers and family in the evolution of criminal and delinquent forms of behavior suggests that socialization may be the situation variable most intimately involved in the evolution of significant criminality. Although socialization evolves from a number of different sources, one's parents and friends are two of the more important origins of such influence. Given that socialization begins relatively early in life, we can anticipate that the seeds of criminality are planted during the first few years of life. However, it is the dynamic interplay of sundry person and situation variables that captures the true essence of criminal development. This interaction will become the focus of our attention as we move to the next stage in our journey through the maze of research that is criminal science.

7

Correlates of Crime: The Person-Situation Interaction

In our efforts to understand human behavior it is important to consider the fact that each of us is a person functioning in a situational context. Examining this issue from a statistical standpoint, we find that in a two-way analysis of variance there are three main effects, one for variable *A*, one for variable *B*, and one for the interaction between *A* and *B*. A significant interaction between these two variables connotes that the effect of one variable varies or changes at different levels of the other variable. The primary emphasis in this chapter is on the theoretical interaction thought to occur between the person and his or her environmental circumstances. Toward this end we investigate the person × situation interaction as it encompasses certain physical, social, and psychological features of criminal involvement.

As we consider the nature of the person-situation interaction, our attention is drawn to the manner in which the person and situation merge to form a meaningful unit. In a study conducted some 30 years ago, Briggs, Wirt, and Johnson (1961) witnessed an interaction between personality functioning and family and/or social conditions in their effect on juvenile delinquency. The outcome of this study showed that juveniles achieving high scores on MMPI scales 4 (*Pd*), 8 (*Sc*), and 9 (*Ma*) were more apt to engage in a variety of delinquent behaviors than other subjects. However, the delinquency of adolescents in this group rose threefold if they had also encountered at least three separate adverse family events (for example, parental absence, economic hardship) compared to other juveniles who also elevated these three MMPI scales but had no history of adverse family conditions.

In a research study cited earlier it was determined that groups of criminal-justice experts, imprisoned offenders, and general-population respondents provided a number of different answers to queries about the causes of crime (Walters & White, 1988). One criminal justice expert, in fact, remarked that a whole host of factors cause crime and that all of the research in the world will never be able to identify the proper causative factors. This respondent was absolutely correct in asserting that myriad factors are involved in the criminal acts of specific individuals. However, as David Rowe (1987) points out, our purpose in examining the person-situation interaction is not to expound upon the variability found in a single individual but to explain patterns applicable to the overall population.

The person × situation interaction is a focus of attention for theorists operating from a transactional or interactionist perspective. However, many such theorists believe that the person and situation are so fundamentally intertwined that their interaction defies meaningful analysis (Magnusson & Allen, 1983). Rowe (1987), on the other hand, argues that while this may be true, efforts could still be directed at removing certain confounding person variations (like genetics) from the equation. In this chapter we take a somewhat different approach to the issue of interaction. Therefore, rather than concentrating on individual person or situation variables, as we did in the previous two chapters, our discussion focuses on three general behavioral domains in which person × situation interactions operate. First, however we discuss the interaction hierarchy, namely primary versus higher-order interaction.

PRIMARY VERSUS HIGHER-ORDER INTERACTION

A primary-level interaction, in the vernacular of the research scientist, occurs when the relationship between an independent and a dependent measure varies as a function of a second independent variable. Higher-order interactions, on the other hand, involve three or more independent variables. Expounding upon this conceptualization, we refer to primary-level interactions as person × situation transactions occurring relatively early in life, to be followed chronologically by higher-order interactions. Consequently, interpersonal exchanges between an infant and his or her caregiver during the first several years of life constitute a primary level of interaction, while interpersonal relationships in later childhood, some of which may involve this same caregiver, exist as higher-order interactions. The primary-level interaction frequently serves to buttress, promote, and stimulate higher-order interactions.

Within the context of our present review we examine primary and higher-order person × situation interactions as they form along three dimensions: physical, social, and psychological. In each case the primary-level interaction occurs when the child is very young (from birth up until age four or five). As the child approaches school age, he or she takes on greater responsibility and begins interacting with a wider network of physical, social, and psychological factors. Moreover, one's primary-level interactions frequently lay the groundwork and provide the context for later, or higher-order, interactions. As we embark on this third leg of our journey through the correlates of significant criminality, the necessity of considering this amalgamation of person and situational variables will become increasingly more apparent, even to the casual observer.

THE PHYSICAL DOMAIN

Primary-Level Interaction

Primary-level interactions taking place in the physical domain position themselves around the early life task of stimulus modulation (Walters, 1990b). This particular early life task subsists as an attempt by the human organism to handle the surge of environmental information and stimulation impinging upon its senses during the first several years of life. Stimulus modulation, therefore, concerns the manner in which one perceives, interprets, and organizes sensory information in an effort to achieve an optimal level of physiological arousal. Turning our attention to the person and situation variables that seem to be most strongly associated with this particular primary-level interaction, we can see how the complex interplay of different person and situation variables could bring about a variety of different human behaviors.

In Chapter 5 we discussed autonomic nervous system reactivity and arousal level as correlates of significant criminality. These influences may very well be grounded in the early temperament (including the genetic inheritance) and nascent environmental experiences of the infant and young child. Although testosterone is a controversial correlate of crime, there is some evidence to suggest that it not only corresponds with aggressive behavior but may also lead to increased levels of physical activity. Daitzman and Zuckerman (1980), for instance, ascertained that students high in testosterone were also more likely to be high on measures of sensation seeking. Furthermore, differential testosterone levels may help explain why males are eight or nine times more likely to be involved in crime than females (Simon & Sharma, 1979). By way of summary, heredity, temperament, autonomic reactivity, arousal level, and testosterone are the person variables that seem most intimately tied to primary-level interactions in the physical domain.

On the situation side of the equation we find parental discipline and level of environmental stimulation. The role of parenting style and discipline in criminal development was a primary topic in Chapter 6. Both factors appear to play an integral role in the chain of events that lead some children to prefer higher levels of sensory stimulation than others. Likewise, it is difficult to discuss the issue of stimulus modulation without also taking into account the kinds of stimulation to which one is primarily attracted. DeMyer-Gapin and Scott (1977), for instance, report that a group of antisocial children were initially more attentive to novel, as opposed to repetitive, stimuli but wound up habituating more rapidly to both relative to a group of neurotic children.

While a discussion of the individual person and situation variables that contribute to the evolution of stimulus modulation tendencies in children may prove interesting, we must explore the interaction of person and situation variables if we wish to fully comprehend the nature of the stimulus modulation life task. Toward this end, two independently administered studies revealed that children possessing difficult temperaments experience markedly increased rates of delinquency if raised in homes where discipline was dispensed in a less than consistent fashion (Sameroff, Seifer, & Zax, 1982; Werner & Smith, 1977). Similarly, Shostak and McIntyre (1978) observed a person × situation interaction in a subgroup of psychopathic offenders showing preference for higher levels of sensory input on the Kinesthetic Aftereffect Test, although the Zuckerman Sensation Seeking Scale (SSS) failed to differentiate between psychopathic and nonpsychopathic offenders.

Several additional studies confirm that behavioral indices of sensation seeking seem particularly effective in identifying persons exhibiting features of a psychopathic life adjustment. The outcome of a study directed by Borkovec (1970) disclosed that a group of psychopathic delinquents were less aroused by a simple series of tones than groups of "normal" and "neurotic" delinquents. Along similar lines, Cox (1978) observed increased amounts of boredom and drowsiness following a brief period of isolation in college students rating high on sensation seeking and low on socialization. Skrzypek (1969) discerned that in comparison to neurotic delinquents, psychopathic delinquents displayed greater preference for complex stimuli and novel pictures. Finally, in a study previously cited, DeMyer-Gapin and Scott (1977) verified that psychopathic children habituated more rapidly to novel stimuli and engaged in more self-stimulatory behavior (talking, moving around) during the testing session that their neurotic counterparts.

The results of studies such as those reviewed here suggest that from a very early age individuals who eventually develop along criminal lines seek out higher levels of stimulation than most other persons. Although research on the actual nature of the interaction that presumably takes place between the person and his or her situation in effecting sensation seeking tendencies is sparse, it is likely that heredity, temperament, and neurological factors on the person side, and family and general environmental variables on the situation side, are involved in this drive for heightened sensory experience. The data presented in this section, combined with the early theorizing of Quay (1965), leads me to speculate that the developing criminal strives to achieve higher than normal levels of sensation and stimulation in an effort to compensate for a resting arousal level that is lower than normal. In brief, the evolving criminal requires greater modulation of stimuli in order to incur an optimal level of arousal (see Table 7.1).

Higher-Order Interaction

With experience, the aspiring criminal learns that there are numerous activities capable of providing high levels of stimulation and excitement. This awareness may be acquired through imitating the behavior of various models (Bandura, 1969) or shaped by a particular schedule of reinforcement (Skinner, 1938). This might then lead to the development of a particular style of thought that with time and repetition becomes self-reinforcing. An interesting possibility is that

Table 7.1
The Person × Situation Interaction in the Physical Domain

	Person Variables	Situation Variables
	STIMULUS MODULATION	
Primary Level Interaction	Genetic Factors Temperament Autonomic Reactivity Arousal Level Testosterone	Parental Discipline Level of Environmental Stimulation
	INTERNAL-EXTERNAL ORIENTATION	
Higher-Order Interaction	Learning Age Testosterone Cognitive Style	School/Career Aspirations Violent TV Shows Peer Interactions Substance Abuse Ambient Temperature

testosterone may play a role at both the primary and higher-order levels. Schalling (1987), for instance, argues that the link between aggressiveness and testosterone differs as a function of age, the relationship tending to be somewhat stronger after puberty than before. She has also observed that high testosterone adolescent males have learned to achieve their goals by expressing anger and intimidating others.

Speaking of age, this person variable also seems to contribute meaningfully to higher-order interactions occurring in the physical domain. Studies employing primate (Baldwin & Baldwin, 1977) and human (Baldwin, 1984) subjects indicate that stimulation-seeking tendencies peak during mid to late adolescence and follow an age pattern reminiscent of the age-crime curve discussed in Chapter 5. Moreover, research on human subjects denotes that sensation seeking (Zuckerman, 1974) and criminality (Hirschi & Gottfredson, 1983) both decline as one proceeds through the third decade of life. These findings, coupled with the observation that one of the primary motives for crime during late adolescence and early adulthood is excitement (Giordano & Cernovich, 1979), certainly lend credence to the hypothesis that age interacts with early stimulation-enhancement tendencies to bring about a higher-order interaction that we will henceforth refer to as internal-external orientation.

A variety of situational correlates of crime may interface with selected person variables and the early products of primary-level interaction to bring about changes in the higher-order cauldrons of the physical domain. Predominant among the situation variables that have been investigated with higher-order physical domain interactions in the mind are school and/or career aspirations, television violence, peers, substance abuse, and ambient temperature. Glueck and Glueck (1968), for example, discovered that delinquent adolescent males expressed greater boredom with school and a stronger desire to enter adventurous vocations like aviation than nondelinquent male adolescents. In one longitudinally designed investigation, cognitively understimulated subjects were drawn more to "stimulating," and oftentimes violent, television shows than others (Himmelweit & Swift, 1976). It does not take much extrapolation to decipher the implications this relationship may have for those of us interested in forming a deeper appreciation of higher-order interactions occuring in the physical domain.

Of further relevance to this issue is peers. Research suggest that peer groups not only provide delinquents with emotional support but also form a conduit through which a sense of excitement and high drama may be achieved (Panella, Cooper, & Henggeler, 1982). Drugs and alcohol would also appear to contribute to higher-order physical domain interactions to the extent that chemicals characteristically augment, alter, and intensify people's perceptions of events. Finally, certain general environmental conditions, such as ambient temperature (Anderson, 1987), may also enter into higher-order interactions occurring in the physical domain on the situation side of the person × situation interactive equation.

Higher-order interactions taking place in the physical domain of human experience seem to cluster around issues of personal orientation (internalization versus externalization of parental and/or significant other messages and dictates). Consequently, an individual preoccupied with achieving an excessive level of stimulation and excitement will look toward environmental contingencies capable of providing him or her with the greatest opportunity for such experiences. The behavioral pattern associated with such tendencies apparently reflects an external rather than internal orientation. Whereas this issue may be somewhat controversial, the preponderance of evidence on orientation and law-violating behavior intimates that criminals, delinquents, and habitual offenders are more externally oriented than noncriminals (Ross & Fabiano, 1985). An external orientation may therefore be a powerful precursor of subsequent criminality.

THE SOCIAL DOMAIN

Primary-Level Interaction

Bowlby (1973, 1982) argues that humans have an innate need for physical contact with others. He further contends that this need finds its initial satisfaction in the developing relationship between infant and primary caregiver. Since this nascent association serves as a building block for future social relationships, problems existing at an early stage of development will likely affect subsequent behavior. Ainsworth (1979), for instance, reports that well-attached infants tend to grow up more cooperative, sympathetic, and self-reliant than their poorly attached counterparts. More recent research results tend to confirm these preliminary findings (Hazan & Shaver, 1987; LaFreniere & Sroufe, 1985).

Bowlby (1982) maintains that attachment plays a pivotal role in child development, in that a child forms its first internalized working models of others from its interactions with the primary caregiver. Ainsworth (1979), in fact, postulates the presence of a critical period for attachment or bonding, which she places somewhere between the ages of 18 and 36 months. Herbert, Sluckin, and Sluckin (1984) argue, however, that there is no strong evidence in either animal or human studies of a ''critical period'' for mother-infant attachment. Consequently, there is controversy over whether human attachment is determined by the product of social interactions occurring during critical or sensitive periods, although it is fairly well established that attachment provides the child with a secure base from whence he or she explores his or her environment (Ainsworth, 1989).

A variety of behaviors have been considered potential markers of attachment, from smiling (Wolff, 1963) to crying in response to separation (Stayton, Ainsworth, & Main, 1973), to exploring from a secure base (Ainsworth & Wittig, 1969). Perhaps the most frequently cited measure of infant attachment is Ainsworth et al.'s (1978) ''strange situation'' technique. The ''strange situation'' is designed to assess the degree to which the mother instills in her child feelings of trust and security. Within the context of this ''strange situation'' the child is exposed to eight increasingly more stressful situations that incorporate an unfamiliar room, a stranger, and the presence or absence of the mother. Scoring takes place on two levels, the first of which involves cataloging the frequency of specific infant behaviors (for example, proximity seeking, resistance, avoidance). At the second level a group of judges use the interactive category ratings to classify infants as secure, insecure-avoidant, or insecure-anxious/ambivalent. Although the ''strange situation'' has been utilized in research on attachment in infants, studies addressing the reliability and validity of this instrument have produced results which are equivocal and inconclusive (Goldsmith & Alansky, 1987; Lamb, 1987).

Hazan and Shaver (1987) measured attachment in adults by conceptualizing love as a bonding process and then analyzed the results of a series of questionnaires they had published in a local newspaper. Examining the recollections of early childhood relationships, current affectional bonds, and indices of self-perception, they obtained empirical support for the theoretical conceptualizations of Bowlby and Ainsworth in two large samples of adults. These authors also observed that the distribution of attachment styles in adults—56 percent secure, 24 percent avoidant, 20 percent anxious/ambivalent—corresponded roughly with the distribution found in infants—70 percent secure, 20 percent avoidant, 10 percent anxious/ambivalent (Ainsworth et al., 1978). Main, Kaplan, and Cassidy (1985) have developed an even more elaborate measure of attachment, the Adult Attachment Interview, which may be of particular interest to researchers attempting to measure attachment feelings in adults. Finally, Rowe, Linquist, and

White (1989) determined that adulthood residuals of early attachment feelings—that is, concern about losing the respect of family members—were more important than fear of criminal sanctions in the law-abiding behavior of a large group of noncriminals.

Besides problems with the reliability and validity of current measures of infant attachment, this approach suffers from a second potential limitation—namely, that the relationship between attachment and social behavior may be overestimated because of the use of criterion (''strange situation'') and dependent (mother's rating of a child's social competence) measures that overlap substantially. A difficulty encountered in research probing attachment styles in adults is that avoidant adults and college students tend to idealize their early relationships as a way of avoiding expressions of negative affect or feelings of personal discomfort (Kobak & Sceery, 1988; Main et al., 1985). Hazan and Shaver (1987) add that only with maturity do many of these individuals begin acknowledging the negative aspects of their early interpersonal experiences. This trend appears to be particularly problematic in studies of criminal offenders who, as a group, tend to be rather immature in their dealings with others (Yochelson & Samenow, 1976).

While considering the person-variable side of the primary level-social domain interactive equation, I was struck by how well temperament, with its genetic, prenatal, and neonatal correlatives, seemed to fit into the equation. Constitutional difficulties (Connell, 1976), infant fearfulness (Goldsmith, Bradshaw, & Rieser-Danner, 1986), persistent crying (Thompson, 1986), low birth weight (Bell, 1979), and maternal alcohol abuse during pregnancy (O'Conner, Sigman, & Brill, 1987) have all been shown to adversely affect the eventual attachment behavior of infants. Budding intelligence or responsivenes may also enter into the equation by protecting a child fortunate enough to possess these characteristics against future criminal involvement.

It is clear, then, that person variables may impact on attachment by making it difficult for the mother to experience a positive relationship with her child, while depriving the infant of opportunities to view the mother as a secure base from whence he or she might explore their environment. Traditional theories have tended to downplay the significance of temperament and other person variables in the development of a child-parent bond, although a recent meta-analysis of the attachment literature hints that temperament is at least as strongly associated with indices of attachment as are a variety of maternal attributes (Goldsmith & Alansky, 1987)

The situational side of primary-level interactions in the social domain embodies several different variables. Mothers who are more affectionate (Bates, Maslin, & Frankel, 1985), accepting (Main, Tomasini, & Tolan, 1979), responsive (Blehar, Lieberman, & Ainsworth, 1977), and positive (Roggman, Langlois, & Hubbs-Tait, 1987) raise children who tend to be more securely attached than mothers who lack these characteristics. Probing this issue further, Londerville and Main (1981) ascertained that mothers who employed warmer tones and were less forceful in interacting with their children seemed to produce more securely attached offspring. On the other hand, children exposed to physical abuse and maltreatment have been shown to be insecurely attached to their primary caregiver, even after allowances are made for initial differences in socioeconomic status (Egeland & Sroufe, 1981; Schneider-Rosen & Cicchetti, 1984).

So that we do not overinterpret the potential applicability of attachment research to a science of criminal behavior, it is important to add that not all of the research outcomes have been positive. Hazan and Shaver (1987) note that parental divorce and absence were unrelated to attachment style in two large samples of adult respondents. Rutter (1972), on the other hand, reports that parental absence and attachment may interact in their effect on behavior. Thus, while losing a mother or father may create anxiety in a well-bonded child, such a loss tends to be accompanied by uninhibited, attention-seeking behavior in children who have not formed a strong attachment to their parents. In a meta-analysis of research on maternal characteristics and attachment, Goldsmith and Alansky (1987) found maternal characteristics to be much less predictive of infant and child attachment than has been traditionally posited by proponents of attachment theory.

One possible interpretation of the ambiguous effects recorded by investigators exploring the person and situational correlates of attachment is that the interaction of person and situational variables is more important than individual person and situation variables in defining attachment. Sroufe (1979) writes that attachment has its roots in infancy and is the result of an interaction between the child and his or her caregiver. Worded somewhat differently, the child is an active participant in his or her own experience. Hazan and Shaver (1987, p. 522) add that "we have overemphasized the degree to which attachment style and attachment-related feelings are traits rather than products of unique person-situation interactions." Hence, while the actual combination of person and situation factors contributing to the interplay of variables at the primary level of social interaction may be unique to the individual, the eventual product (attachment style) is a more universal phenomenon that deserves our continued research focus.

In one of the founding studies on early attachment and behavior, Pringle and Bossio (1960) determined that the better adjusted residents of an orphanage were more likely to have spent the first year of life with their mothers, thus having established the seeds of an incipient bond with a primary caregiver. Research consistently demonstrates that securely attached infants tend to grow up to be more curious (Arend, Gove, & Sroufe, 1979), self-reliant (Sroufe, Fox, & Pancake, 1983), socially competent (LaFreniere & Sroufe, 1985), cooperative (Bates, Maslin, & Frankel, 1985; Matas, Arend, & Sroufe, 1978) children than less securely attached infants.

Securely attached infants also develop self-recognition skills more rapidly than less securely attached infants. Schneider-Rosen and Cicchetti (1984), for instance, determined that 73 percent of the 19-month-old infants in their study capable of visual self-recognition had been previously rated as securely attached. Lewis, Feiring, McGuffog, and Jaskir (1984) observed an interaction between attachment style and gender that found securely and insecurely attached female children failing to differ on criteria introduced by Achenbach and Edelbrock (1981) to assess risk for later psychopathology (15% in each group), but registered a significant effect for males in which 40 percent of the insecure (avoidant, anxious/ambivalent) boys satisfied the Achenbach and Edelbrock criteria compared to 6 percent of the securely attached boys.

Though the preponderance of evidence suggests the presence of a meaningful coalition between attachment style and childhood adjustment, this area of research is not without its detractors. In what is perhaps the most disconfirmatory study on this subject to date, Jacobson, Willie, Tianen, and Aytch (1983) determined that contrary to predictions derived from attachment theory, two-year-old children assessed to be securely attached to a primary caregiver were less rather than more likely to engage in positive interactions with peers compared to avoidant or anxious/ambivalent children. Similarly, Tracy, Farish, and Bretherton (1980) witnessed a significant secure-insecure difference on only one of the 16 measures of exploratory competence considered within the context of their investigation. Finally, Bates et al. (1985) report that early maternal perception, but not various attachment variables, correlated with preschool behavior problems at 36 months.

What does the research literature have to say about the attachment behavior of adults? As we mentioned previously, Hazan and Shaver (1987) studied attachment variables in adults by conceptualizing love as an attachment process. The results of this investigation characterize securely attached adults as more trustful and happy, avoidant adults as more fearful of closeness and less accepting of others, and anxious/ambivalent adults as more obsessional and jealous in their self-reported relationships with others. Kobak and Sceery (1988) probed attachment feelings in a sample of 53 first-year college students in hopes that it might shed light on the process of affect regulation. The results that ensued revealed that securely attached subjects were judged by peers to be more ego-resilient and less hostile, while avoidant subjects were viewed as more hostile and less ego-resilient and anxious/ambivalent subjects as more anxious and less ego-resilient. Additionally, the avoidant group expressed stronger feelings of social alienation and interpersonal distance and the anxious/ambivalent group greater feelings of personal distress relative to subjects in the secure condition.

In a dissertation conducted under the supervision of Professors R. A. Arend and L. A. Sroufe, Leah Matas investigated the connection between attachment style and behaviors suggestive of an evolving conduct disorder. Monitoring mother-child transactions, Matas et al. (1978) discovered that poorly attached children were not only more impulsive than their well-attached counterparts but more aggressive as well. Nearly two decades earlier, Gardner, Hawkes, and Burchinal (1961) had determined that children who spent their infancies in a college home management house and were eventually adopted into various homes demonstrated less positive adjustment on a measure of personality compared to a group of matched controls. However, these findings failed to achieve statistical significance. Interestingly, Cadoret and Cain (1980) report that a large percentage of the index subjects in the original Gardner et al. study later received adult diagnoses of antisocial personality disorder.

The possibility that attachment may function as a protective device against the criminogenic effects of other variables has also been investigated. In a study conducted on subjects inhabiting a small Hawaiian island, Werner and Smith (1977) determined that a strong emotional bond between the mother and child served to protect otherwise "vulnerable" children (raised in poverty, prenatal difficulties, early absence of father) from entering into a life of crime. An FBI study (1985) carried out with 36 serial killers makes mention of a possible link between family atmosphere and attachment in a group of criminal offenders. The family histories of many of these men revealed instability, conflict, and evidence of alcohol and/or drug abuse. Even more compelling from an empirical or theoretical standpoint was the observation that many of these individuals experienced a lack of positive relationship within their families of origin and possibly exhibited minimal attachment to others as a result (FBI, 1985).

Hanson, Henggeler, and colleagues (1984) have gathered information on the families of delinquents through the Memphis Delinquency Project. In one study emanating from this project, Henggeler et al. (1985) compared the interaction between criminality and the mother-son relationship in 67 father-absent homes. Mother-son interactions taking place in homes where the adolescent son had a history of violent criminality (rape, robbery, murder) were marked by lower levels of both positive and negative communication than dyads in which the son had been involved in nonviolent criminality (burglary) or no criminality at all. The mothers of sons with a history of violent criminality were also four and one-half times more likely to have been charged with neglect by juvenile authorities than the mothers of nonviolent offenders. Henggeler et al. speculate that the mothers of violent boys had failed to enculturate their sons by virtue of their low involvement in the childrearing process.

Walters and White (1990) compared 48 maximum security offenders with 46 minimum security inmates and 49 college students on a series of paper-and-pencil measures of attachment originally developed by Hazan and Shaver (1987). It was hypothesized that the maximum security group would encompass a greater percentage of insecure-avoidant members than the other two groups by virtue of the fact that many such individuals had participated in crime as a lifestyle rather than as an isolated event (minimum security offenders) or not at all (college students). The results revealed that subjects in the maximum security reported higher levels of anxiety and discomfort with closeness, depending upon others, and having others depend on them, although they did not display greater concern about trust or intimacy than subjects in the minimum security or control conditions. Such findings seem to suggest that lifestyle criminals experience only selected aspects of an avoidant style of attachment, although it is also possible

Table 7.2
The Person × Situation Interaction in the Social Domain

	Person Variables	Situation Variables
	ATTACHMENT	
Primary Level Interaction	Genetic Factors Temperament Intelligence	Parental Attitude/ Absence/Abuse Social/Cultural Environment
	SOCIAL BONDING/EMPATHY	
Higher-Order Interaction	Gender Cognitive Style	Peer Interactions School Parental Absence

that the maximum security offenders were underreporting avoidant thoughts and feelings in an effort to avoid the negative feelings associated with these early interpersonal relationships (see Table 7.2).

Higher-Order Interaction

As the individual matures, attachment feelings formed at the social domain's primary level begin interacting with various person and situation variables in such a way as to shape higher-order interactions centering on the issue of social bonding. The primary difference between social bonding and early attachment concerns the fact that the former is wider in scope than the latter. While attachment style is a prominent precursor of an evolving social bond, this bond envelops aspects of the attachment style as well as one's general attitude toward society and the ability to empathize with others. In advancing his social-control theory of delinquency, Hirschi (1969) argues that delinquency is likely to occur when the person-society bond is weak or nonexistent.

With its foundation in incipient child-parent transactional patterns, the social bond can be gauged by a subject's willingness to submit to the authority of others and respect reasonable restrictions on his or her behavior. Hirschi contends that this social bond is a function of four elements or characteristics: attachment, involvement, commitment, and belief. Accordingly, higher-order interactions taking place in the social domain are similar in many ways to Hirschi's (1969) social bonding conceptualization, though the present formulation places greater emphasis on empathy than can be found in Hirschi's version of social-control theory.

The person variables that seemingly contribute most to the social domain's higher-order interactions are gender and cognitive style. As was mentioned previously, a wide gap exists between males and females in terms of each group's propensity for engaging in criminal activity. While this may have something to do with genetic and/or neurologic factors like testosterone levels, gender variations in socialization may also explain this intriguing outcome. Research, for instance, indicates that females are normally reinforced for being less aggressive and more empathetic than males (Tieger, 1980). As such, gender is likely to enter into the higher-order interaction at the social level. Similarly, a developing cognitive style may also influence the outcome of the social bonding process. Hence, adolescents functioning on the basis of an egocentric, self-centered world view will not only experience greater difficulty bonding to conventional society but may also be less empathetic than adolescents capable of looking beyond themselves and their immediate circumstances.

Peers and school form the nucleus of the situational contingent involved with higher-order interactions occurring in the social domain. In his work with rhesus monkeys, Harlow (1963) noticed that the absence of attachment to a primary caregiver led subjects to attach to peers. Much the same could be said about human beings as relayed in a study by Rohrer and Edmonson (1960) and cross-validated by Panella et al. (1982). Hay (1985) comments that the social attachments children form with their parents during the first three years of life parallel later peer associations and that the child constructs a generalized concept of his or her social world through interactions with both parents and peers. School seems to play at least a facilitative role in how social bonding gets expressed since, as we saw in Chapter 6, the trend is for crime to increase rather than decrease once the child is permanently removed from the socially controlled school environment. Lastly, Magid and McKelvey (1987) view parental absence, particularly working mothers, as contributing to problems with social bonding, although there is very little evidence at this point by which to assess this possibility.

The interaction that transpires between person and situation variables at the higher-order level of the social domain is less well known than the isolated effects of specific person and situational variables. Nevertheless, the end product of this interaction is fairly easy to identify. Hirschi (1969), for example, states that in the absence of strong conventional ties the individual may drift into criminal behavior. Hirschi's theorizing finds support in a study conducted by Kruttschnitt, Heath, and Ward (1986), which identified concordance between weak atttachments at both home and school and a rising rate of violent criminality. However, where schooling experience and family attachment were both associated with violent criminality in white subjects, only the school variable correlated significantly with violent antisociality in black subjects. A possible interaction between attachment and peer relationships was noted in a study administered by Poole and Regoli (1979), where adolescents who were poorly bonded to their parents seemed more susceptible to delinquent peer influence than more strongly bonded adolescents.

Within the context of a more popularized version of the social bonding hypothesis, Magid and McKelvey (1987) outline three residual effects of inadequate bonding. First, since such individuals are not controlled by accepted social norms, they somehow believe that society's rules do not apply to them. Second, because of their lack of empathy these persons view others as objects—or as stepping stones to an objective—rather than as human beings with feelings and goals of their own. Third, because they have not learned to deal maturely with disappointment, these individuals are consumed by hate, anger, and rage, particularly when they don't get their way. A more thorough treatment of these three characteristics can be found in Walters' (1990b) review of the developmental features of lifestyle criminality.

THE PSYCHOLOGICAL DOMAIN

Primary-Level Interaction

During the first year of life the infant takes a global, undifferentiated approach to his or her environment. Over the course of the next several years, however, there is an evolving sense of self that emerges as the child begins differentiating him or herself from the wider social environment. In a classic study on early human development, Lewis and Brooks (1978) surreptitiously placed rouge on the noses of children 9 to 12 months old and 12 to 24 months old. Only the older group reacted to this change in physical appearance, connoting that one must be one to two years of age before being able to experience an appreciation of self. Once this rudimentary sense of personal awareness is established, the individual begins constructing a self-image from primary-level interactions taking place in the psychological domain.

There is research to suggest that body image is indeed one of the earliest components of an evolving self-image. Stone and Church (1979), a pair of developmental psychologists, assert that a clear body schema is not formed until the child is three to four years of age. Thus, physical attributes like body type (Sheldon, 1954) or minor physical anomalies (Mednick & Kandel, 1988) are person variables with obvious relevance to the unfolding self-image, particularly in the early stages of its development. A young boy born with an asthenic physique probably conceives of himself differently than does a more stoutly built youngster, just as a boy with low-seated ears or wide-set eyes thinks of himself in a particular sort of way. Research indicates that physically unattractive people are ignored more often by others and have more negative characteristics attributed to them than more physically atttractive persons (Krebs & Adinolf, 1975). Likewise, the hemispheric organization of the brain may impact on the developing self-schema by directing the child toward certain activities like music and away from others like reading.

Parental attitude appears to be the most important situation variable involved in primary-level interactions occurring in the psychological domain. Operating out of a transactional analytic framework, Steiner (1974) argues that parents shape a child's early view of him or herself through various verbal and nonverbal messages. Verbal labels like *stupid* or *bad*, or negative references to the child "being just like your father" will likely have a different impact than messages of a more positive or constructive nature. Moreover, negative nonverbal messages, which are abundant in an abusive relationship between a parent and child, will lead to very different behavioral outcomes than a pat on the back, warm hug, or encouraging smile.

It should be noted that variables like race and social class may also play an important moderating role in the relationship between self-image and high-rate criminality. Jensen (1972), as a case in point, found negative self-definitions to be associated with delinquency in lower-class white but not black youths, and positive self-esteem to be correlated with delinquency in lower-class black but not white adolescents in a sample of Californian high school students.

A unidimensional conceptualization of self-image fails to do justice to the complexity of primary-level interactions taking place in the psychological domain during the first few years of life. Three investigators from the National Institute of Mental Health conducted a panel study of 1,886 adolescent boys and recorded a significant negative correlation between self-esteem and subsequent delinquency, but add that a converse effect, wherein delinquency involvement bolsters self-esteem, was also observed in several instances (Rosenberg, Schooler, & Schoenbach, 1989). A study in which 1,668 Chinese high school students completed a battery of self-image measures revealed that weak academic self-concept and poor school and parental relationships correlated with an increased frequency of delinquent behavior (Leung & Lau, 1989). Similar to the Rosenberg et al. study, Leung and Lau ascertained that delinquency was also positively correlated with certain aspects of self-concept (social self-image and physical ability). These findings infer that self-image is a complex, multidimensional concept that is both a potential cause and an effect of crime and delinquency.

The interaction between such person variables as perceptual asymmetries or physique and situation variables like parental attitude leads to an emerging sense of self. Harter (1983) argues that the degree of parental support and involvement interacts with a child's deviant behavior to influence self-esteem. Low self-esteem has been found to accompany both juvenile delinquency (Magee, 1964; Patterson, 1986; Silverman, 1964) and adult criminality (Fitts & Hammer, 1969; Wrightsman, 1974). Conger and Miller (1966) compared 184 delinquent and 184 nondelinquent boys matched on age, IQ, ethnicity, and socioeconomic status and discerned that the delinquent boys tended to be more unhappy, worrisome, and dissatisfied than the nondelinquent boys. Hence, an affiliation of delinquency with low self-esteem seems likely, although more research is necessary in order to establish the theoretical underpinnings of this relationship and determine whether deviant behavior causes low (or high) self-esteem, low self-esteem causes deviant behavior, or both are caused by some third variable (Duncan, 1984).

In one of the more exhaustive efforts to obtain an answer to this question, Reckless and others (1956) studied the relationship between self-esteem and delinquency. All sixth-grade teachers in schools located in high-delinquency areas of

Columbus, Ohio, were asked to nominate white males they thought would be least likely to have problems with the legal authorities. After eliminating boys who could not be located or who had police records, the researchers were left with 125 "good boys." The results of this study indicated that these "good boys" obtained high scores on the Responsibility scale and low scores on the Delinquency Proneness scale of the California Personality Inventory, provided self-evaluations that were obedient and law-abiding, reported favorable perceptions of family interactions, and came from homes that were maritally, economically, and residentially stable. One hundred and three of the original 125 "good boys" were located some four years later and 95 of these boys were again nominated for the "good boy" category by their teachers, with just 4 boys experiencing legal trouble since the first study (Scarpitti, Murray, Dinitz, & Reckless, 1960). The 103 original "good boys" characteristically avoided delinquent peers, earned low scores on a seven-item delinquency scale, and reported favorable family relations.

One year after the original "good boy" study, Reckless, Dinitz, and Kay (1957) asked sixth-grade teachers in the same schools as before to nominate boys they believed were likely to be headed for police and juvenile court contact. Of the 108 boys nominated, 24 (23%) had already been in trouble with the law. Data analyses further revealed that the "bad boys" in this study scored significantly higher on the Delinquency Proneness scale and significantly lower on the Responsibility scale compared to the "good boys" from the earlier study. These scales also differentiated between "bad boys" who had and had not experienced previous contact with the legal system. A four-year follow-up revealed that 27 (38.6%) of the 70 "bad boys" who could be located had been in serious and regular contact with the courts during the follow-up period with a mean of three separate contacts (Dinitz, Scarpitti, & Reckless, 1962).

Several years after the original good boy/bad boy studies, Reckless and Dinitz (1972) set out to examine the effect of a delinquency prevention program, the Youth Development Project, on subsequent criminal behavior and self-esteem. Subjects in this study were all male adolescents selected in a manner similar to the original study on "bad boys." These predelinquent subjects were then randomly assigned to either an experimental school program (with an emphasis on remedial reading, respecting the rights of others, and positive role models) or control group (traditional classroom). Follow-up evaluations two to three years later revealed no difference between experimental and control subjects in terms of subsequent delinquent involvement, academic performance, or dropping out of school. Moreover, there were no differences between the two groups on a measure of self-esteem, although the experimental group did display a slight improvement on this measure from pre- to posttest in comparison to a small reduction in scores for subjects in the control condition.

Although data for the Reckless studies were collected some 30 years ago, these studies remain one of the few concerted research efforts to address the issue of self-image and criminality. This is truly unfortunate, since these studies are plagued by serious methodological flaws. Among the more prominent crit-

Table 7.3
The Person × Situation Interaction in the Psychological Domain

	Person Variables	Situation Variables
	SELF-IMAGE	
Primary Level Interaction	Perceptual Asymmetries Physical Attributes	Parental Attitude/ Abuse
	ROLE IDENTITY	
Higher-Order Interaction	Verbal Intelligence Learning/Cognitive Style Physical Attributes (tattoos) Racial/Ethnic Factors	Peer Interactions School Substance Abuse Unemployment

icisms leveled against the research upon which Reckless and his associates constructed their containment theory of criminal involvement is the use of inadequate criteria (for example, teacher nominations) and dependent (that is, scores on two CPI scales) measures, the problem of differential mortality, and a poverty of concise theoretical speculation as to the presumed relationship between criminality and self-esteem (Tangri & Schwartz, 1970). Before research on self-image can progress beyond its promising beginnings, it must formulate more eloquent theoretical models, utilize stronger research designs, and identify measures of self-esteem and self-image that are appreciably more robust than those currently being used. Perhaps a composite index made up of a self-report measure, like Rosenberg's Self-Esteem Scale; a self-evaluation procedure, like the Semantic Differential; and a projective instrument, like the Incomplete Sentence Blank, would provide more valid results than could be obtained with an isolated indicator (see Table 7.3).

Higher-Order Interaction

In presenting his psychosocial theory of human development, Erikson (1963) wrote that self-identity is actually a synthesis of several different elements. A number of these elements derive from earlier stages (or primary-level interactions) of development, while others arise as a function of demands placed on the individual during adolescence. Each of these elements, however, must be integrated into a meaningful system in order to satisfy Erikson's fifth stage of psychosocial development (identify vs. role confusion). In the absence of a clear sense of identity, the individual experiences confusion, anxiety, worry, and uncertainty as to how he or she fits into the wider social network of relationships and roles.

Person variables contributing to the psychological domain's higher-order interaction include verbal intelligence, cognitive style, physical attributes like tattoos, and racial and/or ethnic determinants. In a longitudinal analysis of data collected on Danish subjects, Moffitt et al. (1981) found low verbal intelligence to be strongly associated with a pattern of delinquent behavior. These authors go on to speculate that low verbal abilities interact with various situational variables and limit one's access to certain rewards in school or in the job market. Egan (1982) writes in his book, *The Skilled Helper*, that a history of failure contributes to the development of certain self-defeating attitudes and beliefs, something he refers to as "disabling self talk." Tattoos contribute to the role identity life task by virtue of their self-labeling function and potential for alienating the individual from conventional society (Walters, 1990b). Like a self-defeating cognitive set or tattoos running up and down one's arms, racial and/or ethnic factors may also play a part in the transformation of a simple self-image to a view of one's wider social role (Harris & Lewis, 1974).

Situationally, peers, schools, substance abuse, and unemployment are of prime consideration in the realm of higher-order developments taking place in the psychological domain. A negative role identity may be reinforced by unconcerned parents, troublemaking peers, or an overburdened school system. Dishion, Stouthamer-Loeber, and Patterson (1984) note that a lack of parental supervision and poor school performance not only correlate with low self-esteem but also portend a negative prognosis in terms of future criminality. In a follow-up of Reckless' "good boys," it was determined that the vast majority of individuals in this group were still in school four years later (Scarpitti et al., 1960). Peers and substance abuse may also hold value for those of us interested in comprehending the mechanisms responsible for the evolution of a criminogenic role identity, since both of these situational influences appear capable of reinforcing a destructive self-image and worldview. Finally, Furnham (1984) conceives of unemployment as impacting on crime through a process of self-denigration, while Farrington et al. (1986) discerned that unemployment correlated most convincingly with criminality in youth predisposed by diverse genetic and/or personality factors.

The product of higher-order psychological domain interactions—role identity—differs from the outcome of primary-level interaction—self-image—in several important ways. Whereas self-image is based on such rudimentary elements as body image, expressions of needs, and general character traits, role identity embodies the wider social environment. A person attempting to construct a self-image will compare him or herself with parents, peers, and siblings. The principal goal of the role identity life task, however, concerns the derivation of an appreciation of oneself relative to the society in which one resides. The individual searching for a role identity is, in effect, asking "How do I fit into society?" I submit that someone sporting a prominent tattoo that reads "Born to Lose" has a very different sense of role identity than an individual whose wallet is filled with pictures of his or her spouse and children. These attitudes, which form the basis of higher-order interactions occurring in the psychological domain, seem fertile soil for the production of more generalized patterns of behavior.

CONCLUSION

Now that we have traversed the third leg of our journey through the research foundation of criminal science, it seems appropriate that we briefly review where we have been. First, we saw that certain characteristics of the individual—person variables—display reasonably strong and stable relationships with various indices of criminal involvement. Next, we examined a long list of situational or environmental characteristics that have traditionally been part of the scientific study of crime. Again, we found several variables that correlated with crime in ways that seemed robust, sound, and meaningful. Finally, in this chapter, we studied the person in interaction with his or her environmental circumstances. Though it is impossible to account for all of the individual variations occurring within the infrastructure of the person × situation relationship, it was possible to identify three primary domains or dimensions of coaction.

Besides discussing the context (domain) of the various interactions, we also scanned primary and higher-order interrelationships. Research on topics reviewed in this chapter indicates that the issues of stimulus modulation and locus of orientation (internal vs. external) are intrinsic to primary- and higher-order level interactions occurring in the physical domain, respectively. According to our review of the social-domain research literature, early attachment exists as the primary-level interaction and social bonding and/or empathy as the higher-order interaction. Lastly, the psychological domain gives rise to the individual's search for identity, initially as a means of differentiating him- or herself from the physical environment and later as a means of establishing his or her niche in society. Investigating individual person and situational correlates of crime without taking into account their interrelationships is akin to trying to wind one's way through an unfamiliar city with nothing more than a compass. Appreciating the manner by which person and situation variables interact along major dimensions of human experience provides the same sort of guidance and direction a roadmap affords the bemused motorist.

Though it would be convenient if the physical, social, and psychological domains of human experience were independent, objective reality as well as common sense dictates that these domains interact. As we discussed previously, higher-order interactions occurring in the physical domain contribute to the orientation life task (internal versus external), the latter orientation seemingly more closely affiliated with criminality. Exploring the physical-psychological interaction, Perotti (1978) found low self-esteem (a psychological domain product) to be associated with an unfolding external locus of control (a physical domain product). Matas et al. (1978) maintain that low self-esteem (a psychological domain product) and weak social bonding (a social domain product) often covary, while Wheeler and Kilmann (1983) witnessed a link between high sensation seeking (a physical domain product) and lesser attachment to a marital partner (a social domain product). These findings underscore the necessity of probing the natural interplay of these three dimensions of human experience.

After reviewing interactive research on crime and delinquency I found myself searching for a more definitive conclusion than was possible in the previous two chapters. Regrettably, the absence of solid research findings on issues central to the interactive hypothesis makes it difficult to be any more precise than we were in Chapters 5 and 6. Though it makes good intuitive sense that various person-situation interactive patterns are of prime significance in the development of major criminal characteristics, the research literature on this issue does not lend itself to singular interpretation. If we are to capitalize on the knowledge that interaction is indispensable to the scientific study of crime and criminals, then we must incorporate interactional research designs, multivariate statistics, and improved measures of sensation seeking, attachment, and self-image into our research.

A critical step in our study of person × situation interaction is identifying a methodology capable of furthering our understanding of the interactive process. Social psychologists Bem and Funder (1978) addressed this issue more than a decade ago, but their ideas and comments are as relevant today as they were 14 years ago. Bem and Funder recommend use of a template-matching technique whereby the characteristics of a particular individual are matched against a composite of "ideal" characteristics likely to result in a distinct outcome in a specified situation. Applying this methodology to research on crime and delinquency we could construct templates of person characteristics (for example, age, sex, temperament, IQ, cognitive style) for a variety of different situational contexts (for example, styles of parental discipline, physical home environment, peers, substance abuse) and then determine how specific individuals fit each of the templates. Such a procedure seems well suited to the task of assessing the person × situation interaction as it pertains to various criminal outcomes.

Were we to conclude our discussion of the correlates of crime at this point, we would be culpable of a grave oversight. Though I view the interactionalist approach as essential to the development of knowledge on criminal behavior, I also believe it imperative that we stop short of reifying the person × situation interaction as a complete explanation of human behavior. There are many ways to satisfy high sensation-seeking tendencies other than through crime. Consequently, while a percentage of all persons inclined to seek excitement will enter crime as a means of satisfying this interest, other individuals will choose to pursue excitement in ways that do not bring them in conflict with the law (speed boat racing, skydiving). Similarly, there are more avenues open to the weakly bonded individual than crime, including politics, big business, and vagrancy. Much the same holds true for primary and higher-order interactions specific to the psychological domain—that is, a negative self-image or deleterious role identity is not unique to criminals. These observations point to the significance of personal choice in the criminal development process, the pivot around which Chapter 8 rotates.

8

Correlates of Crime: The Choice Process

If we were to conduct a mega-longitudinal study of the correlates of criminal behavior and had available to us an unlimited supply of cooperative subjects, ample financial resources, sophisticated statistical procedures, and measures that were undeniably reliable and valid, we would probably witness several very interesting relationships. Our multivariate analyses would likely reveal that sundry person and situation variables, to include verbal intelligence, autonomic reactivity, age, substance abuse, peers, and family environment, contribute uniquely to variations observed in measures of criminal involvement. We might trace an even larger portion of the variance to the interaction of variables in three distinct, but not necessarily orthogonal, clusters (stimulus modulation and/or orientation, attachment and/or social bonding and self-image and/or role identity). However, a significant portion of the variance would remain unaccounted for. I would contend that this large block of unlabeled variance represents the variable of personal choice.

Choice has been at the center of the determinism–free will debate from the very beginning. The English philosopher John Locke (1632–1704) was an early advocate of the deterministic approach to human nature. The free-will position, on the other hand, was championed by Jean-Jacques Rousseau (1712–1778), the famous French political philosopher and writer. The determinism–free will debate was taken up in recent years by Carl Rogers and the noted behaviorist B. F. Skinner. Adopting the free-will side, Rogers (1951) asserted that humans are endowed with freedom of choice, which in turn serves as a foundation for change. Positioned at the other end of this intellectual dialogue, Skinner (1971) postulated that human behavior is a function of environmental contingencies and reinforcement histories. Bandura (1977) added further to the debate with his theory that humans are capable of self-determination through self-reinforcement.

At first brush it would appear that there is no reconciling the deterministic and free-choice viewpoints. However, as has been discussed by Goldkamp

(1987), Kierulff (1988), and others, these differing perspectives may actually be complementary, rather than antagonistic—ergo, determinism, as reviewed in Chapters 5 through 7, highlights the internal and external conditions that predispose one to later criminality. The choice or free-will approach, on the other hand, reminds us that despite the effect conditions can have on behavior, one is still an active participant rather than a pawn in the events of one's life. This chapter also differs from the previous three in that while our discussion of internal and external conditions was primarily concerned with what Hirschi and Gottfredson (1986) refer to as criminal involvement, research on choice behavior converges around the theme of criminal events.

As our contrived mega-analysis clearly points out, there is more to criminal behavior than person, situation, and interactive variables. In the absence of serious brain pathology and debilitating emotional disorder there is always the prospect of choice. We make choices when we get out of bed to attend classes or go to work, we make choices when we elect to watch a television program instead of converse with our spouse or children, and we make choices when we decide to steal a car, burglarize a home, or rob a convenience store. Undoubtedly there are developmental constraints placed on the choice process, given that decisions derived by a 6-month-old infant (if we can even use the term *choice* in this situation) are obviously different from those made by a 16-year-old delinquent. With time and experience, however, this 6-month-old infant will gradually develop the ability to make informed choices, a process upon which we focus our attention in this chapter.

THE CRIMINAL AS A DECISION-MAKER

In July 1985, a group of researchers met in Cambridge, England, to discuss decision making and criminality. Several of the more noteworthy papers presented during the conference were subsequently published in a book edited by sociologists Derek Cornish and Ronald Clarke, under the title *The Reasoning Criminal* (1986). In presenting their ideas on decision making and crime, Cornish and Clarke argued that situational variables exert an important impact, not only on the criminal event but also on the decisions the offender makes relative to his or her criminal career. Hirschi (1986) adds that situational variables and characteristics of the individual may directly affect one's decision to engage or not engage in a specific criminal act. Basically, though, the rational approach to crime assumes that the offender seeks to benefit by way of various choices and decisions.

Criminal decision making has been investigated in groups of robbers (Feeney, 1986), burglars (Walsh, 1986), shoplifters (Weaver & Carroll, 1985), commercial thieves (Gibbs & Shelly, 1982), and opiate abusers (Bennett, 1986). Weaver and Carroll, for instance, explored the thinking and decision-making abilities of 17 experienced and 17 novice shoplifters by accompanying them on a trip through a local department store. They determined that both the experts and novices based their verbalized crime–no crime decisions on a simplified model of environmental risks and opportunities. Several of the more salient factors considered in this assessment were store security, physical layout, presence of bystanders, and item characteristics, to include value and size. Normally, however, subjects considered no more than one or two of these factors before rendering a shoplift–no shoplift decision.

Despite the fact that experienced and novice shoplifters in the Weaver and Carroll study tended to rely on oversimplified models of the environment in rendering crime–no crime decisions, different sets of variables were responsible for deterring subjects in each group from engaging in shoplifting behavior. Whereas fear, guilt, and the possibility of apprehension characteristically deterred novices, the more experienced shoplifters were deterred only by strategic difficulties like the size of an item or the presence of security devices. Furthermore, these "experts" approached strategic difficulties as things to be overcome while novices were normally deterred in the face of any strategic roadblock. Weaver and Carroll remark that the prospect of arrest, jail, or fines rarely entered into the crime–no crime decisions of the experienced shoplifters.

The decision-making models of 113 Californian robbers were explored in interviews conducted by Feeney (1986). Feeney found that only half his sample made even rudimentary plans before deciding to engage in the robbery that resulted in their most recent arrest and only 5 percent employed detailed plans. Interestingly, planning increased with the number of robberies committed. Similar to the experienced shoplifters in the Weaver and Carroll (1985) study, only 21 percent of the sample considered apprehension to be a risk they should concern themselves with before embarking on their most recent criminal venture. In further support of Weaver and Carroll's results, Feeney ascertained that first-time robbers more frequently considered the risk of arrest than experienced robbers. Continuation of the criminal pattern of robbers was found to correlate positively with experience and negatively with fear of apprehension. As we might have anticipated, negative thoughts about robbery were strongest in first-time offenders.

The decision to exit crime has also been a topic of investigation. Cusson and Pinsonneault (1986), for instance, interviewed 17 ex-robbers and reviewed several ex-offender biographies in an effort to identify the factors associated with the decision to abandon crime as a way of life. This group of former offenders advised that their decisions were based on a reevaluation of life goals and increased willingness to accept modest incomes. Some of the specific factors mentioned by study participants as instrumental in their decision to desist from crime were shock, such as seeing one's crime partner gunned down, a gradual wearing down of the criminal drive through an accumulation of punishments and incarcerations, the problems associated with serving time as an older inmate, and a building up of fear brought about by the realization that unless they changed their careers, they would be spending the remainder of their lives in prison.

As part of the reevaluation process that precedes desistence from crime, the individual begins to severe his or her ties with past criminal associates. Cusson and Pinsonneault (1986) discuss the case of one offender who resolved to move out of the city in order to avoid all contact with former inmate associates who happened to live in his old neighborhood. Though none of the respondents in their study mentioned jobs as protection against future criminal involvement, Cusson and Pinsonneault found that every one of their subjects was employed in reasonably well-paying, interesting jobs. Steady employment may therefore reinforce the notion that honest work provides a better long-term payoff than crime. Thus, while a number of external factors enter into the decision to desist from crime, of overriding importance is a reevaluation of one's life goals and personal expectations.

CHOOSING CRIME

The economic or utilitarian approach to understanding crime places a premium on choice as a cause of crime. In its classic version, economic theory argues that people commit crimes because the benefits of such activity outweigh the costs (Becker, 1968). The complex interplay of supply and demand leads to a situation whereby the individual selects crime when the perceived utility (cost : benefit ratio) of so doing exceeds the utility of engaging in legitimate activities. More recently, however, additional factors have been entered into the economic equation. Block and Heineke (1975), for example, contend that wealth, the payoff of illegal activities, enforcement practices, punishment effects, and the degree to which an individual is certain that a particular penalty will be administered need also be considered as a part of the utilitarian approach to explaining crime.

Like the utilitarians, Wilson and Herrnstein (1985) propose that criminal behavior is controlled by its consequences. However, they expand the notion of reinforcement beyond the simplistic cost : benefit analyses performed by economic-minded theorists, affirming what writers like Waldo and Chiricos (1972) had been asserting since the early 1970s that choice is a perceptual process and that it is one's subjective interpretation of an event, not the event itself, which is reinforcing or punishing. Wilson and Herrnstein further argue that the valence attached to a particular reinforcer or punisher may vary depending upon the time of day, relative satiation or deprivation of that contingency, and characteristics like intelligence, impulsivity, and bonding to conventional social norms. Like the utilitarian theorists, however, the essence of Wilson and Herrnstein's argument is that people choose between competing criminal and noncriminal alternatives.

Suspicious of inferences made about individual-level processes like choice from aggregate-level data, Piliavin et al. (1986) probed the impact of perceived sanctions on self-reported criminality. The results of this study, however, failed to identify a significant deterrent effect for perceived sanctions. Arguing for the necessity of aggregate-level research on choice, Heineke (1988) maintains that microlevel analyses, such as the ones conducted by Piliavin et al. (1986), are subject to a variety of conceptual, statistical, and practical limitations. Heineke adds further that if one can demonstrate that actual rewards and sanctions are a monotonic function of perceived rewards and sanctions, the former could legitimately replace the later in research on choice. As Matsueda, Piliavin, and Gartner (1988) point out in responding to this critique, however, there are at least as many problems with Heineke's argument as there are with the original Piliavin et al. study, not to mention the fact that it fails to address the problems of aggregation, measurement error, and identification, all of which appear to limit the meaningfulness of economic research on criminal choice.

Two additional individual-level studies provide circumscribed support for the rational-choice explanation of crime. Witte (1980) collected data on the status of 641 men released from North Carolina prisons and witnessed modulating probabilities of crime based on permutations of variables like age and employment status; and in a study of 1,171 property offenses committed by juveniles and adjudicated by a family court in Honolulu, Hawaii, Ghali (1982) discovered that the decision to engage in certain criminal acts is a dynamic function of factors like age and history of prior court referrals. However, the fact that offending patterns vary by occupational status or criminal background is not bona fide confirmation of the rational choice position. In fact, Paternoster (1987), in a review of research on the perceived certainty and severity of punishment, concludes that there is little evidence in support of a causal nexus between either the perceived certainty or perceived severity of punishment and self-reported criminality. If anything, asserts Paternoster, criminal involvement may be a cause of sanction-linked perceptions through modification of a person's assessment of the certainty and severity of punishment.

While results such as those obtained by Piliavin et al. (1986) and reviewed by Paternoster (1987) shed doubt on the utility of the economic approach to crime, they do not necessarily eliminate the possibility of a choice–criminal behavior relationship. As Johnson and Payne (1986) point out, research in the field of cognitive psychology has demonstrated rather convincingly that the human ability to process, store, and access information is limited. Consequently, most of us develop heuristic strategies that facilitate memory storage and accelerate the rate at which information is retained but at the cost of increased error. Like Piliavin et al., information-processing theorists hypothesize that it is not the objective characteristics of a situation, but one's internal representation of that situation, that drives behavior. However, because we are imperfect information processors, this internal representation embraces only part of the picture (Johnson & Payne, 1986). This may help explain why choice and/or deterrence research conducted at the individual level often fails to provide support for the rational choice hypothesis.

Carroll (1978) explored this issue in a study carried out on groups of adult and juvenile offenders and nonoffenders. After presenting subjects with a three-outcome gambling task that varied along four dimensions—probability of getting away with a crime, probability of capture, the amount of money obtained if successful, the penalty if caught—Carroll asked subjects to evaluate 72 crime opportunities. The results of this study indicate that subjects frequently based their decisions on a single dimension to the exclusion of the other three. Though individual subjects showed consistent preferences for a particular dimension, only minor variations were noted between groups (age, criminal status). In fact, the only difference noted among the choices offered by offenders and nonoffenders was that the offenders viewed all criminal opportunities as more desirable than did the nonoffenders.

Based on the results of this study, Carroll (1978) concluded that a "psychological" explanation of human choice, wherein the individual makes decisions utilizing a simple, often unidimensional analysis of criminal opportunities, is more accurate than the purely "economic" interpretations of choice that portray the individual as making exhaustive, complex calculations leading to an optimal decision. Similar results were obtained in a study of British burglars (Hough, 1987). It would appear, then, that the human decision-making process is, by nature and necessity, limited. As such, we must search for research paradigms that take these imperfections into account. With the various failings of the human decision-making process clearly in mind, we turn our attention to a model of criminal choice behavior.

A MODEL OF CRIMINAL CHOICE AND DECISION MAKING

One of the chief mistakes made by researchers utilizing computer simulations to study the process of human problem solving has been the tacit assumption that the inner workings of the human mind can be replicated by a computer. Whereas computers function on the basis of circuitry, rules, and binary logic, the human learning sequence is grounded in conditioned responses, successive approximations, trial and error, and the strengthening of associational bonds through repetition. While the human mind processes information less efficiently and has significantly less storage space than most modern-day computers, it is capable of several functions the computer is not. Prominent among these are the mind's capacity for ingenuity, propensity for self-evaluation, and ability to act on unfamiliar information.

It would seem that the computer and human mind each possess certain strengths and advantages, although they are hardly interchangeable. There are, nevertheless, several commonalities in the way computers and human beings process information. In fact, I have taken the liberty of borrowing terms, concepts, and procedures from the computer science field in deriving a model of criminal decision-making and choice. Even though the focus of the present discourse is on criminal decision making, this model (which is portrayed in Figure 8.1) seems applicable to the general human decision-making process as well.

Figure 8.1
A Model of Criminal Decision Making

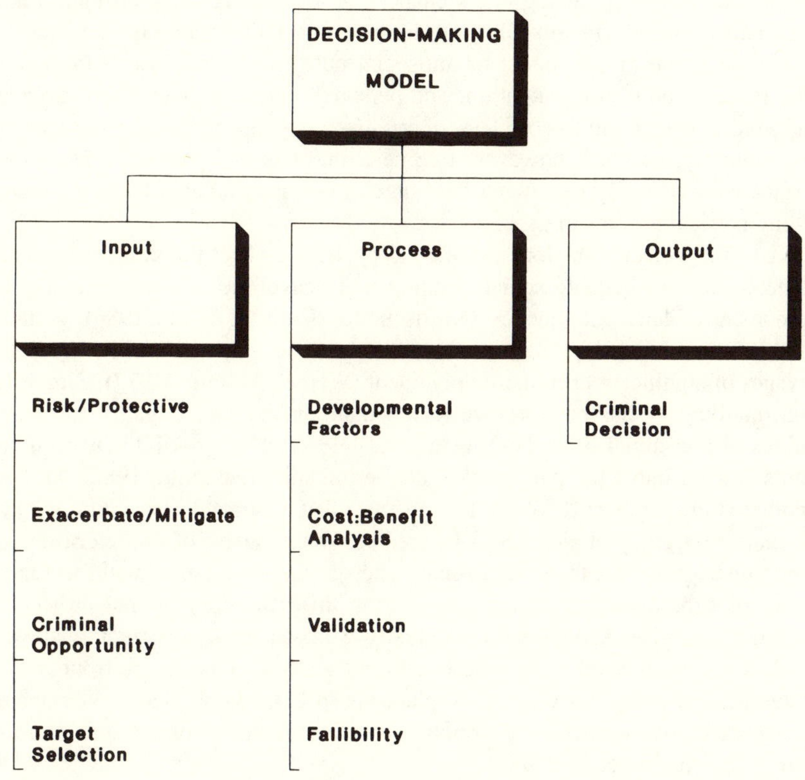

Input

Though I remain steadfast in the opinion that choice is fundamental to the commission of criminal acts, it is important that we not overlook the fact that person, situation, and developmental variables can affect the choice process itself. The input stage of the decision-making process, therefore, provides the context within which decisions are made. Although these contextual considerations serve to limit one's options, they do not determine one's choices. Consequently, while a person's decisions are influenced by such input variables as risk and protective factors, exacerbating and mitigating factors, criminal opportunity, and target selection, these variables are not the aggregate cause of one's choices, though they do operate in concert with specific characteristics of the identified decision maker. In other words, the individual is an active participant in the sequence of events that gave rise to criminal forms of behavior.

Risk and Protective Factors. Risk factors serve to enhance the probability of a particular individual engaging in a pattern of delinquent or criminal behavior. Protective factors, on the other hand, serve to shield one from criminogenic influences, thereby reducing one's chances of developing along criminal lines. Risk and protective factors illustrate how certain individuals may be more or less more prone to delinquent or antisocial outcomes. They also help explain why research on person, situation, and person × situation interaction variables has yielded several robust correlates of criminal involvement. Rather than causing law-violating behavior, however, I contend that risk and protective factors interface with crime by narrowing the range of options available to an individual at any particular point in time.

Risk and protective factors are often at opposite ends of the same continuum. Hence, while inadequate social bonding may leave one vulnerable to the development of later delinquency (Kruttschnitt, Heath, & Ward, 1986), a stable mother-son relationship may protect an otherwise vulnerable child from the ravages of significant criminal involvement (Werner & Smith, 1977). Similarly, high intelligence has been known to inoculate an individual against the temptations of a criminal lifestyle (Kandel et al., 1988) while low IQ may facilitate one's descent into a life pattern of violent criminality (Heilbrun, 1982). Still yet another study (Osborn & West, 1980) shows that continued association with an all-male peer group at ages 18 to 19 predicts greater levels of future criminality while disengagement from an all-male peer group corresponds with decreased levels of subsequent criminality. Data from this same longitudinal project revealed that high-risk boys who eventually went on to become recidivistic offenders had been rated as lacking in concentration at age 8, more troublesome at age 10, and were more likely to be placed in special schools at age 11 compared to high-risk boys who did not display a recidivistic pattern of subsequent criminality (Farrington et al., 1988).

It is worth mentioning that risk and protective factors do not exist independent of other variables, but are part of a wider interlocking network within which the person × situation interaction operates. Sports, while they have been shown to exert a protective effect on black and small-town white youth, are normally ineffective in shielding urban white youth from future criminal involvement (Rutter & Giller, 1984). Leisure activities, in fact, can serve to increase one's risk of future criminality under one set of circumstances and protect otherwise vulnerable adolescents from other criminogenic influences under another set of conditions. The results of a study directed by Agnew and Petersen (1989), for instance, confirmed that time spent in unsupervised peer-oriented social activities correlated positively with delinquency, while time spent in organized leisure activities and noncompetitive sports correlated negatively with delinquency. Shyness is a variable that demonstrates an even more dramatic effect, serving as a risk factor with some individuals and as a protective factor with others. McCord (1987) asserts that children rated as shy and nonaggressive by their teachers at age seven or eight were less likely to be arrested and convicted during the next

40 years, while children rated shy and aggressive were more likely to encounter legal problems during this same 40-year period.

The family seems to be a particularly powerful source of risk and protective influence. Briggs, Wirt, and Johnson (1961) discerned that adverse family circumstances (for example, parental absence, economic hardship) placed male adolescents at a disadvantage in terms of subsequent delinquency development, particularly if these features were accompanied by elevated scores on three MMPI scales: 4 (*Pd*), 8 (*Sc*), and 9 (*Ma*). Hathaway and Monachesi (1963), on the other hand, discovered that children achieving "adverse" MMPI configurations were protected by positive family characteristics like good communication and the presence of strong affectional ties within the family. In a cross-sectional analysis of vandalism in a northern English city, Gladstone (1980) determined that criminal behavior was least likely in situations where the parents carefully monitored the peer-group activities of their offspring.

Positive family relationships may help protect a child against later criminality by providing an effective network of social support as well as ideas and values that inoculate the child against later criminal involvement. Negative family influences, on the other hand, tend to have a multiplicative effect on a child's risk for later delinquency. Hence, Rutter and colleagues (1975) identified six risk factors (low social status, large family size, paternal criminality, maternal psychiatric history, severe marital discord, involvement with the social service administration) that seemed to exert a synergistic effect on the behavior of the adolescents in their study. While the presence of only one risk factor was no more criminogenic than a complete absence of risk factors, the presence of two factors increased a subject's vulnerability to delinquency fourfold, with similar multiplicative increments as the number of active risk factors mounted.

The longitudinal research of West and Farrington (1973) illustrates how risk factors elevate one's chances of engaging in later criminality without determining such behavior. They observed that 13 percent of their sample of 400 working-class delinquents (including 17 recidivists) failed to qualify as high-risk subjects as measured by family criminality and the presence of at least two of the following six additional characteristics: born illegitimate, four or more siblings, permanently separated from one or both parents before age 15, family on welfare, residing in slum housing, under the supervision of social service administration at least once. West and Farrington also identified a number of high-risk youth who did not engage in criminal behavior. Though these high-risk individuals were often socially maladjusted in ways other than delinquency (for example, substance abuse, social isolation, poor work record), a few seemed to have escaped their backgrounds to become happy, successful, contributing members of society. Such findings reaffirm my original contention that risk and protective factors serve to limit and expand, respectively, one's options but do not determine one's choices.

Exacerbating and Mitigating Factors. Where risk and protective factors are designed to explain criminal involvement, exacerbating and mitigating factors are more relevant when it comes to describing specific criminal events. Consequently, they tend to be more situationally influenced than risk and protective factors. This does not mean, however, that a risk factor cannot also play an exacerbating role or that a protective factor cannot also exert a mitigating effect under a discrete set of circumstances. Drugs, for instance, not only serve to increase the possibility of criminal involvement (risk factor) but also play a significant role in the unfolding of various criminal events (exacerbating factor). Along similar lines, a strong social bond may serve to protect one from becoming involved in a criminal lifestyle while empathy for a potential victim might mitigate against committing a specific criminal act. A variable like ambient temperature, on the other hand, would seem generally restricted to an exacerbating or mitigating role in its impact on criminal outcomes.

Felson (1986) argues that the criminal event entails a convergence of person and situation variables over time and space. Assessing the contextual features of serious assault, Felson and Steadman (1983) discerned that person and choice factors, like the desire for retaliation, played a central role in serious assault and homicide. However, they also noted that specific behaviors on the part of both the victim and various bystanders influenced how the violent scenario played out. In Felson and Steadman's original study it was determined that victims were more likely to have been killed when they were intoxicated, physically aggressive, or in possession of a weapon. Follow-up analyses of these data revealed that third parties often played a role in the eventual outcome of a potentially violent event, either as antagonists or mediators (Felson, Ribner, & Siegel, 1984).

The routine-activities approach to crime postulates that three elements must be present for a predatory criminal act to occur: a motivated offender, a suitable target, and the absence of capable guardians against crime (Cohen & Felson, 1979b). This theory borrows liberally from the social and physical ecological perspectives and considers Hawley's (1950) time-space concepts of rhythm, tempo, and timing. Miethe, Stafford, and Long (1987) investigated the relationship between nighttime activities away from home and crime, and observed concordance in the case of property offenses but not in the case of violent crimes. They attribute the lack of a routine-activities effect for violent crime to the spontaneous nature of this category of offense. However, Kennedy and Forde (1990) explored this issue further and found that routine activities accounted for a significant portion of the variance in both violent and property crimes, but for very different reasons. Routine activities appear to exert their effect on violent crime by exposing offenders and victims to conflict situations, while they influence property crime by identifying salient criminal opportunities.

Another portentous feature of the situational context of a criminal event pertinent to exacerbating and mitigating factors is the manner in which decision alternatives are presented to the individual. Tversky and Kahneman (1981) observed that two formerly identical choice alternatives evoked markedly different preferences when phrased in slightly different ways. From these results Tversky and Kahneman concluded that the mode through which alternatives, options, and possibilities are framed can have a vibrant impact on the decisions one derives. It would appear that both the situational context and the manner in which this context is presented are essential to understanding the role exacerbating and mitigating factors play in the rise of specific criminal events.

Criminal Opportunity. Our discussion of input variables would be incomplete without consideration of criminal opportunities. The study of criminal opportunities dates back to the pioneering work of Merton (1938) and Cloward and Ohlin (1960) and is particularly relevant when we examine crime rates. Weather and seasonal variations in crime doubtlessly suggest the prospect that particular crimes are more common during certain seasons or months of the year (assault during the summer for instance), when the opportunity for human interaction is more apparent. Additionally, research shows that property crimes are more prominent in developed as opposed to underdeveloped countries, and in urban as opposed to rural communities, and suggests that one's access to material goods is at least as important as personal and situational factors in understanding the crime of a given region, country, or area. Finally, while Newman's (1972) notion of "defensible space" has been much maligned, there is qualified support for his claim that certain forms of crime can be reduced by limiting criminal opportunities via specific architectural modifications.

The impact of opportunity on crime rates has been documented in research studies administered since the early 1960s. Wilkins (1964), for instance, related that a large portion of the variance in auto theft in England between the years 1938 and 1961 could be attributed to the number of automobiles available. Felson and Cohen (1977), on the other hand, discerned that burglary rates in the United States between 1950 and 1972 were a multiplicative function of three variables—proportion of the population between the ages of 15 and 24, percent of "primary individual" households, and mobility of various property targets (for example, weight of the average television set), the last two of which provide increased opportunities for crime. In a similar vein, Gould (1969) witnessed a correlation of .98 between the amount of currency available in U.S. banks and the number of bank robberies taking place between 1944 and 1965. Finally, Walsh (1978) notes a parallel between the rise of shoplifting offenses in England, circa 1950 to 1960, and a thirteenfold increase in the number of self-service grocery stores available to potential thieves.

Since it is common knowledge that one cannot steal a car that does not exist or rob a bank that is devoid of funds, what then does the study of opportunity really tell us about crime and criminals? We might answer this question by reminding the reader that a consideration of criminal-opportunity issues not only provides us with insight into the temporal, geographical, and seasonal ebb and flow of crime (Sparks, 1980), but also furnishes us with clues crucial to comprehending specific criminal events. Opportunity restricts our access to specific criminal rewards and helps direct our attention to certain goals and away from others. Few people have available to them the opportunities for such large-scale scams as were perpetuated by the likes of stocktrader Ivan Boesky or televangelist Jim Bakker, although the opportunity for other forms of crime can nearly always be found in an open society.

This discussion of criminal opportunity should not be construed as lending support to the misguided notion that criminals sit around waiting for a criminal opportunity to appear. Unlike most noncriminals, the career or lifestyle criminal is constantly searching for new criminal opportunities; and in a world populated by persons naïve to the ways of the criminal, such opportunities abound. Recidivistic offenders characteristically approach their environments and others in ways that differ substantially from the perspective of noncriminals. Even when not actively pursuing antisocial plans, the habitual criminal is alert to illicit opportunities—an unlocked car door, unattended purse, or unsuspecting citizen. Like a championship football team whose defense habitually forces the opposition into turning over the ball, the high-rate offender capitalizes on whatever nascent opportunities are available in forging a criminal way of life.

This hypersensitivity to criminal opportunities was present at an early age in bank robber Willie "The Actor" Sutton:

> The first day at the new school I noticed that the teacher put her pocketbook in the desk drawer. I also noticed that when we were dismissed for the morning recess she left the room too. I served to notice all of this automatically. That very first day, as we all moved down the hall toward the schoolyard, I mumbled something about having forgotten my handkerchief and slipped back into the empty classroom. It took about ten seconds to reach into the drawer of the teacher's desk, open her pocketbook and grab one of the dollar bills that lay in it (Sutton, 1953, p. 47).

Even though the nine-year-old Sutton saw a criminal opportunity that would have been overlooked by most noncriminals, the actual criminal events one chooses to engage in are still a function of the opportunities available to that individual at any particular point in time.

Target Selection. Cousin to the issue of opportunity is the question of target selection. Several factors are considered by offenders in identifying potential human and property targets. Some of the more popular considerations are proximity, accessibility, potential yield, and timing (Hough, 1987). Given the knowledge that offenders rarely traverse a significant distance for the purpose of committing a criminal act, persons and areas in close physical proximity to the offender are at greatest risk for victimization. The accessibility of a particular target and the absence of capable guardians against crime (Cohen & Felson, 1979b) are also frequently taken into account by offenders searching for a target upon which to unleash their antisocial inclinations. The perceived value or potential yield provided by the target is a further consideration, although offender judgments in this regard are often flawed and oversimplified (Carroll, 1978). Timing enters into decisions involving target selection to the extent that certain times of the day, days of the week, or seasons of the year are more or less conducive to the commission of various criminal acts.

A potential victim's lifestyle may also influence his or her vulnerability to victimization. In the original presentation of their lifestyle theory of criminal victimization, Hindelang, Gottfredson, and Garofalo (1978) examined ways in which persons leave themselves vulnerable to victimization by the company they keep and the general activities in which they engage. Victimization rates are two to three times higher in persons whose lifestyle brings them into regular contact with strangers in potentially conflict-promoting environments like discos and bars, although there is no victimization-enhancing effect for persons involved in structured social activities like organized clubs and religious functions (Garofalo, 1987). It seems likely, then, that certain lifestyle features of potential victims may be taken into account by offenders searching for a potential target.

Process

Once the relevant data are entered into a computer, the machine shifts into a processing mode, whereby the information is analyzed by way of existing programs, formats, and procedures. There is also a processing step in the human decision-making sequence that finds its expression in the evaluation, organization, and interpretation of input data. However, unlike a computer the human decision maker does more than apply logic and rules to the information presented. First, the human decision-making process is affected by developmental factors. Second, human problem solving is not only more flexible than the binary logic of the computer but also provides for the possibility of creative solutions that are not necessarily tied to the immediate situational context. Third, the human analytic process is less efficient and more susceptible to error than is the methodology of the computer. These three factors are critical in promoting a fuller appreciation of the information-processing stage of human decision making.

Developmental Context. Just as there is a situational context (input) to human decision making, so there is also a developmental context. The humanistic notion that we are born with the capacity for free will seems as credulous as it is optimistic. It appears that the infant responds to internal drives (hunger) and external circumstances (warm ambient temperature), but does not actively choose or select one behavior over another. Interestingly enough, from an early age the child learns that certain behaviors are more likely to get a parental response than other behaviors. This would seem to suggest the presence of an incipient sensitivity and a budding selectivity in the actions of even the very young child.

Where a strict behaviorist might argue that an infant is ''conditioned'' to respond in a particular fashion, and that there is no need for the intermediary concept of choice, I contend that early learning actually reflects the onset of decision-making capability. For as the child begins to realize that certain behaviors are rewarded and other actions are punished, we see the advent of internalized representations of events, situations, and people. This mental representation process is not only central to the theorizing of information-processing theorists but is also crucial in the minds of developmental psychologists like

Piaget (1954). According to Piaget, a child entering into the preoperational stage of cognitive development (around age two) begins relying on internal representations through symbols, images, and language. By age seven most children have graduated to the concrete operational stage, in which fundamental principles of nature such as the law of cause and effect are beginning to be grasped.

Piaget (1954) also theorized about moral development, although Kohlberg (1976) is the individual whose name is most clearly associated with this particular area of research endeavor. Building on Piaget's earlier work, Kohlberg proposed six stages of moral development embedded in three levels. There is ample evidence that younger children tend to function at lower stages of moral development than older children. However, Kohlberg's assertion that the moral reasoning skills of delinquents are inferior to those exhibited by age-matched peers has not always found confirmation in the empirical research literature (Morash, 1981). Moreover, studies show that responses on a moral dilemma task demonstrate minimal concordance with actual behavior (Blasi, 1980; Kupfersmid & Wonderly, 1980).

Conative development, which concerns an individual's capacity for self-control, also seems relevant to our discussion on personal choice and responsibility. Mischel (1974) writes that impulse control expands with age, although the results of one study indicate that children as young as three are capable of delaying gratification (Schwarz, Schrager, & Lyons, 1983). Therefore, while it appears likely that an infant does not engage in informed decision making, the capacity to choose evolves rapidly and matures in response to various changes occurring in the young child. In a review of the literature on cognitive, moral, and conative development and criminal liability in children, Dalby (1985) concludes that by age 7 most children satisfy rudimentary criteria for criminal responsibility, while nearly all children are liable from a criminal justice standpoint by age 14. Dalby is quick to point out, however, that not all same-aged children are functioning at the same development level.

A young child operates largely on the basis of information provided by his or her immediate environment (family members). However, as this child grows older he or she is exposed to extrafamilial sources of information through contact with peers, school officials, television, and the criminal justice system. In conjunction with this evolving self-awareness comes a concomitant broadening of the options available to the individual along with an expanding ability to make informed decisions. As such, we need to consider development variables as delimiting a person's information-processing capabilities—factors which recede in significance as the individual matures. It would also appear advisable, then, that we replace the outmoded concept of innate or absolute free will with the more reasoned hypothesis that choice behavior unfolds and one's options expand as a function of cognitive development and a widening sphere of environmental experience.

Cost : Benefit Analysis. Decisions are characterized by three primary elements: (1) a set of alternatives; (2) a set of outcomes or payoffs; (3) an assessment of the probability of achieving said outcomes (Johnson & Payne, 1986). Economic theorists like Becker (1968) argue that the assessment of outcomes takes place in the form of a cost : benefit analysis. The human decision maker, according to Becker, weighs the relative advantages and disadvantages of committing a specific criminal act against the advantages and disadvantages of a legitimate enterprise. There are several factors that enter into the cost : benefit analysis, although one's ability to delay gratification and work for long-term benefit, referred to by Wilson and Herrnstein (1985) as one's time horizon, is particularly vital to the eventual outcome of one's internal deliberations. Other factors that often enter into the equation include one's stated motive for engaging in crime and the fallibility of the human decision-making process, both of which are discussed later in this section. If in the end the cost : benefit ratio for crime exceeds the cost : benefit ratio for no crime then, according to economically oriented theorists, the individual will elect crime. Conversely, if the cost : benefit ratios are in the opposite direction, then the individual will select legitimate avenues of goal attainment.

While it very well may be that the human decision-making process falls along the lines of a cost : benefit analysis, there are several problems with the manner in which this process has been conceptualized by economic-minded tacticians. For one, choice appears to be a perceptual process. The deterrent value of specific punishers and the attractiveness of selected reinforcers is largely a function of how they are perceived by the individual (Waldo & Chiricos, 1972). What is more, there is evidence that human choice is a fallible, psychologically oriented process rather than an efficient, economically oriented process (Carroll, 1978). Finally, the bulk of theorizing on the economic aspects of crime has apparently failed to take into account a number of important advances made in the field of psychology relative to the effects of specific reinforcement and punishment contingencies.

Regarding the point just made, Wilson and Herrnstein (1985) remind us that there are two types of reinforcers—primary and secondary. Primary reinforcers attain this status through satisfaction of an innate need like hunger or thirst. Secondary reinforcers, on the other hand, achieve their effect by being paired with a primary reinforcer through a process of classical conditioning. The primary reinforcer not only lays the groundwork for such secondary reinforcers as money, material goods, and prestige but also provides us with a link to the biological bases of behavior. Various schedules of reinforcement are then formed by way of a process of operant conditioning, modeling, and choice behavior.

Schedules of reinforcement take the cost : benefit process a step further by showing how the individual weighs alternatives in light of the rewards and punishments he or she has been exposed to in the past. This reinforcement history exerts a profound effect on the behavior of the individual, since satisfaction of the drive for excitement, acceptance by antisocial peers, or rapid acquisition of material goods can be especially reinforcing, particularly if one rarely gets punished for violations of the moral code. Research, in fact, has demonstrated that fear of punishment and estimates of imminent apprehension both decline with criminal experience (Feeney, 1986; Weaver & Carroll, 1985). This does not mean, however, that we are prisoners of our own reinforcement histories, since we all have the ability, with age, to emit behaviors that have never before been rewarded or refrain from engaging in actions that have been richly reinforced in the past.

Validation. There are multifarious reasons why people engage in criminal action. Some like the easy money, others the excitement, and still others the power it seemingly provides them. Though it is difficult to organize these criminal motives into meaningful categories, to do so facilitates our understanding of the criminal decision-making process and provides an avenue through which opportunity and target selection might be paired with a specific criminal event. Validation affords the offender a psychological rationale for his or her violations of societal laws and the personal rights of others. The validation process operates on the basis of a motivational set designed to justify, direct, and organize current and future displays of criminal conduct.

A study of robbers carried out by Feeney (1986) determined that 60 percent of those interviewed reported engaging in robbery as a quick means to accrue large sums of money for drugs, clothes, or late-model automobiles. The remaining subjects (40%) stated that they engaged in robbery as a way of obtaining excitement, achieving a sense of power and control over others, and expressing angry feelings. In a second study, Carroll (1978) discerned that the positive aspects of a situation (money) seemed more important than the negative aspects (probability of getting caught) in directing the behavior of criminal offenders. More recently, Walters and White (1988) discovered that the offenders in their sample gave several reasons for their involvement in crime, but one of the more common explanations was the express desire for more money.

Based more on clinical experience than research data, there are four general motives considered to be important in validating criminal activity: anger and rebellion, excitement and pleasure, power and control, and greed and laziness. The anger and rebellion motive reflects the hostility, resentment, and acrimony some offenders direct at the community because of a perceived sense of societal injustice. Excitement and pleasure are prominent in the criminal activities of adolescents and young adults and provide for immediate gratification of self-centered desires. Our third motive, power and control, reveals why some offenders put a premium on gaining power and control over others. Finally, greed and laziness can be observed in crimes inspired by the desire to accumulate material goods (to include money) as rapidly and effortlessly as possible. The validation process and the four motives that compose it, are discussed in greater detail by Walters (1990b).

Fallibility. Maultsby (1975), the founder of Rational Behavior Therapy (RBT), asserts that we are all fallible human beings. This is particularly evident when it comes to the manner in which we analyze and process information. Alexander Pope is frequently credited with using the phrase, "to err is human";

well, it is also quite common for humans to rely on oversimplified environmental models in making decisions (Carroll, 1978). According to the results of a participant-observer study of professional shoplifters, habitual offenders weigh alternatives utilizing an oversimplified, often unidimensional, decision-making approach (Weaver & Carroll, 1978). This is probably one of the pitfalls into which many offenders, novice as well as professional, fall once they embrace the criminal lifestyle. To a large extent, continued involvement in lawbreaking activity augments these persons' chances of arrest in the future.

As was discussed previously, developmental factors place limits on one's ability to process information. The natural imperfection of the human decision-making process does much the same thing. Being human, we are subject to information loss and the drawing of erroneous inferences. This occurs, in part, because people are in the habit of considering only a portion of the relevant facts and sometimes focus on irrelevant information in rendering their decisions. Accordingly, the human decision maker will never be as efficient as a computer, but then again, the computer will probably never be able to capture the creativity, ingenuity, and charity of the human decision maker. In short, the innate limitations of the human mind need to be taken into account when examining the process of decision making, criminal or otherwise.

Output

The output, as conceptualized by the present model of criminal decision making, is a product of the input and processing stages. Information presented to the individual (input) is analyzed in such a manner (process) as to bring about a final outcome. This decision is influenced but not determined by the person, situation, and interactive variables discussed in previous chapters. Although the output decision is largely dichotomous in nature (crime–no crime), there are additional features of the criminal situation that must also be decided upon—that is, selecting a crime partner or deciding to go it alone; choosing the time frame in which the criminal act is to be carried out; formulating a precise plan of criminal action.

It is noteworthy that Feeney (1986) found a minimal degree of formal planning in the criminal schemes of many of his experienced robbers. This would suggest that an interaction exists between choice behavior and cognitive style, particularly as one gravitates toward increased levels of criminal involvement. Pearson and Weiner (1985) discuss behavioral consequences and feedback factors in their integrated theory of delinquency and crime, which may have something to contribute to the output stage of our decision-making model of criminal behavior. In fact, the reinforcement and punishment of behaviors emanating from one's decisions provide useful information about whether to continue or desist from a particular chain of behavior, whether this behavior is criminal or noncriminal in nature.

CONCLUSION

Returning to the mega-analysis with which we began this chapter, we can see that if we were able to effectively measure choice behavior, such conduct would account for much of the variance that had previously gone unexplained. Unfortunately, describing this measure in theoretical terms is much easier than deriving an operationalized meter of choice behavior. The decision-making model described in this chapter is offered in the spirit of cooperation as it encourages greater integration, creativity, and collaboration on the part of researchers and theorists, but should in no way be viewed as authoritative or conclusive. As we complete the final leg of our journey through the maze of correlates that comprise significant criminality, it should be kept in mind that if the model of criminal decision making discussed in this chapter inspires researchers to look at the issue of criminal choice in greater detail, then it will have fulfilled its author's intentions.

PART IV

THEORY

9

Models and Theories of Criminal Behavior

Organizing the often disparate results of criminal science research into a coherent, integrated, and useful system of theoretical constructs can be a genuinely challenging task. Empirical data do not always fit comfortably within the framework of contemporary models and theories of criminal behavior. Moreover, outcomes generated by the same data set are sometimes inconsistent, incongruous, and seemingly irreconcilable. The temptation to force these results into existing theories and models is consequently strong. It is also apparent that reviews of the literature have occasionally been selective in that findings consonant with the reviewer's perspective are conceded greater credence than less favorable outcomes. While the tendency to slant the results or review of particular areas of research endeavor in favor of one's biases is understandable, it is by no means justified—not if our goal is to make the study of criminal behavior more scientific.

Walters (1990b) examined eight theories of criminality with the aid of six criteria borrowed from Maddi (1976). For the purpose of the present discussion we group these criteria into two primary categories: operationality and testability and fertility and efficacy. The first criterion cluster asks whether the theory is clear, concise, and open to survey and review. The second criterion cluster concerns itself with the dual issue of fruitfulness and empirical validity. In other words, does the theory stimulate empirical and theoretical inquiry, and if so, how does it fare under such scrutiny? Although a theory can never be proven or deemed unconditionally valid (Walters, 1990b), it can be found untenable, void, or lacking in support. It is the responsibility of criminal scientists everywhere to dispassionately evaluate current theories of crime causation, discarding those that do not meet our requirements, revising those that are incomplete, and devising new theories where gaps in knowledge exist.

In this chapter we entertain six theories or models of criminal behavior subdivided into four categories: person-oriented, situation-oriented, interactive, and choice. It is not surprising that the author of the person-oriented theory we discuss (Hare) is a psychologist, since person-oriented theories are based largely on the study of individual differences. Situation-oriented theorists, on the other hand, emphasize the role of environmental factors in crime genesis and are represented here by Cohen's (1955) subcultural deviance model of delinquency development and the labeling perspective (Lemert, 1972; Schur, 1971). Interactive theories consider the complex interplay of person and situation factors as depicted in Mednick's (1977) biosocial model of law-abiding behavior and Hirschi's (1969) social bonding version of control theory. Finally, choice theorists, though not negating the role person and situation variables can play in crime genesis, focus their attention on the process of decision making as it relates specifically to crime.

PERSON-ORIENTED THEORY

There is probably no such thing as a theory of criminal behavior that considers only person variables. There are, however, models that elevate person variables to a position of preeminence over situational, interactive, and choice variables. The person-oriented theory reviewed in this section is Hare's (1970) response perseveration model of psychopathy.

Hare's Response Perseveration Model

Robert D. Hare (1970), a psychologist and professor at the University of British Columbia in Vancouver, postulates that a neurologically based deficit in the ability to avoid engaging in perseverative activity is a prime cause of psychopathy and serious criminal conduct. Attempting to explain the recidivistic offender's irresponsibility, impulsiveness, and apparent inability to learn from his or her past mistakes, Hare noticed a similarity in the actions of habitual criminals and animals whose brains had been lesioned (McCleary, 1966). Doren (1987) states that Hare's theory can be organized into three principle tenets. First, psychopaths and criminals are presumed to be suffering from lesions of the limbic system. Second, these ablations are said to interfere with the organism's ability to inhibit ongoing behavior. Third, this loss of inhibitory control leads to a perseveration of situationally dominant responses irrespective of the long-term consequences of these actions.

Hare (1970) based much of his early theorizing about the perseverative tendencies of criminals on animal research signaling the presence of a relationship between limbic system damage and deficits in behavioral control and passive avoidance learning (McCleary, 1966). Lesioned limbic areas, such as the septum (Lubar, 1964), anterior caudate nucleus (Fox, Kimble, & Lickey, 1964), hippocampus (Teitelbaum & Milner, 1963), insular cortex (Pare & Dumas, 1965), and amygdala (Bacon & Stanley, 1963) have been shown to interfere with behavioral inhibition in rats, cats, and dogs. Ursin, McCleary, and Linck (cited in McCleary, 1966) trained 20 rats, half of whom had portions of their limbic system ablated, to run from the middle of a single-lane maze to a goal box located at one end. Once this response had been learned, the researchers shocked the rats while they ate the food contained in the goal box. All ten of the nonlesioned rats, but only one of the lesioned rats, subsequently learned to avoid the goal box by running to the opposite end of the maze. Four of the lesioned rats remained in the start box and the other five ran to the goal box despite the fact this action was inevitably followed by electrical shock.

Although animal research clearly demonstrates that animals whose limbic systems have been ablated are subject to more frequent displays of perseverative action than nonlesioned animals, it is difficult to generalize these findings to antisocial behavior in humans. In an effort to extend the issue of cortical damage and perseverative behavior to humans, Hare examined the results of electroencephalograph (EEG) studies on psychopaths and criminals. Early research on this issue suggested gross cortical immaturity on the part of criminal offenders that was vaguely reminiscent of EEG findings obtained in samples of normal adolescents (Ehrlich & Keogh, 1956; Ellingson, 1954). Kurland, Yeager, and Arthur (1963) recorded EEG anomalies in the more highly aggressive and psychopathic subjects they tested. However, Walters and White (1988) argue that EEG abnormalities may be the result rather than cause of crime, since involvement in a criminal lifestyle may increase one's risk for certain categories of brain pathology (for example, head damage from fights, generalized dysfunction from chronic drug usage). Petersen et al. (1982), however, observed a connection between EEG irregularities measured at age 1 to 15, and before subjects had experienced their inaugural arrest and later convictions for theft.

Despite the seeming support EEG results lend a neurological interpretation of crime, there are several problems with this area of research. As the reader may recall, EEG findings are only about 60 percent accurate (Filskov & Goldstein, 1974), with a false positive rate of between 15 and 20 percent (Mayo, 1976). Moreover, from 30 to 68 percent of the psychopaths and criminals included in these research investigations have failed to record anomalous EEGs (Volavka, 1987). Reviewing the results of EEG research on criminal offenders, Syndulko (1978) uncovered a higher-than-normal rate of EEG abnormality, but acknowledged no difference when offenders were compared with noncriminal psychiatric patients. Even if research determines that cortical dysfunction is part of the criminal profile, there is as of yet no conclusive proof that such problems are responsible for the self- and other-destructive actions of the typical high-rate offender.

A third area of research enlisted in support of a neurological interpretation of crime centers on measures of electrodermal reactivity. Borkovec (1970) was one of the first investigators to discover that psychopathic offenders exposed to auditory tones evidenced smaller electrodermal responses than noncriminal controls. Hare and Quinn (1971) observed similar results in a group of psychopaths evaluated for habituation to the cardiac-orienting response, while Loeb and Mednick (1977) discovered that children later convicted of serious criminality recorded lower initial skin-conductance responses than children with no subsequent history of criminal involvement. Hare (1982) later determined that a high psychopathic group was less reactive than normal subjects to an aversive stimulus that could be avoided, although there were no group differences when the aversive stimulus was unavoidable. Perhaps psychopaths and criminals respond to escape-option situations the way many of us respond to situations in which escape is not possible. Though research addressing the issue of electrodermal reactivity in social rule-breakers adds substance to Hare's position on diminished responsiveness in habitual criminal offenders, it does not localize this deficit in the limbic region of the brain nor does it necessarily indicate the presence of a perseverative deficit as has been hypothesized by Hare.

Perseverative deficits have been demonstrated, however, in paradigms in which behavioral tasks have been employed. Newman, Widom, and Nathan (1985) provided monetary rewards to subjects who responded to positive stimuli and monetary punishments to subjects who responded to negative stimuli, and found that psychopathic delinquents committed significantly more passive avoidance[1] errors than nonpsychopathic controls on a task where earning a reward competed with avoiding punishment. However, there were no differences between psychopaths and controls when subjects were reinforced for responding to positive stimuli and rewarded for failing to respond to negative stimuli. This led Newman et al. to conclude that the deficit was one of passive avoidance rather than lack of motivation or ability on the part of psychopathic subjects. The relationship between psychopathy and impaired passive avoidance learning was subsequently replicated in two follow-up experiments (Newman & Kosson, 1986; Newman, Patterson, & Kosson, 1987). These developments provide sustenance to the argument that a weakness in the psychopath's ability to inhibit certain behavioral outcomes serves as a foundation for the perseveration of a situationally dominant response, although they reveal nothing about the origin of this alleged deficit.

In evaluating Hare's theory it is important that we keep in mind the criteria of operationality/testability and fertility and efficacy. Hare's theory seems to encounter problems when either set of criteria is considered. First, researchers have been unable to derive a robust and reliable behavioral measure of limbic system damage in humans. Both EEG recordings and electrodermal reactivity have been used to appraise the brain activity of psychopaths and criminal offenders, although both are patently ineffective in localizing cortical dysfunction (Wedding, Horton, & Webster, 1986). It has also been argued that Hare's theory is lacking in comprehensiveness (Doren, 1987). Hare has sought to remedy this by implicating additional neurological features (for example, perceptual asymmetry) in the crime development sequence (Hare & Connolly, 1987). However, to date the theory continues to be incomplete and significantly less thorough than some of the other theories we discuss later in this chapter.

[1]Passive avoidance is a research paradigm wherein the subject learns not to make a response to a warning signal in order to avoid a noxious stimulus.

Regarding the fertility and efficacy criterion cluster, Hare's theory has generated a fair amount of research, but the results have been only partly supportive of his three founding theorems. There is virtually no empirical substantiation for Hare's first postulate that psychopaths suffer from lesions in the limbic region of the brain. Although animal research (McCleary, 1966) tends to corroborate Hare's second—lesions of the limbic system result in a loss of ability to inhibit ongoing behavior—and third—the loss of ability to inhibit ongoing activity leads to perseveration of situationally dominant behavior regardless of the long-term consequences—postulates, we would do well to remind ourselves that these studies were the origin of many of Hare's ideas and therefore not an adequate test of the theory's validity. Moreover, the results of several animal studies suggest that once the lesioned animal is allowed to practice a task, response perseveration drops off dramatically (McCleary, 1966). It is highly unlikely that the same could be said of psychopaths and high-rate offenders to which Hare is attempting to generalize this research. Hare's model, like most person-oriented theories, is lacking in comprehensiveness, precision, and empirical support, largely because it probes only a small portion of the relevant data.

SITUATION-ORIENTED THEORY

In contrast to person-oriented theories, which highlight the role of individual factors in crime genesis, situation-oriented approaches direct their attention to environmental circumstances and conditions. Differential association (Sutherland & Cressey, 1978), social strain (Merton, 1957), and the group conflict approach, as represented by the Marxist school of criminology (Colvin & Pauly, 1983), have all taken up the banner of situationally oriented concerns.

Situation-oriented theory can probably be traced back to the Chicago school of criminology. Sometime around 1920 the sociology department at the University of Chicago embarked on a program of research into the effects of urban living on the human condition, with particular emphasis on the development of patterns of criminal conduct. The theorizing of such notables as Robert Parks, Ernest Burgess, Clifford R. Shaw, and Henry D. McKay showed how social disorganization, rapid urbanization, wide-spectrum population shifts, and the transmission of criminal values all helped shape the criminal and delinquent outcomes of persons living in the Chicago metropolitan area. In this section we find ourselves examining two models—Cohen's (1955) subculture of delinquency theory and the labeling perspective—with clear ties to the pioneering work of the Chicago school.

Cohen's Subculture of Delinquency Theory

Albert Cohen's (1955) work on delinquent subcultures reveals the influence of Edwin Sutherland and Robert Merton. Sutherland's differential association theory (Sutherland & Cressey, 1978) and Merton's (1957) social strain theory therefore serve as preambles to our discussion of Cohen's subculture of delinquency interpretation of criminal involvement.

Differential Association Theory. Sutherland (1939) proposed that criminal behavior is learned in association with others, especially peers. Hence, a person exposed to an excess of definitions favorable to violations of the law and an absence of definitions unfavorable to social violations would be expected to be drawn to delinquent solutions to their problems (Cohen, Lindesmith, & Schuessler, 1956). Sutherland's differential association theory of criminal involvement can be summarized in five basic postulates: (1) crime, like any behavior, is learned; (2) criminal behavior is learned in intimate association with those who commit crime; (3) criminal outcomes are a function of the frequency, intensity, duration, and priority of these associations; (4) cultural conflict subserves the differential association process; (5) individual differences are only important to the extent that they impact on one's associations. According to Sutherland, differential association involves not only the learning of the actual techniques of crime but of motives, attitudes, drives, and rationalizations favorable to violations of the law as well (Sutherland & Cressey, 1978).

Early research on differential association was generally supportive of major aspects of the theory, but there were several postulates that received less than full support. Short (1957), for instance, determined that delinquency was strongly correlated with the intensity of associations but much less so with their frequency, duration, or priority. Enyon and Reckless (1961) ascertained that associations with delinquent peers predicted both officially recorded and self-reported criminality, while Voss (1964) noted a positive correlation between one's rate of association with delinquent peers and one's own level of delinquent activity. More recently, Reinarman and Fagan (1988) observed a differential-association effect in juveniles that was largely independent of the social class of the subject's neighborhood.

Jaquith (1981) carried out an evaluation of the differential-association interpretation of causality in the case of substance use and discovered that alcohol and marijuana intake in adolescents was reasonably well accounted for by the differential association theorem, although allowances need to be made for the differential impact of peer pressure and variations in internalized definitions of behavior favorable and unfavorable to violations of the law. Orcutt (1987) has also studied marijuana usage in teenagers and young adults and has obtained results supportive of the basic tenets of differential association theory. Crossing motivation with associations, Orcutt determined that college students expressing unfavorable attitudes toward marijuana tended to avoid the use of this substance regardless of the number of friends semiactively involved in its use. In a similar vein, students communicating more favorable views on marijuana were likely to be users themselves if at least one of their four closest friends were also semiregular users. Of students holding a neutral opinion about the use of marijuana, however, the rate of usage depended largely on their associations—marijuana usage rates approaching zero if such individuals had no close friends who used the substance but rising to around 50 percent when two or more of the subject's four closest friends were semiregular smokers of marijuana.

Despite the wide empirical support differential association theory has enjoyed over the years, the theory is not beyond reproach. First, Sutherland failed to adequately explain why budding outlaws turn to delinquent peers rather than to their parents or more conforming peers in deriving definitions of appropriate conduct (Wilson & Herrnstein, 1985). Second, Sutherland postulates a certain degree of specificity in crime based on the theory that criminals learn both the motivation and techniques of crime by way of their associations. Unfortunately for differential association theory, research has fairly conclusively demonstrated that crime specialization is largely a myth (Smith, Smith, & Noma, 1984; Wolfgang et al., 1972). Third, it is always possible that criminal associations are the result, rather than the cause, of criminal involvement. Finally, it has been argued that critical hypotheses and other features of Sutherland's theory are untestable (Cressey, 1960), although many aspects of the theory have, in fact, been successfully tested (Orcutt, 1987; Matsueda, 1988; Tittle et al., 1986).

Social Strain Theory. The noted French sociologist Emile Durkheim (1938) coined the term *anomie* to describe a state of normlessness brought about by certain adverse social conditions. From this, Merton (1957) formulated a social strain theory of criminal involvement. Merton proposed that a society instills in its citizenry aspirations for upward mobility and a desire for selected goals. However, when legitimate avenues to goal attainment are blocked, anomie or strain sets in, which in turn compels the individual to violate the law in order to attain these goals. Lower-class persons are viewed by Merton as more susceptible to the ravages of anomie because they are more regularly thwarted in their efforts to participate in the economic rewards of the wider society. As such, social class assumes a prominent position in Merton's theory, although research outcomes on the proposed nexus between social class and crime (Tittle, Villemez, & Smith, 1978) and the connection between income inequality and crime (Messner, 1981; Stack, 1982) tend to run counter to Merton's formulations.

Merton assumed in his theorizing that humans are conforming organisms who only violate the law when the disjunction between goals and means becomes so great that the individual believes he or she can no longer pursue socially sanctioned goals via legitimate channels. Society and certain social variables are, according to strain theorists, responsible for the majority of crime being committed in the world today. According to Merton, a society that emphasizes goals over the means to obtain these goals, and that restricts access to opportunities for legitimate advancement, is establishing the conditions for anomie and future criminality. Strain theorists have long argued that once a person is removed from a situation of anomie or frustration, negative behavior will recede. However, when this hypothesis has been tested with pupils dropping out of high school it has been largely refuted by results showing such persons engaging in more rather than less crime upon leaving school (Shavit & Rattner, 1988; Thornberry, Moore, & Christenson, 1985).

Several investigators have obtained results indicating that between 10 and 30 percent of the variance in selected measures of criminal and/or delinquent outcome can be attributed to independent variables purportedly reflecting social strain (Brennan & Huizinga, 1975; Cernkovitch & Giordano, 1987; Stack, 1983). Conversely, Hirschi (1969) contends that commitment to conventional aims is sufficient to explain results such as these, and that there is no need to bring goals-means disjunction into the picture. Farnworth and Leiber (1989) arrived at a somewhat different conclusion, however, in a study of Seattle, Washington, adolescents. Operationalizing disjunction as incongruence between educational aspirations and expectations rather than between economic goals and educational means, Farnworth and Leiber uncovered a moderate association between disjunction and utilitarian or property-oriented crime and a slight, but significant, relationship between disjunction and nonutilitarian crime.

Strain theory has been faulted by Bahr (1979) for being too general and imprecise, and by Elliott and Voss (1974) for failing to account for criminality in persons raised in middle-class home environments. Furthermore, Merton has been taken to task for not explaining why most working-class youth do not become involved in significant levels of criminality and of those who do engage in crime, why many desist before becoming adults (Hirschi, 1969). It has also been noted that, contrary to predictions derived from strain theory, high aspirations in working-class youth are inversely rather than directly correlated with subsequent criminality (Elliott & Voss, 1974; Hirschi, 1969). Finally, the performance of strain theory in comparisons contrasting it with other interpretations of criminal involvement (for example, social control theory) is unimpressive (Hepburn, 1976; Stack, 1982; Thornberry et al., 1985) and the operationality of terms like goal-means disjunction and blocked opportunities are so weak as to make proper evaluation of Merton's theory exceedingly difficult.

Cohen's Model. Since Cohen studied under both Sutherland and Merton, it seems only natural that his approach should reflect the influence of both mentors. Sutherland's principal contribution to the subculture of delinquency interpretation of criminal involvement was instilling in Cohen an understanding of how people learn to act in association with others. Merton, on the other hand, helped Cohen develop an appreciation for subcultures as a major avenue of investigation. Merging these two trends in criminological thought, Cohen derived a theory that saw delinquent youth forming a subculture whose values and ideals differed substantially from those held by the wider society.

Cohen (1955) theorized that lower-class boys are encouraged to strive for middle-class goals. However, since significantly fewer legitimate opportunities exist for these lower-class individuals, they experience what Cohen refers to as status frustration. Many such individuals attempt to handle their negative feelings of frustration by seeking status among similarly alienated peers, says Cohen. The theory goes on to postulate that these individuals subsequently assemble into gangs where they can justify their common cause, learn the attitudes and actions of crime, and rebel collectively against the wider society whom they view as responsible for their misfortune.

There are nine "middle class" values that lower-class male youth experiencing a sense of status frustration are hypothesized to reject: (1) responsibility; (2) rationality; (3) ambition; (4) self-control; (5) development of skills for conventional success; (6) cultivation of manners and courtesy; (7) respect for other people's property; (8) postponement of immediate gratification in favor of long-term goals; and (9) the necessity of wholesome recreation (Cohen, 1955). The delinquent subculture takes these values and, for the most part, reverses them so that irresponsibility and laziness are valued over accountability and ambition. The gang then takes on the role of an opportunity structure through which the members of the delinquent subculture strike back at a society they believe has abandoned them.

School is thought by Cohen (1955) to be a primary vehicle by which young people are taught middle-class values. As such, children who do not succeed in this environment will likely rebel, not only against the authority of the school but against the authority of the wider society as well. Cohen, like Merton (1957), would predict that since the school creates a sense of status frustration in many lower-class pupils, dropping out of school should be followed by decreased rather than increased levels of subsequent criminality. Although early research on crime and school dropout rates was generally supportive of this supposition (compare Elliott, 1966; Elliott & Voss, 1974), more recent studies show an accelerating rate of criminal involvement in delinquency-prone students dropping out of school (compare Bachman, O'Malley, & Johnston, 1978; Polk et al., 1981; Shavit & Rattner, 1988; Thornberry et al., 1985).

There is little substantiation for many of the other "strain" features of Cohen's theory, to include the assumption that most delinquents feel frustrated by middle-class expectations (Downes, 1966; Hirschi, 1969) or that most lower-class youth strive for success as defined by middle-class values (Kitsuse & Dietrick, 1959; Lemert, 1972). Strain theory also predicts that females should contribute more to the crime rate than they apparently do since they have traditionally been denied access to many forms of societally defined success (Harris, 1977). In probing this issue further, Simon and Baxter (1989) note that women in less socially and economically progressive nations do not engage in crime any more often than women living in more progressive countries. Furthermore, changes in economic opportunities over time apparently had no appreciable effect on the criminal activities of females in the 31 nations surveyed by these two investigators.

The differential association component of Cohen's (1955) theory has received far greater empirical support than has the strain component. It is reasonably well established, for example, that peers play a cardinal role in delinquency development (Elliott, Huizinga, & Ageton, 1985; Hanson et al., 1984; West, 1982) and that the majority of crimes committed by juveniles occur in the company of others (Petersilia, Greenwood, & Lavin, 1978). However, though delinquency frequently originates in groups, it is not normally a function of gang-related activity, a primary focus of Cohen's theorizing (Rutter & Giller, 1984). Consequently, while there has been some confirmation of the learning and associational aspects of Cohen's subculture of delinquency theory, its operationality/testability is limited while its fertility/efficacy is only slightly better than average, and perhaps below that which could be achieved through a straight differential association interpretation of the data.

Cloward and Ohlin (1960), architects of the opportunity theory of delinquency involvement, have argued that instead of just one delinquent subculture, there are at least three distinct deviant subcultures: the criminal, the violent, and the retreatist. The criminal subculture is populated by delinquents who have had the opportunity to observe and interact with professional thieves who encourage criminality but reject violent, gang-related activities. The violent subculture contains adolescents who have had little contact with professional criminals but who have had the opportunity to observe those who choose violent solutions to their problems. Persons in the violent subculture treat aggression as a means to an end—securing peer status. The retreatist subculture is marked by heavy drug usage and addiction and is stocked with juveniles whose access to legitimate, criminal, and violent opportunities has been seriously curtailed.

The Labeling Perspective

Because proponents of the labeling perspective view individual differences in crime to be principally a consequence of societal labeling practices, it will be treated as a situation-oriented approach to criminal science theorizing. Labeling theorists fervently argue that society is partly responsible for crime owing chiefly to the attributions and labels it uses to identify certain of its members (Plummer, 1979; Schur, 1971). The criminal is, in effect, a victim of his or her environment and the labeling practices of the society in which he or she resides. The labeling perspective is an extension of attribution theory and symbolic interactionalism and, as such, places primary emphasis on the effects labels have on a person's self-image (Lemert, 1951), as well as the manner in which they restrict one's access to societally sanctioned goals and legitimate opportunities for advancement (Tannenbaum, 1938).

Youthful offenders, according to labeling theorists, are tagged from the moment they first come into contact with the criminal justice system. As the theory goes, a youthful offender once labeled begins to isolate him or herself from conventional society, while seeking the companionship of similarly labeled peers. In a study directed by Gold and Williams (1969) adolescents apprehended for illegal activities and later processed through the juvenile court system were shown to commit a larger number of subsequent offenses relative to a matched group of nonapprehended control subjects. After reviewing the literature on labeling and delinquent behavior, Rutter and Giller (1984) concluded that official processing through the criminal justice system tends to enhance the prospect of future offending. Thus, while a court appearance may not be perceived by most juvenile offenders as stigmatizing (Foster, Dinitz, & Reckless, 1972), employers (Buikhuisen & Dijksterhuss, 1971), teachers (Balch, 1972), and family members (Snyder, 1971) do not typically share this view.

In a 10- to 25-year follow-up of previously adjudicated delinquents in two Pennsylvania counties, Brown et al. (1989) ascertained a direct association between the length of elapsed time between first contact with the juvenile justice system and adjudication as a delinquent and later adult convictions. Disposition (probation vs. placement), on the other hand, had no discernable effect on the rate of adult conviction. Similar results were obtained in the Racine cohort study, which found the best adult outcomes for the 98 subjects who had been immediately referred and sanctioned (Shannon, 1982). Steadman and Felson (1984) also failed to unearth support for the labeling perspective when they studied police handling of incidents involving adult ex-offenders, ex-mental patients, and general population subjects. Contrary to predictions generated by labeling theory, police offenders were no more likely to arrest ex-offenders or ex-mental patients than they were general population subjects. Findings such as these run counter to the assumptions labeling theorists have about the effect of early adjudication on later criminality.

A fundamental limitation of labeling theory is that it fails to account for deviant and criminal actions engaged in prior to one's involvement in the criminal justice system (Bahr, 1979; Rutter & Giller, 1984). Labeling theorists have argued, in response, that this shortcoming is overshadowed by the theory's ability to predict secondary deviation, the process by which deviant acts assume a self-identifying function (Douglas, 1970; Lemert, 1972). Newton and Shelden (1975) interviewed 36 male youths incarcerated in a minimum security juvenile facility and found evidence of both a primary and secondary deviance effect. However, since this study was based on retrospective accounts of personal experiences with deviant behavior and social control agencies, these results are open to a variety of alternative interpretations. Moreover, Newton and Shelden failed to include a control group of youthful offenders who had engaged in criminality but had not been processed through the juvenile court system. In a like manner, reviews of the research literature on labeling, like that conducted by Mahoney (1974), uncover only modest support for the secondary deviation hypothesis. Thus, while labeling and secondary deviance may help elucidate certain features of the criminal profile, this perspective is not without certain drawbacks, to include a paucity of empirical confirmation for major components of the model.

Besides being restricted in scope, labeling theory is probably more applicable to certain groups than others. A court appearance may be more traumatic for a middle-class youth than a lower-class one and so may more readily result in a negative labeling effect in the former than in the latter (Ageton & Elliott, 1974; Thornberry, 1971). Research conducted by Ageton and Elliott (1974) and

Thomas (1977) further reveals that the labeling effect is weakest for persons most likely to be processed through the criminal justice system. Elliott and colleagues concluded that negative labeling is an attenuating process that exerts its primary effect on adolescents with prior commitment to the conventional social order (Elliott, Ageton, & Canter, 1979). Additional research is required in order to determine whether an interaction between labeling and individual characteristics like commitment is actually at work in creating a negative attribution outcome for certain groups but not others.

There are two founding propositions on which labeling theory rests, neither of which appears to have received much in the way of corroborative support. The first premise states that "extralegal" factors (gender, race, social class) hold more weight than "legal" factors (offense severity, criminal record) when it comes to assigning sanctions to a particular individual. Most scholars agree that extralegal factors play only a small role in criminal justice decision making (Gove, 1980; Tittle, 1975), although Sampson (1986) uncovered evidence of a mild ecological bias in the arrest practices of police officers taking part in a study on police decision making.

A second major assumption of labeling theorists that has attracted criticism from the field holds that state intervention actually creates career or lifestyle criminals. Opponents counter, however, that in addition to the mixed outcomes achieved in studies on the causal nature of labeling effects (Bazemore, 1985; Palamara, Cullen, & Gersten, 1986; Shannon, 1982), research intimates that many high-rate offenders were heavily involved in crime long before coming into contact with the criminal justice system (Mankoff, 1971). Such findings have led Hirschi (1975) to conclude that criminal justice labeling has no appreciable effect on subsequent criminality.

The labeling perspective has unquestionably created much debate and re-evaluation. However, relevant research studies have mustered only a modicum of support for the underlying postulates and tenets of the labeling approach to criminological theory. Moreover, the model's scope is exceedingly narrow and it fails to address such fundamental issues as the process of initial crime development, the role of nonlabeling environmental factors in the criminal development process, and the prospect of personal choice and responsibility. Even more serious than the equivocal empirical findings generated by research on the labeling perspective is the use of imprecisely defined terms and hazy conceptualizations. Until the labeling process is more precisely defined and the scope of the theory expanded, the labeling perspective will remain an interesting but incomplete explanation of crime and its causation.

INTERACTIVE THEORY

Interactive theories consider the complex interplay of person and situation variables as they impact on and explain criminal development. Most of us would agree that person- and situation-oriented models are hampered by oversimplicity.

Although interactional theories, by virtue of their augmented complexity, may have greater face validity than their person- and situation-oriented counterparts, the true test of their utility rests with their ability to organize the plethora of data that have grown up around the important question of crime genesis. The Quay (1977) revision of sensation-seeking theory qualifies as an interactive model to the extent that a biological propensity for stimulation seeking is postulated to interact with parenting style. In this section we explore two additional interactive theories: Mednick's biosocial model and Hirschi's social control theory.

Mednick's Biosocial Theory

Professor Sarnoff A. Mednick proposed a biosocial model of law-abiding behavior in the introductory chapter of a book entitled *The Biosocial Bases of Criminal Behavior* (Mednick & Christiansen, 1977). Arguing that man is an inherently asocial being who is motivated primarily by self-interest and immediate gratification, Mednick set out to explain how people learn to live law-abiding lives rather than criminal ones. Borrowing from Mowrer's (1960) work on fear and avoidance learning, Mednick postulated that the acquisition of law-abiding behavior requires the assemblage of distinctive individual characteristics and the establishment of specific environmental conditions. He attested that if deficiencies were present in either area, the learning of law-abiding behavior would be deficit, fragmentary, or altogether nonexistent.

In much the same manner as Hare (1970) linked autonomic reactivity with criminality, Mednick (1977) proposed that deficits in passive avoidance learning (eluding fear by avoiding behaviors one has been punished for in the past) are at the heart of the criminalization process. Rapid dissipation of the autonomic responses associated with fear and anxiety was thought by Mednick to promote effective learning of the passive avoidance response. Slow dissipation of anxiety and fear, on the other hand, was hypothesized to result in incomplete acquisition of passive avoidance learning. A subset of individuals therefore have trouble anticipating the negative consequences of their actions, either because their parents were remiss in properly training them or because their autonomic reactions are inadequate to the task of forging an effective bond between stimulus and response. These are the type individuals Mednick postulates as being at increased risk for later criminality.

There is reasonably good empirical documentation of slower-than-normal rates of electrodermal response and recovery in certain offender groups, particularly those diagnosed psychopathic, habitual, or recidivistic (Hare, 1975; Siddle, Nicol, & Foggitt, 1973). Mednick (1977) contends that genetics may play a role in the autonomic difficulties experienced by high-rate offenders, an argument which is strengthened by the observation that electrodermal responsiveness is associated with estimates of high heritability (Bell et al., 1977). Moreover, a recent review of the literature on heredity and crime by Walters and White (1989a) finds support for the presence of a modest yet significant crime-gene connection. Nevertheless, research on the interactive effects of heredity and environment on criminal outcomes is, at best, mixed—some studies showing an interactive relationship (Mednick et al., 1977) and others advising that the effects of biology and environment are largely independent and noninteractive (Cadoret & Cain, 1980; Gabrielli & Mednick, 1984).

The studies on autonomic reactivity reviewed thus far can be faulted for failing to evaluate the causal nature of the proposed link between autonomic functioning and serious criminality. This is because electrodermal abnormalities may just as easily be the result, as they are the cause, of later criminal conduct. For this very reason the Mauritius Project was conceived, developed, and implemented (Schulsinger et al., 1975). As part of this project the autonomic reactions and behaviors of all three-year-old children in the Mauritius (an island in the Indian Ocean) villages of Vacoas and Quatre Bornes were assessed and then correlated with behavioral measures taken several years later.

Venables (1987) offers some preliminary findings on the Mauritius subjects as they enter early adolescence. He indicates first that there was no apparent relationship between heart rate and antisocial behavior or between phasic skin conductance and antisocial behavior at either age 9 or 11. Even though tonic skin conductance abnormalities were observed in subjects who eventually engaged in delinquent behavior, this outcome occurred in the high-SES group only—a finding which is consistent with Mednick's (1977) supposition that genetic factors play a more important role in the criminal activities of higher, as opposed to lower, SES subjects. In general, the Mauritius Project has produced preliminary results that run counter to those obtained with adults—namely, that higher rather than lower levels of autonomic response measured at age three were associated with subsequent delinquent behavior (Venables, 1987). Perhaps autonomic factors play a variable role in criminal development contingent upon the subject's age at the time the measures are taken.

The operationality and testability of Mednick's theory appear to be rather strong. However, there are problems with the way several of the variables central to Mednick's theorem have been conceptualized. For one, it is doubtful whether a slow electrodermal recovery, as measured in the laboratory, has clear behavioral referents in real life (Trasler, 1987). Further, electrodermal recovery has been shown to be generally unstable over time and across situations (Levander et al., 1979). The sensitivity and specificity of electrodermal recovery as a measure of criminological tendencies have also been brought into question by studies showing that only a subgroup of offenders exhibit extended electrodermal recovery times and that groups other than criminals (for example, depressives, hyperactives) also record longer-than-normal electrodermal recovery times (Buikhuisen, Eurelings-Bontekoe, & Host, 1989). Finally, there is controversy over whether the "recovery limb" of the electrodermal response even adequately measures anxiety and/or fear dissipation. Edelberg and Muller (1977) obtained results that led them to conclude that the "recovery limb" was actually measuring attention more than it was anxiety or arousal. Thus, while Mednick's theory has been moderately fruitful, its empirical validity remains uncertain as we search for robust and generalizable measures of anxiety recovery.

One final criticism of Mednick's theory is that it fails to fully articulate the interaction postulated to exist between the genetic and/or biologic features of anxiety dissipation and the environmental features of family atmosphere and disciplinary practice. A thorough reading of Mednick's theory reveals that he may be proposing an additive rather than interactive effect: ''If there are lacks in either of these spheres (family training, individual physiological characteristics) the learning of law-abidance will be incomplete, retarded and/or unsuccessful'' (Mednick, 1977, p. 1). However, as Thornberry (1987) reminds us, a truly interactive theory does more than specify a set of variables; it actually clarifies the process of interaction. This is an area in which Mednick's theory unquestionably falls short of the mark and one which, along with increased methodological rigor in defining the biosocial criterion measures, needs to be addressed if the theory is to contribute to our understanding of criminal behavior.

Hirschi's Social Control Theory

Travis Hirschi, a professor of sociology at the University of Arizona in Tucson, is responsible for the development of a model that emphasizes the role of social bonding in preventing persons from engaging in criminal action. Like Mednick, Hirschi is concerned with how people learn to avoid criminal involvement rather than with how people learn to engage in law-violating behavior, since he assumes that humans are, by nature, self-centered and hedonistic. Hirschi posits that criminal action occurs when the individual fails to bond with conventional social groups like the family, school, and pro-social peers, which under normal circumstances would aid the individual in learning to suppress antisocial inclinations. Though trained as a sociologist, Hirschi considers person (age, gender, intelligence) as well as the situational (socializing agents) variables in the formulation of his theory of human behavior.

From the very beginning, Hirschi (1969) proposed that social bonding was based on four key elements. One such element is attachment which, according to Hirschi, exists in the form of ties between the individual and major agents of socialization—most notably, parents, teachers, and community leaders. The second major element in Hirschi's theory is commitment to the conventional social order. With commitment comes an investment in conformity and the development of goals incompatible with illegal action. The third feature of Hirschi's theory, involvement, guides the person's participation in conventional activities. The fourth key element is belief, which mirrors confidence in the moral validity of societal rules and norms. Utilizing an independent sample of subjects, Hindelang (1973) noted the presence of an inverse relationship between delinquency and measures of all four of Hirschi's key elements. Wiatrowski, Griswold, and Roberts (1981), on the other hand, found support for attachment, involvement, and belief, but not commitment.

Hirschi (1969) subjected his theory to empirical scrutiny by administering questionnaires to 4,000 high school students. The results of this study provided support for all four key elements and charted a negative relationship between measures of family, school, community, and peer attachment on the one hand and delinquency on the other. In cross-validating Hirschi's original investigation, Hindelang (1973) conferred corroborative verification on the validity of many of Hirschi's ideas, although he recorded a direct relationship between peer attachment and delinquency where Hirschi had uncovered an inverse or negative association. It would seem that peer attachment exerts a bi-directional effect on criminal involvement dependent, of course, on the peers (deviant or conventional) with whom one associates. The majority of studies carried out on Hirschi's version of social control theory have yielded generally positive outcomes (Austin, 1977; Bahr, 1979; Jensen & Eve, 1976; Poole & Regoli, 1979).

The cross-national validity of Hirschi's theory was substantiated in a study administered on a large sample of Australian secondary school students (Mak, 1990). In this study, 52 percent of the variance in self-reported delinquency was explained by a multivariate composite consisting of social control, personal control (empathy, impulse control), and background (age, sex, broken home) measures. When social control theory is compared to other popular models of crime causation, the results are often more supportive of Hirschi's theorems than they are of the other formulations. Contrasting Hirschi's social control model with Merton's strain paradigm, Stack (1982) ascribed greater explanatory power to Hirschi's position. The outcome of studies showing that dropping out of school demonstrates an accelerating (as control theory would predict) rather than decelerating (as strain theory would predict) effect on subsequent criminality (Bachman, O'Malley, & Johnston, 1978; Polk et al., 1981; Shavit & Rattner, 1988; Thornberry et al., 1985) is further evidence of control theory's empirical superiority over anomie and/or strain interpretations. Hirschi's theory is less clearly preeminent when compared to Sutherland's differential association model, although even here the advantage appears to go to Hirschi's social control theory (Hepburn, 1976; Jensen, 1972; Poole & Regoli, 1979).

The majority of studies on Hirschi's (1969) social bonding and/or control theory have been conducted on groups of male delinquents. Linquist, Smusz, and Doerner (1985), however, unveiled qualified support for Hirschi's theorems in a sample of adult male probationers. Testing three of Hirschi's key elements, Linquist et al. ascertained a strong relationship between commitment and success on probation, a moderate relationship between involvement and probation outcome, but no relationship when attachment and probation were correlated. Paternoster et al. (1983) uncovered support for several of Hirschi's ideas in a sample of college students interviewed about such behaviors as marijuana use and petty thievery. In addition, Hirschi's ideas appear applicable to female delinquency (Hindelang, 1973; Jensen & Eve, 1976; Warren, 1983) and the results of one study (Rosenbaum, 1987) suggest that social control–based hypotheses may be more predictive of female as opposed to male patterns of offending.

Hirschi's social bonding and/or control model has stimulated as much research, debate, and inquiry as any modern theory of criminal behavior. Moreover, it characteristically fares well under empirical scrutiny, particularly when contrasted with other theories of crime genesis. However, the theory remains operationally weak in the sense that many of its terms, to include deviance, are not explicitly defined (Bernard, 1987). Further, Colvin and Pauley (1983) castigate Hirschi for failing to specify how bonds are formed or broken, and question whether bonding is an all-or-nothing phenomenon as was inferred in Hirschi's original writings. Social bonding theory also fails to address the issue of noncriminal outcomes in a healthy proportion of individuals possessing weak social bonds. Despite problems with precision and operationality, Hirschi's interactive theory of criminal involvement will likely continue to make a substantial contribution to the criminal science research effort.

CHOICE THEORY

Choice formulations, first introduced in Chapter 8 of this volume, are more concerned with criminal events than with criminal development. The criminal decision-making process will therefore assume center stage in this review of choice theory. The rational choice perspective has been selected for the purpose of illustrating issues common to choice theories of criminal conduct.

Rational Choice Theory

The economic or rational choice perspective is a variant of deterrence theory. In addition to considering the utility of crime, the primary focus of deterrence theory, economic models of criminal behavior consider the utility that might reasonably be anticipated through one's involvement in noncriminal forms of activity. As such, the decision to participate in illegality entails contrasting the cost : benefit ratio of crime with the cost : benefit ratio of noncrime. In an article published in the *Journal of Political Economy*, Becker (1968) established the parameters of an economic theory of criminal conduct. Becker painstakingly outlined the steps normally taken by an individual contemplating the crime–no crime question in formulating his economic perspectus. The underlying premise of this approach is that the individual rationally weighs the available alternatives and then selects the optimal solution.

The rational choice perspective considers not only the decision-making patterns of the individual but the availability and distribution of economic resources as well. It would follow, then, that crime should rise during periods of economic recession because of a concomitant reduction in legitimate employment opportunities. Studies on this issue have generated mixed outcomes, although the evidence insinuates that there is minimal relationship between crime and economic hardship (Orsagh & Witte, 1981). Even in studies clearly demonstrating a crime-economics connection, the effect is not overly impressive. Hence, Freeman (1983) calculates that a 50 percent reduction in unemployment would attenuate crime by a margin of no more than 5 percent. It appears that while criminal and noncriminal opportunities play a critical role in criminal development, their action is much more complex than rational choice theorists have proposed.

While aggregate-level studies (Brier & Fienberg, 1980; Cook, 1980) are generally supportive of the rational choice perspective, individual-level studies are much less so (Piliavin et al., 1986). This seems somewhat paradoxical, in light of the fact that rational choice theory is designed to provide insight into the individual decision-making process that gives rise to corollary criminal events. A further flaw in rational choice theory is the artificiality of many of the research studies upon which the rational choice model is based. The majority of such inquiries are either self-report surveys of relatively minor offenses (smoking marijuana, shoplifting, fighting) or laboratory-based investigations of questionable generalizability. Until this situation is remedied, rational choice theory will be ill equipped to answer the questions utmost in the minds of criminal scientists.

There are serious questions about the validity of the assumption, central to economic theories of crime, that the human decision-making process is rational, efficient, and dedicated to finding the optimal solution in any particular situation. Research suggests that serious crime is often more impulsive and expressive than it is rational and profit oriented (Fattah, 1982). Studies probing the dynamics of shortcut decision making (Corbin, 1980) and perseverative choice selection (Einhorn & Hogarth, 1978) argue against the efficacy of the human decision-making process, while investigations such as those conducted by Carroll (1978), Weaver and Carroll (1985), and Cimler and Beach (1981) bring into serious question the supposition, central to rational choice theory, that people seek to optimize their utilities.

If raising the cost of crime fails to produce the results we are seeking, then perhaps reducing the benefits of crime or raising the benefits of noncrime would prove more fruitful. Cook (1977), for one, has argued that crime can be controlled by lowering the benefits of crime. This might be accomplished by legalizing certain activities (drugs) that, in turn, would substantially reduce the profit one might reasonably anticipate from involvement in such activities. Resources could also be directed at expanding the incentive for pro-social, noncriminal forms of behavior by way of income augmentation or other social programs. Where increased attention to the relative benefits of crime and noncrime is worthy of further attention, there are no clear indications at this point that such focus would be any more effective than the current practice of raising the costs of crime. Furthermore, research suggests that costs and benefits are highly subjective and so less amenable to wide-spectrum implementation than has been postulated in the past by rational choice theorists.

Early empirical studies on the economic or rational choice approach to crime causation were based principally on bivariate analyses correlating crime with selected indices of economic well-being. Over the past two decades multivariate statistics and complex mathematical formulae have frequently graced the pages of journals reporting the results of economic research on crime. Such a development, however, does not change the fact that the economic viewpoint has not been particularly helpful in shedding light on the fundamental features of criminal choice. Whereas this model is moderately fertile in terms of its ability to stimulate new research and ongoing scholarly debate, it has not fared as well on the empirical investigative front (Piliavin et al., 1986). This model also suffers from restricted generalizability and meaningfulness because of the circumscribed nature of many of its hypotheses, concepts, and procedures. This is not to say that choice is unimportant in comprehending crime but that the rational choice perspective is less than fully satisfactory in clarifying the role of choice in the criminal science sequence.

CONCLUSION

In a previous publication (Walters, 1990b) I reviewed eight theories of criminal action, three of which (labeling, social control, rational choice) are highlighted here. The introduction of three additional theories (Hare, Mednick, Cohen), however, fails to alter my previous conclusion: despite the fact that major theories of criminal conduct attract attention to prominent, and potentially meaningful, features of the criminal profile, they all suffer from a common malady, conceptual myopia. In other words, current theories of crime causation are short on breadth. Although each theory addresses itself to a subset of relevant issues, these issues are unduly circumscribed, as well as narrow, and tend to reflect only a relatively small portion of the total picture. Integration is not only advisable but necessary. For this reason, we might want to take note of some of the integrative concepts advanced by Thornberry in his recent article on criminological theory.

Thornberry (1987) writes that conditions and behavior are reciprocally interactive, and he reviews three trends in current criminological thought with which he takes issue. On the first count, he finds fault with the unidirectional nature of most theories of criminal behavior and argues persuasively that delinquency is as much a cause of various social maladies as it is a result of these same social conditions. Thornberry inventories research on unemployment (Thornberry & Christenson, 1984), occupational attainment (Kandel & Logan, 1984), and dropping out of school (Thornberry et al., 1985) in support of his position. Second, Thornberry criticizes the field of criminology for failing to take developmental considerations into account when postulating intervariable relationships. On the third point, Thornberry contends that most theories make little or no mention of how contextual catalysts like social class or minority group status affect these intervariable relationships by modifying the interactional effects of social and developmental agents.

Within the confines of his interactive theory of delinquent involvement, Thornberry (1987) proposes a network of interlocking causal variables that operate in ways discussed in Akers' (1977) reformulation of the differential association doctrine, Hirschi's (1969) social bonding version of social control theory, and Miller's (1958) work on the subculture of poverty. Thornberry proposes that initial attachment to one's parents is critical in the development of commitment to the conventional social order in childhood and early adolescence. As the child grows older there is an accompanying shift that finds attachment to one's peers, the authority of school, and identification with the youth culture assuming increased importance in fostering commitment to a noncriminal lifestyle. Late adolescence and early adulthood usher in further developmental changes that find employment, college, the military, and marriage increasingly more important in promoting commitment to the conventional social order. Thornberry is quick to add, however, that these developmental changes take place within the context of a person's position in the social structure, so that someone raised in a home that provides economic security, stable family relationships, and pro-social role models has a greater stake in conformity and is less apt to choose certain delinquent solutions than someone raised in an impoverished neighborhood in which antisocial role models abound.

It is obvious that more thought needs to be devoted to the development and expansion of criminal science theory. Thornberry (1987), as well as Pearson and Weiner (1985), offer important insights into how interactional and interdisciplinary issues can be meaningfully integrated into our theories of criminal involvement and criminal events. Much of the data presently exist; it is just a matter of finding a workable theoretical infrastructure upon which to rest the morass of seemingly irreconcilable outcomes gathered over the past several decades. Though we can never prove the absolute truth or utility of a theory, we can with just a few exceptions (Hirschi, Sutherland) cast a disapproving glare on major portions of most current theories of criminal conduct. The paradox seems to be that criminological theories have attempted to explain too wide a spectrum of criminal activity with just a few generalized principles. Consequently, theorists have offered us models that promise much more than they can deliver. The goal of criminal science theory, on the other hand, is the development of models that promise less and deliver more.

10

A Multi-Pattern Theory of Criminal Involvement

The multi-pattern theory of criminal involvement is based, first on homogeneous groupings, second on the three *C*'s (conditions, choice, and cognition), and third on the interaction of person and situation variables along three dimensions (physical, social, and psychological). As we saw in Chapter 9, wide-scale or omnibus theories of criminology sabotage their well-intended efforts by adopting too vast a perspective on criminal science issues. Reflecting for a moment, it makes intuitive sense that there may be as many reasons for crime as there are persons who violate the law. It is also well within the realm of possibility that the reasons for crime might cluster into a finite number of patterns. Since theory is, by definition, a reductionistic attempt to organize empirical findings into a meaningful framework, it becomes necessary to constrict one's focus at some point in the process. Instead of reducing data at the explanatory stage, as is the practice of omnibus theories of criminal conduct, a more efficacious approach might be to narrow data at the definitional stage. This, in turn, would permit a more comprehensive review of the dynamic interactive relationship between individual person and situation variables.

Past efforts to categorize offenders have met with limited success, in part because the criteria employed have been uncertain and in many cases, ambiguous. Several of the early criminologists classified offenders by crime category (murder, robbery, assault, rape, burglary, larceny, other). However, research has consistently shown that most offenders do not specialize (Wolfgang, Thornberry, & Figlio, 1987), although there may be crimes certain offenders choose to avoid for personal, moral, or sentimental reasons (Walters, 1990b). Several categorizing schemes have been found useful for the purpose of clinical classification (see Chapter 3, Volume 2) but are less well suited to clearing away the confusion that presently envelops criminal science theory. This is because most offender classification systems lack a consistent structural framework with which to make sense of the massive array of information currently known to criminal scientists. In this chapter we see how the three *C*'s form the descriptive boundaries of a multi-pattern theory of criminal involvement.

Taking the first *C*—that of conditions—we discern the significance of the individual, the individual's situational context, and the interaction between the two. Though conditions do not cause crime in a direct sense, they do facilitate its expression by restricting a person's options. Selection of the criminal option constitutes the middle stage in the criminal development sequence, a stage known as choice. An underlying assumption of the multi-pattern approach to human behavior is that crime cannot be understood without taking into account choice and decision making. The third and final stage in the criminal developmental sequence is cognition—the thinking style which arises out of the conditions in one's life and the decisions one makes relative to these conditions. Cognitions fortify the criminal choices and direct the specific pattern of criminality toward its logical conclusion.

It is essential that we appreciate the dynamic nature of the conditions-choice-cognition sequence that constitutes the multi-pattern theory of criminal involvement. Though conditions normally set the criminal developmental sequence in action, followed in succession by choice and cognition, this is an overly simplistic approach to crime explanation. Choice, in fact, is not possible in situations where self-talk is absent or intent cannot be formed. The criminological thinking style that evolves from the choices one makes in response to various life conditions can impact on the individual's decisions and on how he or she interprets various environmental conditions and events. Hence, as Thornberry (1987) so eloquently argues, the causal order of conditions, choice, and cognition is multidirectional, thereby creating a dynamic system of mutually dependent forces. This complex system of interlocking influences provides the theoretical infrastructure of the multi-pattern theory of criminal involvement. However, the criteria by which individual theoretical patterns are defined exist as three domains of person × situation interaction.

As was noted in Chapter 7, primary-order person × situation interactions gather along three dimensions: the physical (stimulus modulation), the social (attachment), and the psychological (self-image). Walters (1990b) argues that problems in all three areas characterize the criminal lifestyle. It seems logical, then, that complications in just one or two of these domains might result in divergent patterns of criminal conduct. Specific problems with the stimulus modulation, attachment, and self-image life tasks therefore constitute the criteria around which the multi-pattern theory of criminal conduct is structured. We begin by discussing the pattern defined by problems in all three domains, a pattern referred to as lifestyle criminality.

THE LIFESTYLE CRIMINAL

The notion of a criminal lifestyle rests on the proposition established by research that a majority of crime is committed by a small portion of the total criminal population. As a case in point, Wolfgang, Figlio, and Sellin (1972) determined that 6 percent of the males born in the city of Philadelphia in 1945 accounted for 51 percent of all crimes committed by the cohort. Shannon (1982) observed parallel results in a sample of subjects born in Racine, Wisconsin. Enlisting divergent methodologies, the career criminality concept has been verified in groups of subjects from Washington, D.C. (Blumstein & Cohen, 1979), California (Petersilia, Greenwood, & Lavin, 1978), Ohio (Figgie Corporation, 1988), London, England (West & Farrington, 1977), Ireland (Russel, 1964), Peru (Cooper, 1971), and Japan (Kobayashi, Ono, Ooe, & Sakumichi, 1982). With the criminal lifestyle conceptualization in its proper historical and cultural context, we move next into a discussion on how this pattern is defined and how a system of conditions, choice, and cognition form a conduit through which this lifestyle flows.

Definition

There are actually two definitions of *lifestyle criminality*, one behavioral, the other phenomenological. The behavioral definition holds that crime can be conceptualized as a lifestyle characterized by irresponsibility, self-indulgence, interpersonal intrusiveness, and social rule breaking (Walters, 1990b). The critical aspect of this definition is that it conceives of crime in lifestyle terms. Persons falling within the purview of the criminal lifestyle engage in crime as part of a wider lifestyle in which global irresponsibility, unrestrained hedonism, interpersonal violations, and blatant disregard for societal norms, laws, and mores predominate. This does not mean that crime can only be understood as a lifestyle—to the contrary, this is the underlying rationale for constructing a multi-pattern theory of criminal conduct—just that one of several patterns exists as a lifestyle.

The phenomenological or psychological definition of *lifestyle criminality* asserts that the lifestyle criminal sets himself up to fail in ways that are dramatic and destructive to himself and to others (Walters, 1990b). The dramatic feature of this definition is the by-product of inadequate resolution of the stimulus modulation life task that finds the individual seeking higher than normal levels of sensory stimulation. The other-destructive element can be traced to the lifestyle offender's problems with attachment and subsequent failure to bond with others. The self-destructive component is an expression of the lifestyle criminal's inadequate handling of the self-image life task and eventual development of a negative and isolative view of himself. In the end, these features merge, exacerbating the individual's fear of intimacy, commitment, and failure and opening the door to future criminal decisions and the development of a criminal mentality.

Conditions

As was explicitly laid out in Chapters 5 and 6, there is a plethora of internal and external factors that might potentially contribute to future criminal involvement. However, it is presumed that person × situation interactions occurring in three primary areas of human endeavor (physical, social, and psychological) constitute the foundation upon which the criminal lifestyle is erected. These three sets of interactive influences give rise to the early developmental life tasks of stimulus modulation, social attachment, and self-image, the improper resolution of which are seen as preconditions for future lifestyle criminality.

In the physical domain we find the early life task of stimulus modulation. Here the individual works toward establishing an optimal level of sensory stimulation. The early life task of attachment is the product of a person × situation interaction taking place in the social domain. It should come as no surprise that this early life task has important implications for future interpersonal relationships. Finally, interactions taking place in the psychological domain help define the subject's self-image. This third early life task has a great deal to do with whether the individual views him or herself as a worthwhile and potentially successful human being.

The early life tasks are normally resolved within the first four to five years of life. The transition from early to later life tasks appears to be at least partly a function of the subject's entrance into a world outside his or her immediate family. This demonstrates the critical role of contextual factors during this transitional phase of development. Biological agents are probably also involved in the progression from early to later life tasks, in that major neurological changes occur between the ages of four and six. In the end, the lifestyle criminal resolves the early life tasks in ways that lead him to seek excitement, avoid meaningful interpersonal relationships, and view himself in a largely negative light.

With resolution of the early life tasks, the individual moves on to the later life tasks (Walters, 1990b). Analogous to their early life counterparts, the later life tasks organize themselves into three dimensions of interaction: physical, social, and psychological. The physical domain gives rise to the later life task of defining an internal versus external life orientation, while the social dimension incorporates the later life task of empathy and social bonding. Role identity is the overriding theme of higher-order interactions occurring in the psychological domain, a task that addresses one's manner of integration into the wider social environment. These later life tasks are never fully resolved but, rather, guide development over the entire lifespan, and in the case of the lifestyle criminal, direct behavior toward negative and destructive solutions to the problems of everyday living.

The multi-pattern theory of criminal involvement is dynamic rather than deterministic. Variables are seen as existing in a constant state of transition, flux, and interaction, although it is sometimes necessary to survey the static picture in order to obtain an appreciation of the isolated segments which comprise the overall picture. We also need to keep in mind that despite the protuberance of primary and higher-order interactions, as represented by the early and later life tasks, independent person and situation variables and choice factors also impact on the development of criminal patterns of behavior. Consequently, an individual may have problems negotiating all three early life tasks yet still not engage in a lifestyle pattern of criminality because of the choices he or she makes relative to these early life tasks.

As the present discussion implies, conditions do not determine behavior but, rather, place one at increased or decreased risk for subsequent problems—in this case, legal difficulties. Conditions therefore exert two categories of action on behavior. First, they may serve a risk or protective function. The risk function increases one's liability for later criminal involvement, while the protective function decreases this liability. Second, conditions may demonstrate an exacerbating or mitigating effect on behavior. Hence, they may augment one's chances of being involved in a specific criminal event (exacerbation) or minimize such a possibility (mitigation). Without belaboring the point, conditions do not impel one to commit crimes; rather, they narrow or widen one's options relative to some particular future course of action.

Choice

The argument has been advanced that choice enters into the causal equation because conditions serve only to modify the available options rather than determine one's choices. It is claimed further that it is the attitude one adopts toward the early and later life tasks, not the tasks themselves, that triggers future criminal involvement. This is why not all persons possessing high sensation-seeking tendencies, weak social attachments, and negative self-images function along criminal lines. In sum, crime cannot be understood without making reference to choice and the decision-making process.

The decision-making model outlined in Chapter 8 serves as the structure by which the multi-pattern theory of criminal conduct can be understood. This model breaks the sequence into input, process, and output. At the input stage we find risk and protective factors, exacerbating and mitigating factors, opportunity, and target selection issues. Hence, various life conditions, situational considerations, and opportunity to commit a specific criminal act function as precursors to the actual criminal choice. This information is then subjected to a cost : benefit analysis of available options, although the developmental status, motivational mindset, and reinforcement history of the individual, not to mention the fallibility of the human decision-making process, all play key roles in the processing stage of criminal decision making. The output constitutes a decision by the actor to either engage in or refrain from engaging in a specific criminal act.

As the phenomenological definition of lifestyle criminality suggests, the recidivistic offender is driven to lose in ways which are both dramatic and destructive. The evolving life decision to lose is a founding premise of the lifestyle model of criminality (Walters, 1990b). This mentality is not an inherited trait but emanates from the decisions a person makes relative to the conditions of his or her life. It is, in truth, a failure of development in which the habitual offender decides that he or she would rather lose on his or her terms than take a chance at conventional success and risk possible failure (Walters, 1990b). The person reasons that he or she cannot lose if he or she does not try. Existential fears, therefore, fuel the evolving life decision to lose in a manner that is dramatic and destructive to oneself and to others. The outcome is still based on choice, however, and as such, the capacity for change lies with the individual.

Choice is defined by the multi-pattern theory of criminal involvement as the ability to select alternative options from those available at any particular point in time. This should not be confused with the ubiquitous sense of free will espoused by early classical theorists. One must take into account the developmental, situational, and motivational context of choice when examining the decision-making process. Although cost : benefit analysis is afforded a prominent position in this theory, the outcome is often less than fully optimal, since the thinking upon which it is based is less than fully rational. It is of overriding significance, therefore, that we appreciate, dissect, and study the choice process that seems to stimulate development of criminal patterns of deportment.

Cognition

The thinking style that unfolds in support of the lifestyle criminal's decision to act in irresponsible and law-violating ways exerts a formidable influence on subsequent behavior. In fact, criminological thinking emerges for the express purpose of buttressing and nourishing the evolving criminal lifestyle. This belief system is composed of eight primary categories of irrational thought that in the end provide the formula by which one might fulfill the evolving life decision to lose in a manner both dramatic and destructive. Each of these eight cognitive features of lifestyle criminality is discussed individually, commencing with mollification.

Mollification. The lifestyle criminal can often be heard blaming someone other than him or herself for the difficulties his or her illegalities have created. Through mollification the individual shifts responsibility for past criminal actions onto other persons and external circumstances. One's early upbringing, the courts, and society at large are favorite targets of offenders bent on mollifying their criminal excursions by transferring blame to the conditions of their life. Mollification can also take the form of berating the victims of one's crimes or downplaying the seriousness of injuries incurred by victims. From time to time the offender may encounter inequalities, hardships, and injustices that do, in fact, exist. What he or she needs to realize, however, is that this does not excuse, justify, or mitigate the severity of the individual's own law-breaking behavior and actions.

Cutoff. The lifestyle criminal often has trouble dealing effectively with frustration. As such, he or she will seemingly ''fly off the handle'' at the slightest provocation, frequently embarrassing family, friends, and acquaintances. What many theorists fail to realize is that the criminal will use angry outbursts to control, intimidate, and manipulate others. In fact, he or she may use anger to further a criminal career by way of a cognitive mechanism Yochelson and Samenow (1976) refer to as the cutoff. The cutoff may consist of a simple phrase (''fuck it''), visual image, or musical theme, but all with the common goal of eliminating anxieties, concerns, and deterrents that would otherwise prevent the individual from participating in a given criminal act. In addition to the internal cutoffs previously mentioned, the individual might also invoke an external cutoff by consuming alcohol and/or drugs.

Entitlement. The lifestyle criminal fancies him or herself a special person—someone entitled to violate the laws of society with impunity. Not that most criminals adopt an anarchistic view of the world; it's just that they don't see the law as directly applying to them. This attitude of entitlement supplies the lifestyle offender with permission to violate the laws of society and intrude into the private lives of others. Entitlement encompasses three primary facets: ownership, uniqueness, and misidentification (Walters, 1990b). Ownership refers to a mind-set wherein the habitual felon convinces himself that if he or she is strong, smart, or arrogant enough to procure something from another, then he or she must be entitled to it. Uniqueness has its foundation in early life experiences that lead the evolving lifestyle criminal to the conclusion that he or she is different from others and therefore justified in taking whatever steps deemed necessary to achieve a stated criminal objective. Finally, the recidivistic lifestyle offender will misidentify wants and privileges as needs and rights, thereby establishing the necessity of obtaining these desires at all costs.

Power Orientation. The lifestyle criminal adopts a rather simplistic view of the world. He or she divides the world into two broad categories—strong and weak—and goes about applying these criteria to individuals encountered on a daily basis. The lifestyle criminal sizes up people, situations, and events based on an oversimplified mental assessment of relative strength, reasoning that those persons he or she perceives as weak can be used, manipulated, or intimidated to personal advantage. The power orientation is directed toward gaining a sense of power and control over one's environment and consists of two cognitive elements: the zero state and power thrust (Yochelson & Samenow, 1976). The zero state is experienced as feelings of behavioral debilitation and impuissance, while the power thrust is the offender's attempt to gain power and control over others through manipulation, intimidation, or physical force. Many lifestyle offenders have found the power thrust an effective solution to zero-state feelings, although with short-term relief comes negative long-term consequences.

Sentimentality. Sentimentality is a term Yochelson and Samenow (1976) use to describe the way offenders express tender feelings and aesthetic interests for the purpose of self-gratification. Like mollification, sentimentality is used by the lifestyle offender to justify criminal activity, but instead of pointing to various environmental injustices, the habitual lawbreaker uses sentimentality to cite episodes in which he or she engaged in some positive action, as if this somehow excuses their past criminality. Whether the subject sentimentalizes through concern for an injured animal, coaching a Little League team, or bestowing gifts on family and friends purchased with ill-gotten funds, the bottom line is that these good deeds are often enacted for other than altruistic reasons. In short, sentimentality is a selfish attempt by the individual to prove that he or she really is a "good person" despite a life pattern of crime and predation.

Superoptimism. There is nothing wrong with a healthy sense of optimism and self-confidence. The lifestyle criminal, however, goes well beyond the limits of reason in adopting what Yochelson and Samenow (1976) refer to as a superoptimistic attitude. Experience has taught the lifestyle offender that he or she gets away with the majority of serious crimes committed. Over time this growing realization crystallizes into an attitude of invincibility, wherein the individual believes he or she can do and get away with just about any criminal act. Superoptimism continues to grow with each successful criminal venture until the person eventually sets him or herself up for failure and subsequent arrest. Superoptimism, not the law enforcement establishment, is what catches most criminals (Walters & White, 1989b).

Cognitive Indolence. Examining the behavioral characteristics of habitual criminality we see that irresponsibility is a major component of the criminal lifestyle. In this regard, Walters (1990b) argues that the lifestyle criminal is as lazy in thought as he or she is in behavior. As such, he or she is easily bored, overly accepting of personal ideas, and continually in search of shortcuts, despite the fact that these shortcuts are frequently fraught with strife and conflict. Many times the lifestyle criminal ends up inviting failure because he or she lacks criticalness of thought and the capacity for realistic self-appraisal. This may occur despite the presence of average to above-average intellectual ability. Problem solving and goal setting are two additional skills hindered by the cognitive indolence that pervades the thinking of the typical habitual offender.

Discontinuity. The lifestyle criminal lacks direction in both behavior and thinking. Behaviorally, this is reflected in a sporadic work history, poor school performance, absence of stable long-term interpersonal relationships, and serious financial mismanagement. Cognitively, this lack of direction is expressed as discontinuity. Defined as inconsistency in thought and behavior, discontinuity is one of the few behaviors lifestyle criminals display on a fairly consistent basis (Walters, 1990b). Because of a focus that finds external control taking precedence over self-discipline, the lifestyle offender is frequently distracted by environmental events and encounters difficulty following through on initially good intentions. This lack of persistence makes it troublesome for the lifestyle offender to maintain commitments over time and is a major cause of both recidivism and the "failure" of rehabilitative programming.

Interconnections

The interconnections that link conditions, choice, and cognition are complex, multifaceted, and bidirectional. Walters (1990b) discusses the bonds that tie specific behavioral, motivational, and cognitive features of lifestyle criminality together. Thus, while all aspects of the criminal lifestyle are interconnected, there are certain behaviors that tend to correlate more convincingly with specific motives and cognitive patterns than others. Research, however, must be carried out in order to determine whether these clusters are, in fact, empirically valid. The only clue to their veridicality at this point is that they appear to make theoretical sense and have been found useful in understanding clinical case study material (Walters, 1990b).

The Serial Killer: A Lifestyle Criminal in Profile

At first brush it would appear that serial killers differ substantially from the prototypical lifestyle criminal. After all, research shows that nearly all serial murderers are Caucasian, were raised in middle-class two-parent homes, and possess above-average to superior intellectual ability (FBI, 1985)—certainly not the standard profile of a lifestyle criminal. Despite their advantaged backgrounds and better than average abilities, however, these individuals seem locked in a pattern of school failure, poor work performance, and strained interpersonal relationships. Referencing the three early life tasks, nearly all 36 of the subjects taking part in a FBI study (1985) experienced problems with social bonding, high mental energy levels (as represented by violent sexual fantasies), and self-esteem. It would appear that instead of being an enigma, the serial murderer is actually an epitome of lifestyle criminality.

One serial killer, Ted Bundy, is estimated to have been responsible for the brutal murders of from 36 to over 300 women (Holmes & DeBurger, 1985). Although the focus of Bundy's criminal lifestyle was on expressing anger toward, and gaining control over, women—particularly women with long hair parted in the middle—he was known to have committed other serious crimes as well (burglary, larceny). Following his escape from a jail cell in western Colorado, Bundy chose to steal in order to support the lavish lifestyle to which he felt entitled rather than taking the time to find legitimate employment (Rule, 1989). Irresponsibility, self-indulgence, interpersonal intrusiveness, and social rule breaking were all part of the lifestyle Ted Bundy fashioned for himself. The loser's mentality was clearly evident in Bundy's decision to flee to a state (Florida) known for its conservative policies on crime and willingness to utilize capital punishment. That Bundy set himself up for failure should be obvious; that there are criminal offenders who direct themselves toward success is less apparent but warrants further investigation.

OTHER PATTERNS

If the lifestyle criminal is said to have major problems negotiating the three early life tasks, it stands to reason that other patterns involving one, two, or none of these patterns are also possible. There are seven patterns other than the aforementioned lifestyle prototype (high sensation seeking, weak attachment, poor self-image) that are theoretically possible extensions of the developmental scheme presented in this chapter. These include: (1) high sensation seeking and weak attachment; (2) high sensation seeking and poor self-image; (3) weak attachment and poor self-image; (4) high sensation seeking alone; (5) weak attachment alone; (6) poor self-image alone; and (7) adequate resolution of the three early life tasks. The third pattern (weak attachment and poor self-image) will not be discussed since it seems to represent a relatively minor variation on the criminal lifestyle theme. The six remaining patterns, on the other hand, appear to represent distinct entities that require additional scrutiny. The objective here is to briefly discuss these six patterns in an attempt to explore possibilities that might then be followed up by research and further theoretical probing.

High Sensation Seeking and Poor Self-Image: Low Rate–High Risk Offender

Lifestyle patterns of criminal conduct encompass a high rate (frequency) and risk (severity) of antisocial activity. Other combinations are possible, however. The low rate–high risk offender, for example, engages in criminal behavior on an intermittent basis. Though infrequent, these periodic episodes of acting out behavior are characteristically intense and violent in nature and frequently result in tragedy for both the victim and offender. That is because these relatively brief bouts of frequently violent criminality are atypical or uncharacteristic of the low rate–high risk offender's normal demeanor as related by persons familiar with his or her everyday behavior. It is commonly reported that these brief stretches of criminality are bounded by much longer periods of law-abiding and socially congruent behavior. However, closer observation reveals the existence of marital, relationship, and mental health problems even during periods in which criminality is absent.

The low rate–high risk offender is reasonably well attached to others. This is the primary reason why, unlike the lifestyle criminal, he or she does not engage in a regular pattern of criminal violation. Under most circumstances, therefore, the low rate–high risk offender considers the feeling and rights of others. Problems persist, however, because this group of individuals exhibits high sensation-seeking tendencies and a weak self-image. These developmental contingencies lead to a chronic state of inner turmoil and personal dissatisfaction that may periodically ignite problems of a more criminal nature, particularly if the level of environmental stress is high. As a result, mental health issues and environmental change or pressure are normally much more intimately tied to the criminal actions of the low rate–high risk offender than is typically the case with lifestyle patterns of antisocial adjustment.

High sensation-seeking tendencies and poor self-image alone do not bring about a low rate–high risk pattern of criminality. As we saw with the criminal lifestyle, the aspiring lifestyle felon makes certain choices that interact with the three life tasks to bring about a pattern of negative behavior that is repeated over and over again. Consequently, choice is crucial to the development of the low rate–high risk pattern. It is noteworthy that the low rate–high risk concept is similar in many ways to what has been referred to in the MMPI literature as overcontrolled hostility (Megargee, Cook, & Mendelsohn, 1967). Such persons are said to exert rigid control over feelings of anger and hostility but also tend to act out in extremely aggressive fashion if provoked. The low rate–high risk profile is also roughly analogous to a DSM-III-R (American Psychiatric Association, 1987) diagnosis of Intermittent Explosive Disorder.

The cognitive characteristics of the low rate–high risk perpetrator promulgate around two primary themes: (1) a tendency to deny emotions, which then build up over time, and (2) an inability to effectively cope with stress and frustration. The first characteristic has its roots in two cognitive strategies, controversion and amplification. Controversion refers to the fact that bad feelings are denied, go unacknowledged, and tend to proliferate over time. This eventually leads to amplification wherein these feelings are expressed in a single violent or irresponsible volley of emotion and activity triggered by a specific, and oftentimes relatively minor, event. The second behavior characteristic (poor stress tolerance) ties in with the cutoff referenced earlier in our review of the criminal lifestyle. Entitlement and power-oriented thinking, on the other hand, are not generally part of the low rate–high risk profile.

High Sensation Seeking and Weak Attachment: Quasisuccessful Malefactor

In many ways this pattern is similar to the criminal lifestyle. As is normally the case with the lifestyle offender, the quasisuccessful malefactor owns a fairly extensive record of past criminal action. Unlike the lifestyle offender, however, the quasisuccessful felon is moderately successful in his or her criminal pursuits. This is because he or she does not possess the negative self-image that leads the lifestyle criminal to engage in patently self-defeating behavior from the very beginning. Although many more quasisuccessful lawbreakers elude detection than is the case with their lifestyle counterparts, most end up in some form of legal trouble eventually, their success being as ephemeral as it is mercuric.

The conditions that mark the quasisuccessful pattern are poor attachment to others, which opens the door to intrusive action, and a high need for excitement, which paves the way for thrill-seeking interests. Since the self-image life task has been resolved reasonably well by this group of individuals, we do not see the drive toward self-destruction so characteristic of lifestyle patterns of criminal involvement. However, owing to the fact that the quasisuccessful pattern is more similar than it is different from the criminal lifestyle, most members of this genre eventually encounter failure, albeit less dramatically than do lifestyle offenders. Also, because of a close psychological proximity to the lifestyle pattern, it is not long before most quasisuccessful malefactors find themselves drawn to a lifestyle paradigm of criminal involvement.

The belief system used by the quasisuccessful malefactor to support his or her criminal decisions is heavily ladden with such cognitive schema as entitlement and power orientation. Sentimentality may also be a favorite cognitive maneuver of the quasisuccessful malefactor, but discontinuity and superoptimism are rarely part of the clinical picture. This, in fact, is what helps the quasilegal felon avoid the level of life failure that so epitomizes lifestyle patterns of criminal conduct. It is noteworthy that the quasilegal malefactor might well serve as the midpoint in the amoral manipulator–lifestyle criminal continuum, one end representing the most successful and the other end the least successful group of offenders.

High Sensation Seeking: Thrill-Seeking Outlaw

The thrill-seeking outlaw is usually younger than most other categories of offender and normally exits from crime earlier than subjects in most other groups. This is because the focus of this particular pattern of lawbreaking behavior is on excitement and pleasure, a motive which normally subsides or "burns out" early on in the criminal sequence (Walters, 1990b). The crimes committed by this group of individuals are dedicated to generating a maximal level of excitement, exhilaration, and thrills. Gang-related activity and such crimes as auto theft for the purpose of driving an automobile around town for a few hours and then abandoning it appear to be particularly attractive to an individual following a thrill-seeking pattern of criminal involvement.

The stimulus modulation life task appears to be the seat of many of the thrill-seeking outlaw's difficulties. This individual views higher than normal levels of sensory stimulation as optimal, and often places him or herself in situations designed to trigger excitement and a modulating pattern of environmental stimulation. This group of individuals is reasonably well attached to others and, as such, the excitement-generating actions they pursue are not typically of a directly injurious nature. The self-image life task is also not a major problem for the thrill-seeking outlaw, a fact which provides many of these individuals with the opportunity to exit the pattern before it becomes terminally self-destructive.

The interaction between person and situation variables is particularly evident in illegal actions that take on a thrill-seeking veneer. As Quay (1977) posits, the child's proclivity for action-oriented behavior interacts with certain features of the environment to bring about a specific outcome. If the child is reinforced for excitement-engendering activity, he or she will tend to become immersed in such behavior on a more regular basis. Peers can be a particularly potent source of reinforcement for the thrill-seeking outlaw, and when the thrill-seeking subject may have occasion to engage in directly aggressive action, it is often in the company of peers who serve as a collective cutoff for the type deterrents that normally prevent these persons from engaging in seriously intrusive activities.

The criminal demeanor of the thrill-seeking outlaw is directed at maximizing sensory stimulation. Consequently, these individuals rely heavily on the self-indulgent cognitions of sentimentality and superoptimism. Cognitive indolence is also quite commonly observed in this pattern, as is the cognitive operation of amphetamization whereby one's thoughts and ideas become self-stimulatory and self-reinforcing in and of themselves. The power orientation may be present, but it is usually only seen within the context of one's peer group or gang. Entitlement, on the other hand, is probably not a major component of the thrill-seeking pattern.

Weak Attachment: Amoral Manipulator

The amoral manipulator engages in crimes that are primarily economic in nature. These individuals normally function on the ''fringes'' of illegality in the sense that, instead of directly assaulting society's institutions or its members, they entertain hustles, swindles, scams, and other unethical but quasilegal acts. Stated somewhat differently, these persons have learned to manipulate the system to their personal advantage. These are the Ivan Boeskys, Jim Bakkers, and Michael Milkins of the world. Owing to the nature of the crimes and quasilegal acts committed by these individuals, they are rarely sent to prison, and if they are it is normally for a relatively brief period of time in a minimum security institution. This is because they are often powerful members of the community whose illegal actions are viewed as less threatening than those displayed by the typical lifestyle offender or quasisuccessful malefactor.

It is a fundamental tenet of the multi-pattern theory of criminal involvement that amoral manipulators are weakly bonded to others. Consequently, they have trouble empathizing with other people and have little or no compunction about manipulating, lying, or cheating as a way of obtaining their self-serving goals. The amoral manipulator, by virtue of having adequately resolved the stimulus modulation and self-image life tasks, eschews violence and physical aggression. In fact, he or she realizes that the road to success in crime and quasilegality is not to be found in outward displays of intrusive behavior. Although intrusive actions may be part of the amoral pattern, they tend to be covert and indirect rather than overt and conspicuous.

Unlike the lifestyle criminal, who engages in crime as a means of validating his loser's life decision, the amoral manipulator is geared toward success. The amoral manipulator is, in fact, driven to succeed at any cost. The primary motive for crimes committed by this group of individuals is greed, but without the associated laziness witnessed in lifestyle offenders (Walters, 1990b). The amoral manipulator has learned that greed-based goals are more likely to be realized if accompanied by industry rather than by indolence. It is not uncommon, however, for the amoral manipulator to find his or her victories superficial, hollow, and empty, which in turn fuels the drive for power, control, and self-aggrandizement.

Instead of being consumed with self-doubt and uncertainty, the amoral manipulator is confident and self-centered. He must, however, learn to modify this thinking in ways that allow this other-destructive pattern to continue. Interviewing a group of white-collar criminals convicted of fraud, embezzlement, and sundry tax violations, Benson (1985) witnessed a pattern of rationalization in which subjects denied their guilt through cognitive distortions similar in many ways to mollification and sentimentality. Conversely, superoptimism, cognitive indolence, and discontinuity are rarely part of the amoral picture since one must be realistic, goal oriented, and focused in order to obtain the level of success enjoyed by most individuals following an amoral approach to the accumulation of interpersonal power and material wealth.

Poor Self-Image: High Rate–Low Risk Offender

The high rate–low risk offender, as the term suggests, regularly participates in criminal, antisocial, and self-destructive activities. However, in contrast to the crimes committed by the typical lifestyle criminal, the illegal acts perpetrated by the high rate–low risk offender have a much lower probability of detection and carry with them less severe penalties should the subject be apprehended. The overriding emphasis of this pattern centers on the construction of a losing lifestyle characterized by self-indulgence and irresponsibility. This includes drug addiction, prostitution, and habitual gambling—activities which carry the losing lifestyle of the high rate–low risk offender to its logical conclusion. Where drugs and gambling may be part of the criminal lifestyle, they are to a large extent the lifestyle in high rate–low risk patterns of offending. Thus, where drugs and gambling are self-indulgent expressions of a criminal lifestyle, the high rate–low risk offender turns this around and uses crime to implement and support a drug or gambling lifestyle.

The high rate–low risk offender is probably ambivalently attached to others but does not display the utter lack of empathy that forms the basis of interpersonal relationships for the avoidantly attached lifestyle criminal. Though self-indulgent, the high rate–low risk felon does not exhibit the chronic level of tension and internal stimulation found in the low rate–high risk offender. The fundamental predicament of the high rate–low risk offender is, as the model suggests, a poor self-image. Harboring a great many self-denigrating thoughts about him or herself, the high rate–low risk offender engages in behaviors that aid in the development of a losing lifestyle, although the failure of the high rate–low risk offender is nowhere near as dramatic, intense, or serious as the failure displayed by the high rate–high risk offender.

Adequate Resolution of Early Life Tasks: Casual Rule Violator

The frequency and severity of crimes committed by the casual rule violator are typically both low and normally of a more petty nature than the infractions perpetrated by the typical lifestyle, quasisuccessful, or for that matter amoral manipulating offender. I base this assertion on the proposition that casual rule violators have less of a stake or investment in crime than do persons described in previous sections. Consequently, casual rule violators seldom get caught for their transgressions, and when they do they almost never serve time. Not that casual rule violators are immune from involving themselves in significant criminality; it's just that serious lawlessness is much more the exception than the rule when it comes to casual patterns of criminal conduct.

The casual rule violator is thought to have adequately negotiated the three early life tasks of stimulus modulation, attachment, and self-image. Theoretically, if a problem exists it will involve the later life tasks. The cognitive features delineated in our discussion on the criminal lifestyle may be present in the casual offender as well, but in isolated form. In the lifestyle criminal, these eight characteristics are so intertwined that one criminal thought leads to another, which in turn leads to yet another, and so on in much the same manner as an avalanche gathers momentum as it travels downhill. The casual rule violator, on the other hand, may express entitlement at one point and sentimentality at another, but rarely are they intertwined to the point where one set of beliefs automatically ties into a second set of criminal thoughts and ideas.

In this chapter we have discussed seven forms of criminal involvement (eight if we count the weak attachment, poor self-image pattern separate from the criminal lifestyle) and seen that each has its own unique features. However, there is one characteristic all eight patterns seemingly have in common, whether we consider the lifestyle, amoral, or casual variety of criminal conduct. This communal attribute is the driven quality of behavior that seems to arise with continued involvement in criminal activity. Continued "success" in crime (not getting caught) seems to breed not only superoptimism but a drive for continued involvement in criminal activities. It's clear that both Ted Bundy (lifestyle criminal) and Jim Bakker (amoral manipulator) were driven beyond rational understanding as they found themselves eluding the negative long-term consequences of their criminal ventures. However, the casual rule violator can also get caught up in crime. This is what makes successful crime so elusive, even for persons who have adequately resolved the three early life tasks.

CONCLUSION

As was previously stated, the multi-pattern theory of criminal involvement is by no means deterministic in its conceptualizations or philosophy. Choice continues to play a critical role in the criminal development sequence, no matter which of the eight patterns is present. Hence, someone who is poorly bonded to others, possesses a seemingly insatiable desire for excitement, and holds to a negative self-view does not automatically embrace the criminal lifestyle. Nor is the fact that one has adequately resolved the stimulus modulation, attachment, and self-image life tasks a guarantee that one will renounce all forms of criminal temptation and opportunity. Movement into any of the eight patterns of criminal involvement presupposes the individual's ability to choose. Consequently, conditions and choice must be present and a belief system put into place before a particular criminal pattern can emerge.

Figure 10.1
The Eight Patterns of Criminal Involvement Conceptualized as a Semidynamic System

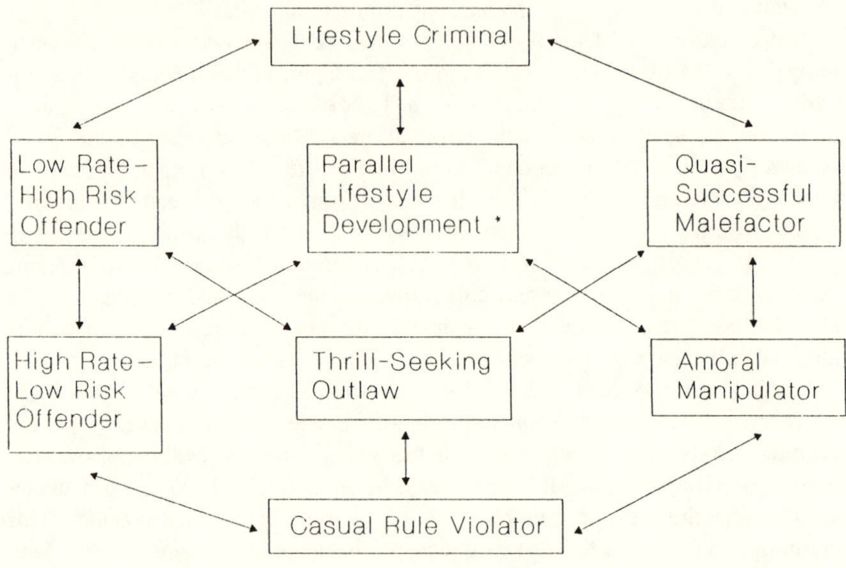

I believe it is worth reiterating that the multi-pattern theory of criminal involvement is partly dynamic, in that the boundaries between different patterns are semipermeable. The reader may recall that the early life tasks are resolved, for better or worse, by around age five. Although the outcome of the early life tasks cannot be altered, the product of the later life tasks continues to change over the course of one's lifetime. As such, one might traverse boundaries and move from one pattern to another by virtue of changes taking place in how one is negotiating a particular later life task. Rarely, however, does one move beyond an adjacent pattern (see Figure 10.1). Therefore, while moving from the quasisuccessful level to the thrill-seeking level would certainly be feasible, shifting from the lifestyle level to the amoral level is much less likely.

Epilogue

Professor Lee Ellis (1988) of Minot State University in North Dakota examined published research on a variety of crime-related issues, the goal being to ascertain the "universal" demographic correlates of criminality. Defining *universality* as an overriding preponderance of effects obtained in 12 or more independent studies conducted in at least five different nations, Ellis applied his criteria to the available data. In the process he unearthed seven universal demographic correlates of criminality, five of which (parental absence, number of siblings, race, lower socioeconomic status, high urbanization) were thought to cluster into a more general familial and/or socialization factor. The two remaining correlates (age, gender) were ostensibly independent of one another and the five familial and/or socialization variables. These findings would appear to support Ellis' claim that replicable demographic correlates of criminal behavior do, in fact, exist.

The outcome of Ellis' (1988) review spotlights the presence of three reasonably autonomous correlates of criminal action, each of which seems to possess a fair degree of generalizability across studies and populations. Additional person and situation variables were shown in Chapters 5 and 6 to be consequential in the evolution of criminal forms of behavior. Besides Ellis' demographic measures (for example, age, gender, race), genetic factors, temperament, intelligence, cognitive style, and several other person variables have been found to exert a potentially meaningful effect on criminality. Likewise, where the present volume corroborates Ellis' findings on the importance of family factors in criminal development, it also demonstrates that crime is linked to drugs, peers, the physical environment, and several other situation-oriented considerations. Though individual person and situation variables are vital to the criminal development sequence, the person × situation interaction is even more crucial for our purposes here.

As was discussed in Chapter 7, the person × situation interaction occurs in three primary domains (physical, social, and psychological), which in turn give rise to the stimulus modulation or orientation, attachment or social bonding, and self-image or role identity life tasks. These three general themes are the residual outcome of a never-ending series of interactions taking place between the person and his or her environment. Consequently, if we are to understand criminal conduct we must first comprehend the person × situation interaction so essential to the behavior of all criminal offenders. Without benefit of an underlying philosophy of criminal science we will likely find ourselves in a morass of conflicting and incompatible research findings.

The scientific method is one of several procedures capable of assisting us in our quest to comprehend and explain the world around us. In an effort to acquire knowledge, scientists set out to reject the null hypothesis of no effect or relationship. In truth, all attempts to accumulate new knowledge center on rejecting rather than accepting hypotheses, since there are a multitude of alternative explanations for any single positive finding. Accordingly, we cannot justifiably accept a hypothesis, although we can most assuredly reject it. Truth can therefore be conceptualized as an ideal absence of falsehood that is never fully realized. We approach this ideal, however, when we conduct sound investigations and the overriding majority of outcomes prevent us from rejecting the pertinent hypotheses. Data provide us with a vehicle by which we might entertain, organize, and debunk various hypotheses—a poverty of disconfirmatory evidence being the only legitimate means by which we might demonstrate the growing validity of suppositional relationships.

It is a fundamental premise of the criminal science approach to the study of lawbreaking behavior that more information is preferable to less information. In point of fact, this is the common ground upon which the five foundations of criminal science rest—the eternal pursuit of knowledge on the nature of crime and the behavior of criminals. Within the bounds of this first volume we have explored three of the foundations and discovered that crime must be considered within a historical and cultural context, subjected to ongoing empirical scrutiny, and conceptualized in ways capable of organizing available data into a manageable theoretical framework. In the final analysis, more information and knowledge is better than less information and knowledge.

There are studies that bring into question the incremental validity of psychometric data (Garb, 1984). In other words, simply appending more psychometric information to a multivariate equation does not necessarily bolster one's ability to predict certain behaviors. Such a finding seems to run counter to the argument that more data are better than less. However, if we examine several of the studies reviewed by Garb we note that the weak incremental validity of many forms of personality assessment can be traced to the fact that in many cases the additional data were superfluous, extraneous, or peripheral to the questions raised by the investigator. So that we might more properly evaluate the five foundations of criminal science investigation we must focus on data, techniques, and measures that are pertinent, properly organized, and skillfully applied.

In this first volume of a text introducing the reader to the science of criminal investigative practice, we have surveyed the contextual, correlative, and theoretical foundations of criminal science, the goal being to reject specious relationships and highlight potentially meaningful ones. Beyond the obvious need for more research, we must approach criminal science inquiry from a somewhat difference perspective than we have in the past. Among the pertinent issues deserving greater attention are discussions of internal versus external sources of social control, the role of the person $\times$ situation interaction in crime genesis, and the development of a multi-patterned theory of criminality. Our next step will be to make practical use of the information and knowledge developed in this volume. As such, the focus of the second volume in this series is on assessment, prediction, and intervention.

References

Achenbach, T. M., & Edelbrock, C. S. (1981). Behavioral problems and competencies reported by parents of normal and disturbed children aged 4 through 16. *Monographs of the Society for Research in Child Development, 46* (1, Serial No. 188).

Adams, J. T. (1927). Provincial society, 1690–1763. In A. M. Schlesinger & D. R. Fox (eds.), *A history of American Life in Twelve Volumes* (Volume III). New York: Macmillan.

Adler, A. (1927). *The practice and theory of individual psychology*. New York: Harcourt, Brace, & World.

Adler, F. (1977). The interaction between women's emancipation and female criminality: A cross-cultural perspective. *International Journal of Criminology and Penology, 5*, 101–112.

———. (1983). *Nations not obsessed with crime*. Littleton, CO: Fred B. Rothman.

Ageton, S. S. (1983). The dynamics of female delinquency, 1976–1980. *Criminology, 21*, 555–584.

Ageton, S. S., & Elliott, D. S. (1974). The effects of legal processing on delinquent orientations. *Social Problems, 22*, 87–100.

Agnew, R. (1990). Adolescent resources and delinquency. *Criminology, 28*, 535–566.

Agnew, R., & Petersen, D. M. (1989). Leisure and delinquency. *Social Problems, 36*, 332–350.

Ahlstrom, W. M., & Havighurst, R. J. (1971). *Four hundred losers: Delinquent boys in high school*. San Francisco: Jossey-Bass.

Ainsworth, M. D. S. (1979). Infant-mother attachment. *American Psychologist, 34*, 932–937.

———. (1989). Attachments beyond infancy. *American Psychologist, 44*, 709–716.

Ainsworth, M. D. S., Blehar, M. C., Waters, E., & Wall, S. (1978). *Patterns of attachment: A psychological study of the strange situation*. Hillsdale, NJ: Lawrence Erlbaum.

Ainsworth, M. D. S., & Wittig, B. A. (1969). Attachment and exploratory behavior of one-year-olds in a strange situation. In B. M. Foss (ed.), *Determinants of infant behavior: Vol. 4* (pp. 111–136). New York: Barnes & Noble.

Akers, R. L. (1977). *Deviant behavior: A social learning approach*. Belmont, CA: Wadsworth.

Alexander, M., & McCaslin, C. (1974). Criminality in heroin addicts before, during and after methadone treatment. *American Journal of Public Health Supplement, 64,* 51–56.

Allan, E. A., & Steffensmeier, D. J. (1989). Youth, unemployment, and property crime: Differential effects on job availability and job quality of juvenile and young adult arrest rates. *American Sociological Review, 54,* 107–123.

Allan, L. J. (1978). Child abuse: A critical review of the research and the theory. In J. P. Martin (ed.), *Violence and the Family* (pp. 43–79). Chichester, England: John Wiley.

Allen, G. F. (1987). Where are we going in criminal justice? Some insights from the Chinese criminal justice system. *International Journal of Offender Therapy and Comparative Criminology, 31,* 101–110.

Allport, G. W. (1961). *Pattern and growth in personality*. New York: Holt, Rinehart, & Winston.

American Psychiatric Association. (1987). *Diagnostic and statistical manual of mental disorders* (3rd edition, revised). Washington, DC: Author.

Anastasi, A. (1982). *Psychological testing*. New York: Macmillan.

Anderson, C. A. (1987). Temperature and aggression: Effects on quarterly, yearly, and city rates of violent and nonviolent crime. *Journal of Personality and Social Psychology, 52,* 1161–1173.

Anderson, C. A., & Anderson, D. C. (1984). Ambient temperature and violent crime: Tests of the linear and curvilinear hypotheses. *Journal of Personality and Social Psychology, 46,* 91–97.

Anderson, E. (1978). *A place on the corner*. Chicago: University of Chicago Press.

Andrew, J. M. (1978). Laterality on the tapping test among legal offenders. *Journal of Clinical Child Psychology, 7,* 149–150.

———. (1982). Memory and violent crime among delinquents. *Criminal Justice and Behavior, 9,* 364–371.

Anglin, M. D., Brecht, M. L., Woodward, J. A., & Bonett, D. G. (1986). An empirical study of maturing out: Conditional factors. *International Journal of the Addictions, 21,* 233–246.

Anglin, M. D., McGlothlin, W. H., & Speckart, G. (1981). The effects of parole on methadone patients' behavior. *American Journal of Drug and Alcohol Abuse, 8,* 153–170.

Anglin, M. D., & Speckart, G. (1986). Narcotics use, property crime and dealing: Structural dynamics across the addiction career. *Journal of Quantitative Criminology, 2,* 355–375.

———. (1988). Narcotics and crime: A multisample, multimethod analysis. *Criminology, 26,* 197–233.

Appleton's Annual Cyclopaedia. (1887). *1887 Cyclopaedia: Volume XXVII*. New York: Author.

Archer, D., & Gartner, R. (1984). *Violence and crime in cross-national perspective*. New Haven, CT: Yale University Press.

Arend, R., Gove, F. L., & Sroufe, L. A. (1979). Continuity of individual adaptation from infancy to kindergarten: A predictive study of ego-resiliency and curiosity in preschoolers. *Child Development, 50,* 950–959.

Arthurs, R. G. S., & Cahoon, E. B. (1964). A clinical and electroencephalographic survey of psychopathic personality. *American Journal of Psychiatry, 120,* 875–882.

Asnis, S. F., & Smith, R. C. (1978). Amphetamine abuse and violence. *Journal of Psychedelic Drugs, 10,* 371–379.

Austin, R. L. (1977). Commitment, neutralization, and delinquency. In T. N. Ferdinand (ed.), *Juvenile delinquency: Little brother grows up* (pp. 121–137). Beverly Hills, CA: Sage.

———. (1978). Race, father-absence, and female delinquency. *Criminology, 15,* 487–504.

Bachman, J. G., Green, S., & Wirtanen, I. D. (1971). *Youth in Transition: Volume 3. Dropping out—Problem or symptom?* Ann Arbor, MI: University of Michigan Institute for Social Research.

Bachman, J. G., O'Malley, P. M., & Johnston, J. (1978). *Youth in Transition: Volume 6. Adolescence to adulthood—Change and stability in the lives of young men.* Ann Arbor, MI: University of Michigan Institute for Social Research.

Bacon, S. (1963). Alcohol, alcoholism, and crime. *Crime and Delinquency, 9,* 1–14.

Bacon, W. E., & Stanley, W. C. (1963). Effects of deprivation level in puppies on performance maintained by a passive person reinforcer. *Journal of Comparative and Physiological Psychology, 56,* 783–785.

Bahr, S. J. (1979). Family determinants and effects of deviance. In W. R. Burr, R. Hill, F. I. Nye, & I. L. Reiss (eds.), *Contemporary theories about the family: Volume I. Research-based theories* (pp. 615–643). New York: Free Press.

Bailey, W. C. (1979). The deterrent effect of the death penalty for murder in Ohio: A time series analysis. *Cleveland State Law Review, 28,* 51–70.

———. (1984). Poverty, inequality, and city homicide rates. *Criminology, 22,* 531–550.

Balch, R. (1972). *Negative reactions to delinquent labels in a junior high school.* Unpublished Ph.D. Dissertation, University of Oregon.

Baldwin, J. D. (1984). Thrill and adventure seeking and the age distribution of crime: Comment on Hirschi and Gottfredson. *American Journal of Sociology, 90,* 1326–1330.

Baldwin, J. D., & Baldwin, J. I. (1977). The role of learning phenomena in the ontogeny of exploration and play. In S. Chevalier-Skolnikoff & F. E. Poirier (eds.), *Primate bio-social development* (pp. 343–406). New York: Garland.

Ball, J. C., Rosen, L., Flueck, J. A., & Nurco, D. N. (1981). The criminality of heroin addicts: When addicted and when off opiates. In J. A. Inciardi (ed.), *The drugs-crime connection* (pp. 39–65). Beverly Hills, CA: Sage.

Ball, J. C., Shaffer, J. W., & Nurco, D. N. (1983). The day-to-day criminality of heroin addicts in Baltimore: A study in the continuity of offense rates. *Drug and Alcohol Dependence, 12,* 119–142.

Bandura, A. (1969). *Principles of behavior modification.* New York: Holt, Rinehart, & Winston.

———. (1977). *Social learning theory.* Englewood Cliffs, NJ: Prentice-Hall.

Bandura, A., Ross, D., & Ross, S. A. (1963). Imitation of film-mediated aggressive models. *Journal of Abnormal and Social Psychology, 66,* 3–11.

Banfield, E. C. (1974). *The unheavenly city revisited.* Boston, MA: Little, Brown & Company.

Barnes, H. E. (1926). *The repression of crime*. New York.

Barnes, H. E., & Teeters, N. K. (1943). *New horizons in criminology*. New York: Prentice-Hall.

Baron, L., & Straus, M. A. (1987). Four theories of rape: A macrosociological analysis. *Social Problems, 34,* 467–488.

Baron, R. A. (1972). Aggression as a function of ambient temperature and prior anger arousal. *Journal of Personality and Social Psychology, 21,* 183–189.

Baron, R. A., & Ransberger, V. M. (1978). Ambient temperature and the occurrence of collective violence: The "long hot summer" revisited. *Journal of Personality and Social Psychology, 36,* 351–360.

Baron, R. M., & Needel, S. P. (1980). Toward an understanding of the differences in the responses of humans and other animals to density. *Psychological Review, 87,* 320–326.

Bates, J. E., Maslin, C. A., & Frankel, K. A. (1985). Attachment, security, mother-child interaction, and temperament as predictors of behavior-problem ratings at age three years. *Monographs of the Society for Research in Child Development, 50,* (1–2, Serial No. 209).

Baumrind, D. (1978). Parental disciplinary patterns and social competence in children. *Youth and Society, 9,* 239–276.

Bayley, D. (1976). *Forces of order: Police behavior in Japan and the United States*. Berkeley, CA: University of California Press.

Bazemore, G. (1985). Delinquency reform and the labeling perspective. *Criminal Justice and Behavior, 12,* 131–169.

Bean, P. T., & Wilkinson, C. K. (1988). Drug taking, crime and the illicit supply system. *British Journal of Addictions, 83,* 533–539.

Bearison, D. J., & Cassel, T. Z. (1975). Cognitive decentration and social codes: Communication effectiveness in young children from differing family contexts. *Developmental Psychology, 11,* 29–36.

Becker, G. S. (1968). Crime and punishment: An economic approach. *Journal of Political Economy, 76,* 169–217.

Beckerman, A., & Fontana, L. (1989). Vietnam veterans and the criminal justice system: A selected review. *Criminal Justice and Behavior, 16,* 412–428.

Bee, H. L., Van Egeren, L. F., Streissguth, A. P., Nyman, B. A., & Leckie, M. S. (1969). Social class differences in maternal teaching strategies. *Developmental Psychology, 11,* 726–734.

Bell, B., Mednick, S. A., Gottesman, I. I., & Sergeant, J. (1977). Electrodermal parameters in male twins. In S. A. Mednick & K. O. Christiansen (eds.), *Biosocial bases of criminal behavior* (pp. 217–225). New York: Gardner.

Bell, P. A., & Baron, R. A. (1976). Aggression and heat: The mediating role of negative affect. *Journal of Applied Social Psychology, 6,* 18–30.

Bell, P. A., & Fusco, M. E. (1986). Linear and curvilinear relationships between temperature, affect, and violence: Reply to Cotton. *Journal of Applied Social Psychology, 16,* 802–807.

Bell, P. A., Garnand, D. B., & Heath, D. (1984). Effects of ambient temperature and seating arrangement on personal and environmental evaluations. *Journal of General Psychology, 110,* 197–200.

Bell, R. Q. (1979). Parent, child, and reciprocal influences. *American Psychologist, 34,* 821–826.

Belson, A. (1978). *Televised violence and the adolescent boy*. Westmead, England: Saxon House, Teakfield Limited.

Bem, D. J., & Funder, D. C. (1978). Predicting more of the people more of the time: Assessing the personality of situation. *Psychological Review, 85,* 485–501.

Bennahum, D. A. (1971). Tattoos of heroin addicts in New Mexico. *Rocky Mountain Medical Journal, 68,* 63–66.

Bennett, I. (1960). *Delinquent and neurotic children*. New York: Basic Books.

Bennett, R. R., & Lynch, J. P. (1990). Does a difference make a difference? Comparing cross-national crime indicators. *Criminology, 28,* 153–182.

Bennett, T. (1986). A decision-making approach to opioid addiction. In D. B. Cornish & R. V. Clarke (eds.), *The reasoning criminal: Rational choice perspectives on offending* (pp. 83–103). New York: Springer-Verlag.

Bennett, T., & Wright, R. (1984). The relationship between alcohol use and burglary. *British Journal of Addictions, 79,* 431–437.

Benson, M. L. (1985). Denying the guilty mind: Accounting for involvement in a white-collar crime. *Criminology, 23,* 583–607.

Berger, A. S., & Simon, W. (1974). Black families and the Moynihan report: A research evaluation. *Social Problems, 22,* 146–161.

Berger, R. J. (1989). Female delinquency in the emancipation era: A review of the literature. *Sex Roles, 21,* 375–399.

Berk, R. A., Lenihan, K. J., & Rossi, P. H. (1980). Crime and poverty: Some experimental evidence from ex-offenders. *American Sociological Review, 45,* 766–786.

Berkowitz, L., & Geen, R. G. (1966). Film violence and the cue properties of available targets. *Journal of Personality and Social Psychology, 3,* 525–530.

Berkowitz, L., & Macaulay, J. (1971). The contagion of criminal violence. *Sociometry, 34,* 328–360.

Berkowitz, L., & Rawlings, E. (1963). Effects of film violence on inhibitions against subsequent aggression. *Journal of Abnormal and Social Psychology, 66,* 405–412.

Bernard, T. J. (1987). Structure and control: Reconsidering Hirschi's concept of commitment. *Justice Quarterly, 44,* 409–424.

Berry, R. E., & Boland, J. P. (1977). *The economic cost of alcohol abuse*. New York: Free Press.

Biderman, A. D., & Reiss, A. J. (1967). On exploring the "dark figure" of crime. *Annals of the American Academy of Political and Social Science, 374,* 733–748.

Black, W. A., & Gregson, R. A. (1973). Time perspective, purpose in life, extroversion and neuroticism in New Zealand prisoners. *British Journal of Social and Clinical Psychology, 12,* 50–60.

Blasi, A. (1980). Bridging moral cognition and moral action: A critical review of the literature. *Psychological Bulletin, 88,* 1–45.

Blau, J. R., & Blau, P. M. (1982). The cost of inequality: Metropolitan structure and violent crime. *American Sociological Review, 47,* 114–129.

Blehar, M. C., Lieberman, A. F., & Ainsworth, M. D. S. (1977). Early face-to-face interaction and its relation to later infant-mother attachment. *Child Development, 48,* 182–194.

Block, C. R. (1984). *Is crime seasonal?* Chicago: Statistical Analysis Center, Illinois Criminal Justice Information Authority.

Block, M. K., & Heineke, J. M. (1975). A labor theoretic analysis of the criminal choice. *American Economic Review, 65,* 314–325.

Blumstein, A., & Cohen, J. (1979). Estimation of individual crime rates from arrest records. *Journal of Criminal Law and Criminology, 70,* 561–585.

Bohman, M. (1971). A comparative study of adopted children, foster children, and children in their biological environment born after undesired pregnancies. *Acta Paediatrica Scandinavica, 60* (Suppl. 221), 5–38.

———. (1978). Some genetic aspects of alcoholism and criminality: A population of adoptees. *Archives of General Psychiatry, 35,* 269–276.

Bohman, M., Cloninger, C. R., Sigvardsson, S., & von Knorring, A-L. (1982). Predisposition to petty criminality in Swedish adoptees: I. Genetic and environmental heterogeneity. *Archives of General Psychiatry, 39,* 1233–1241.

Borgstrom, C. A. (1939). Eine serie von kriminellen zwilligen. *Archiv fur Rassen-und Gesellschaftsbiologie, 33,* 334–343.

Borkovec, T. D. (1970). Autonomic reactivity to sensory stimulation in psychopathic, neurotic, and normal juvenile delinquents. *Journal of Consulting and Clinical Psychology, 35,* 217–222.

Bornstein, R. A., & Matarazzo, J. D. (1982). Wechsler VIQ versus PIQ differences in cerebral dysfunction: A literature review with emphasis on sex differences. *Journal of Clinical Neuropsychology, 4,* 319–334.

Bottomley, A. K., & Coleman, C. A. (1980). Police effectiveness and the public: The limitations of official crime rates. In R. V. G. Clarke & J. M. Hough (eds.), *The effectiveness of policing*. Farnborough, England: Gower.

Bouhdiba, A. (1965). *Criminalite et changements sociaux en Tunisie*. Tunis: University of Tunis.

Boulanger, G. (1986). Violence and Vietnam veterans. In G. Boulanger & C. Kadushin (eds.), *The Vietnam veteran redefined* (pp. 70–79). Hillsdale, NJ: Lawrence Erlbaum.

Bowlby, J. (1973). *Attachment and loss: Volume 2. Separation: Anxiety and anger*. New York: Basic Books.

Bowlby, J. (1982). *Attachment and loss: Volume 1. Attachment*. New York: Basic Books (originally published in 1969).

Boyer, P. (1978). *Urban masses and moral order in America, 1820–1920*. Cambridge, MA: Harvard University Press.

Braithwaite, J. (1979). *Inequality, crime, and public policy*. London: Routledge & Kegan Paul.

———. (1981). The myth of social class and criminality reconsidered. *American Sociological Review, 46,* 36–57.

Braithwaite, J., & Braithwaite, V. (1980). Effects of income inequality and social democracy on homicide. *British Journal of Criminology, 20,* 45–53.

Brecher, M., Wang, B. W., Wong, H., & Morgan, J. P. (1988). Phencyclidine and violence: Clinical and legal issues. *Journal of Clinical Psychopharmacology, 8,* 397–401.

Brennan, P. A., & Mednick, S. A. (1990). A reply to Walters & White: "Heredity and crime." *Criminology, 28,* 657–661.

Brennan, T., & Huizinga, D. (1975). *Theory validation and aggregate national data*. Integration report of the Office of Youth Opportunity Research, FY 1975. Boulder, CO: Behavioral Research Institute.

Brenner, H. M. (1976). *Estimating the social costs of national economic policy: Implications for mental and physical health and criminal aggression.* Paper No. 5, Joint Economic Committee, Congress of the United States. Washington, DC: U.S. Government Printing Office.

Brier, N. (1989). The relationship between learning disability and delinquency: A review and reappraisal. *Journal of Learning Disabilities, 22,* 546–553.

Brier, S. S., & Fienberg, S. E. (1980). Recent economic modeling of crime and punishment: Support for the deterrence hypothesis? In S. E. Fieberg & A. J. Reiss (eds.), *Indicators of crime and criminal justice: Quantitative studies* (pp. 82–97). Washington, DC: U.S. Government Printing Office.

Briggs, P. F., Wirt, R. D., & Johnson, R. (1961). An application of prediction tables to the study of delinquency. *Journal of Consulting Psychology, 25,* 46–50.

Broder, P. K., Dunivant, N., Smith, E. C., & Sutton, L. P. (1981). Further observations on the link between learning disabilities and juvenile delinquency. *Journal of Educational Psychology, 73,* 838–850.

Brody, E. B., & Brody, N. (1976). *Intelligence: Nature, determinants, and consequences.* New York: Academic Press.

Brody, S. R. (1977). *Screen violence and film censorship—A review of research.* Home Office Research Study No. 35. London: H.M.S.O.

Brown, W. K., Miller, T. P., Jenkins, R. L., & Rhodes, W. A. (1989). The effect of early juvenile court adjudication on adult outcome. *International Journal of Offender Therapy and Comparative Criminology, 33,* 177–183.

Buikhuisen, W., Bontekoe, E. H. M., van der Plas-Korenhoff, C., & van Buuren, S. (1984). Characteristics of criminals: The privileged offender. *International Journal of Law and Psychiatry, 7,* 301–313.

Buikhuisen, W., & Dijksterhuss, P. H. (1971). Delinquency and stigmatization. *British Journal of Criminology, 11,* 185–187.

Buikhuisen, W., Eurelings-Bontekoe, E. H. M., & Host, K. B. (1989). Crime and recovery time: Mednick revisited. *International Journal of Law and Psychiatry, 12,* 29–40.

Buikhuisen, W., & Meijs, B. W. G. P. (1983). A psychosocial approach to recidivism. In K. T. van Dusen & S. A. Mednick (eds.), *Prospective studies of crime and delinquency* (pp. 99–115). Boston: Kluwer-Nijhoff Publishing.

Buikhuisen, W., van der Plas-Korenhoff, C., & Bontekoe, E. H. M. (1985). Parental home and deviance. *International Journal of Offender Therapy and Comparative Criminology, 29,* 201–210.

Bull, R. (1982). Physical appearance and criminality. *Current Psychological Reviews, 2,* 269–282.

Bureau of Justice Statistics. (1981a). *Measuring crime.* Washington, DC: Author.

———. (1981b). *Veterans in prison.* Washington, DC: Author.

———. (1983a). *Prisoners and alcohol.* Washington, DC: Author.

———. (1983b). *Prisoners and drugs.* Washington, DC: Author.

———. (1988a). *Criminal victimization in the United States, 1986.* Washington, DC: Author.

———. (1988b). *Profile of state prison inmates, 1986.* Washington, DC: Author.

———. (1988c). *Report to the nation on crime and justice* (2nd ed.). Washington, DC: Author.

———. (1988d). *The seasonality of crime victimization.* Washington, DC: Author.

Burns, R. S., & Lerner, S. E. (1978). Phencyclidine deaths. *Journal of the American College of Emergency Physicians, 7,* 135–141.

Burr, A. (1987). Chasing the dragon. *British Journal of Criminology, 27,* 333–357.

Burt, M. R. (1983). Justifying personal violence: A comparison of rapists and the general public. *Victimology, 8,* 131–150.

Busch, K. A., & Schnoll, S. H. (1985). Cocaine—Review of current literature and interface with the law. *Behavioral Sciences and the Law, 3,* 283–298.

Busia, K. A. (1966). Social survey of Sekondi-Takorade. In R. Hauser (ed.), *Social implications of industrialization and urbanization in Africa south of the Sahara.*

Buss, A., & Plomin, R. (1984). *Temperament: Early developing personality traits.* Hillsdale, NJ: Lawrence Erlbaum.

Cadoret, R. J. (1978). Psychopathology in adopted away offspring of biologic parents with antisocial behavior. *Archives of General Psychiatry, 35,* 176–184.

Cadoret, R. J., & Cain, C. (1980). Sex differences in predictors of antisocial behavior in adoptees. *Archives of General Psychiatry, 37,* 941–951.

Cadoret, R. J., Cain, C., & Crowe, R. R. (1983). Evidence for a gene-environment interaction in the development of adolescent antisocial behavior. *Behavior Genetics, 13,* 301–310.

Cadoret, R. J., O'Gorman, T., Troughton, E., & Heywood, E. (1985). Alcoholism and antisocial personality: Interrelationships, genetic and environmental factors. *Archives of General Psychiatry, 42,* 161–167.

Cahalan, D. (1970). *Problem drinkers.* San Francisco: Jossey-Bass.

Cahalan, D., & Room, R. (1972). Problem drinking among American men aged 21–59. *American Journal of Public Health, 62,* 1473–1482.

Camp, B. W. (1977). Verbal mediation in young aggressive boys. *Journal of Abnormal Psychology, 86,* 145–153.

Campbell, D. T., & Stanley, J. C. (1966). *Experimental and quasi-experimental designs for research.* Chicago: Rand McNally.

Canter, R. (1982). Sex differences in self-report delinquency. *Criminology, 20,* 378–398.

Cantor, D., & Land, K. C. (1985). Unemployment and crime rates in the post-World War II United States: A theoretical and empirical analysis. *American Sociological Review, 50,* 317–332.

Caplan, N. S. (1965). Intellectual functioning. In H. C. Quay (ed.), *Juvenile delinquency* (pp. 100–138). Princeton: Van Nostrand.

Card, J. (1983). *Lives after Vietnam.* Lexington, MA: D. C. Heath.

Carlsmith, J. M., & Anderson, C. A. (1979). Ambient temperature and the occurrence of collective violence: A new analysis. *Journal of Personality and Social Psychology, 37,* 337–344.

Carlsson, G. (1977). Crime and behavioral epidemiology: Concepts and applications to Swedish data. In S. A. Mednick & K. O. Christiansen (eds.), *Biosocial bases of criminal behavior* (pp. 25–43). New York: Gardner.

Carr, R. R., & Meyers, E. J. (1980). Marijuana and cocaine: The process of change in drug policy. In Drug Abuse Council, *The facts about "drug abuse"* (pp. 153–189). New York: Free Press.

Carroll, J. S. (1978). A psychological approach to deterrence: The evaluation of crime opportunities. *Journal of Personality and Social Psychology, 36,* 1512–1520.

Carroll, J. S., & Weaver, F. (1986). Shoplifters' perceptions of crime opportunities: A process-tracing study. In D. B. Cornish & R. V. Clarke (eds.), *The reasoning criminal: Rational choice perspectives on offending* (pp. 19–38). New York: Springer-Verlag.

Cernkovich, S. A., & Giordano, P. C. (1987). Family relationships and delinquency. *Criminology, 25,* 295–321.

Chaiken, J., & Chaiken, M. (1982). *Varieties of criminal behavior.* Santa Monica, CA: Rand Corporation.

Chambliss, W., & Nagasawa, R. (1969). On the validity of official statistics: A comparative study of white, black and Japanese high school boys. *Journal of Research in Crime and Delinquency, 6,* 71–77.

Chambliss, W. J., & Ryther, T. E. (1975). *Sociology: The discipline and its direction.* New York: McGraw-Hill.

Chappell, D., Geis, G., Schaefer, S., & Siegel, L. (1971). Forcible rape: A comparative study of offenses known to the police in Boston and Los Angeles. In J. M. Henslin (ed.), *Studies in the sociology of sex* (pp. 169–190). New York: Appleton-Century-Crofts.

Chatz, T. L. (1972). Management of male adolescent sex offenders. *International Journal of Offender Therapy, 2,* 109–115.

Chein, I., Gerard, D. L., Lee, R. S., & Rosenfeld, E. (1964). *The road to H: Narcotics, delinquency, and social policy.* New York: Basic Books.

Chiricos, T. G. (1987). Rates of crime and unemployment: An analysis of aggregate research evidence. *Social Problems, 34,* 187–212.

Christiansen, K. O. (1970). Crime in a Danish twin population. *Acta Geneticae Gemellologiae: Twin Research, 19,* 323–326.

———. (1974). Seriousness of criminality and concordance among Danish twins. In R. Hood (ed.), *Crime, criminology, and public policy* (pp. 63–77). London: Heinemann.

Christie, N. (1974). Criminological data as indicators on contemporary society. In *Crime and Industrialization* (pp. 144–155). Stockholm: Scandinavian Research Council for Criminology.

Cimler, E., & Beach, L. R. (1981). Factors involved in juveniles' decisions about crime. *Criminal Justice and Behavior, 8,* 275–286.

Clarke, D. G., & Blackenburg, W. (1972). Trends in violent content in selected mass media. In G. A. Comstock & E. Rubinstein (eds.), *Television and social behavior: Volume I* (pp. 188–243). Washington, DC: U.S. Government Printing Office.

Clark, N. H. (1976). *Deliver us from evil: An interpretation of American prohibition.* New York: Norton.

Cleckley, H. (1976). *The mask of sanity* (5th ed.). St. Louis: Mosby.

Clelland, D., & Carter, T. J. (1980). The new myth of class and crime. *Criminology, 18,* 319–336.

Clifford, W. (1967). *Juvenile delinquency in Zambia.* United Nations Publication, SOA/SD/CS3.

———. (1976). *Crime control in Japan.* Boston: Lexington.

Climent, C. E., & Ervin, F. R. (1972). Historical data in the evaluation of violent subjects. *Archives of General Psychiatry, 27,* 621–624.

Clinard, M. B., & Abbott, D. J. (1973). *Crime in developing countries: A comparative approach.* New York: John Wiley.

Cloninger, C. R., & Guze, S. B. (1973). Psychiatric illness in the families of female criminals: A study of 288 first-degree relatives. *British Journal of Psychiatry, 122,* 697–703.

Cloninger, C. R., Reich, T., & Guze, S. B. (1975a). The multifactorial model of disease transmission: II. Sex differences in the familial transmission of sociopathy (antisocial personality). *British Journal of Psychiatry, 127,* 11–22.

———. (1975b). The multifactorial model of disease transmission: III. Familial relationships between sociopathy and hysteria (Briquet's Syndrome). *British Journal of Psychiatry, 127,* 23–32.

Cloninger, C. R., Sigvardsson, S., Bohman, M., & von Knorring, A-L. (1982). Predisposition to petty criminality in Swedish adoptees: II. Cross-fostering analysis of gene-environment interaction. *Archives of General Psychiatry, 39,* 1242–1247.

Cloward, R. A., & Ohlin, L. E. (1960). *Delinquency and opportunity.* New York: Free Press.

Cohen, A. K. (1955). *Delinquent boys.* New York: Free Press.

Cohen, A., Lindesmith, A., & Schuessler, K. (1956). *The Sutherland papers.* Bloomington, IN: Indiana University Press.

Cohen, J. (1969). *Statistical power analysis for the behavioral sciences.* New York: Academic Press.

Cohen, L. E., & Felson, M. (1979a). On estimating the social costs of national economic policy: A critical examination of the Brenner study. *Social Indicators Research, 6,* 251–259.

———. (1979b). Social change and crime rate trends: A routine activity approach. *American Sociological Review, 44,* 588–608.

Cohen, L. E., & Land, K. C. (1987). Age structure and crime: Symmetry versus asymmetry and the projection of crime rates through the 1990s. *American Sociological Review, 52,* 170–183.

Cohen, M. A. (1988). Some new evidence on the seriousness of crime. *Criminology, 26,* 343–353.

Cohn, E. G. (1990). Weather and crime. *British Journal of Criminology, 30,* 51–64.

Cole, A. C. (1934). The irrepressible conflict, 1850–1865. In A. M. Schlesinger & D. R. Fox (eds.), *A history of American life in twelve volumes* (volume VII). New York: Macmillan.

Coleman, J. S., Campbell, E. Q., Hobson, C. J., McPartland, J., Mood, A. M., Weinfield, F. D., & York, R. L. (1966). *Equality of educational opportunity.* Washington, DC: Office of Education.

Coleman, J. S., Hoffer, T., & Kilgore, S. (1982). *High school achievement: Public, Catholic, and private schools compared.* New York: Basic Books.

Collins, J. J. (1981). Alcohol careers and criminal careers. In J. J. Collins (ed.), *Drinking and crime* (pp. 152–206). New York: Guilford.

Colvin, M., & Pauly, J. (1983). A critique of criminology: Toward an integrated structural-Marxist theory of delinquent production. *American Journal of Sociology, 89,* 513–551.

Comstock, G. A. (1980). *Television in America.* Beverly Hills, CA: Sage.

Conger, J. J., & Miller, W. C. (1966). *Personality, social class, and delinquency.* New York: John Wiley.

Connell, D. B. (1976). *Individual differences in attachment: An investigation into stability, implications, and relationships to the structure of early language development.* Unpublished doctoral dissertation, Syracuse University.

Cook, P. J. (1975). The correctional carrot: Better jobs for parolees. *Policy analysis, 1,* 11–54.

———. (1977). Punishment and crime: A critique of current findings concerning the preventive effects of punishment. *Law and Contemporary Problems, 41,* 164–204.

———. (1980). Research on criminal deterrence: Laying the groundwork for the second decade. In N. Morris & M. Tonry (eds.), *Crime and justice: An annual review of research: Vol. 2* (pp. 211–268). Chicago: University of Chicago Press.

Cook, R. F., Fosen, R. H., & Pacht, A. (1971). Pornography and the sex offender: Patterns of previous exposure and arousal effects of pornographic stimuli. *Journal of Applied Psychology, 55,* 503–511.

Cook, T. D., Kendzierski, D., & Thomas, S. (1983). The implicit assumption of television research: An analysis of the 1982 NIMH report on television and behavior. *Public opinion quarterly, 47,* 161–201.

Coons, R. M. (1981, February). *Learning disabilities and criminality.* Paper presented at Winnipeg Congress.

Cooper, H. H. A. (1971). Crime, criminals, and prisons in Peru. *International Journal of Offender Therapy and Comparative Criminology, 15,* 135–148.

———. (1975). Medico-legal problems in Peru. *International Journal of Offender Therapy and Comparative Criminology, 19,* 191–196.

Corbin, R. M. (1980). Decisions that might not get made. In T. S. Wallsten (ed.), *Cognitive processes in choice and decision behavior.* Hillsdale, NJ: Lawrence Erlbaum.

Cornish, D. B., & Clarke, R. V. (eds.). (1986). *The reasoning criminal: Rational choice perspectives on offending.* New York: Springer-Verlag.

Cotton, J. L. (1986). Ambient temperature and violent crime. *Journal of Applied Social Psychology, 16,* 786–801.

Cowie, J., Cowie, V., & Slater, E. (1968). *Delinquency in girls.* London: Heinemann.

Cox, D. N. (1978). Psychophysiological correlates of sensation seeking and socialization during reduced stimulation. *Dissertation Abstracts International, 39,* (1-B), 372.

Craft, M., Fabisch, W., Stephenson, G., Burnand, G., & Kerridge, D. (1962). 100 admissions to a psychopathic unit. *Journal of Mental Science, 108,* 564–583.

Cressey, D. R. (1966). Crime. In R. K. Merton & R. A. Nisbet (eds.), *Contemporary social problems* (pp. 136–192). Chicago: Harcourt, Brace.

Cripe, C. A. (1990). Studying Japanese prisons: An informal tour of two institutions. *Federal Prison Journal, 1,* 35–41.

Crowe, R. R. (1972). The adoptive offspring of women criminal offenders: A study of arrest records. *Archives of General Psychiatry, 27,* 600–603.

———. (1974). An adoption study of antisocial personality. *Archives of General Psychiatry, 31,* 785–791.

Cullen, F. T., Larson, M. T., & Mathers, R. A. (1985). Having money and delinquent involvement: The neglect of power in delinquency theory. *Criminal Justice and Behavior, 12,* 171–192.

Cullen, F. T., Link, B. G., Travis, L. F., & Wozniak, J. F. (1985). Consensus in crime seriousness: Empirical reality or methodological artifact? *Criminology, 23,* 99–118.

Curtis, L. (1974). *Criminal violence.* Lexington, MA: D. C. Heath.

Cusson, M., & Pinsonneault, H. P. (1986). The decision to give up crime. In D. Cornish

& R. Clarke (eds.), *The reasoning criminal: Rational choice perspectives on offending* (pp. 72–82). New York: Springer-Verlag.

Czudner, G. (1985). Changing the criminal. *Federal Probation, 49,* 64–66.

Daitzman, R., & Zuckerman, M. (1980). Disinhibitory sensation seeking, personality and gonadal hormones. *Personality and Individual Differences, 1,* 103–110.

Dalby, J. T. (1985). Criminal liability in children. *Canadian Journal of Criminology, 27,* 137–145.

Dalby, J. T., Schneider, R. D., Arboleda-Florez, J. (1982). Learning disorders in offenders. *International Journal of Offender Therapy and Comparative Criminology, 26,* 145–151.

Dalgard, O. S., & Kringlen, E. (1976). A Norwegian twin study of criminality. *British Journal of Criminology, 16,* 213–232.

Danziger, S., & Wheeler, D. (1975). The economics of crime: Punishment or income redistribution. *Review of Social Economy, 33,* 113–131.

Darity, W., & Myers, S. L. (1983). Changes in black family structure: Implications for welfare dependency. *American Economic Review, 73,* 59–64.

Datesman, S. K., & Scarpitti, F. R. (1980). The extent and nature of female crime. In S. K. Datesman & F. R. Scarpitti (eds.), *Women, crime and justice* (pp. 3–64). New York: Oxford.

Davids, A., & Falkof, B. B. (1975). Juvenile delinquents then and now: Comparison of findings from 1959 and 1974. *Journal of Abnormal Psychology, 84,* 161–164.

Davids, A., Kidder, C., & Reich, M. (1962). Time orientation in male and female juvenile delinquents. *Journal of Abnormal and Social Psychology, 64,* 239–240.

Davidson, J. M., Camargo, C. A., & Smith, E. R. (1979). Effects of androgen on sexual behavior in hypogonadal men. *Journal of Clinical Endocrinology and Metabolism, 48,* 955–958.

Davis, B. (1982). The PCP epidemic: A critical review. *The International Journal of Addictions, 17,* 1137–1155.

Davis, J. R. (1983). *The relation between crime and unemployment—An economic model.* Paper presented at the annual meeting of the American Society of Criminology.

DeFeudis, F. V., & Schauss, A. G. (1987). The role of brain monoamine metabolite concentrations in arsonists and habitually violent offenders: Abnormalities of criminals or social isolation effects? *International Journal of Biosocial Research, 9,* 27–30.

DeFronzo, J. (1983). Economic assistance to impoverished Americans. *Criminology, 21,* 119–136.

———. (1984). Climate and crime: Tests of an FBI assumption. *Environment and Behavior, 16,* 185–210.

Demaree, R. G., & Neman, J. F. (1976). Criminality indicators before, during, and after treatment for drug abuse: DARP research findings. In Research Triangle Institute, *Drug use and crime* (P3–259–167). Springfield, VA: National Technical Information Service.

Demaris, O. (1970). *America the violent.* New York: Cowles.

DeMyer-Gapin, S., & Scott, T. J. (1977). Effect of stimulus novelty on stimulation seeking in antisocial and neurotic children. *Journal of Abnormal Psychology, 86,* 96–98.

DeRen, G., Diligent, M. B., & Petiet, G. (1973). The tattoo and the personality of the tattooed. *Medical Legal Dommage Corporation, 6,* 309.

Devine, J. A., Sheley, J. F., & Smith, M. D. (1988). Macroeconomic and social-control policy influences on crime rate changes, 1948–1985. *American Sociological Review, 53,* 407–420.

DeWolfe, A. S., & Ryan, J. J. (1984). Wechsler performance IQ > verbal IQ index in a forensic sample: A reconsideration. *Journal of Clinical Psychology, 40,* 291–294.

Dietz, P. E., & Rada, R. T. (1982). Battery incidents and batterers in a maximum security hospital. *Archives of General Psychiatry, 39,* 31–34.

Dinitz, S., Scarpitti, F. R., & Reckless, W. C. (1962). Delinquency vulnerability: A cross group and longitudinal analysis. *American Sociological Review, 27,* 515–517.

Dishion, T. J., Stouthamer-Loeber, M., & Patterson, G. R. (1984). *The monitoring construct* [OSLC technical report]. (Available from OSLC, 207 East 5th, Suite 202, Eugene, OR 97401).

Dixson, A. F. (1980). Androgens and aggressive behavior in primates: A review. *Aggressive Behavior, 6,* 37–67.

Donnerstein, E. (1984). Pornography: Its effect on violence against women. In N. M. Malamuth & E. Donnerstein (eds.), *Pornography and sexual aggression* (pp. 53–81). Orlando, FL: Academic Press.

Doren, D. M. (1987). *Understanding and treating the psychopath.* New York: John Wiley.

Douglas, J. D. (ed.). (1970). *Observations of deviance.* New York: Random House.

Downes, D. (1966). *The delinquent solution: A study of subcultural theory.* London: Routledge & Kegan Paul.

Drapkin, I (1983). Criminology: Intellectual history. In S. H. Kadish (editor-in-chief), *Encyclopedia of crime and justice: Volume I* (pp. 547–556). New York: Free Press.

Driver, M. V., West, L. R., & Faulk, M. (1974). Clinical and EEG studies of prisoners charged with murder. *British Journal of Psychiatry, 125,* 583–587.

Dugdale, R. L. (1877). *The Jukes: A study of crime, pauperism, disease, and heredity.* New York: G. P. Putnam.

Duncan, G. J. (1984). *Years of poverty, years of plenty.* Ann Arbor, MI: Survey Research Center, Institute of Social Research.

Dunivant, N. (1982). *The relationship between learning disabilities and juvenile delinquency.* Williamsburg, VA: National Center for State Courts (NCSCR-072).

DuPont, R. L., & Greene, M. H. (1973). The dynamics of a heroin addiction epidemic. *Science, 181,* 716–741.

Durkheim, E. (1938). *The rules of sociological method* [transl. S. A. Solovay & J. H. Mueller]. New York: Free Press.

———. (1951). *Suicide: A study in sociology* [transl. J. A. Spaulding & G. Simpson]. New York: Free Press.

Duster, T. (1987). Crime, youth unemployment, and the black urban underclass. *Crime and Delinquency, 33,* 300–316.

Eck, J. E., & Riccio, L. J. (1979). Relationship between reported crime rates and victimization survey results: An empirical and analytical study. *Journal of Criminal Justice, 7,* 293–308.

Eckerman, W. C., Bates, J. D., Rachal, J. V., & Poole, W. K. (1971). *Drug usage and arrest charges: A study of drug usage and arrest charges among arrestees in six metropolitan areas of the United States* (Final report BNDD contract no. J-70–35). Washington, DC: Drug Enforcement Administration.

Edelberg, R., & Muller, M. (1977). *The status of electrodermal recovery measures.* Paper presented to the Society for Psychophysiological Research, Philadelphia, PA.

Edgar, P. (1977). *Children and screen violence.* St. Lucia, Australia: University of Queensland Press.

Edwards, E. D., & Goldner, N. S. (1975). Criminality and addiction: Decline of client criminality in a methadone treatment program. In E. C. Senay, V. Shorty, & H. Alksne (eds.), *Developments in the field of drug abuse.* Cambridge, MA: Schenkman Press.

Edwards, J. N., & Fuhrman, E. R. (1985). The constancy of crime hypothesis: Historical evidence for Plymouth Colony. *Qualitative Sociology, 8,* 149–158.

Egan, G. (1982). *The skilled helper.* Belmont, CA: Wadsworth.

Egeland, B., & Sroufe, L. A. (1981). Attachment and early maltreatment. *Child Development, 52,* 44–52.

Ehrenkranz, J., Bliss, E., & Sheard, M. H. (1974). Plasma testosterone: Correlation with aggressive behavior and social dominance in man. *Psychosomatic Medicine, 36,* 469–475.

Ehrlich, I. (1975). The deterrent effect of capital punishment: A question of life and death. *American Economic Review, 65,* 397–417.

Ehrlich, S. K., & Keogh, R. P. (1956). The psychopath in a mental institution. *Archives of Neurology and Psychiatry, 76,* 286–295.

Einhorn, H. J., & Hogarth, R. M. (1978). Confidence in judgment: Persistence in the illusion of validity. *Psychological Review, 85,* 395–416.

Eisenberg, J., Langner, T. S., & Gersten, J. C. (1975). Differences in the behavior of welfare and non-welfare children in relation to parental characteristics. *Journal of Community Psychology, 3,* 311–340.

El Bacha, A. (1962). Quelques aspects particuliers de la delinquance juvenile dans certaines ville du royaume du maroc. *International Review of Criminal Policy, 20,* 21–23.

Elder, G. H., Caspi, A., & Downey, G. (1983). Problem behavior in family relationships: A multigenerational analysis. In A. Sorensen, F. Weinert, & L. Sherrod (eds.), *Human development: Interdisciplinary prospective* (pp. 93–118). Hillsdale, NJ: Lawrence Erlbaum.

Ellingson, R. J. (1954). Incidence of EEG abnormality among patients with mental disorders of apparently nonorganic origin: A critical review. *American Journal of Psychiatry, 111,* 263–275.

Ellinwood, E. H. (1971). Assault and homicide associated with amphetamine abuse. *American Journal of Psychiatry, 127,* 1170–1175.

Elliott, D. S. (1966). Delinquency, school attendance, and school dropout. *Social Problems, 13,* 307–314.

Elliott, D. S., & Ageton, S. S. (1980). Reconciling race and class differences in self-reported and official estimates of delinquency. *American Sociological Review, 45,* 95–110.

Elliott, D. S., Ageton, S. S., & Canter, R. J. (1979). An integral theoretical perspective on delinquent behavior. *Journal of Research in Crime and Delinquency, 16,* 3–27.

Elliott, D. S., Ageton, S. S., Huizinga, D., Knowles, D. A., & Canter, R. J. (1983). *The prevalence and incidence of delinquent behavior: 1976–1980*. Boulder, CO: Behavioral Research Institute.

Elliott, D. S., Huizinga, D., & Ageton, S. S. (1985). *Explaining delinquency and drug use*. Beverly Hills, CA: Sage.

Elliott, D. S., Knowles, B. A., & Canter, R. J. (1981). *The epidemiology of delinquent behavior and drug use among American adolescents*. [National Youth Survey Project Report No. 14]. Boulder, CO: Behavioral Research Institute.

Elliott, D. S., & Voss, H. (1974). *Delinquency and dropout*. Lexington, MA: D. C. Heath.

Ellis, L. (1988). The victimful-victimless crime distinction, and seven universal demographic correlates of victimful criminal behavior. *Personality and Individual Differences, 9,* 525–548.

Ellis, P. L. (1982). Empathy: A factor in antisocial behavior. *Journal of Abnormal Child Psychology, 2,* 123–133.

Elmer, E. (1977). *Fragile families, troubled children*. Pittsburg: University of Pittsburg Press.

Empey, L. T. (1978). *American delinquency*. Homewood, IL: Dorsey.

Engendorf, A., Kadushin, C., & Laufer, R. S. (1981). *Legacies of Vietnam: Comparative adjustment of veterans and their peers*. Washington, DC: U.S. Government Printing Office.

Enyon, T. G., & Reckless, W. C. (1961). Companionships at delinquency onset. *British Journal of Criminology, 2,* 167–168.

Epps, P., & Parnell, R. W. (1952). Physique and temperament of women delinquents compared with women undergraduates. *British Journal of Medical Psychology, 25,* 249–255.

Erickson, M. L., & Empey, L. T. (1963). Court records, undetected delinquency, and decision-making. *Journal of Criminal Law, Criminology and Police Science*, *54,* 456–469.

———. (1965). Class position, peers, and delinquency. *Sociology and Social Research, 49,* 268–282.

Erikson, E. H. (1963) *Childhood and society* (2nd ed.). New York: Norton.

Eron, L. D., Huesmann, L. R., Lefkowitz, M. M., & Walder, L. O. (1972). Does television cause aggression? *American Psychologist, 27,* 253–263.

Ewing, J. A. (1967). Addictions II: Non-narcotic addictive agents. In A. N. Freedman & H. S. Kaplan (eds.), *Comprehensive Textbook of Psychiatry* (pp. 1003–1011). Baltimore: Williams & Wilkins.

Fagan, J., Weis, J. G., & Cheng, Y-T. (1990). Delinquency and substance abuse among inner-city students. *Journal of Drug Issues, 20,* 351–402.

Fagan, J., & Wexler, S. (1987). Family origins of violent delinquents. *Criminology, 25,* 643–669.

Faiman, C., & Winter, J. S. D. (1974). Gonadotrophins and sex hormone patterns in puberty: Clinical data. In M. M. Grumbach, G. D. Grave, & F. E. Mayer (eds.), *Control of the onset of puberty* (pp. 2–44). New York: John Wiley.

Farley, F. (1986). The big T in personality. *Psychology Today, 20,* 44–52.

Farley, F. H., & Farley S. V. (1972). Stimulus-seeking motivation and delinquent behavior among institutionalized delinquent girls. *Journal of Consulting and Clinical Psychology, 39,* 94–97.

Farley, F. H., & Sewell, T. (1976). Test of an arousal theory of delinquency: Stimulus-seeking in delinquent and nondelinquent black adolescents. *Criminal Justice and Behavior, 3,* 315–320.

Farnworth, M. (1984). Family structure, family attributes, and delinquency in a sample of low-income, minority males and females. *Journal of Youth and Adolescence, 13,* 349–364.

Farnworth, M., & Lieber, M. J. (1989). Strain theory revisited: Economic goals, educational means, and delinquency. *American Sociological Review, 54,* 263–274.

Farrington, D. P. (1979). Environmental stress, delinquent behavior, and convictions. In I. G. Sarason & C. D. Spielberger (eds.), *Stress and Anxiety: Volume 6.* Washington, DC: Hemisphere.

———. (1988). Advancing knowledge about delinquency and crime: The need for a coordinated program of longitudinal research. *Behavioral Sciences and the Law, 6,* 307–331.

Farrington, D. P., Gallagher, B., Morley, L., St. Ledger, R. J., & West, D. J. (1986). Unemployment, school leaving, and crime. *British Journal of Criminology, 26,* 335–356.

———. (1988) Are there any successful men from criminogenic backgrounds? *Psychiatry, 51,* 116–130.

Fattah, E. H. (1982). A critique of deterrence research with particular reference to the economic approach. *Canadian Journal of Criminology, 24,* 79–90.

Faulkner, H. U. (1931). The quest for social justice, 1898–1914. In A. M. Schlesinger & D. R. Fox (eds.), *A history of American life in twelve volumes* (Volume XI). New York: Macmillan.

Fauman, B. J., & Fauman, M. A. (1982). Phencyclidine abuse and crime: A psychiatric perspective. *Bulletin of the American Association of Psychiatry and the Law, 10,* 171–176.

Faupel, C. E. (1987). Heroin use and criminal careers. *Qualitative Sociology, 10,* 115–131.

Faupel, C. E., & Klockars, C. B. (1987). Drugs-crime connections: Elaborations from the life histories of hard-core heroin addicts. *Social Problems, 34,* 54–68.

Federal Bureau of Investigation. (1985). The men who murdered. *FBI Law Enforcement Bulletin, 54,* 1–5.

———. (1988). *Crime in the United States, 1987.* Washington, DC: U.S. Government Printing Office.

Feeney, F. (1986). Robbers as decision-makers. In D. B. Cornish & R. V. Clarke (eds.), *The reasoning criminal: Rational choice perspectives on offending* (pp. 53–71). New York: Springer-Verlag.

Feldman, R. A., Caplinger, T. E., & Wodarski, J. S. (1983). *The St. Louis conundrum: The effective treatment of antisocial youths.* Englewood Cliffs, NJ: Prentice-Hall.

Felson, M. (1986). Linking criminal choices, routine activities, informal control, and criminal outcomes. In D. B. Cornish & R. V. Clarke (eds.), *The reasoning criminal: Rational choice perspectives on offending* (pp. 119–128). New York: Springer-Verlag.

Felson, M., & Cohen, L. E. (1977). *Criminal acts and community structure: A routine activity approach.* Working papers in applied social statistics, Department of Sociology, University of Illinois at Urbana-Champaign.

Felson, R. B., Ribner, S. A., & Siegel, M. S. (1984). Age and the effect of third parties during criminal violence. *Sociology and Social Research, 68,* 452–462.

Felson, R. B., & Steadman, H. J. (1983). Situational factors in disputes leading to criminal violence. *Criminology, 21,* 59–74.

Ferdinand, T. N. (1967). The criminal patterns of Boston since 1846. *American Journal of Sociology, 73,* 84–99.

———. (1970). Demographic shifts and criminality: An inquiry. *British Journal of Criminology, 10,* 169–175.

Ferreira, A. J., & Winter, W. D. (1968). Information exchange and silence in normal and abnormal families. *Family Process, 7,* 251–276.

Feshback, S., & Singer, R. D. (1971). *Television and aggression: An experimental field study.* San Francisco: Jossey-Bass.

Field, L. H., & Williams, M. (1970). The hormonal treatment of sexual offenders. *Medicine, Science, and the Law, 10,* 27–34.

Figgie Corporation. (1988). *The Figgie Report: Part VI. The business of crime: The criminal perspective.* Richmond, VA: Figgie International Inc.

Filskov, S. B., & Goldstein, S. G. (1974). Diagnostic validity of the Halstead-Reitan Neuropsychological Battery. *Journal of Consulting and Clinical Psychology, 42,* 383–388.

Finlayson, D. S., & Loughran, J. L. (1976). Pupils' perceptions in high and low delinquency schools. *Educational Research, 18,* 138–145.

Fitts, W. H., & Hammer, W. T. (1969). *The self-concept and delinquency.* Research Monograph No. 1, Nashville Mental Health Centre, Nashville, TN.

Fitzhugh, K. B. (1973). Some neurological features of delinquent subjects. *Perceptual and Motor Skills, 36,* 494.

Forslund, M. (1970). A comparison of negro and white crime rates. *Journal of Criminal Law, Criminology, and Police Science, 61,* 214–217.

Foster, J. D., Dinitz, S., & Reckless, W. C. (1972). Perceptions of stigma following public intervention for delinquent behavior. *Social Problems, 20,* 202–209.

Fox, S. S., Kimble, D. P., & Lickey, M. E. (1964). Comparison of caudate nucleus and septal-area lesions on two types of avoidance behavior. *Journal of Comparative and Physiological Psychology, 58,* 380–386.

Freedman, D. G. (1979). Ethnic differences in babies. *Human Nature, 2,* 36–43.

Freedman, J. L. (1984). Effect of television violence on aggression. *Psychological Bulletin, 96,* 227–246.

Freeman, R. B. (1983). Crime and unemployment. In J. Q. Wilson (ed.), *Crime and public policy* (pp. 89–106). San Francisco: Institute for Contemporary Studies.

Freud, S. (1922). *Beyond the pleasure principle.* London: International Psychoanalytic Press.

Friedman, H. L., & Johnson, R. L. (1972). Mass media use and aggression: A pilot study. In G. A. Comstock & E. A. Rubinstein (eds.), *Television and social behavior: Volume 3. Television and adolescent aggressiveness* (pp. 336–360). Washington, DC: U.S. Government Printing Office.

Friedrich, L. K., & Stein, A. H. (1973). Aggressive and prosocial television programs and the natural behavior of preschool children. *Monographs of the Society for Research in Child Development, 38* (Serial No. 151).

Fuchs, V. R. (1983). *How we live: An economic perspective on Americans from birth to death.* New York: Basic Books.

Furnham, A. (1984). Unemployment, attribution theory and mental health: A review of the British literature. *International Journal of Mental Health, 13,* 51–67.

Gabrielli, W. F., & Mednick, S. A. (1980). Sinistrality and delinquency. *Journal of Abnormal Psychology, 89,* 654–661.

———. (1984). Urban environment, genetics, and crime. *Criminology, 22,* 645–652.

Garafalo, R. (1914). *Criminology*. London: Heinemann.

Garb, H. N. (1984). The incremental validity of information used in personality assessment. *Clinical Psychology Review*, *4*, 641–655.

Gardner, D. B., Hawkes, G. R., & Burchinal, L. G. (1961). Noncontinuous mothering in infancy and development in later childhood. *Child Development, 32*, 225–234.

Garofalo, J. (1987). Reassessing the lifestyle model of criminal victimization. In M. R. Gottfredson & T. Hirschi (eds.), *Positive Criminology* (pp. 23–42). Newbury Park, CA: Sage.

Garland, D. (1985). The criminal and his science. *British Journal of Criminology, 25,* 109–137.

Gendreau, P., & Ross, R. R. (1987). Revivification of rehabilitation: Evidence from the 1980s. *Justice Quarterly, 4,* 349–407.

George, C., & Main, M. (1980). Abused children: Their rejection of peers and caregivers. In T. M. Field, S. Goldberg, D. Stern, & A. M. Sostek (eds.), *High risk infants and children: Adult and peer interactions* (pp. 293–312). New York: Academic Press.

Ghali, M. A. (1982). The choice of crime: An empirical analysis of juveniles' criminal choice. *Journal of Criminal Justice, 10,* 433–442.

Gibbens, T. C. N. (1963). *Psychiatric studies of Borstal lads*. London: Oxford University Press.

Gibbs, J. J., & Shelly, P. L. (1982). Life in the fast lane: A retrospective view by commercial thieves. *Journal of Research in Crime and Delinquency. 19,* 299–330.

Gibbs, J. T. (1982). Personality patterns of delinquent females: Ethnic and socialization variations. *Journal of Clinical Psychology, 38,* 198–206.

Gilbert, M., & Gravier, B. (1982). *Cerebral dysfunction, homicide and psychosis: Case study*. Montreal: Institut Philippe-Pinel.

Gillespie, R. W. (1975). *Economic factors in crime and delinquency: A critical review of the empirical evidence*. Washington, DC: National Institute of Law Enforcement and Criminal Justice.

Giordano, P., & Cernkovich, S. (1979). On complicating the relationship between liberation and delinquency. *Social Problems, 26,* 467–481.

Gladstone, F. J. (1980). *Co-ordinating crime prevention effects*. Home Office Research Study No. 62. London: Her Majesty's Stationery Office.

Glueck, S., & Glueck, E. (1950). *Unraveling juvenile delinquency*. New York: Commonwealth Fund.

———. (1968). *Delinquents and nondelinquents in perspective*. Cambridge, MA: Harvard University Press.

———. (1974). *Of delinquency and crime*. Springfield, IL: Thomas.

Goddard, H. H. (1914). *Feeble-mindedness: Its causes and consequences*. New York: Macmillan.

Gold, M., & Reimer, D. J. (1975). Changing patterns of delinquent behavior among

Americans 13 through 16 years old: 1967–1972. *Crime and Delinquency Literature, 7,* 483–517.

Gold, M., & Williams, J. R. (1969). National study of the aftermath of apprehension. *Prospectus, 3,* 3–12.

Goldkamp, J. S. (1987). Rational choice and determinism. In M. R. Gottfredson & T. Hirschi (eds.), *Positive criminology* (pp. 125–137). Newbury Park, CA: Sage.

Goldman, H. (1977). The limits of clockwork: The neurobiology of violent behavior. In J. P. Conrad & S. Dinitz (eds.), *In fear of each other* (pp. 43–76). Lexington, MA: D. C. Heath.

Goldsmith, H. H., & Alansky, J. A. (1987). Maternal and infant temperamental predictors of attachment: A meta-analytic review. *Journal of Consulting and Clinical Psychology, 55,* 805–816.

Goldsmith, H. H., Bradshaw, D. L., & Rieser-Danner, L. A. (1986). Temperamental dimensions as potential developmental influences on attachment. In J. V. Lerner & R. M. Lerner (eds.), *New directions for child development: Temperament and psychosocial interaction in infancy and childhood* (pp. 5–34). San Francisco: Jossey-Bass.

Goldsmith, H. H., & Campos, J. J. (1982). Toward a theory of infant temperament. In R. N. Emde & R. J. Harmon (eds.), *The development of attachment and affiliative systems* (pp. 161–193). New York: Plenum.

Goldstein, P. J. (1981). Getting over: Economic alternatives to predatory crime among street drug users. In J. A. Inciardi (ed.), *The drugs-crime connection* (pp. 67–84). Beverly Hills, CA: Sage.

Goodwin, D. W., Crane, B., & Guze, S. B. (1971). Felons who drink: An 8-year follow-up. *Quarterly Journal of Studies on Alcohol, 32,* 136–147.

Gordon, R. A. (1975). Examining labeling theory: The case of mental retardation. In W. Gove (ed.), *The labeling of deviance* (pp. 83–146): New York: John Wiley.

Gorenstein, E. E. (1982). Frontal lobe functions in psychopaths. *Journal of Abnormal Psychology, 91,* 368–379.

Goring, C. (1913). *The English convict.* London: Her Majesty's Stationery Office.

Gottfredson, G. D. (1981). Schooling and delinquency. In S. E. Martin, L. B. Sechrest, & R. Redner (eds.), *New directions in the rehabilitation of criminal offenders* (pp. 424–469). Washington, DC: National Academy Press.

———. (1983, May). *The school action effectiveness study: Interim summary of the alternative education evaluation.* Paper distributed by the Center for Social Organization of Schools, Johns Hopkins University, Baltimore, MD.

Gottfredson, M. R., & Hirschi, T. (1987). The positive tradition. In M. R. Gottfredson & T. Hirschi (eds.), *Positive criminology* (pp. 9—22). Newbury Park, CA: Sage.

Gough, H. G. (1948). A sociological theory of psychopathy. *American Journal of Sociology, 53,* 359–366.

———. (1965). Cross-cultural validation of a measure of asocial behavior. *Psychological Reports, 17,* 379–387.

Gould, L. C. (1969). Juvenile entrepreneurs. *American Journal of Sociology, 74,* 710–720.

Gove, W. R. (ed.) (1980). *The labeling of deviance: Evaluating a perspective* (2nd ed.). Beverly Hills, CA: Sage.

Goy, R. W. (1968). Organizing effects of androgen on the behavior of rhesus monkeys.

In R. P. Michael (ed.), *Endocrinology and human behavior* (pp. 12–31). London: Oxford University Press.

Goy, R. W., Wolf, J. E., & Eisele, S. G. (1977). Experimental female hermaphroditism in rhesus monkeys: Anatomical and psychological characteristics. In J. Money & H. Musaph (eds.), *Handbook of sexology* (pp. 139–156). Amsterdam: Elsevier/North Holland Biomedical Press.

Greenberg, D. F. (1979). Delinquency and the age structure of society. In S. L. Messinger & E. Bittner (eds.), *Criminology review yearbook* (pp. 586–620). Beverly Hills, CA: Sage.

———. (1985). Age, crime, and social explanation. *American Journal of Sociology, 91,* 1–21.

Greenberg, S. W. (1976). The relationship between crime and amphetamine abuse: An empirical review of the literature. *Contemporary Drug Problems, 5,* 101–130.

———. (1981). Alcohol and crime: A methodological critique of the literature. In J. J. Collins (ed.), *Drinking and crime* (pp. 70–109). New York: Guilford.

Greenberg, S. W., & Adler, F. (1974). Crime and addiction: An empirical analysis of the literature, 1920–1973. *Contemporary Drug Problems, 3,* 221–267.

Greene, B. T. (1981). An examination of the relationship between crime and substance abuse/use in a drug/alcohol treatment population. *International Journal of the Addictions, 16,* 627–645.

Greene, E. B. (1943). The revolutionary generation, 1763–1790. In A. M. Schlesinger & D. R. Fox (eds.), *A history of American life in twelve volumes* (Volume IV). New York: Macmillan.

Greene, R. L. (1980). *The MMPI: An interpretive manual.* New York: Grune & Stratton.

Greenwood, P. W. (1983). Controlling the crime rate through imprisonment. In J. Q. Wilson (ed.), *Crime and public policy* (pp. 251–269). New Brunswick, NJ: Transaction Books.

Greer, S. (1964). Study of parental loss in neurotics and sociopaths. *Archives of General Psychiatry, 11,* 177–180.

Grier, P. E. (1988). Cognitive problem-solving skills in anti-social rapists. *Criminal Justice and Behavior, 15,* 501–514.

Griffitt, W., & Veitch, R. (1971). Hot and crowded: Influences of population density and temperature on interpersonal affective behavior. *Journal of Personality and Social Psychology, 17,* 92–98.

Grinspoon, L. (1977). *Marihuana reconsidered.* Cambridge, MA: Harvard University Press.

Gurr, T. R. (1977). Crime trends in modern democracies since 1945. *International Annals of Criminology, 16,* 41–85.

———. (1981). Historical trends in violent crime: A critical review of the evidence. In M. Tonry & N. Morris (eds.), *Crime and justice: An annual review of research. Vol. 3* (pp. 295–353). Chicago: University of Chicago Press.

———. (1989). Historical trends in violent crime: Europe and the United States. In T. R. Gurr (ed.), *Violence in America, Vol. I: The history of crime* (pp. 21–54). Newbury Park, CA: Sage.

Guze, S. B., Tuason, V. B., Gatfield, P. D., Stewart, M. A., & Picken, B. (1962). Psychiatric illness and crime with particular reference to alcoholism: A study of 223 criminals. *Journal of Nervous and Mental Disease, 134,* 512–521.

Guze, S. B., Wolfgram, E. D., McKinney, J. K., & Cantwell, D. P. (1967). Psychiatric illness in the families of convicted criminals: A study of 519 first-degree relatives. *Diseases of the Nervous System, 28,* 651–659.

Hall, C. S., & Lindzey, G. (1970). *Theories of personality.* New York: John Wiley.

Haller, M. H. (1989). Bootlegging: The business and politics of violence. In T. R. Gurr (ed.), *Violence in America, Vol. I: The history of crime* (pp. 146–162). Newbury Park, CA: Sage.

Hammersley, R., Forsyth, A., Morrison, V., & Davies, J. B. (1989). The relationship between crime and opioid use. *British Journal of Addictions, 84,* 1029–1043.

Hamparian, D. M., Schuster, R., Dinitz, S., & Conrad, J. P. (1978). *The violent few.* Lexington, MA: Lexington/D. C. Heath.

Hansmann, H. B., & Quigley, J. M. (1979). *Population heterogeneity and the sociogenesis of homicide.* Working Paper No. 824. Institute for Social and Policy Studies, Yale University.

Hanson, C. L., Henggler, S. W., Haefele, W. F., & Rodick, J. D. (1984). Demographic, individual, and family relationship correlates of serious and repeated crime among adolescents and their siblings. *Journal of Consulting and Clinical Psychology, 52,* 528–538.

Hare, R. D. (1970). *Psychopathology: Theory and research.* New York: John Wiley.

———. (1975). Psychopathy. In P. Venables & M. Christie (eds.), *Research in psychophysiology* (pp. 325–348). New York: John Wiley.

———. (1978). Electrodermal and cardiovascular correlates of psychopathy. In R. D. Hare & D. Schalling (eds.), *Psychopathic behavior* (pp. 107–144). New York: John Wiley.

———. (1979) Psychopathy and laterality of cerebral function. *Journal of Abnormal Psychology, 88,* 605–610.

———. (1982). Psychopathy and physiological activity during anticipation of an aversive stimulus in a distraction paradigm. *Psychophysiology, 19,* 266–271.

———. (1984). Performance of psychopaths on cognitive tasks related to frontal lobe function. *Journal of Abnormal Psychology, 93,* 133–140.

Hare, R. D., & Connolly, J. F. (1987). Perceptual asymmetries and information processing in psychopaths. In S. A. Mednick, T. E. Moffitt, & S. A. Stack (eds.), *The causes of crime: New biological approaches* (pp. 218–238). New York: Cambridge University Press.

Hare, R. D., & Forth, A. E. (1985). Psychopathy and lateral preference. *Journal of Abnormal Psychology, 94,* 541–546.

Hare, R. D., & McPherson, L. M. (1984). Psychopathy and perceptual asymmetry during verbal dichotic listening. *Journal of Abnormal Psychology, 93,* 141–149.

Hare, R. D., & Quinn, M. J. (1971). Psychopathy and autonomic conditioning. *Journal of Abnormal Psychology, 77,* 223–235.

Harlow, H. F. (1963). The maternal affectional system. In B. M. Foss (ed.), *Determinants of infant behavior* (Vol. 2, pp. 3–29). New York: John Wiley.

Harper, M. A., Morris, M., & Bleyerveld, J. (1972). The significance of an abnormal EEG in psychopathic personalities. *Australian and New Zealand Journal of Psychiatry, 6,* 214–224.

Harries, K. D., Stadler, S. J., & Zdorkowski, R. T. (1984). Seasonality and assault: Exploration in inter-neighborhood variation, Dallas 1980. *Annals of the Association of American Geographers, 74,* 590–604.

Harris, A. R. (1977). Sex and theories of deviance: Toward a functional theory of deviant type-scripts. *American Sociological Review, 42,* 3–16.

Harris, A. R., & Lewis, M. (1974). *Race and criminal deviance: A study of youthful offenders.* Paper presented at the annual meeting of the American Sociological Association.

Harris, R. J. (1975). *A primer of multivariate statistics.* New York: Academic Press.

Harry, B. (1983). Movies and behavior among hospitalized mentally disordered offenders. *Bulletin of the American Academy of Psychiatry and the Law, 11,* 359–364.

———. (1987). Tattoos, body experience, and body image boundary among violent male offenders. *Bulletin of the American Academy of Psychiatry and the Law. 15,* 171–178.

Harter, S. (1983). Developmental perspectives on the self system. In E. M. Hetherington (ed.), *Handbook of child psychology: Vol. 4. Socialization, personality, and social development* (pp. 108–173). New York: John Wiley.

Hartjen, C. A., & Priyadarsini, S. (1984). *Delinquency in India: A comparative analysis.* New Brunswick, NJ: Rutgers University Press.

Hartman, D. P. (1969). Influence of symbolically modeled instrumental aggression and pain cues on aggressive behavior. *Journal of Personality and Social Psychology, 11,* 280–288.

Hartup, W. W. (1983). Peer relations. In E. M. Hetherington (ed.), *Handbook of child psychology: Vol. 4. Socialization, personality, and social development* (pp. 413–457). New York: John Wiley.

Haskell, M. R., & Yablonsky, L. (1978). *Criminology: Crime and criminality* (2nd ed.). Chicago: Rand McNally.

Hathaway, S. R., & Monachesi, E. D. (1963). *Adolescent personality and behavior: MMPI patterns of normal, delinquent, dropout, and other outcomes.* Minneapolis: University of Minnesota Press.

Hauser, R. (1978). *Kurzlehrbuch des schweizerischen strafprozessrechts.*

Hawley, A. (1950). *Human ecology: A theory of community structure.* New York: Ronald.

Hay, D. F. (1985). Learning to form relationships in infancy: Parallel attainments with parents and peers. *Developmental Review, 5,* 122–161.

Hayim, G. J. (1973). *Changes in criminal behavior of heroin addicts in the Addiction Research and Treatment Corporation: Interim report of the first years of treatment.* Washington, DC: U.S. Government Printing Office.

Hayes, J., & Bensch, M. (1981). The P > V sign on the WISC-R and recidivism in delinquents. *Journal of Consulting and Clinical Psychology, 49,* 480–481.

Hazama, H. (1976). Historical changes in life styles of industrial workers. In H. Patrick (ed.), *Japanese industrialization and its social consequences* (pp. 21–51). Berkeley, CA: University of California Press.

Hazan, C., & Shaver, P. (1987). Romantic love conceptualized as an attachment process. *Journal of Personality and Social Psychology, 52,* 511–524.

Hazelwood, R. R., & Douglas, J. E. (1984). The random killers. *Newsweek,* p. 100.

Heath, L., Kruttschnitt, C., & Ward, D. (1986). Television and violent criminal behavior: Beyond the Bobo doll. *Victims and violence, 1,* 177–190.

Heilbrun, A. B. (1982). Cognitive models of criminal violence based upon intelligence and psychopathy levels. *Journal of Consulting and Clinical Psychology, 50,* 546–557.

Heineke, J. M. (1988). Crime, deterrence, and choice: Testing the rational behavior hypothesis. *American Sociological Review, 53,* 303–305.

Helfrich, A. A., Crowley, T. J., Atkinson, C. A., & Post, R. D. (1982). A clinical profile of 136 cocaine abusers. In L. S. Harris (ed.), *Problems of drug dependence, 1982* (pp. 343–350). NIDA Research Monograph Series No. 43.

Henderson, M., & Hewstone, M. (1984). Prison inmates' explanations for interpersonal violence: Accounts and attributions. *Journal of Consulting and Clinical Psychology, 52,* 789–794.

Henggeler, S. W., Hanson, C. L., Borduin, C. M., Watson, S. M., & Brunk, M. A. (1985). Mother-son relationships of juvenile felons. *Journal of Consulting and Clinical Psychology, 53,* 942–943.

Henggeler, S. W., McKee, E., & Borduin, C. M. (1989). Is there a link between maternal neglect and adolescent delinquency? *Journal of Clinical Child Psychology, 18,* 242–246.

Hennigan, K. M., Del Rosario, M. L., Heath, L., Cook, T. D., Wharton, J. D., & Calder, B. J. (1982). Impact of the introduction of television on crime in the United States: Empirical findings and theoretical implications. *Journal of Personality and Social Psychology, 42,* 461–477.

Henshel, R. L., & Carey, S. (1975). Deviance, deterrence and knowledge of sanctions. In R. L. Henshel & R. A. Silverman (eds.), *Perceptions in criminology* (pp. 54–73). New York: Columbia University Press.

Hepburn, J. R. (1976). Criminology: Testing alternative models of delinquent causation. *Journal of Criminal Law and Criminology, 67,* 450–460.

Herbert, M., Sluckin, W., & Sluckin, A. (1984). Mother-to-infant "bonding." *Annual Progress in Child Psychiatry and Child Development,* 63–84.

Herzog, E., & Sudia, C. E. (1973). Children in fatherless families. In B. M. Caldwell & H. N. Riccuti (eds.), *Review of child development research: Volume 3* (pp. 141–232). Chicago: University of Chicago Press.

Hetherington, E. M., Cox, M., & Cox, R. (1979). Play and social interaction in children following divorce. *Journal of Social Issues, 35,* 26–49.

Hetherington, E. M., Stouwie, R., & Ridberg, E. H. (1971). Patterns of family interaction and child rearing attitudes related to three dimensions of juvenile delinquency. *Journal of Abnormal Psychology, 77,* 160–176.

Himmelweit, H. T., & Swift, B. (1976). Continuities and discontinuities in media usage and taste: A longitudinal study. *Journal of Social Issues, 32,* 133–156.

Hindelang, M. J. (1973). Causes of delinquency: A partial replication and extension. *Social Problems, 20,* 471–487.

———. (1978). Race and involvement in common law personal crimes. *American Sociological Review, 46,* 461–474.

———. (1979). Sex differences in criminal activity. *Social Problems, 27,* 143–156.

———. (1981). Variations in sex-race-age-specific incident rates of offending. *American Sociological Review, 43,* 93–109.

Hindelang, M. J., Gottfredson, M. R., & Garofalo, J. (1978). *Victims of personal crime: An empirical foundation for a theory of personal victimization.* Cambridge, MA: Ballinger.

Hindelang, M. J., Hirschi, T., & Weis, J. G. (1979). Correlates of delinquency: The illusion of discrepancy between self-report and official measures. *American Sociological Review, 44,* 995–1014.

Hindelang, M. J., Hirschi, T., & Weis, J. G. (1981). *Measuring delinquency*. Beverly Hills, CA: Sage.

Hindelang, M. J., & McDermott, M. J. (1981). *Juvenile criminal behavior: An analysis of rates and victim characteristics*. Washington, DC: U.S. Government Printing Office.

Hinshaw, S. P. (1987). On the distinction between attentional deficits/hyperactivity and conduct problems/aggression in child psychopathology. *Psychological Bulletin, 101,* 443–463.

Hirschi, T. (1969). *Causes of delinquency*. Berkeley, CA: University of California Press.

———. (1972). Social class and crime. In G. W. Thielbar & S. D. Feldman (eds.), *Issues in social inequality* (pp. 503–520). Boston: Little, Brown.

———. (1975). Labeling theory and juvenile delinquency: An assessment of the evidence. In W. R. Gove (ed.), *The labeling of deviance: Evaluating a perspective* (pp. 181–201). Beverly Hills, CA: Sage.

———. (1986). On the compatibility of rational choice and social control theories of crime. In D. B. Cornish & R. V. Clarke (eds.), *The reasoning criminal: Rational choice perspectives on offending* (pp. 105–118). New York: Springer-Verlag.

Hirschi, T., & Gottfredson, M. (1983). Age and the explanation of crime. *American Journal of Sociology, 89,* 552–584.

———. (1985). Age and crime, logic and scholarship: Comment on Greenberg. *American Sociological Review, 91,* 22–27.

———. (1986). The distinction between crime and criminality. In T. F. Hartnagel & R. A. Silverman (eds.), *Critique and explanation: Essays in honor of Gwynne Nettler*. New Brunswick, NJ: Transaction Books.

Hirschi, T., & Hindelang, M. J. (1977). Intelligence and delinquency: A revisionist review. *American Sociological Review, 42,* 571–587.

Hirschi, T., & Selvin, H. (1967). *Delinquency research*. New York: Free Press.

Hoffman, J. J., Hall, R. W., & Bartsch, T. W. (1987). On the relative importance of "psychopathic" personality and alcoholism on neuropsychological measures of frontal lobe dysfunction. *Journal of Abnormal Psychology, 96,* 158–160.

Holmes, R. M., & DeBurger, J. E. (1985). Profiles in terror: The serial murderer. *Federal Probation, 49,* 29–34.

Hooton, E. A. (1939). *The American criminal: An anthropological study*. Cambridge, MA: Harvard University Press.

Hough, E. (1907). *The story of the outlaw*. New York.

Hough, M. (1987). Offenders' choice of target: Findings from victim surveys. *Journal of Quantitative Criminology, 3,* 355–369.

Howard, J. (1784). *State of prisons in England and Wales*. London.

Huesmann, L. R., Lagerspetz, K., & Eron, L. D. (1984). Intervening variables in the TV violence-aggression relation: Evidence from two countries. *Developmental Psychology, 20,* 746–775.

Huesmann, L. R., & Eron, L. D. (1985). Cognitive processes and the persistence of aggressive behavior. *Developmental Psychology, 10,* 243–251.

Huesmann, L. R., Eron, L. D., Lefkowitz, M. M., & Walder, L. O. (1984). The stability of aggression over time and generations. *Developmental Psychology, 20,* 1120–1134.

Huizinga, D., & Elliott, D. S. (1987). Juvenile offenders: Prevalence, offender incidence, and arrest rates by race. *Crime and Delinquency, 33,* 206–223.

Humphries, D., & Wallace, D. (1980). Capitalist accumulation and urban crime, 1950–1971. *Social Problems, 28,* 179–193.

Hunt, D., Spunt, B., Lipton, D., Goldsmith, D., & Strug, D. (1987). The costly bonus: Cocaine related crime among methadone treatment clients. *Advances in Alcohol and Substance Abuse, 6,* 107–122.

Hutchings, B., & Mednick, S. A. (1975). Registered criminality in the adoptive and biological parents of registered male criminal adoptees. In R. R. Fieve, D. Rosenthal, & H. Brill (eds.), *Genetic research in psychiatry* (pp. 105–116). Baltimore: Johns Hopkins University Press.

Inciardi, J. A. (1979). Heroin use and street crime. *Crime and Delinquency, 25,* 335–346.

———. (1986). *The war on drugs: Heroin, cocaine, crime, and public policy.* Palo Alto, CA: Mayfield.

Irwin, J. (1970). *The felon.* Englewood Cliffs, NJ: Prentice-Hall.

Jacobson, J. L., Willie, D. E., Tianen, R. L., & Aytch, D. M. (1983, April). *The influence of infant-mother attachment on toddler sociability with peers.* Paper presented at the meeting of the Society for Research in Child Development, Detroit, MI.

Jacoby, J. E., Weiner, N. A., Thornberry, T. P., & Wolfgang, M. E. (1973). Drug use in a birth cohort. In National Commission on Marijuana and Drug Abuse, *Drug use in America: Problems in perspective* (pp. 300–343). Washington, DC: U.S. Government Printing Office.

Jaffe, L. T., & Archer, R. P. (1987). The prediction of drug use among college students from the MMPI, MCMI, and sensation seeking scales. *Journal of Personality Assessment, 51,* 243–253.

Jamieson, K. M., & Flanagan, T. J. (eds.) (1989). *Sourcebook of criminal justice statistics—1988.* Washington, DC: Bureau of Justice Statistics.

Janis, I. L., Mahl, G., Kagan, J., & Holt, R. (1969). *Personality: Dynamics, development, and assessment.* New York: Harcourt, Brace, and World.

Jacquith, S. M. (1981). Adolescent marijuana and alcohol use. *Criminology, 19,* 271–280.

Jarvis, G., & Parker, H. (1989). Young heroin users and crime: How do the 'new users' finance their habits. *British Journal of Criminology, 29,* 175–185.

Jencks, C. S. (1979). *Who gets ahead? The determinants of economic success in America.* New York: Basic Books.

Jensen, A. R. (1980). *Bias in mental testing.* New York: Macmillan.

Jensen, G. F. (1972). Parents, peers, and delinquent action. A test of the differential association perspective. *American Journal of Sociology, 78,* 562–575.

Jensen, G., & Eve, R. (1976). Sex differences in delinquency. *Criminology, 13,* 427–448.

Jessor, R., & Jessor, S. L. (1977). *Problem behavior and psychosocial development: A longitudinal study of youth.* New York: Academic Press.

Joe, T. (1987). Economic inequality: The picture in black and white. *Crime and Delinquency, 33,* 287–299.

Johnson, A., & Burke, E. C. (1955). Parental permissiveness and fostering in child rearing and their relationship to juvenile delinquency. *Proceedings of the Staff Meetings of the Mayo Clinic, 30,* 557–565.

Johnson, B. D., Goldstein, P. J., Preble, E., Schmeidler, J., Lipton, D. S., Spunt, B.,

& Miller, T. (1985). *Taking care of business: The economics of crime by heroin abusers*. Lexington, MA: Lexington Books.

Johnson, E., & Payne, J. (1986). The decision to commit a crime: An information-processing analysis. In D. B. Cornish & R. V. Clarke (eds.), *The reasoning criminal: Rational choice perspectives on offending* (pp. 39–52). New York: Springer-Verlag.

Johnson, R. E. (1978). *A shopkeeper's millennium: Society and revivals in Rochester, New York, 1815–1837*. New York: Hill & Wang.

Johnson, R. E., Marcos, A. C., & Bahr, S. J. (1987). The role of peers in the complex etiology of adolescent drug use. *Criminology, 25,* 323–340.

Jolin, A., & Gibbons, D. C. (1987). Age patterns in criminal involvement. *International Journal of Offender Therapy and Comparative Criminology, 31,* 237–260.

Jones, E. T. (1976). Crime change patterns in American cities. *Journal of Criminal Justice, 4,* 333–340.

Jurkovic, G. J., & Prentice, N. M. (1977). Relation of moral and cognitive development to dimensions of juvenile delinquency. *Journal of Abnormal Psychology, 86,* 414–420.

Kagan, J. (1978). The baby's elastic mind. *Human Nature, 1,* 66–73.

Kagan, J., Kearsely, R. B., & Zelazo, P. R. (1978). *Infancy: Its place in human development*. Cambridge, MA: Harvard University Press.

Kalish, C. B. (1988). International crime rates. *Bureau of Justice Statistics Special Report*. Washington, DC: Department of Justice.

Kandel, D. B., & Logan, J. A. (1984). Patterns of drug use from adolescence to young adulthood I: Periods of risk for initiation, continued risk and discontinuation. *American Journal of Public Health, 74,* 660–667.

Kandel, E., Brennan, P. A., Mednick, S. A., & Michelson, N. M. (1989). Minor physical anomalies and recidivistic adult violent criminal behavior. *Acta Psychiatrica Scandinavica, 79,* 103–107.

Kandel, E., Mednick, S. A., Kierkegaard-Sorensen, L., Hutchings, B., Knop, J., Rosenberg, R., & Schulsinger, F. (1988). IQ as a protective factor for subjects at high risk for antisocial behavior. *Journal of Consulting and Clinical Psychology, 56,* 224–226.

Kaplan, H. B. (1980). *Deviant behavior in defense of self*. New York: Academic Press.

Kaplan, J. (1970). *Marijuana—The new prohibition*. New York: World Publishing.

———. (1984). Alcohol, law enforcement and criminal justice. In The American Assembly (ed.), *Alcoholism and related problems* (pp. 78–90). Englewood Cliffs, NJ: Prentice-Hall.

Kavanagh, G. W. (1928). *The criminal and his allies*. Indianapolis.

Kay, H. (1972). Weaknesses in the television-causes-aggression analysis by Eron et al. *American Psychologist 27,* 970–973.

Kazdin, A. E. (1985). *Treatment of antisocial behavior in children and adolescents*. Homewood, IL: Dorsey.

———. (1987). Personal communication: October 1987 (cited in Magid & McKelvey, 1987).

Kehrer, C., & Mittra, S. S. (1978). Pennsylvania offers a good approach to assisting incarcerated veterans. *American Journal of Corrections, 40,* 6–9.

Kellam, S. G., Adams, R. G., Brown, H. C., & Ensminger, M. E. (1982). The long-term evolution of the family structure of teenage and older mothers. *Journal of Marriage and the Family, 44,* 539–554.

Kennedy, L. W., & Forde, D. R. (1990). Routine activities and crime: An analysis of victimization in Canada. *Criminology, 28,* 137–152.

Kerlinger, F. N. (1973). *Foundations of behavioral research* (2nd ed.) New York: Holt, Rinehart, and Winston.

Kierkegaard-Sorensen, L. D., & Mednick, S. A. (1977). A prospective study of predictors of criminality: A description of registered criminality in high-risk and low-risk families. In S. A. Mednick & K. O. Christiansen (eds.), *Biosocial bases of criminal behavior* (pp. 229–244). New York: Gardner.

Kierulff, S. (1988). Sheep in the midst of wolves: Personal-responsibility therapy with criminal personalities. *Professional Psychology: Research and Practice, 19,* 436–440.

Kilpatrick, D. G., Sutker, P. B., & Smith, A. D. (1976). Deviant drug and alcohol use. In M. Zuckerman & C. D. Spielberger (eds.), *Emotions and anxiety: New concepts, methods and applications* (pp. 247–278). Hillsdale, NJ: Lawrence Erlbaum.

Kipnis, D., & Wagner, W. (1967). Character structure and response to leadership power. *Journal of Experimental Research in Personality, 2,* 16–24.

Kipper, D. A. (1977). The Kahn Test of Symbol Arrangement and criminality. *Journal of Clinical Psychology, 33,* 777–781.

Kitsuse, J. I., & Dietrick, D. C. (1959). Delinquent boys: A critique. *American Sociological Review, 24,* 208–215.

Kleinman, P. H., & Lukoff, I. F. (1975). *Methadone maintenance—Modest help for a few. Part I.* New York: Columbia University School of Social Work. (mimeo).

Kloss, G. (1976). *West Germany: An introduction.* New York: John Wiley.

Kobak, R. R., & Sceery, A. (1988). Attachment in late adolescence: Working models, affect regulation, and representations of self and others. *Child Development, 59,* 135–146.

Kobayashi, Y., Ono, N., Ooe, A., & Sakumichi, S. (1982). Professionalization of violent criminals and characteristics of their criminal situations. *Tohoku Psychologica Folia, 41,* 107–115.

Kohlberg, L. (1976). Moral stages and moralization: The cognitive-developmental approach. In T. Lickona (ed.), *Moral development and behavior* (pp. 31–53). New York: Holt, Rinehart and Winston.

Kolb, L. (1925). Drug addiction and its relation to crime. *Mental Hygiene, 9,* 74–89.

Koppel, H. (1987). Lifetime likelihood of victimization. *Bureau of Justice Statistics Technical Report.* Washington, DC: Department of Justice.

Kornhauser, R. R. (1978). *Social sources of delinquency: An appraisal of analytic models.* Chicago: University of Chicago Press.

Kosson, D. S., & Newman, J. P. (1986). Psychopathy and the allocation of attentional capacity in a divided-attention situation. *Journal of Abnormal Psychology, 95,* 257–263.

Kranz, H. (1936). *Lebenschieksale krimineller zwillinge.* Berlin: Springer-Verlag.

Kratcoski, P. C., & Kratcoski, J. E. (1977). The balance of social status groupings within schools as an influencing variable on the frequency and character of delinquent behavior. In P. C. Friday & V. L. Stewart (eds.), *Juvenile justice: International perspectives* (pp. 160–171). New York: Praeger.

Kraut, R. E. (1976). Deterrent and definitional influences on shoplifting. *Social Problems, 23,* 358–368.

Krebs, D., & Adinolf, A. A. (1975). Physical attractiveness, social relations, and personality style. *Journal of Personality and Social Psychology, 31,* 245–253.

Krohn, M. O. (1976). Inequality, unemployment and crime: A cross-national analysis. *Sociological Quarterly, 17,* 303–313.

Krout, J. A., & Fox, D. R. (1944). The completion of independence, 1790–1830. In A. M. Schlesinger & D. R. Fox (eds.), *A history of American life in twelve volumes* (Volume V). New York: Macmillan.

Kruttschnitt, C., Heath, L., & Ward, D. A. (1986). Family violence, television viewing habits, and other adolescent experiences related to violent criminal behavior. *Criminology, 24,* 235–267.

Krynicki, V. E. (1978). Cerebral dysfunction in repetitively assaultive adolescents. *Journal of Nervous and Mental Disease, 166,* 59–67.

Kulich, B. A. (1975). A look at a juvenile prison. *Proxis der Kinderpsychologie und Kinderpsychiatrie, 24,* 107–110.

Kupfersmid, J. H., & Wonderly, D. M. (1980). Moral maturity: Failure to find a link. *Journal of Youth and Adolescence, 9,* 249–261.

Kupperstein, L. R., & Wilson, W. C. (1971). Erotica and antisocial behavior: An analysis of selected social indicator statistics. *Technical Report of the Commission on Obscenity and Pornography* (Volume 7). Washington, DC: U.S. Government Printing Office.

Kurland, H. D., Yeager, C. T., & Arthur, R. J. (1963). Psychophysiological aspects of severe behavior disorders. *Archives of General Psychiatry, 8,* 599–604.

Kutchinsky, B. (1983). *Law, pornography, and crime: The Danish experience.* London: Martin Robertson.

Kvaraceus, W. C. (1945). *Juvenile delinquency and the school.* New York: World Books.

Lab, S. P., & Hirschel, J. D. (1988). Climatological conditions and crime: The forecast is . . . ? *Justice Quarterly, 5,* 281–299.

LaFreniere, P. J., & Sroufe, L. A. (1985). Profiles of peer competence in preschoolers: Interrelations between measures, influences of social ecology, and relation to attachment history. *Developmental Psychology, 21,* 56–69.

Lamb, M. E. (1987). Predictive implications of individual differences in attachment. *Journal of Consulting and Clinical Psychology, 55,* 817–824.

Land, K. C., McCall, P. L., & Cohen, L. E. (1990). Structural covariates of homicide rates: Are there any invariances across time and social space. *American Journal of Sociology, 95,* 922–963.

Landolfi, J., & Leclair, D. P. (1976). *Profile of Vietnam era veterans incarcerated in Massachusetts correctional institutions.* Boston: Massachusetts Department of Corrections.

Lane, R. (1979). *Violent death in the city: Suicide, accident, and murder in 19th century Philadelphia.* Cambridge, MA: Harvard University Press.

———. (1980). Urban police and crime in nineteenth century America. In N. Morris & M. Tonry (eds.), *Crime and Justice: An annual review of research. Volume 2* (pp. 1–43.). Chicago: University of Chicago Press.

———. (1989). On the social meaning of homicide trends in America. In T. R. Gurr (ed.), *Violence in America, Vol. I: The history of crime* (pp. 55–79). Newbury Park, CA: Sage.

Lange, J. (1930). Crime and destiny (transl. C. Haldane). New York: Charles Boni.

Langevin, R., Paitich, D., Orchard, B., Handy, L., & Russon, A. (1983). Childhood and family background of killers seen for psychiatric assessment: A controlled study. *Bulletin of the American Academy of Psychiatry and the Law, 11,* 331–341.

Laub, J. (1983). Patterns of offending in urban and rural areas. *Journal of Criminal Justice, 11,* 129–142.

Laub, J. H., & Sampson, R. J. (1988). Unraveling families and delinquency: A reanalysis of the Gluecks' data. *Criminology, 26,* 355–380.

Laosa, L. M., & Brophy, J. E. (1972). Effects of sex and birth order on sex-role development and intelligence among kindergarten children. *Developmental Psychology, 6,* 409–415.

LeBlanc, M., Biron, L., & Pronovost, L. (1979). *Psycho-social development and delinquency evolution.* University of Montreal (mimeo).

Lee, C. C. (1985). Successful rural black adolescents: A psychosocial profile. *Adolescence, 20,* 129–142.

Lefkowitz, M. M., Eron, L. D., Walder, L. O., & Huesmann, L. R. (1977). *Growing up to be violent: A longitudinal study of the development of aggression.* New York: Pergamon.

Lefton, L. A. (1985). *Psychology* (3rd ed.). Boston: Allyn & Bacon.

LeGras, A. M. (1934). *Psychose en criminaliteit bij tweelingen.* Utrecht: University of Utrecht.

Leibrich, J. (1986). Pitfalls in criminal justice evaluation research: Sampling measurement, and design problems. *Federal Probation, 50,* 31–35.

Lemert, E. M. (1951). *Social Pathology.* New York: McGraw-Hill.

———. (1972). *Human deviance, social problems and social control* (2nd ed.). Englewood Cliffs, NJ: Prentice-Hall.

Leung, K., & Lau, S. (1989). Effects of self-concept and perceived disapproval of delinquent behavior in school children. *Journal of Youth and Adolescence, 18,* 345–359.

Levander, S. E., Schalling, D. S., Lidberg, L., Bartfai, A., & Lidberg, Y. (1980). Skin conductance recovery time and personality in a group of criminals. *Psychophysiology, 17,* 105–111.

Levander, S. E., Schalling, D., Lidberg, L., & Lidberg, Y. (1979). *Electrodermal recovery time, stress and psychopathy.* (Report from the Laboratory for Clinical Stress Research, No. 59). Stockholm: Karolinska Institute.

Levene, R., & Zeffaroni, E. (1978). *Los codigos penales Latino-americanos: Volume 3.*

Levine, J. (1976). The potential for crime overreporting in criminal victimization surveys. *Criminology, 14,* 307–330.

Levinson, D., Darrow, C., Klein, E., Levinson, M., & McKee, B. (1978). *The seasons of a man's life.* New York: Knopf.

Lewis, M., & Brooks, J. (1978). Self-knowledge and emotional developments. In M. Lewis & L. A. Rosenblum (eds.), *The development of affect* (pp. 205–226). New York: Plenum.

Lewis, M., Feiring, C., McGuffog, C., & Jaskir, J. (1984). Predicting psychopathology in six-year-olds from early social relations. *Child Development, 55,* 123–136.

Lewis, O. F. (1922). *The development of American prisons and prison conditions.* Albany, NY.

Leyens, J. P., Camino, L., Parke, R. D., & Berkowitz, L. (1975). Effects of movie violence on aggression in a field setting as a function of group dominance and cohesion. *Journal of Personality and Social Psychology, 32,* 346–360.

Liazos, A. (1972). The poverty of the sociology of deviance: Nuts, sluts, and perverts. *Social Problems,* 103–120.

Linquist, C. A., Smusz, T. D., & Doerner, W. (1985). Causes of conformity: An application of control theory to adult misdemeanant probationers. *International Journal of Offender Therapy and Comparative Criminology, 29,* 1–14.

Little, W. R., & Ntsekhe, V. R. (1959). Social class background of young offenders from London. *British Journal of Delinquency, 10,* 130–135.

Loeb, J., & Mednick, S. A. (1977). A prospective study of predictors of criminality: Electrodermal response patterns. In S. A. Mednick & K. O. Christiansen (eds.), *Biosocial bases of criminal behavior* (pp. 245–254). New York: Gardner.

Loeber, R. (1982). The stability of antisocial and delinquent child behavior: A review. *Child Development, 53,* 1431–1446.

———. (1990). Development and risk factors of juvenile antisocial behavior and delinquency. *Clinical Psychology Review, 10,* 1–41.

Loeber, R., & Dishion, T. (1983). Early predictors of male delinquency: A review. *Psychological Bulletin, 94,* 68–99.

Loeber, R., & Snyder, H. N. (1990). Rate of offending in juvenile careers: Findings of constancy and change in lambda. *Criminology, 28,* 97–109.

Loftin, C. (1980). Alternative estimates of the impact of certainty and severity of punishment on levels of homicide in American states. In S. E. Fienberg & A. J. Reiss (eds.), *Indicators of crime and criminal justice: Quantitative studies.* Washington, DC: U.S. Government Printing Office.

Loftin, C., & Hill, R. (1974). Regional subculture and homicide: An examination of the Gastil-Hackney thesis. *American Sociological Review, 39,* 714–724.

Loftin, C., McDowall, D., & Boudouris, J. (1989). Economic change and homicide in Detroit, 1926–1979. In T. R. Gurr (ed.), *Violence in America: Vol. I. The history of crime* (pp. 163–177). Newbury Park, CA: Sage.

Loftin, C., & Parker, R. N. (1985). An error-in-variable model of the effect of poverty on urban homicide rates. *Criminology, 23,* 269–287.

Lombroso, C. (1911). *Crime, its causes and remedies.* Boston: Little, Brown.

Londerville, S., & Main, M. (1981). Security of attachment, compliance, and maternal training method in the second year of life. *Developmental Psychology, 17,* 289–299.

Long, S. K., & Witte, A. D. (1981). Current economic trends: Implications for crime and criminal justice. In K. N. Wright (ed.), *Crime and criminal justice in a declining economy* (pp. 69–143). Cambridge, MA: Oelgeschlager, Gunn & Hain.

Lowenstein, L. (1978). The bullied and non-bullied child. *Bulletin of the British Psychological Society, 31,* 316–318.

Lubar, J. F. (1964). Effect of medial cortical lesions on the avoidance behavior of the cat. *Journal of Comparative and Physiological Psychology, 58,* 38–46.

Lueger, R., & Cadman, W. (1982). Variables associated with recidivism and program-termination of delinquent adolescents. *Journal of Clinical Psychology, 38,* 861–863.

Lykken, D. (1957). A study of anxiety in the sociopathic personality. *Journal of Abnormal and Social Psychology, 55,* 6–10.

Maccoby, E. E., & Jacklin, C. N. (1974). *The psychology of sex differences*. Stanford, CA: Stanford University Press.

Maccoby, E., Johnson, J., & Church, R. (1958). Community integration and the social control of juvenile delinquency. *Journal of Social Issues, 14,* 38–51.

MacDonald, J. M. (1976). *Psychiatry and the criminal* (3rd ed). Springfield, IL: Charles C. Thomas.

Maddi, S. A. (1976). *Personality theories: A comparative analysis* (3rd ed.). Homewood, IL: Dorsey Press.

Maddux, J. V., & Desmond, D. P. (1979). Crime and treatment of heroin users. *International Journal of the Addictions, 14,* 891–904.

Magee, R. D. (1964). Correlates of aggressive defiant classroom behavior in elementary school boys: A factor analytic study. *Dissertation Abstracts, 2,* 1340–1341.

Magid, K., & McKelvey, C. A. (1987). *High risk*. New York: Bantam Books.

Magnusson, D., & Allen, V. L. (1983). *Human development: An interactional perspective*. New York: Academic Press.

Mahoney, A. R. (1974). The effect of labeling upon youths in the juvenile justice system: A review of the evidence. *Law and Society Review, 8,* 583–614.

Main, M., Kaplan, N., & Cassidy, J. (1985). Security in infancy, childhood, and adulthood: A move to the level of representation. *Monographs of the Society for Research in Child Development, 50,* (1–2, Serial No. 209).

Main, M., Tomasini, L., & Tolan, W. (1979). Differences among mothers of infants judged to differ in security. *Developmental Psychology, 15,* 472–473.

Mak, A. S. (1990). Testing a psychosocial control theory of delinquency. *Criminal Justice and Behavior, 17,* 215–230.

Malina, R. M. (1973). Biological substrata. In K. S. Miller & R. M. Dreger (eds.), *Comparative studies of blacks and whites in the United States* (pp. 52–123). New York: Seminar Press.

Mankoff, M. (1971). Societal reaction and career deviance: A critical analysis. *Sociological Quarterly, 12,* 204–218.

Manne, S. H., Kandel, A., & Rosenthal, D. (1962). Differences between performance IQ and verbal IQ in a severely sociopathic population. *Journal of Clinical Psychology, 18,* 73–77.

Marciniak, R. D. (1986). Implications to forensic psychiatry of post-traumatic stress disorder: A review. *Military Medicine, 151,* 434–437.

Martinson, R. (1974). What works? Questions and answers about prison reform. *Public Interest, 10,* 22–54.

Mark, V. H., & Ervin, F. R. (1970). *Violence and the brain*. New York: Harper & Row.

Masters, F., & Greaves, D. (1967). The Quasimodo complex. *British Journal of Plastic Surgery, 20,* 204–210.

Matarazzo, J. (1972). *Wechsler's measurement and appraisal of adult intelligence* (5th ed.). Baltimore, MD: Williams & Wilkins.

Matas, L., Arend, R. A., & Sroufe, L. A. (1978). Continuity of adaptation in the second year: The relationship between quality of attachment and later competence. *Child Development, 49,* 547–556.

Matsueda, R. L. (1982). Testing control theory and differential association: A causal modeling approach. *American Sociological Review, 47,* 489–504.

———. (1988). The current state of differential association theory. *Crime and Delinquency, 34,* 277–306.

Matsueda, R. L., & Heimer, K. (1987). Race, family structure, and delinquency: A test of differential association and social control theories. *American Sociological Review, 52,* 826–840.

Matsueda, R. L., Piliavin, I., & Gartner, R. (1988). Economic assumptions versus empirical research. *American Sociological Review, 53,* 305–309.

Matthews, R. (1979). Testosterone levels in aggressive offenders. In M. Sandler (ed.), *Psychopharmacology of aggression* (pp. 123–130). New York: Raven Press.

Matza, D. (1964). *Delinquency and drift.* New York: John Wiley.

Maultsby, M. C. (1975). *Help yourself to happiness through rational self-counseling.* New York: Institute for Rational Living.

Maume, D. J. (1989). Inequality and metropolitan rape rates: A routine activity approach. *Justice Quarterly, 6,* 513–527.

Mayo Clinic. (1976). *Clinical examinations in neurology.* Philadelphia: Saunders.

McBride, D. C. (1981). Drugs and violence. In J. A. Inciardi (ed.), *The drugs-crime connection* (pp. 105–123). Beverly Hills, CA: Sage.

McBride, D. C., & McCoy, C. (1982). Crime and drugs: The issues and literature. *Journal of Drug Issues, 12,* 137–151.

McCandless, B. R., Persons, W. S., & Roberts, A. (1972). Perceived opportunity, delinquency, race, and body build among delinquent youth. *Journal of Consulting and Clinical Psychology, 38,* 281–287.

McCarthy, E. D., Langner, T. S., Gersten, J. C., Eisenberg, J. G., & Orzeck, L. (1975). Violence and behavior disorders. *Journal of Communication, 25,* 71–85.

McCleary, R. A. (1966). Response-modulating functions of the limbic system: Initiation and suppression. In E. Stellar & J. M. Sprague (eds.), *Progress in physiological psychology* (Vol. 1, pp. 209–272). New York: Academic Press.

McCord, J. (1979). Some child-rearing antecedents of criminal behavior in adult men. *Journal of Personality and Social Psychology, 37,* 1477–1486.

———. (1982). A longitudinal view of the relationship between parental absence and crime. In J. Gunn & D. P. Farrington (eds.), *Abnormal offenders, delinquency, and the criminal justice system* (pp. 113–128). Chichester, England: John Wiley.

———. (1987). *Aggression and shyness as predictors of problems: Another view.* Presented at the biennial meeting of the Society for Research in Child Development, Baltimore, MD.

———. (1988). Parental behavior in the cycle of aggression. *Psychiatry, 51,* 14–23.

McCord, J., & McCord, W. (1958). The effects of parental role model on criminality. *Journal of Social Issues, 14,* 66–75.

McCord, J., McCord, W., & Thurber, E. (1963). The effects of maternal employment on lower class boys. *Journal of Abnormal and Social Psychology, 67,* 177–182.

McCord, W., McCord, J., & Zola, I. K. (1959). *Origins of crime: A new evaluation of the Cambridge-Somerville study.* New York: Columbia University Press.

McDermott, M. J., & Hindelang, M. J. (1981). Juvenile criminal behavior in the United States: Its trends and implications. Washington, DC: Office of Juvenile Justice and Delinquency Prevention.

McGhee, J. D. (1984). *Running the gauntlet: Black men in America.* New York: National Urban League.

McGlothlin, W. H., Anglin, M. D., & Wilson, B. D. (1978). Narcotic addiction and crime. *Criminology, 16,* 293–315.

McGlothlin, W. H., & West, L. (1968). The marijuana problem: An overview. *American Journal of Psychiatry, 125,* 370–378.

McGrath, R. D. (1989). Violence and lawlessness on the western frontier. In T. R. Gurr (ed.), *Violence in America, Vol. 1: A history of crime* (pp. 122–145). Newbury Park, CA: Sage.

Mednick, B., Reznick, C., Hocevar, D., & Baker, R. (1987). Long-term effects of parental divorce on young adult male crime. *Journal of Youth and Adolescence, 16,* 31–45.

Mednick, S. A. (1977). A biosocial theory of the learning of law-abiding behavior. In S. A. Mednick & K. O. Christiansen (eds.), *Biosocial bases of criminal behavior* (pp. 1–23). New York: Gardner.

Mednick, S. A., Brennan, P., & Kandel, E. (1988). Predisposition to violence. *Aggressive Behavior, 14,* 25–33.

Mednick, S. A., & Christiansen, K. O. (eds.). (1977). *Biosocial bases of criminal behavior*. New York: Gardner.

Mednick, S. A., Gabrielli, W. F., & Hutchings, B. (1984). Genetic influences in criminal convictions: Evidence from an adoption cohort. *Science, 224,* 891–894.

Mednick, S. A., & Kandel, E. S. (1988). Congenital determinants of violence. *Bulletin of the American Academy of Psychiatry and the Law, 16,* 101–109.

Mednick, S. A., Kierkegaard-Sorensen, L., Hutchings, B., Knop, J., Rosenberg, R., & Schulsinger, F. (1977). An example of biosocial interactive research: The interplay of socioenvironmental and individual factors in the etiology of criminal behavior. In S. A. Mednick & K. O. Christiansen (eds.), *Biosocial bases of criminal behavior* (pp. 9–23). New York: Gardner.

Meehl, P. E., & Rosen, A. (1955). Antecedent probability and the efficacy of psychometric signs, patterns, or cutting scores. *Psychological Bulletin, 52,* 194–216.

Megargee, E. I. (1972). *The California Psychological Inventory Handbook*. San Francisco: Jossey-Bass.

Megargee, E. I., Cook, P. E., & Mendelsohn, G. A. (1967). Development and validation of an MMPI scale of assaultiveness in overcontrolled individuals. *Journal of Abnormal Psychology, 72,* 519–528.

Meisenhelder, T. (1977). An exploratory study of exiting from criminal careers. *Criminology, 15,* 319–334.

Meltzer, L. J., Levine, M. D., Karniski, W., Palfrey, J. S., & Clarke, S. (1984). An analysis of the learning styles of adolescent delinquents. *Journal of Learning Disabilities, 17,* 600–608.

Menard, S., & Elliott, D. S. (1990). Longitudinal and cross-sectional data collection and analysis in the study of crime and delinquency. *Justice Quarterly, 7,* 11–55.

Menzies, F. (1971). Preferences in television content among violent persons. *FCI Research Reports,* No. 3.

Merton, R. K. (1938). Social structure and anomie. *American Sociological Review, 3,* 672–682.

———. (1957). *Social theory and social structure*. New York: Free Press of Glencoe.

Messner, S. F. (1980). Income inequality and murder rates: Some cross-sectional findings. In R. Tomasson (ed.), *Comparative Social Research: Vol. 3* (pp. 185–198). Greenwich, CT: JAI Press.

———. (1982). Poverty, inequality, and the urban homicide rate: Some unexpected findings. *Criminology, 20,* 103–114.

———. (1984). The "dark figure" and composite indexes of crime: Some empirical exploration of alternative data sources. *Journal of Criminal Justice, 12,* 435–444.

———. (1986). Television violence and violent crime: An aggregate analysis. *Social Problems, 33,* 218–235.

Messner, S. F., & Tardiff, K. (1986). Economic inequality and levels of homicide: An analysis of urban neighborhoods. *Criminology, 24,* 297–317.

Michael, R. P., & Zumpe, D. (1987). Annual rhythms in human violence and sexual aggression in the United States and the role of temperature. *Social Biology, 30,* 263–278.

Miele, F. (1979). Cultural bias in the WISC. *Intelligence, 3,* 149–164.

Miethe, T. D., Stafford, M. C., & Long, J. S. (1987). Social differentiation in criminal victimization: A test of routine activities lifestyle theories. *American Sociological Review, 52,* 184–194.

Milavsky, J. R. (nd). TV and violence. *National Institute of Justice Crime File: Study Guide*. Washington, DC: National Institute of Justice.

Milavsky, J. R., Kessler, R. C., Stipp, H., & Rubens, W. S. (1982). *Television and aggression: A panel study*. New York: Academic Press.

Milgram, S., & Shotland, R. L. (1973). *Television and antisocial behavior: Field experiments*. New York: Academic Press.

Miller, L. (1988). Neuropsychological perspectives on delinquency. *Behavioral Sciences and the Law, 6,* 409–428.

Miller, W. B. (1958). Lower class culture as a generating milieu of gang delinquency. *Journal of Social Issues, 14,* 5–19.

Ministry of Justice, Japan. (1970). *Criminal Justice in Japan*. Tokyo: Author.

Mischel, W. (1969). Continuity and change in personality. *American Psychologist, 24,* 1012–1018.

———. (1974). Processes in delay of gratification. *Advances in Experimental Psychology, 7,* 249–292.

Mitchell, S., & Rosa, P. (1981). Boyhood behavior problems as precursors of criminality: A fifteen-year follow-up study. *Journal of Child Psychology, 22,* 19–33.

Moffitt, T. (1987). Parental mental disorder and offspring criminal behavior: An adoption study. *Psychiatry, 50,* 346–360.

Moffitt, T. E., Gabrielli, W. F., Mednick, S. A., & Schulsinger, F. (1981). Socioeconomic status, IQ, and delinquency. *Journal of Abnormal Psychology, 90,* 152–156.

Monahan, T. P. (1957). Family status and the delinquent child: A reappraisal and some new findings. *Social Forces, 35,* 250–258.

Money, J., Wiedeking, C., Walker, P., Migeon, C., Meyer, W., & Borgaonkar, D. (1975). 47,XYY and 46,XY males with antisocial and/or sex-offending behavior: Antiandrogen therapy plus counseling. *Psychoneuroendocrinology, 1,* 165–178.

Monkkonen, E. H. (1981). A disorderly people? Urban order in the nineteenth and twentieth centuries. *Journal of American History, 68,* 536–559.

———. (1989). Diverging homicide rates: England and the United States, 1850–1875. In T. R. Gurr (ed.), *Violence in America, Vol. I: The history of crime* (pp. 80–101). Newbury Park, CA: Sage.

Monroe, R. R., & Mickle, W. A. (1967). Alpha-chloralose activated EEG in psychiatric patients. *Journal of Nervous and Mental Disease, 144,* 59–68.

Moore, W. (1963). *Social change*. Englewood Cliffs, NJ: Prentice-Hall.

Morash, M. A. (1981). Cognitive developmental theory: A basis for juvenile correctional reform? *Criminology, 19,* 360–371.

Morbidity and Mortality Weekly Reports. (1982). National surveillance of cocaine use and related health consequences. *Center for Disease Control, 31,* 265–268, 273.

Moss, H. A. (1967). Sex, age, and state as determinants of mother-infant interaction. *Merrill-Palmer Quarterly, 13,* 19–36.

Mott, J. (1981). Criminal involvement and penal response. In G. Edwards & C. Busch (eds.), *Drug problems in Britain: A review of ten years* (pp. 217–243). London: Academic Press.

Mowrer, O. H. (1960). *Learning theory and behavior*. New York: John Wiley.

Murchison, C. (1926). *Criminal intelligence*. Worchester, MA: Clark University Press.

Murdoch, B. D. (1972). Electroencephalograms, aggression and emotional maturity in psychopathic and non-psychopathic prisoners. *Psychologia Africana, 14,* 216–231.

Murphy, L. B., & Moriarity, A. E. (1976). *Vulnerability, coping and growth: From infancy to adolescence*. New Haven, CT: Yale University Press.

Murray, C. A. (1976). *The link between learning disabilities and juvenile delinquency: Current theory and knowledge*. Washington, DC: National Institute for Juvenile Justice and Delinquency Prevention.

Myerhoff, H. L., & Myerhoff, B. G. (1966). Field observation of middle class 'gangs.' In R. Giallombardo (ed.), *Juvenile delinquency: A book of readings* (3rd ed., pp. 295–304). New York: John Wiley.

Naffine, N., & Gale, F. (1989). Testing the nexus: Crime, gender, and unemployment. *British Journal of Criminology, 29,* 144–156.

Nagel, W. H. (1967). Juvenile delinquency in Thailand. *United Nations Report*.

Nahas, G. G. (1973). *Marihuana—Deceptive weed*. New York: Raven.

Nathan, P. E. (1988). The addictive personality in the behavior of the addict. *Journal of Consulting and Clinical Psychology, 56,* 183–188.

National Institute on Alcohol Abuse and Alcoholism. (1978). *Third special report to the Congress on alcohol and health*. Washington, DC: U.S. Government Printing Office.

National Institute of Mental Health (1982). *Television and behavior: Ten years of scientific progress and implications for the eighties*. Washington, DC: U.S. Government Printing Office.

Neale, J. M., & Liebert, R. M. (1973). *Science and behavior: An introduction to methods of research*. Englewood Cliffs, NJ: Prentice-Hall.

Nelson, J. F. (1980). Alternative measures of crime: A comparison of the Uniform Crime Reports and the National Crime Survey in twenty-six American cities. In D. F. Georges-Abeyie & K. D. Harries (eds.), *Crime: A spatial perspective* (pp. 77–92). New York: Columbia University Press.

Nettler, G. (1978). *Explaining crime* (2nd ed.). New York: McGraw-Hill.

Neufeldt, V. (ed.). (1988). *Webster's new world dictionary* (3rd ed.). New York: Simon & Schuster.

Newcomb, M. D., & McGee, L. (1989). Adolescent alcohol use and other delinquent behaviors: A one-year longitudinal analysis controlling for sensation seeking. *Criminal Justice and Behavior, 16,* 345–369.

Newman, G. (1976). *Comparative deviance: Perception and law in six cultures*. New York: Elsevier.

Newman, G. (1982). The implications of tattooing in prisoners. *Journal of Clinical Psychiatry, 43,* 231–234.

Newman, J. P., & Kosson, D. S. (1986). Passive avoidance learning in psychopathic and nonpsychopathic offenders. *Journal of Abnormal Psychology, 95,* 252–256.

Newman, J. P., Patterson, C. M., & Kosson, D. S. (1987). Response prevention in psychopaths. *Journal of Abnormal Psychology, 96,* 145–148.

Newman, J. P., Widom, C. S., & Nathan, P. E. (1985). Passive avoidance in syndromes of disinhibition: Psychopathy and extraversion. *Journal of Personality and Social Psychology, 48,* 1316–1327.

Newman, O. (1972). *Defensible space: Crime prevention through urban design.* New York: MacMillan.

Newton, C. H., & Shelden, R. G. (1975). The delinquent label and its effect on future behavior: An empirical test of Lemert's levels of deviance. *International Journal of Criminology and Penology, 3,* 229–241.

New York Times. (July 27, 1971).

Nicholi, A. M. (1983). The nontherapeutic use of psychoactive drugs. *New England Journal of Medicine, 308,* 925–933.

Nielson, J., & Tsuboi, T. (1970). Correlation between stature, character disorder and criminality. *British Journal of Psychiatry, 116,* 145–150.

Nurco, D. N. (1987). Drug addiction and crime: A complicated issue. *British Journal of Addictions, 82,* 7–9.

Nurco, D. N., Cisin, I. H., & Ball, J. C. (1985). Crime as a source of income for narcotic addicts. *Journal of Substance Abuse Treatment, 2,* 113–115.

Nurco, D. N., Cisin, I. H., & Balter, M. B. (1981). Addict careers I. A new typology. *International Journal of the Addictions, 16,* 1305–1325.

Nurco, D. N. & DuPont, R. L. (1977). A preliminary report on crime and addiction with a community-wide population of narcotic addicts. *Drug and Alcohol Dependence, 2,* 109–121.

O'Connor, M. J., Sigman, M., & Brill, N. (1987). Disorganization of attachment in relation to maternal alcohol consumption. *Journal of Consulting and Clinical Psychology, 55,* 831–836.

Ogloff, J. R., & Wong, S. (1990). Electrodermal and cardiovascular evidence of a coping response in psychopaths. *Criminal Justice and Behavior, 17,* 231–245.

Ohlesen, W. H., Gibbs, F. A., & Adams, C. L. (1970). EEG studies of criminals. *Clinical EEG, 1,* 92–100.

Okasha, A. A., Sadek, A., & Moneim, S. A. (1975). Psychological and electroencephalographic studies of Egyptian murderers. *British Journal of Psychiatry, 126,* 34–40.

Olweus, D. (1980). Familial and temperamental determinants of aggressive behavior in adolescent boys: A causal analysis. *Developmental Psychology, 16,* 644–660.

Orcutt, J. D. (1987). Differential association and marijuana use: A closer look at Sutherland (with a little help from Becker). *Criminology, 25,* 341–358.

Organization for Economic Cooperation and Development. (1980). *High Level Conference on the Employment of Women,* April 17–18.

Orsagh, T., & Witte, A. D. (1981). Economic status and crime: Implications for offender rehabilitation. *Journal of Criminal Law and Criminology, 72,* 1055–1071.

Osborn, S. G., & West, D. J. (1980). Do young delinquents really reform? *Journal of Adolescence, 3,* 99–114.

Osborne, R. T., & McGurk, F. C. J. (1982). *The testing of Negro intelligence, Vol. 2*. Athens, GA: Foundation for Human Understanding.

Osgood, D. W., O'Malley, P. M., Bachman, J. G., & Johnston, L. D. (1989). Time trends and age trends in arrests and self-reported illegal behavior. *Criminology, 27,* 389–417.

Palamara, F., Cullen, F. T., & Gersten, J. C. (1986). The effects of police and mental health intervention on juvenile deviance: Specifying contingencies in the impact of formal reaction. *Journal of Health and Social Behavior, 27,* 90–105.

Panella, D. H., Cooper, P. F., & Henggeler, S. W. (1982). Peer relations in adolescence. In S. W. Henggeler (ed.), *Delinquency and adolescent psychopathology: A family ecological systems approach* (pp. 139–161). Littleton, MA: Wright-PSG.

Pare, W. P., & Dumas, J. P. (1965). The effects of insular neocortical lesions on passive and active behavior in the rat. *Psychonomic Science, 2,* 87–88.

Parke, R. D., Berkowitz, L., Leyens, J. P., West, S., & Sebastian, R. J. (1977). Some effects of violent and nonviolent movies on the behavior of juvenile delinquents. In L. Berkowitz (ed.), *Advances in experimental social psychology* (pp. 136–172). New York: Academic Press.

Parker, H., Newcombe, R., & Bakx, K. (1986). *Heroin and crime*. Liverpool: University of Liverpool Press.

Parker, R., & Smith, D. (1979). Deterrence, poverty and type of homicide. *American Journal of Sociology, 85,* 614–624.

Paternoster, R. (1987). The deterrent effect of the perceived certainty and severity of punishment: A review of the evidence and issues. *Justice Quarterly, 4,* 173–217.

Paternoster, R., Saltzman, L. E., Waldo, G. P., & Chiricos, T. G. (1983). Perceived risk and social control: Do sanctions really deter? *Law and Society Review, 17,* 457–479.

Patterson, G. R. (1986). Performance models for antisocial boys. *American Psychologist, 41,* 432–444.

Patterson, G. R., & Dishion, T. J. (1985). Contributions of families and peers to delinquency. *Criminology, 23,* 63–79.

Pearson, F. S., & Weiner, N. A. (1985). Criminology: Toward an integration of criminological theories. *Journal of Criminal Law and Criminology, 76,* 116–150.

Pellegrini, R. J. (1987). Nuclear fallout and criminal violence: Preliminary inquiry into a new, biogenic predisposition hypothesis. *International Journal of Biosocial Research, 9,* 125–143.

Pentland, B., & Rothman, G. (1982). Incarcerated Vietnam-service veterans—Stereotypes and realities. *Journal of Correctional Education, 33,* 10–14.

Perrotti, J. (1978). *The effects of direct decision therapy on some personality and behavioral characteristics in juvenile delinquents*. Unpublished doctoral dissertation, United States International University. (University Microfilms No. 7909843).

Petersen, I., Matousek, M., Mednick, S. A., Volavka, J., & Pollock, V. (1982). EEG antecedents of thievery. *Acta Psychiatrica Scandinavica, 62,* 331–338.

Petersilia, J., Greenwood, P. W., & Lavin, M. (1978). *Criminal careers of habitual felons*. Washington, DC: U.S. Government Printing Office.

Peterson, D. R., & Becker, W. C. (1965). Family interaction and delinquency. In H. C. Quay (ed.), *Juvenile delinquency: Research and theory* (pp. 63–99). Princeton, NJ: Van Nostrand.

Peterson, M. A., & Braiker, H. B. (1980). *Doing crime: A survey of California prison inmates*. Santa Monica, CA: Rand.

Phillips, D. (1983). The impact of mass media violence on U.S. homicides. *American Sociological Review, 48,* 560–568.

Phillipson, M. (1974). *Understanding crime and delinquency: A sociological introduction*. Chicago: Aldine.

Piaget, J. (1954). *The construction of reality in the child*. New York: Basic Books.

Piliavin, I., & Gartner, R. (1981). *The impact of supported work on ex-offenders*. New York: Manpower Demonstration Research Corporation.

Piliavin, I., Gartner, R., Thornton, C., & Matseuda, R. L. (1986). Crime, deterrence, and rational choice. *American Sociological Review, 51,* 101–119.

Platt, J. J., Spivak, G., & Shure, M. B. (1976). *The problem-solving approach to adjustment*. San Francisco: Jossey-Bass.

Plaut, T. F. (1967). *Alcohol problems: A report to the nation by the Cooperative Commission on the Study of Alcoholism*. New York: Oxford University Press.

Plummer, K. (1979). Misunderstanding labeling perspectives. In D. Downes & P. Rock (eds.), *Deviant interpretations*. London: Martin Robinson.

Polk, K., Adler, C., Bazemore, G., Blake, G., Cordray, S., Coventry, G., Galvin, J., & Temple, M. (1981). *Becoming adult: An analysis of maturational development from age 16 to 30 of a cohort of young men*. Final report of the Marion County Youth Study, University of Oregon, Eugene, OR.

Polk, K., & Schafer, W. E. (1972). *Schools and delinquency*. Englewood Cliffs, NJ: Prentice-Hall.

Pontius, A. A. (1972). Neurological aspects in some types of delinquency, especially among juveniles: Toward a neurological model of ethical action. *Adolescence, 7,* 289–308.

Poole, E. D., & Regoli, R. M. (1979). Parental support, delinquent friends, and delinquency: A test of interactional effects. *Journal of Criminal Law and Criminology, 70,* 188–193.

Pope, C. E. (1979). Race and crime revisited. *Crime and Delinquency, 25,* 347–357.

Pottieger, A. E. (1981). Sample bias in drugs/crime research: An empirical study. In J. A. Inciardi (ed.), *The drugs-crime connection* (pp. 207–237). Beverly Hills, CA: Sage.

Powers, E., & Witmer, H. (1951). *An experiment in the prevention of delinquency: The Cambridge-Somerville Youth Study*. New York: Columbia University Press.

Pringle, M. L. K., & Bossio, V. (1960). Early prolonged separations and emotional adjustment. *Journal of Child Psychology and Psychiatry, 1,* 37–48.

Prinz, R. J., Conner, P. A., & Wilson, C. C. (1981). Hyeractive and aggressive behavior in childhood: Intertwined dimensions. *Journal of Abnormal Child Psychology, 9,* 191–202.

Pulkkinen, L. (1980). The child in the family. *Nordisk Pykologi, 32,* 147–157.

———. (1982). Self-control and continuity from childhood to late adolescence. In P. B. Baltes & O. G. Brim (eds.), *Lifespan development and behavior: Vol. 4* (pp. 63–105). New York: Academic Press.

Pupura, P. P. (1979). Police activity and the full moon. *Journal of Police Science and Administration, 7,* 350–353.

Quay, H. C. (1965). Psychopathic personality as pathological stimulation-seeking. *American Journal of Psychiatry, 122,* 180–183.

———. (1977). Psychopathic behavior: Reflections on its nature, origins, and treatment. In I. C. Uzgiris & F. Weizmann (eds.), *The structuring of experience* (pp. 371–383). New York: Plenum.

Quinney, R. (1966). Structural characteristics, population areas, and crime rates in the United States. *Journal of Criminal Law, Criminology and Police Science, 57,* 42–52.

Quiroga, H. S. (1957, Jan/Mar). *Jornadas Industrialis.*

Rada, R. T., Laws, D. R., & Kellner, R. (1976). Plasma testosterone levels in the rapist. *Psychosomatic Medicine, 38,* 257–268.

Raine, A. (1982). *Psychophysiology, psychometrics, and socialization.* Unpublished doctoral dissertation, University of York.

Raine, A., & Venables, P. H. (1981). Classical conditioning and socialization: A biosocial interaction. *Personality and Individual Differences, 2,* 273–283.

———. (1988). Skin conductance responsivity in psychopaths to orienting, defensive, and consonant-vowel stimuli. *Journal of Psychophysiology, 2,* 221–225.

Raine, A., Venables, P. H., & Williams, M. (1990). Autonomic orienting responses in 15-year-old male subjects and criminal behavior at age 24. *American Journal of Psychiatry, 147,* 933–937.

Rafter, N. H. (1985). Gender, prisons, and prison history. *Social Science History, 9,* 233–247.

Rand, M. R. (1987). Violent crime trends. *Bureau of Justice Statistics Special Report.* Washington, DC: Department of Justice.

Rankin, J. H., & Wells, L. E. (1990). The effect of parental attachments and direct control on delinquency. *Journal of Research in Crime and Delinquency, 27,* 140–165.

Rauma, D., & Berk, R. A. (1982). Crime and poverty in California: Some quasi-experimental evidence. *Social Science Research, 11,* 318–351.

Reasons, C. E. (1975). The addict as a criminal. *Crime and Delinquency, 21,* 19–27.

Reckless, W. C., & Dinitz, S. (1972). *The prevention of juvenile delinquency: An experiment.* Columbus, OH: Ohio State University Press.

Reckless, W. C., Dinitz, S., & Kay, B. (1957). The self component in potential delinquency and potential non-delinquency. *American Sociological Review, 22,* 566–570.

Reckless, W. C., Dinitz, S., & Murray, E. (1956). Self-concept as an insulator against delinquency. *American Sociological Review, 21,* 744–746.

Reid, J. B., Taplin, P. S., & Loeber, R. (1981). A social interactional approach to the treatment of abusive families. In R. B. Stuart (ed.), *Violent behaviors: Social learning approaches to prediction, management, and treatment* (pp. 83–101). New York: Brunner/Mazel.

Reid, S. T. (1982). *Crime and criminology* (3rd ed.). New York: Holt, Rinehart, & Winston.

Reinarman, C., & Fagan, J. (1988). Social organization and differential association: A research note from a longitudinal study of violent juvenile offenders. *Crime and Delinquency, 34,* 307–327.

Reiss, A. J. (1971). *The police and the public.* New Haven, CT: Yale University Press.

Reiss, A. J., & Rhodes, A. L. (1961). The distribution of juvenile delinquency in the social class structure. *American Sociological Review, 26,* 720–732.

Renzetti, C. M., & Curran, P. J. (1981, November). *Women, crime, and gender roles:*

A critical reappraisal. Paper presented at the annual meeting of the American Society of Criminology, Washington, DC.

Rescorla, R. A., & Wagner, A. R. (1972). A theory of Pavlovian conditioning: Variations in the effectiveness of reinforcement and nonreinforcement. In A. M. Black & W. F. Prokasy (eds.), *Classical conditioning. II: Current research and theory* (pp. 64–99). New York: Appleton-Century-Crofts.

Research Triangle Institute. (1976). *Drug use and crime.* Springfield, VA: National Technical Information Service. (PB–259 167).

Richardson, J. F. (1970). *The New York police, colonial times to 1901.* New York: Oxford University Press.

Ro, C-H. (1971). Seoul. In A. A. Laquian (ed.), *Rural urban migrants and metropolitan development* (pp. 161–165). Toronto: Intermet Metropolitan Studies Series.

Roberts, J. V., & Gabor, T. (1990). Lombrosian wine in a new bottle: Research on crime and race. *Canadian Journal of Criminology, 32,* 291–313.

Robins, L. N. (1966). *Deviant children grown up: A sociological and psychiatric study of sociopathic personality.* Baltimore: Williams & Wilkins.

———. (1978). Aetiological implications in studies of childhood histories relating to antisocial personality. In R. D. Hare & D. Schalling (eds.), *Psychopathic behavior: Approaches to research* (pp. 255–271). Chichester, England: John Wiley.

Robins, L. N., Darvish, H. S., & Murphy, G. E. (1970). The long-term outcome for adolescent drug users: A follow-up study of 76 users and 146 non-users. In J. Zubin & A. M. Freedman (eds.), *The psychopathology of adolescence* (pp. 159–178). New York: Grune & Stratton.

Robins, L. N., West, P. A., & Herjanic, B. L. (9175). Arrests and delinquency in two generations: A study of black urban families and their children. *Journal of Child Psychology and Psychiatry, 16,* 125–140.

Rogers, C. R. (1951). *Client-centered therapy.* Boston: Houghton-Mifflin.

Roggman, L. A., Langlois, J. H., & Hubbs-Tait, L. (1987). Mothers, infants, and toys: Social play correlates of attachment. *Infant behavior and development, 10,* 233–237.

Rogosa, D. (1980). A critique of cross-lagged correlation. *Psychological Bulletin, 88,* 245–258.

Rohrer, J. H., & Edmonson, M. S. (eds.). (1960). *The eighth generation: Cultures and personalities of New Orleans Negroes.* New York: Harper.

Roizen, J. (1981). Alcohol and criminal behavior among blacks: The case for research on special populations. In J. J. Collins (ed.), *Drinking and crime* (pp. 207–252). New York: Guilford.

Roizen, J., & Schneberk, D. (1977). Alcohol and crime. *Special Report to the National Institute of Alcohol Abuse and Alcoholism.* Washington, DC: U.S. Government Printing Office.

Rosanoff, A. J., Handy, L. M., & Rosanoff, I. A. (1934). Criminality and delinquency in twins. *Journal of Criminal Law and Criminology, 24,* 923–934.

Rosen, L., Lalli, M., & Savitz, L. (1975) *City life and delinquency: The family and delinquency.* Unpublished report submitted to the National Institute for Juvenile Justice and Delinquency Prevention.

Rosenbaum, J. L. (1987). Social control, gender, and delinquency: An analysis of drug, property and violent offenders. *Justice Quarterly, 4,* 117–132.

Rosenberg, M., Schooler, C., & Schoenbach, C. (1989). Self-esteem and adolescent problems: Modeling reciprocal effects. *American Sociological Review, 54,* 1004–1018.

Rosenquist, C. M., & Megargee, E. I. (1969). *Delinquency in three cultures*. Austin, TX: University of Texas Press.

Rosenthal, D. (1975). Heredity in criminality. *Criminal Justice and Behavior, 2,* 3–21.

Ross, R. R., & Fabiano, E. A. (1985). *Time to think: A cognitive model of delinquency prevention and offender rehabilitation*. Johnson City, TN: Institute of Social Sciences and Art.

Rossi, P. H., Berk, R. A., & Lenihan, K. J. (1980). *Money, work, and crime*. New York: Academic Press.

Rothbart, M. K., & Derryberry, D. (1981). Development of individual differences in temperament. In M. E. Lamb & A. L. Brown (eds.), *Advances in developmental psychology: Vol. I* (pp. 37–86). Hillsdale, NJ: Lawrence Erlbaum.

Rotton, J., & Frey, J. (1985). Air pollution, weather, and violent crimes: Concomitant time-series analysis of archival data. *Journal of Personality and Social Psychology, 49,* 1207–1220.

Rowe, A., Lindquist, J. H., & White, O. Z. (1989). A note on the family and crime in the United States. *Psychological Reports, 65,* 1001–1002.

Rowe, A. R., & Tittle, C. R. (1977). Life-cycle changes and criminal propensity. *Sociological Quarterly, 18,* 223–236.

Rowe, D. C. (1983). Biometrical genetic models of self-reported delinquent behavior: A twin study. *Behavior Genetics, 13,* 473–489.

———. (1987). Resolving the person-situation debate: Invitation to interdisciplinary dialogue. *American Psychologist, 42,* 218–227.

Rowe, D. C., & Osgood, D. W. (1984). Heredity and sociological theories of delinquency: A reconsideration. *American Sociological Review, 49,* 526–540.

Rubin, R. T. (1987). The neuroendocrinology and neurochemistry of antisocial behavior. In S. A. Mednick, T. E. Moffitt, & S. A. Stack (eds.), *The causes of crime: New biological approaches* (pp. 239–262). New York: Cambridge University Press.

Rule, A. (1989). *The stranger beside me*. New York: Signet.

Rushton, J. P. (1987, November). *Population differences in rule-following behaviour: Race evolution and crime*. Paper presented at the 39th annual meeting of the American Society of Criminology, Montreal.

Russel, M. (1964). The Irish delinquent in England. *Studies, 53,* 18–24.

Rutter, M. (1972). *Maternal deprivation reassessed*. New York: Penguin Books.

Rutter, M., & Giller, H. (1984). *Juvenile delinquency: Trends and perspectives*. New York: Guilford.

Rutter, M., Maughan, B., Mortimore, P., Ouston, J., & Smith, A. (1979). *Fifteen thousand hours: Secondary schools and their effects on children*. Cambridge, MA: Harvard University Press.

Rutter, M., Yule, B., Quinton, D. Rowlands, O., Yule, W., & Berger, M. (1975). Attainment and adjustment in two geographical areas: III. Some factors accounting for area differences. *British Journal of Psychiatry, 126,* 520–533.

Saccuzzo, D. P., & Lewandowski, D. G. (1976). The WISC as a diagnostic tool. *Journal of Clinical Psychology, 60,* 327–337.

Sagel-Grande, I. (1987). Some aspects of criminality and criminology in the German Democratic Republic (GDR). *International Journal of Offender Therapy and Comparative Criminology, 31,* 91–100.

Sameroff, A. J., Seifer, R., & Zax, M. (1982). Early development of children at risk for emotional disorder. *Monographs of the Society for Research in Child Development, 47,* (Serial No. 199).

Sampson, R. J. (1985). Structural sources of variation in race-age-specific rates of offending across major U.S. cities. *Criminology, 23,* 647–673.

———. (1986). Effects of socioeconomic context on official reaction to juvenile delinquency. *American Sociological Review, 51,* 876–885.

Sampson, R. J., & Castellano, T. C. (1982). Economic inequality and personal victimisation. *British Journal of Criminology, 22,* 363–385.

Sanchez, J. E., & Johnson, B. D. (1987). Women and the drugs-crime connection: Crime rates among drug abusing women at Rikers Island. *Journal of Psychoactive Drugs, 17,* 205–216.

Sarbin, T. R., Allen, V. L., & Rutherford, E. E. (1965). Social reinforcement, socialization, and chronic delinquency. *British Journal of Social and Clinical Psychology, 4,* 179–184.

Sarri, R. C. (1983). Gender issues in juvenile justice. *Crime and Delinquency, 29,* 381–397.

———. (1987). Unequal protection under the law: Women and the criminal justice system. In J. Figueira-McDonough & R. C. Sarri (eds.), *The trapped woman: Catch–22 in deviance and control* (pp. 394–426). Newbury Park, CA: Sage.

Sattler, J. M. (1982). *Assessment of children's intelligence and special abilities* (2nd ed.). Boston: Allyn & Bacon.

Sayed, Z. A., Lewis, S. A., & Brittain, R. P. (1969). An electroencephalographic and psychiatric study of thirty-two insane murderers. *British Journal of Psychiatry, 115,* 415–424.

Scarpitti, F. R., Murray, E., Dinitz, S., & Reckless, W. C. (1960). The "good" boy in a high delinquency area: Four years later. *American Sociological Review, 25,* 555–558.

Schalling, D. (1978). Psychopathy-related personality variables and the psychophysiology of socialization. In R. D. Hare & D. Schalling (eds.), *Psychopathic behavior: Approaches to research* (pp. 85–106). New York: John Wiley.

———. (1987). Personality correlates of plasma testosterone levels in young delinquents: An example of person-situation interaction? In S. A. Mednick, T. E. Moffitt, & S. A. Stack (eds.), *The causes of crime: New biological approaches* (pp. 282–291). New York: Cambridge University Press.

Schlesinger, A. M. (1945). The rise of the city, 1878–1898. In A. M. Schlesinger & D. R. Fox (eds.), *A history of American life in twelve volumes* (Volume 10). New York: Macmillan.

———. (1986). *The cycles of American history*. Boston: Houghton-Mifflin.

Schmidt, D. E., & Keating, J. P. (1979). Human crowding and personal control: An integration of the research. *Psychological Bulletin, 86,* 680–700.

Schneider-Rosen, K., & Cicchetti, D. (1984). The relationship between affect and cognition in maltreated infants: Quality of attachment and development of visual self-recognition. *Child Development, 55,* 648–658.

Schroeder, R. C. (1980). *The politics of drugs*. Washington, DC: Congress Quarterly Press.

Schulman, M. (1987, April). *Why isn't there more street crime?* Paper presented to the Columbia University Seminar in Moral Education, New York City.

Schulsinger, F. (1972). Psychopathology: Heredity and environment. *International Journal of Mental Health, 1,* 190–206.

Schulsinger, F., Mednick, S. A., Venables, P. H., Raman, A. C., & Bell, B. (1975). The early detection and prevention of mental illness: The Mauritius Project. A preliminary report. *Neuropsychobiology, 1,* 166–179.

Schultz, J. W. (1982). Trauma, crime and the affirmative defense. *Colorado Law Review, 11,* 2401–2403.

Schur, E. M. (1971). *Labeling deviant behavior: Its sociological implications.* New York: Harper & Row.

Schwartz, R. H. (1984). Marijuana: A crude drug with a spectrum of under-appreciated toxicity. *Pediatrics, 83,* 455–458.

Schwarz, J. C., Schrager, J. B., & Lyons, A. E. (1983). Delay of gratification by preschoolers: Evidence for the validity of the choice paradigm. *Child Development, 54,* 620–625.

Schweinhart, L. J., & Weikart, D. P. (1983). The effect of the Perry Preschool Program on youths through age 15—A summary. In Consortium for Longitudinal Studies, *As the twig is bent: The lasting effects of preschool programs* (pp. 71–101). Hillsdale, NJ: Lawrence Erlbaum.

Scott, J. E., & Schwalm, L. A. (1988). Rape rates and the circulation rates of adult magazines. *Journal of Sex Research, 24,* 241–250.

Scott, P. (1966). Gangs and delinquent groups in London. In R. Giallombardo (ed.), *Juvenile delinquency: A book of readings* (pp. 319–334). New York: John Wiley.

Sellin, T. (ed.), (1967). *Capital punishment.* New York: Harper & Row.

———. (1983). Preface. In F. Adler, *Nations not obsessed with crime* (pp. xvii–xviii). Littleton, CO: Fred B. Rothman.

Selltiz, C., Jahoda, M., Deutch, M., & Cook, S. W. (1959). *Research methods in social relations* (rev. ed.). New York: Holt.

Shaffer, J. W., Nurco, D. N., Ball, J. C., Kinlock, T. W., Duszynski, K. R., & Langrod, J. (1987). The relationship of preaddiction characteristics to the types and amounts of crime committed by narcotic addicts. *International Journal of the Addictions, 22,* 153–165.

Shaffer, J. W., Nurco, D. N., & Kinlock, T. W. (1984). A new classification of narcotic addicts based on type and extent of criminal activity. *Comprehensive Psychiatry, 25,* 315–328.

Shannon, L. W. (1982). *Assessing the relationship of adult criminal careers to juvenile careers: A summary.* Washington, DC: Office of Juvenile Justice and Delinquency Prevention.

Shapiro, S. K., & Garfinkel, B. D. (1986). The occurrence of behavior disorders in children: The interdependence of attention deficit disorder and conduct disorder. *Journal of the American Academy of Child Psychiatry, 25,* 809–819.

Shasby, G., & Kingsley, R. F. (1978). A study of behavior and body type in troubled youth. *Journal of School Health, 48,* 103–107.

Shavit, Y., & Rattner, A. (1988). Age, crime, and the early life course. *American Journal of Sociology, 93,* 1457–1470.

Shaw, C. R., & McKay, H. D. (1942). *Juvenile delinquency and urban areas.* Chicago: University of Chicago Press.

Shaw, D. M., Churchill, C. M., Noyes, R., & Loeffelholz, P. L. (1987). Criminal behavior and post-traumatic stress disorder in Vietnam veterans. *Comprehensive Psychiatry, 28,* 403–411.

Sheldon, W. (1954). *Atlas of men.* New York: Harper.

Shelley, L. I. (1981). *Crime and modernization: The impact of industrialization and urbanization on crime.* Carbondale, IL: Southern Illinois University Press.

Shoham, S. G., Rahav, G., Markowski, R., Chard, F., Neuman, F., Ben-Haim, M., Baruch, L., Esformes, Y., Schwarzman, Z., Rubin, R., Mednick, S., & Buickhuisen, W. (1987). Family parameters of violent prisoners. *Journal of Social Psychology, 127,* 83–91.

Shore, M. F. (1971). Psychological theories of the causes of antisocial behavior. *Crime and Delinquency, 17,* 456–468.

Short, J. F. (1957). Differential association and delinquency. *Social Problems, 4,* 233–239.

Short, J. F., & Nye, F. I. (1957). Reported behavior as a criterion of deviant behavior. *Social Problems, 5,* 207–213.

Short, J. F., & Strodtbeck, F. L. (1965). *Group process and gang delinquency.* Chicago: University of Chicago Press.

Short, J. F., Tennyson, R. A., & Howard, K. I. (1966). Behavior dimensions of gang delinquency. In R. Giallombardo (ed.), *Juvenile delinquency: A book of readings* (pp. 287–306). New York: John Wiley.

Shostak, D. A., & McIntyre, C. W. (1978). Stimulation-seeking behavior in three delinquent personality types. *Journal of Consulting and Clinical Psychology, 46,* 582.

Shover, N. (1983). The later stages of ordinary property offender careers. *Social Problems, 31,* 208–218.

Sickles, R. C., Schmidt, P., & Witte, A. D. (1979). An application of the simultaneous Tobit model: A study of the determinants of criminal recidivism. *Journal of Economics and Business, 31,* 166–171.

Siddle, D. A. T. (1977). Electrodermal activity and psychopathy. In S. A. Mednick & K. O. Christiansen (eds.); *Biosocial bases of criminal behavior* (pp. 89–108). New York: Gardner.

Siddle, D. A. T., Nicol, A. R., & Foggitt, R. H. (1973). Habituation and over-extinction of the GSR component of the orienting response in anti-social adolescents. *British Journal of Social and Clinical Psychology, 12,* 303–308.

Siegel, R. A. (1978). Probability of punishment and suppression of behavior in psychopathic and nonpsychopathic offenders. *Journal of Abnormal Psychology, 87,* 514–522.

Siegel, R. K. (1982). Cocaine smoking. *Journal of Psychoactive Drugs, 14,* 271–359.

Silberman, C. E. (1978). *Criminal violence, criminal justice.* New York: Random House.

Silverman, L. P., & Spruill, N. L. (1977). Urban crime and the price of heroin. *Journal of Urban Economics, 4,* 80–103.

Silverman, L. P., Spruill, N. L., & Levine, D. (1975). *Urban crime and heroin availability.* Arlington, VA: Public Research Institute.

Silverman, M. T. (1964). The relationship between self-esteem and aggression in two social classes. *Dissertation Abstracts, 25,* 2616.

Simon, R. J., & Baxter, S. (1989). Gender and violent crime. In N. A. Weiner & M. E. Wolfgang (eds.), *Violent crime, violent criminals* (pp. 171–197). Newbury Park, CA: Sage.

Simon, R. J., & Sharma, N. (1979). Women and crime: Does the American experience generalize? In F. Adler & R. J. Simon (eds.), *The criminology of deviant women* (pp. 391–400). Boston: Houghton Mifflin.

Simonds, J. F., & Kashani, J. (1980). Specific drug use and violence in delinquent boys. *American Journal of Drug and Alcohol Abuse, 7,* 305–322.

Simons, R. L., Robertson, J. F., & Downs, W. R. (1989). The nature of the association between parental rejection and delinquent behavior. *Journal of Youth and Adolescence, 18,* 297–310.

Simpson, D. D., & Sells, S. B. (1982). Effectiveness of treatment for drug abuse: An overview of the DARP research program. *Advances in Alcohol and Substance Abuse, 2,* 7–29.

Siringo, C. A. (1885). *A Texas cowboy*. Chicago.

Skinner, B. F. (1938). *The behavior of organisms*. New York: Appleton-Century-Crofts.

———. (1971). *Beyond freedom and dignity*. New York: Knopf.

Skogan, W. G. (1977). The changing distribution of big-city crime: A multi-city time series analysis. *Urban Affairs Quarterly, 13,* 33–48.

Skrzypek, G. J. (1969). Effect of perceptual isolation and arousal on anxiety, complexity preference, and novelty preference in psychopathic and neurotic delinquents. *Journal of Abnormal Psychology, 74,* 321–329.

Slater, E. (1953). Genetic investigations in twins. *Journal of Mental Science, 99,* 44–52.

Slosson, P. W. (1931). The great crusade and after, 1914–1928. In A. M. Schlesinger & D. R. Fox (eds.), *A history of American life in twelve volumes* (Volume XII). New York: Macmillan.

Small, J. G. (1966). The organic dimension of crime. *Archives of General Psychiatry, 15,* 82–89.

Smith, D. A., & Paternoster, R. (1987). The gender gap in theories of deviance: Issues and evidence. *Journal of Research in Crime and Delinquency, 24,* 140–172.

Smith, D. A., & Visher, C. A. (1980). Sex and involvement in deviance/crime: A quantitative review of the empirical literature. *American Sociological Review, 45,* 691–701.

Smith, D. A., Visher, C. A., & Davidson, L. A. (1984). Equity and discretionary justice: The influence of race on police arrest decisions. *Journal of Criminal Law and Criminology, 75,* 234–249.

Smith, D. R., Smith, W. R., & Noma, E. (1984). Delinquent career-lines: A conceptual link between theory and juvenile offenses. *Sociological Quarterly, 25,* 155–172.

Smith, G. M., & Fogg, C. P. (1978). Psychological predictors of early use, late use, and nonuse of marijuana among teenage students. In D. B. Kandel (ed.), *Longitudinal research on drug use: Empirical findings and methodological issues* (pp. 101–113). Washington, DC: Hemisphere.

Snyder, E. C. (1971). The impact of the juvenile court hearing on the child. *Crime and Delinquency, 17,* 180–190.

Sparks, R. F. (1980). Criminal opportunities and crime rates. In S. E. Fienberg & A. J. Reiss (eds.), *Indicators of crime and criminal justice: Quantitative studies* (pp. 18–28). Washington, DC: Bureau of Justice Statistics.

Speckart, G., & Anglin, M D. (1985). Narcotics and crime: An analysis of existing evidence for a causal relationship. *Behavioral Sciences and the Law, 3,* 259–282.

———. (1986). Narcotics use and crime: An overview of recent research advances. *Contemporary Drug Problems, 13,* 741–769.

Spinetta, J. J., & Rigler, D. (1972). The child-abusing parent: A psychological review. *Psychological Bulletin, 77,* 296–304.

Sroufe, L. A. (1979). The coherence of individual development: Early care, attachment, and subsequent developmental issues. *American Psychologist, 34,* 834–841.

Sroufe, L. A., Fox, N. E., & Pancake, V. R. (1983). Attachment and dependency in developmental perspective. *Child Development, 54,* 1615–1627.

Stack, S. (1982). Social structure and Swedish crime rates. *Criminology, 20,* 499–513.

Stack, S. (1983). Homicide and property crime: The relationship of anomie. *Aggressive Behavior, 9,* 339–344.

Stark, R. (1979). Whose status counts? *American Sociological Review, 44,* 668–669.

Stattin, H., & Magnusson, D. (1989). The role of early aggressive behavior in the frequency, seriousness, and types of later crime. *Journal of Consulting and Clinical Psychology, 57,* 710–718.

Stattin, H., Magnusson, D., & Reichel, H. (1989). Criminal activity at different ages: A study based on a Swedish longitudinal research population. *British Journal of Criminology, 29,* 368–385.

Stayton, D. J., Ainsworth, M. D. S., & Main, M. B. (1973). Development of separation behavior in the first year of life: Protest, following, and greeting. *Developmental Psychology, 9,* 213–225.

Steadman, H. J., & Felson, R. B. (1984). Self-reports of violence: Ex-mental patients, ex-offenders, and the general population. *Criminology, 22,* 321–342.

Stefanov, I., & Naumov, N. (1974). Bulgaria. In *Population policy in developed countries.*

Steffensmeier, D. J., & Allan, E. A. (1988). Sex disparities in arrests by residence, race, and age: An assessment of the gender convergence/crime hypothesis. *Justice Quarterly, 5,* 53–80.

Steffensmeier, D. J., Allan, E. A., Harer, M. D., & Streifel, C. (1989). Age and the distribution of crime. *American Journal of Sociology, 94,* 803–831.

Steffensmeier, D. J., & Cobb, M. J. (1981). Sex differences in urban arrest patterns, 1934–79. *Social Problems, 29,* 37–49.

Steffensmeier, D. J., & Harer, M. D. (1987). Is the crime rate really falling? An ''aging'' U.S. population and its impact on the nation's crime rate, 1980–1984. *Journal of Research in Crime and Delinquency, 24,* 23–48.

Stein, A. H., & Friedrich, L. K. (1972). Television content and young children's behavior. In J. P. Murray, E. A. Rubinstein, & G. A. Comstock (eds.), *Television and social learning* (pp. 202–317). Rockville, MD: National Institute of Mental Health.

Steiner, C. (1974). *Scripts people live: Transactional analysis of life scripts.* New York: Bantam Books.

Stephens, R. C., & Ellis, R. D. (1975). Narcotic addicts and crime: Analysis of recent trends. *Criminology, 12,* 474–488.

Stewart, C. H. M., & Hemsley, D. R. (1984). Personality factors in the taking of criminal risks. *Personality and Individual Differences, 5,* 119–122.

Stewart, J. K. (1986). The urban strangler: How crime causes poverty in the inner city. *Police Review, 37,* 6–10.

Stockwell, E. G., Wicks, J. W., & Adamchak, D. J. (1978). Research needed on socioeconomic differentials in U.S. mortality. *Public Health Reports, 93,* 666–672.

Stone, L. J., & Church, J. (1979). *Childhood and adolescence: A psychology of the growing person* (4th ed.). New York: Random House.

Straus, M. A., Gelles, R. J., & Steinmetz, S. K. (1980). *Behind closed doors: Violence in the American family.* Garden City, NY: Anchor/Doubleday.

Stumpfl, F. (1936). *Die ursprunge des verbrechens am Lebenslauf von Zwillingen.* Leipzig: Georg Thieme Verlag.

Sunley, R. (1955). Early nineteenth-century American literature on child rearing. In M. Mead & M. Wolfenstein (eds.), *Childhood in contemporary cultures* (pp. 150–167). Chicago: University of Chicago Press.

Sutherland, E. H. (1931). Mental deficiency and crime. In K. Young (ed.), *Social attitudes* (pp. 357–375). New York: Holt.

———. (1939). *Principles of criminology* (3rd ed.). Philadelphia: Lippincott.

Sutherland, E. H., & Cressey, D. R. (1978). *Principles of criminology* (10th ed.). New York: Harper & Row.

Sutker, P. B., Archer, R. P., & Allain, A. N. (1978). Drug abuse patterns, personality characteristics and relationships with sex, race, and sensation seeking. *Journal of Consulting and Clinical Psychology, 40,* 635–644.

Sutker, P. B., Moan, C. E., & Allain, A. N. (1983). Assessment of cognitive control in psychopathic and normal prisoners. *Journal of Behavioral Assessment, 5,* 275–287.

Sutton, W. (with Q. Reynolds) (1953). *I, Willie Sutton.* New York: Farrar, Straus, & Young.

Suzuki, Y. (1977). *Criminal law reform in Japan.* UNAFEI, Resource Material Series (No. 13).

Sviridoff, M., & McElroy, J. E. (1984). *Employment and crime.* New York: Vera Institute of Justice.

Sykes, G. M., & Matza, D. (1970). Techniques of delinquency. In M. E. Wolfgang, L. Savitz, & N. Johnston (eds.), *The sociology of crime and delinquency* (2nd ed, pp. 292–299). New York: John Wiley.

Syndulko, K. (1978). Electrocortical investigations of sociopathy. In R. D. Hare & D. Schalling (eds.), *Psychopathic behavior: Approaches to research* (pp. 145–156). New York: John Wiley.

Tagaki, P., & Platt, T. (1978). Behind the gilded ghetto: An analysis of race, class and crime in Chinatown. *Crime and Social Justice, 9,* 2–25.

Tangri, S. S., & Schwartz, M. (1970). Self-concept research. In M. E. Wolfgang, L. Savitz, & N. Johnston (eds.), *The sociology of crime and delinquency* (pp. 406–416). New York: John Wiley.

Tannenbaum, F. (1938). *Crime and the community.* Boston: Ginn.

Tarter, R. E. (1988). Are there inherited behavioral traits that predispose to substance abuse? *Journal of Consulting and Clinical Psychology, 56,* 189–196.

Tarter, R. E., Hegedus, A. M., Alterman, A. I., & Katz-Garris, L. (1983). Cognitive capacities of juvenile violent, nonviolent and sexual offenders. *Journal of Nervous and Mental Disease, 171,* 564–567.

Taylor, J. P., & Gammon, C. B. (1975). Effects of type and dose of alcohol on human physical aggression. *Journal of Personality and Social Psychology, 32,* 169–175.

Taylor, T., & Watt, D. C. (1977). The relation of deviant symptoms and behaviour in a normal population to subsequent delinquency and maladjustment. *Psychological Medicine, 7,* 163–169.

Teitelbaum, H., & Milner, P. (1963). Activity changes following partial hippocampal lesion in rats. *Journal of Comparative and Physiological Psychology, 56,* 284–289.

Temple, M., & Ladouceur, P. (1986). The alcohol-crime relationship as an age-specific phenomenon: A longitudinal study. *Contemporary Drug Problems, 15,* 89–115.

Tennenbaum, D. J. (1977). Personality and criminality: A summary and implications of the literature. *Journal of Criminal Justice, 5,* 225–235.

Tennyson, R. A. (1967). Family structure and delinquent behavior. In M. W. Klein (ed.), *Juvenile gangs in context* (pp. 57–69). Englewood Cliffs, NJ: Prentice-Hall.

Terry, C. E., & Pellens, M. (1928). *The opium problem.* New York: Haddon Craftsman.

Thomas, A., & Chess, S. (1977). *Temperament and development.* New York: Brunner/Mazel.

Thomas, A., Chess, S., & Birch, H. G. (1963). *Behavioral individuality in early childhood.* New York: New York University Press.

Thomas, A., Chess, S., & Birch, H. G. (1968). *Temperament and behavior disorders in children.* New York: New York University Press.

Thomas, A., Chess, S., & Korn, S. J. (1982). The reality of difficult temperament. *Merrill-Palmer Quarterly, 28,* 1–20.

Thomas, C. W. (1977). *The effects of legal sanctions on juvenile delinquency: A comparison of the labeling and deterrent perspectives.* Final Report, LEAA Grants 75-NI-99-0031 and 76-NI-99-0050. Bowling Green State University, Bowling Green, OH.

Thomas, D. S. (1925). *Social aspects of the business cycle.* London: George Routledge & Sons.

Thompson, R. A. (1986). Temperament, emotionality, and infant cognition. In J. V. Lerner & R. M. Lerner (eds.), *Temperament and social interaction in infants and children* (pp. 35–53). San Francisco: Jossey-Bass.

Thornberry, T. P. (1971). *Punishment and crime: The effect of legal dispositions on subsequent criminal behavior.* Unpublished doctoral dissertation, University of Pennsylvania.

———. (1987). Toward an interactional theory of delinquency. *Criminology, 25,* 863–892.

Thornberry, T. P., & Christenson, R. L. (1984). Unemployment and criminal involvement: An investigation of reciprocal causal structures. *American Sociological Review, 49,* 398–411.

Thornberry, T. P. & Farnworth, M. (1982). Social correlates of criminal involvement: Further evidence on the relationship between social status and criminal behavior. *American Sociological Review, 47,* 505–518.

Thornberry, T. P., Moore, M., & Christenson, R. L. (1985). The effect of dropping out of high school on subsequent criminal behavior. *Criminology, 23,* 3–18.

Thrasher, F. W. (1927). *The gang.* Chicago: University of Chicago Press.

Tieger, T. (1980). On the biological basis of sex differences in aggression. *Child Development, 51,* 943–963.

Tienari, P. (1963). Psychiatric illnesses in identical twins. *Acta Psychiatric Scandinavica, 39* (Suppl. 171).

Tittle, C. R. (1975). Deterrents or labeling? *Social Forces, 53,* 399–410.

———. (1983). Social class and criminal behavior: A critique of the theoretical foundation. *Social Forces, 62,* 334–358.

Tittle, C. R., Burke, M. J., & Jackson, E. F. (1986). Modeling Sutherland's theory of differential association: Toward an empirical clarification. *Social Forces, 65,* 405–432.

Tittle, C. R., Villemez, W. J., & Smith, D. A. (1978). The myth of social class and criminality: An empirical assessment of the empirical evidence. *American Sociological Review, 43,* 643–656.

Toby, J., & Toby, M. L. (1961). *Low school status as a predisposing factor in subcultural delinquency.* New Brunswick, NJ: Rutgers University (mimeo).

Tracy, R. L., Farish, G. D., & Bretherton, I. (1980, April). *Exploration as related to infant-mother attachment in one-year-olds.* Paper presented at the International Conference on Infant Studies, New Haven, CT.

Trasler, G. (1987). Some cautions for the biological approach to crime causation. In S. A. Mednick, T. E. Moffitt, & S. A. Stack (eds.), *The causes of crime: New biological approaches* (pp. 7–24). New York: Cambridge University Press.

Trial Magazine. (1977). *The forgotten men,* pp. 20–21.

Tuchfeld, B. S., Clayton, R., & Logan, J. (1982). Alcohol, drug use and delinquent and criminal behaviors among male adolescents and young adults. *Journal of Drug Issues, 12,* 185–198.

Turner, A. G. (1981). The San Jose recall study. In R. G. Lehnen & W. G. Skogan (eds.), *The national crime survey: Working papers, Vol. I: Current and historical perspectives* (pp. 22–27). Washington, DC: Bureau of Justice Statistics.

Tversky, A., & Kahneman, D. (1981). The framing of decisions and the psychology of choice. *Science, 211,* 281–299.

United Nations. (1977). *Report of the Secretary-General on Capital Punishment.* United Nations Report No. A/32/199.

United Nations Bureau of Social Affairs. (1967). *Juvenile delinquency in India.* SOA/SD/CS.2.

United Nations Economic and Social Council. (1971). *Capital punishment.* United Nations No. E/4947.

United States Commission on Obscenity and Pornography. (1970). *Report of the United States Commission on Obscenity and Pornography.* Washington, DC: author.

Van Dusen, K. T., Mednick, S. A., Gabrielli, W. F., & Hutchings, B. (1983). Social class and crime in an adoption cohort. *Journal of Criminal Law and Criminology, 74,* 249–269.

Van Vechten, C. C. (1942). Differential criminal case mortality in selected jurisdictions. *American Sociological Review, 7,* 833–839.

Van Voorhis, P., Cullen, F. T., Mathers, R. A., & Garner, C. C. (1988). The impact of family structure and quality of delinquency: A comparative assessment of structural and functional factors. *Criminology, 26,* 235–261.

Venables, P. H. (1987). Autonomic nervous system factors in criminal behavior. In S. A. Mednick, T. E. Moffitt, & S. A. Stack (eds.), *The causes of crime: New biological approaches* (pp. 110–136). New York: Cambridge University Press.

Venables, P. H., Mednick, S. A., Schulsinger, F., Raman, A. C., Bell, B., Dalais, J. C., & Fletcher, R. P. (1978). Screening for risk of mental illness. In G. Serban (ed.), *Cognitive defects in development of mental illness* (pp. 273–303). New York: Brunner/Mazel.

Virkkunen, M., Nuutila, A., Goodwin, F. K., & Linnoila, M. (1987). Cerebrospinal fluid monoamine metabolite levels in male arsonists. *Archives of General Psychiatry, 44,* 241–247.

Vogel, E. G. (1979). *Japan as number one: Lessons for America.* Cambridge, MA: Harvard University Press.

Volavka, J. (1987). Electroencephalogram among criminals. In S. A. Mednick, T. E. Moffitt, & S. A. Stack (eds.), *The causes of crime: New biological approaches* (pp. 137–145). New York: Cambridge University Press.

Voss, H. L. (1964). Differential association and reported delinquent behavior: A replication. *Social Problems, 12,* 78–85.

Voss, H. L., & Stephens, R. C. (1973). Criminality history of narcotic addicts. *Drug Forum, 2,* 191–202.

Wadsworth, M. E. J. (1976). Delinquency, pulse rates and early emotional deprivation. *British Journal of Criminology, 16,* 245–256.

———. (1980). Early life events and later behavioral outcomes in a British longitudinal study. In S. B. Sells, R. Crandall, M. Roff, J. S. Strauss, & W. Pollin (eds.), *Human functioning in longitudinal perspective* (pp. 168–177). Baltimore: Williams & Wilkins.

Wagner, M. W., & Almeida, L. (1987). Geophysical variables and behavior: XXXVII. Lunar phase, "no," weekend, "yes," month, "sometimes." *Perceptual and Motor Skills, 64,* 949–950.

Waldo, G. P., & Chiricos, T. G. (1972). Perceived penal sanctions and self-reported criminality: A neglected approach to deterrence research. *Social Problems, 19,* 522–540.

Waldo, G. P., & Dinitz, S. (1967). Personality attributes of the criminal: An analysis of research studies, 1950–65. *Journal of Research in Crime and Delinquency, 4,* 185–202.

Waldrop, M., & Halverson, C. (1971). Minor physical anomalies and hyperactive behavior in young children. *Exceptional Infant, 2,* 343–380.

Walker, N. (1971). *Crimes, courts, and figures: An introduction to criminal sanctions.* United Kingdom: Penguin.

Walsh, A. (1987). Cognitive functioning and delinquency: Property versus violent offenses. *International Journal of Offender Therapy and Comparative Criminology, 31,* 285–289.

Walsh, A., & Beyer, J. (1986). Wechsler performance-verbal discrepancy and antisocial behavior. *Journal of Social Psychology, 126,* 419–420.

Walsh, A., Petee, T. A., & Beyer, J. A. (1987). Intellectual imbalance and delinquency: Comparing high verbal and high performance IQ delinquents. *Criminal Justice and Behavior, 14,* 370–379.

Walsh, D. P. (1978). *Shoplifting: Controlling a major crime.* London: Macmillan.

Walsh, D. (1986). Victim selection procedures among economic criminals: The rational choice perspective. In D. B. Cornish & R. V. Clarke (eds.), *The reasoning criminal: Rational choice perspectives on offending* (pp. 39–52). New York: Springer-Verlag.

Walters, G. D. (1990a). Heredity, crime, and the killing-the-bearer-of-bad-news syndrome: A reply to Brennan and Mednick. *Criminology, 28,* 663–667.

———. (1990b). *The criminal lifestyle: Patterns of serious criminal conduct.* Newbury Park, CA: Sage.

Walters, G. D., Solomon, G. S., & Walden, V. R. (1982). Use of the MMPI in predicting psychotherapeutic persistence in groups of male and female outpatients. *Journal of Clinical Psychology, 38,* 80–83.

Walters, G. D., & Walters, C. M. (1991). Examining the relationship between airborne pollen levels and 911 calls for assistance. *International Journal of Offender Therapy and Comparative Criminology, 35,* 162–166.

Walters, G. D., & White, T. W. (1987). *Examining lifestyle criminality: The Leavenworth 500.* Unpublished manuscript, United States Penitentiary, Leavenworth, KS.

———. (1988). Crime, popular mythology, and personal responsibility. *Federal Probation, 52,* 18–26.

———. (1989a). Heredity and crime: Bad genes or bad research? *Criminology, 27,* 455–485.

———. (1989b). The thinking criminal: A cognitive model of lifestyle criminality. *Criminal Justice Research Bulletin, 4,* No. 4.

———. (1990). Attachment and social bonding in maximum and minimum security prison inmates. *American Journal of Criminal Justice, 15,* 54–69.

Ward, D. A., Jackson, M., & Ward, R. E. (1969). Crimes of violence by women. In D. J. Mulvihill & M. M. Tumin (eds.), *Crimes of violence* (pp. 843–909). Washington, DC: U.S. Government Printing Office.

Warren, M. Q. (1983). Applications of interpersonal-maturity theory to offender populations. In W. S. Laufer & J. M. Day (eds.), *Personality theory, moral development, and criminal behavior* (pp. 23–50). Lexington, MA: Lexington Books.

Warren, M. Q., & Rosenbaum, J. L. (1987). Criminal careers of female offenders. *Criminal Justice and Behavior, 13,* 393–418.

Washton, A. M., & Gold, M. S. (1984). Chronic cocaine abuse: Evidence for adverse effects on health and functioning. *Psychiatric Annals, 14,* 733, 737–739, 743.

Walters, E., & Crandall, V. J. (1964). Social class and observed maternal behavior from 1940 to 1960. *Child Development, 35,* 1021–1032.

Waters, L. K., & Kirk, W. E. (1968). Stimulus-seeking motivation and risk-taking behavior in a gambling situation. *Educational and Psychological Measurement, 28,* 549–550.

Watts, W. D., & Wright, L. S. (1990). The relationship of alcohol, tobacco, marijuana, and other illegal drug use to delinquency among Mexican-American, black, and white adolescent males. *Adolescence, 25,* 171–181.

Weaver, F. M., & Carroll, J. S. (1985). Crime perceptions in a natural setting by expert and novice shoplifters. *Social Psychology Quarterly, 48,* 349–359.

Wechsler, D. (1967). *Manual for the WPPSI.* New York: Psychological Corporation.

———. (1974). *Manual for the WISC-R.* New York: Psychological Corporation.

———. (1981). *Manual for the WAIS-R.* New York: Psychological Corporation.

Wedding, D., Horton, A. M., & Webster, J. (1986). *The neuropsychology handbook: Behavioral and clinical perspectives.* New York: Springer.

Weil, T. E., Black, J. K., Blutstein, H. I., McMorris, D. S., Munson, F. P., & Townsend, C. (1972). *Area handbook for Peru.* Washington, DC: U.S. Government Printing Office.

Weinstein, L., & Sackhoff, J. (1987). Adler is right. *Bulletin of the Psychonomic Society, 25,* 201.

Weis, J. (1973). *Delinquency among the well-to-do.* Unpublished doctoral dissertation, University of California, Berkeley.

Wells, L. E., & Rankin, J. H. (1988). Direct parental controls and delinquency. *Criminology, 26,* 263–285.

Werner, E. E., & Smith, R. S. (1977). *Kauai's children come of age,* Honolulu: University of Hawaii Press.

Wertenbaker, T. J. (1927). The first Americans, 1607–1690. In A. M. Schlesinger & D. R. Fox (eds.), *A history of American life in twelve volumes* (Volume 2). New York: Macmillan.

West, D. J. (1982). *Delinquency: Its roots, careers, and prospects.* Cambridge, MA: Harvard University Press.

West, D. J., & Farrington, D. P. (1973). *Who becomes delinquent*? London: Heinemann.

———. (1977). *The delinquent way of life: Third report of the Cambridge study in delinquent development.* London: Heinemann.

Wheeler, J., & Kilmann, P. R. (1983). Comarital sexual behavior: Individual and relationship variables. *Archives of Sexual Behavior, 12,* 295–306.

White, J. L., Moffitt, T. E., Earls, F., Robins, L., & Silva, P. A. (1990). How early can we tell?: Predictors of childhood conduct disorder and adolescent delinquency. *Criminology, 28,* 507–533.

White, J. L., Moffitt, T. E., & Silva, P. A. (1989). A prospective replication of the protective effects of IQ in subjects at high risk for juvenile delinquency. *Journal of Consulting and Clinical Psychology, 57,* 719–724.

Wiatrowski, M. D., Griswold, D. B., & Roberts, M. K. (1981). Social control theory and delinquency. *American Sociological Review, 46,* 525–541.

Widom, C. S. (1989). The cycle of violence, *Science, 244,* 160–166.

Wiederanders, M. R. (1981). Some myths about the employment problems of young offenders. *Federal Probation, 45,* 9–12.

Wilkins, D. (1964). *Social deviance: Social policy, action and research.* London: Tavistock.

Wilkinson, K. (1980). The broken home and delinquent behavior: An alternative interpretation of contradictory findings. In T. Hirschi & M. Gottfredson (eds.), *Understanding crime: Current theory and research* (pp. 21–42). Beverly Hills, CA: Sage.

Williams, D. (1969). Neural factors related to habitual aggression: Consideration of differences between those habitual aggressives and others who have committed crimes of violence. *Brain, 92,* 503–520.

Williams, J., & Gold, M. (1972). From delinquent behavior to official delinquency. *Social Problems, 20,* 209–229.

Williams, J. B. (ed.). (1967). *Narcotics and hallucinogens: A handbook* (rev. ed.). Beverly Hills, CA: Glencoe Press.

Williams, J. B. (1974). *Narcotics and drug dependence.* Beverly Hills, CA: Glencoe Press.

Wilson, H. (1980). Parental supervision: A neglected aspect of delinquency. *British Journal of Criminology, 20,* 203–235.

Wilson, J. P. (1978). *Identity, ideology and crisis: The Vietnam veteran in transition, Vol II.* Washington, DC: Disabled American Veterans.

Wilson, J. P., & Zigelbaum, S. D. (1983). The Vietnam veteran on trial: The relation of post-traumatic stress disorder to criminal behavior. *Behavioral Sciences and the Law, 1,* 69–83.

Wilson, J. Q., & Boland, B. (1978). The effect of the police on crime. *Law and Society Review, 12,* 367–390.

Wilson, J. Q., & Cook, P. J. (1985). Unemployment and crime—What is the connection? *The Public Interest, 79,* 3–8.

Wilson, J. Q., & Herrnstein, R. J. (1985). *Crime and human nature.* New York: Simon & Schuster.

Wines, F. H. (1895). *Punishment and reform.* New York.

Winick, C. (1971). Marijuana use by young people. In P. F. Healy & J. P. Manak (eds.), *Drug dependence and abuse resource book.* Chicago: National District Attorneys Association.

Winter, A. (1891). *The New York State Reformatory at Elmira.* London.

Wish, E. D. (1986). PCP and crime: Just another illicit drug? In D. H. Clouet (ed.), *Phencyclidine: An update. NIDA Research Monograph No. 64* (pp. 174–189). Rockville, MD: National Institute of Drug Abuse.

Wish, E. D., Cuadrado, M., & Martorana, J. (1986). Estimates of drug use in intensive supervision probationers: Results from a pilot study. *Federal Probation, 50,* 4–16.

Wish, E. D., Klumpp, K. A., Moorer, A. H., & Brady, E. (1980). *An analysis of drugs and crime among arrestees in the District of Columbia.* Springfield, VA: National Technical Information Service.

Witte, A. (1980). Estimating the economic model of crime with individual level data. *Quarterly Journal of Economics, 94,* 57–84.

Wolf, P. (1971). Crime and development: An international comparison of crime rates. *Scandinavian Studies in Criminology, 3,* 107–121.

Wolff, P. H. (1963). Observations on the early development of smiling. In B. M. Foss (ed.), *Determinants of infant behaviour* (Vol. 2, pp. 113–134). New York: John Wiley.

Wolfgang, M. E. (1967). International criminal statistics: A proposal. *Journal of Criminal Law, Criminology and Police Science, 58,* 65–69.

———. (1981). *Delinquency in a birth cohort II: Some preliminary results.* Paper presented to the Attorney General's Task Force on Violent Crime.

Wolfgang, M. E., Figlio, R. M., & Sellin, T. (1972). *Delinquency in a birth cohort.* Chicago: University of Chicago Press.

Wolfgang, M. E., Figlio, R. M., Tracy, P. E., & Singer, S. I. (1985). *The National Survey of Crime Severity.* Washington, DC: Bureau of Justice Statistics.

Wolfgang, M. E., Thornberry, T. P., & Figlio, R. M. (1987). *From boy to man, from delinquency to crime.* Chicago: University of Chicago Press.

Wolfgang, M. E., & Weiner, N. A. (1982). *Patterns in injurious and violent delinquency in a birth cohort: A preliminary analysis.* Unpublished paper, University of Pennsylvania.

Woodward, M. (1955). The role of low intelligence in delinquency. *British Journal of Delinquency, 5,* 281–303.

Wright, H. H. (1980). Violence and PCP abuse. *American Journal of Psychiatry, 137,* 752–753.

Wrightsman, L. S. (1974). Measures of philosophies of human nature. *Psychological Reports, 14,* 743–751.

Wu, T-C., Tashkin, D. P., Djahed, B., & Rose, J. E. (1988). Pulmonary hazards of smoking marijuana compared with tobacco. *New England Journal of Medicine, 318,* 347–351.

Wurmser, L. (1978). Addictive disorders: Drug dependence. In G. U. Balis, L. Wurmser, E. McDaniel, & R. G. Grenell (eds.), *Clinical psychopathology: The psychiatric foundations of medicine* (pp. 387–428). Boston: Butterworth.

Yablonsky, L. (1966). The delinquent group as a near-group. In R. Giallobardo (ed.), *Juvenile delinquency: A book of readings* (pp. 249–258). New York: John Wiley.

Yager, T., Laufer, R. S., & Gallops, M. S. (1984). Some problems associated with war experience in men of the Vietnam generation. *Archives of General Psychiatry, 41,* 327–333.

Yamamoto, J., Seeman, W., & Lester, B. K. (1963). The tattooed man. *Journal of Nervous and Mental Diseases, 136,* 365–367.

Yeudall, L. T., Fromm-Auch, D., & Davies, P. (1982). Neuropsychological impairment of persistent delinquency. *Journal of Nervous and Mental Diseases, 170,* 257–265.

Yochelson, S., & Samenow, S. E. (1976). *The criminal personality, Vol. I: A profile for change*. New York: Jason Aronson.

———. (1986). *The criminal personality, Vol. III: The drug user*. New York: Jason Aronson.

Yoshimasu, S. (1961). The criminological significance of the family in the light of the studies of criminal twins. *Acta Criminologiae et Medicinae Legalis Japanica, 27,* 117–141.

Zahn, M. A. (1989). Homicide in the twentieth century: Trends, types, and causes. In T. R. Gurr (ed.), *Violence in America, Vol. I: The history of crime* (pp. 216–234). Newbury Park, CA: Sage.

Zahn, M. A., & Bencivengo, M. (1974). Violent death: A comparison between drug users and nondrug users. *Addictive Diseases, 1,* 283–312.

Ziskind, E. (1978). The diagnosis of sociopathy. In R. D. Hare & D. Schalling (eds.), *Psychopathic behaviour: Approaches to research* (pp. 47–54). Chichester, England: John Wiley.

Zuckerman, M. (1974). The sensation seeking motive. In B. A. Maher (ed.), *Progress in experimental personality research: Vol. 7* (pp. 79–148). New York: Academic Press.

———. (1979). *Sensation seeking: Beyond the optimal level of arousal*. Hillsdale, NJ: Lawrence Erlbaum.

Zuckerman, M., Kolin, E. A., Price, L., & Zoob, I. (1964). Development of a sensation-seeking scale. *Journal of Consulting Psychology, 8,* 477–482.

Zuckerman, M., Murtaugh, T. M., & Siegel, J. (1974). Sensation seeking and cortical augmenting-reducing. *Psychophysiology, 11,* 535–542.

Zuckerman, M., Persky, H., Link, K., & Basu, G. K. (1968). Experimental and subject factors determining responses to sensory deprivation, social isolation, and confinement. *Journal of Abnormal Psychology, 73,* 183–194.

Zuckerman, M., Tushup, R., & Finner, S. (1976). Sexual attitudes and experience: Attitude and personality correlates and changes produced by a course in sexuality. *Journal of Consulting and Clinical Psychology, 44,* 7–19.

Author Index

Subject Index

About the Author

GLENN D. WALTERS is coordinator of the comprehensive drug program at the Federal Correctional Institution in Fairton, New Jersey, and has served as a consultant for Mainstream Inc., Topeka, Kansas. He is the author of *The Criminal Lifestyle: Patterns of Serious Criminal Conduct*.